"THE JOURNALS OF JIM ELLIOT
is a book of power based on an actual life."

James Root, "Religion in Review"
Bloomington, Indiana <u>Herald</u>

These are the complete and unabridged journals of a man who died in the service of his Lord, a man who will be remembered for his total commitment and extraordinary devotion. You'll be challenged and chastised as you observe how Jim Elliot yielded his desires...his plans...his LIFE entirely to his Father's will. <u>The Journals of Jim Elliot</u> will endure through the years as a testimony to a courageous man of God, a classic in the missionary tradition, a tribute to a dynamic faith.

Jim Elliot

(October 8, 1927 – January 8, 1956)

The Journals of
JIM ELLIOT

Edited by
Elisabeth Elliot

Power Books

Fleming H. Revell Company
Tarrytown, New York

Unless otherwise identified, Scripture quotations are based on the American Standard Edition of the Revised Bible. Copyright 1901 by Thomas Nelson & Sons. Copyright 1929 by International Council of Religious Education.

Scripture quotations identified KJV are from the King James Version of the Bible.

Scripture quotations identified WEYMOUTH are from WEYMOUTH'S NEW TESTAMENT IN MODERN SPEECH by Richard Francis Weymouth. Published by special arrangement with James Clarke & Company, Ltd., and reprinted by permission of Harper & Row, Publishers, Inc.

Scripture quotations identified PHILLIPS are from THE NEW TESTAMENT IN MODERN ENGLISH (Revised Edition), translated by J. B. Phillips. © J. B. Phillips, 1958, 1960, 1972. Used by permission of Macmillan Publishing Co., Inc.

"Does Jesus Care" by Frank E. Graeff © 1971. Dayspring Music, a division of Word Music, Inc. Used by permission.

Scripture quotations identified CONYBEARE are from *The Epistles of Paul* by William John Conybeare (N.Y.: Charles C. Cook).

Scripture quotations identified THAYER are from *Greek Modern Bible* by J. R. Thayer.

Scripture quotations identified TRENCH are from *Commentary on the Epistles to the Seven Churches in Asia* by Richard Chenevix Trench (N.Y. Scribner's, 1869).

Scripture quotations identified DARBY are from *Synopsis of the Books of the Bible* by J. N. Darby.

Excerpt from "Night Song at Amalfi" reprinted with permission of Macmillan Publishing Co., Inc., from COLLECTED POEMS by Sara Teasdale. Copyright 1915 by Macmillan Publishing Co., Inc., renewed 1943 by Mamie T. Wheless.

Excerpt from "Let It Be Forgotten" reprinted with permission of Macmillan Publishing Co., Inc., from COLLECTED POEMS by Sara Teasdale. Copyright 1920 by Macmillan Publishing Co., Inc., renewed 1948 by Mamie T. Wheless.

Excerpt from TOWARD JERUSALEM by Amy Carmichael used by permission of the publisher, The Society for Promoting Christian Knowledge. American edition published by Christian Literature Crusade.

Diligent effort has been made to locate and secure permission for the inclusion of all copyrighted material in this book. If any such acknowledgments have been omitted, the publisher would appreciate receiving full information so that proper credit may be given in future editions

Library of Congress Cataloging in Publication Data

Elliot, James, 1927-1956.
    The journals of Jim Elliot.

    1. Elliot, James, 1927-1956. 2. Missionaries—
Ecuador—Biography. 3. Missionaries—United States—
Biography. I. Elliot, Elisabeth. II. Title.
BV2853.E3A34   266'.023'0924 [B]   78-16298
ISBN 0-8007-5147-7

Contents

Preface

A few years ago Christ Church of Hamilton, Massachusetts, set up a missionary committee. Among the members were two former missionaries, of whom I was one, and a currently active missionary, the "Flying Priest" of the Quebec-Labrador Mission, the Reverend Robert Bryan. As we became acquainted, Bob was thunderstruck to learn that I was the widow of Jim Elliot. To find in so unlikely a place this living link with a man who, to Bob, was a legend was what startled him. After the meeting he told me that it was the story of Jim's death, along with four other missionaries, at the hands of jungle Indians called Aucas, which had goaded him to become a missionary. "Each generation has its heroes," Bob said. "Sir Wilfred Grenfell inspired my father's generation. Your husband inspired mine."

Bob is only one of hundreds who have told me what the story (recounted in newspapers, magazines, and in a book *Through Gates of Splendor*) has meant to them. I have never counted the pile of letters I have received from readers of Jim's biography, *Shadow of the Almighty*, many of whom said it had the greatest influence in their lives of any book except the Bible. The book quoted heavily from Jim's personal letters and journals.

When, twenty years after his death, a publisher first asked for the rest of the journals, I was hesitant. I had edited them carefully for the biography, trying to include enough to show the true man, trying not to include what seemed too private. There were those who felt despair on reading the biography, for Jim seemed larger than life, too holy, too single eyed to be believed. I felt that such readers had not read very carefully, for the flaws, the flesh, the failures were there. There was no denying, however, the impact of his dedication to God. If that was what the reader remembered, that was as it should be.

Here, then, is the rest. More flaws, flesh, and failures are revealed here. More also is revealed of that consuming thirst to

9

do the will of God. There is, I discover, considerably more of our own love story than I had remembered. To include more than I did of the details of this part of Jim's life would have been disproportionate in the biography but needs no defense in the journals, for they are presented almost in their entirety. The sum of all deletions amounts to perhaps two or three pages. Occasional lapses in grammar, inconsistencies in the spellings of names, and disorders in syntax have been allowed to stand. Notes which I have added for the sake of clarity are in brackets.

The eleventh chapter of the Book of the Epistle to the Hebrews recounts wonderful stories of things done by faith: ". . . these men conquered kingdoms, ruled in justice and proved the truth of God's promises. They shut the mouths of lions, they quenched the furious blaze of fire, they escaped death by the sword. From being weaklings they became strong men and mighty warriors; they routed whole armies of foreigners. Women received their dead raised to life again, while others were tortured . . . exposed to the test of public mockery and flogging, and to being left bound in prison. They were killed by stoning, by being sawn in two . . ." (vv. 33–37 PHILLIPS).

Some, in the twentieth century, were killed by wooden lances. The Hebrews account goes on: "All these won a glowing testimony to their faith, but *they did not then and there receive the fulfillment of the promise.* God had something better planned for our day, and it was not his plan that they should reach perfection without us. Surrounded then as we are by these serried ranks of witnesses, let us strip off everything that hinders us, as well as the sin which dogs our feet, and *let us run the race that we have to run* with patience, our eyes fixed on Jesus, the source and the goal of our faith. For he himself endured a cross . . ." (11:39–12:2 PHILLIPS, italics mine).

ELISABETH ELLIOT

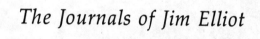

The Journals of Jim Elliot

1

Junior Year at Wheaton College Wheaton, Illinois, 1948

Wheaton is a small liberal-arts college about twenty-five miles west of Chicago. Its motto is "For Christ and His Kingdom." When Jim went there in the fall of 1945, it was with the object of preparing himself for the Lord's service. He eliminated all that he felt would distract him from this objective, dating being one example of such a distraction. He made a habit of getting up early in the morning in order to have uninterrupted time for prayer and Bible study, but it was not until his junior year that he began to keep a journal as a means of self-discipline. Forcing himself to articulate something on paper helped him to concentrate and gave direction to his devotional times.

JANUARY 17 *Genesis 23*   What is written in these pages I suppose will someday be read by others than myself. For this reason I cannot hope to be absolutely honest in what is herein recorded, for the hypocrisy of this shamming heart will ever be putting on a front and dares not to have written what is actually found in its abysmal depths. Yet, I pray, Lord, that You will make these notations to be as nearly true to fact as is possible so that I may know my own heart and be able to definitely pray regarding my gross, though often unviewed, inconsistencies. I do this at the suggestion of Stephen Olford [a young British preacher who was later pastor of Calvary Baptist Church in New York City] whose chapel message of yesterday morning convicted me that my quiet time with God is not what it should be. These remarks are to be written from fresh, daily thoughts given from God in meditation on His Word.

Abraham calls himself a "stranger and a sojourner" in a land he believed God was going to give to him. This is the first time he shows any real inclination to making a home on earth, and how slight it is—only a field, some trees, and a cave in which he can bury his dead. Lord, show me that I must be a stranger, unconcerned and unconnected with affairs below, "looking for a city" (Heb. 13:14). It was when Abraham owned his strangerhood that the sons of Heth called him a "prince of God" (v. 6) among them. Abraham made no attempts to be a prince of men, as had Lot, and they all recognized his character and inheritance (qualities of a prince) as being not "of men" but "of God." Oh, to be known as Israel—a prince with God—no longer as Jacob of the carnal mind.

Help me, Lord, not to "mourn and weep" only for those things, once precious, which You teach me are but dead (whether desires, pleasures, or whatever may be precious to my soul now), but give me a willingness to put them away out of my sight (v. 4). Burying places are costly, but I would own a Machpelah where corpses (dead things in my life) can be put away.

JANUARY 18 *Genesis 24*   Abraham's wisdom in sending his servant instead of his son is excellent instruction for the marriage of "pilgrims." "Beware that thou bring not my son thither again" (v. 7). Abraham knew the tremendous battle it was to leave cultured Ur and become a tent dweller. Isaac must have a wife whose background was at least acquainted with Jehovah (Canaanites were not, but Laban spoke naturally of Jehovah [vv. 31, 50]) and who knew something of the sacrifice of *leaving* for her love. She was dwelling in a house nominally godly, but they lacked the character of strangers. They sought no city. Lord, if thou wouldst join me to a woman, give me one who like Rebekah, unattracted as yet by Isaac's physical characteristics, unhesitatingly said, "I will go." Jewels I can never give her—she must be willing to take only a tent and love, and be able to give comfort (v. 67). This wife was serviceable (bearing water), a second miler ("for thy camels also"), prompt and responsive (she "hastened and ran" [v. 18, 20, 28]), and retiring (she covered herself). Lord Jesus, as one who constitutes part of Thy bride, make me to be all of these.

JANUARY 19 *Genesis 25*   Abraham's jealous guard over Isaac is seen again here. The sons of the concubines must be sent away from the son of promise. There can be no union of flesh and spirit. Is this story of Rebekah's firstborn to teach me that, too? How often I would ask when conscious of inner struggles between the two natures (not infrequently of late), "If such is the case, to what purpose do I live?" (v. 22). And, Lord, teach me as I inquire of Thee that my two natures do vie with each other for manifestation in my life and that that which first conceived in me, the elder of the two, must be servile to my new and younger nature. How I long that the "quiet man," not self-reliant and skilled to suffice himself (v. 27), may overcome, may supplant, trip up the hairy hypocrite. Esau had his own garment and needed no covering for his flesh—how loath is the natural man to renounce his natural covering and don the robes of righteousness. He lives only for today—"what is the birthright to me, I am about to die?"—and despises the fact of God's pronounced blessing upon the firstborn. And always is it so. Cain is supplanted by Abel, Ishmael by Isaac, Esau by Jacob—the new man shall subjugate the old. Thank you, Lord; may my new man be strongest in me today!

JANUARY 19 *2 Timothy 2*   Extra blessings in the evening. Lawful participation in the games demanded training rules (v. 2). The training rules for this life-and-death struggle (Christ in me in the world) are dietary—feed on the right food, get enough, digest it well; and they are also physical (that's not the right word, though)—keep exercising your spiritual muscle; don't get flabby (v. 8). "Remember Jesus Christ, risen!" Not only is He to be remembered in His death, as He asked, but He is risen! Glory to God for such a remembrance!

Verse 9. Systematic Theology, be careful how you tie down the Word to fit into your set and final creeds, systems, dogmas, and organized theistic philosophies. The Word of God is not bound! It's free to say what it will to the individual, and no one can outline it into dispensations which cannot be broken. Don't get it down "cold" but let it live, fresh, warm, and vibrant, so that the world is not binding ponderous books about it, but rather it is shackling you for having allowed it to have free course in your life. That's the apostolic pattern!

Lord, help I pray. I hear the apostle telling me to turn away, and I have no strength to act. "Shun!" (v. 16), "Depart!" (v. 19); "Purge yourself!" (v. 21); "Flee!" (v. 22); "Refuse!" (v. 23). God, grant Paul's firmness to my vacillating spirit!

And those who are arguing about foreknowledge, election, and such—read those verses 14–26 and then look how the apostle is willing to leave it a paradox (vv. 25, 26). "God gives repentance" and "they recover themselves." Yes, yes, I'm naive and glad to be so in such a case.

JANUARY 20   *Genesis 26*   It is as the Word said it should be in the last days. Famine is upon Christendom. Love is grown cold because of the predominance of iniquity. The Son of Man must indeed seek for faith at His coming, for it is scarce. May these two elements, unknown either among Christians or worldlings, be found this day in me, Lord. I would have faith working by love in me. The tendency is to go to Egypt as our fathers have done, even as was Isaac's case. There is a river which does not fail; seemingly Egypt is without famine. But God wants me to find my satisfaction in wells in a famished land, not the river of a fat one.

O Lord, when Christians are going to Egypt and the world for their ideas, their methods, their manner of life, I would hear your word to Isaac, "Go not down . . . dwell in a land I will tell thee of" (v. 2). I would sow in a land of sojourning and in spite of the general famine, would be fruitful so that even worldlings will envy—not to have lands and possessions, but to display a life blessed a hundredfold without having gone to the world for methods of "cultivation." Teach me that wells, known to godly men in past years, must be unstopped, and I would not be surprised as Contention and Enmity (Esek and Sitnah) bar the way to blessing. The world must see plainly that Jahweh is with me (v. 28). Abraham had well trouble with Abimelech, I expect no less.

JANUARY 21 *Genesis 27* "Your speech betrays you." However cleverly I may cover my hands, do acts which make me seem someone I am not, and deceive by the gifts my hand might provide, the ultimate test for who I am is my voice. "The voice is Jacob's voice"—that could not be doubted. Out of a heart that is full of either sweet water or bitter springs, the fountain at my tongue and who or what I really am is at my heart. Clear out the source and fill it with Thy love that my speech may be sound and uncondemned—today!

JANUARY 22 *Genesis 28* God's promise to Abraham was that his seed should be as the dust of the earth and as the stars of heaven (13:16; 15:5). To Isaac it was promised they should be as the stars (26:4) but to Jacob that they should be as dust (v. 14). Stars suggest those children of Abraham which are so by faith—a heavenly people with a heavenly purpose and with heavenly promises. "In Isaac shall thy seed be called" (21:12). Jacob, later Israel, gives his name to the earthly people whose promises, purposes, and character were earthly. The differences of these destinations mark peoples so entirely different that to argue similarities in law, warfare, or inheritance is to be careless in the reading of Scripture.

Verse 16. In my room tonight I wish to awake as Jacob, my namesake, did and, as my soul is struck with the sobriety of the thought, would say, "How dreadful is this place! Jehovah is in this place, and I knew it not" (vv. 17, 16).

JANUARY 23 *Genesis 29* Stones on cave mouths seem just now to be barriers to blessing. On Christ's tomb the stone

sealed life away from those who were dead; when it was rolled
away, there was quickening to spiritual life. In Lazarus's being
raised the stone held the dead from the land of the living;
when removed, there was awakening to belief in Christ. Here
the stone kept the thirsting from getting at refreshment; when
it was taken off, there was revitalizing at high day. Lord,
whatever barrier there is in my life that keeps the waters of life
from freely flowing, I would not wait until all are gathered for
the great removal as these flock tenders would have. Now I ask
that You would point it out and give me power to cast it off. I
would not be like Rachel—beautiful but barren. Give me
Leah's tender eyes that I might be sensitive to the light of Thy
truth and fruitful. I would not cease bearing, though, after
Judah is born. It is often after breaking of the bread, praising
Thee, easy to stop there and not go on to labor in the work,
bearing Issachar, the fifth son whose name is from *to hire*—
service.

JANUARY 24 *Genesis 30*   My cry is Rachel's this morning,
"Give me children, or I die" (v. 1). Lord, I long to be reproduc-
ing Christ in other men, and I wonder if because Thou hast
favored me naturally, as Thou didst Rachel, somehow You
have seen best to withhold fruit. "Judge me and hear my
voice" (v. 6). Take away my reproach, Lord, I would bear a
Joseph.

JANUARY 25 *Genesis 31*   Rachel and Leah manifest an attitude toward their family which I would have toward all
earthly ties. There is now no longer an inheritance for me
down here. I've been bought by the labors of that great
Shepherd who came from afar to gain me as His bride. Lead
on, Lord, whatever God's command is or wherever He may
lead, I am now ready to go. Jacob's leading away from Laban
was influenced by circumstance—"hearing" and "seeing" (vv.
1, 2) and the promise of God, "I will be with thee, go" (v. 3). I
would see the world's countenance different toward me from
before. It has smiled and shown itself congenial, as did Laban,
but now that Thou hast blessed me above measure, it can only

be envious of me as it was of You, Lord Jesus.

Twice Laban was unable to speak good or bad. Here in verse 29 and in 24:50. I find that the world cannot speak good or bad. Whatever it may say, there is no effect in its voice, because the spiritual man is not judged according to man. Jacob, like Paul, was unaffected by man's censure, but the Lord judged them both (1 Cor. 4:1–5).

Peniel. Rachel gave a natural cause for not rising to be hospitable to Laban. Have I ever, Lord, because I am concealing idols within, given physical reasons for not rising in Thy service? Oh, may I be cut off entirely from the world, concealing no longer the false gods. May that in me which holds them be slain as Jacob declared it should be (v. 32).

JANUARY 26 *Genesis 32*   God taught Jacob not to fear Esau but to fear God. Esau could be appeased, and his face seen without hurt. God must be met with, and the crafty man must struggle with him. Jacob left Peniel with a new name and a new walk. No longer was it the walk of self-confident Jacob but the limp of humbled Israel who saw God face to face and lived. Fear not Ἰακωβ, the face of man, but learn to fear the face of God. Lord, I fear to ask for a tryst with Thee, but it must need be before I enter the land of blessing and promise. Will You meet me alone and deal with me as You did with the patriarch. His self-confidence hardly surpasses mine, and I hate myself for this, but I pray that You should give me the broken spirit, the bent look, before I proceed to deal with my brothers— whomever they may be.

JANUARY 27 *Genesis 33*   Three exams in a row (finals, two hours each) left me uneasy last night, and I know I lost contact with the Spirit. I was entirely too talkative, too dogmatic— even argumentative—with David [my brother who was Jim's classmate and fellow member of the wrestling squad] about Christians in politics. I am seeking peace on this subject. Lord, possess my spirit today. A brother gave me a verse yesterday which is a blessing. Proverbs 16:3: "Commit thy works unto the Lord, and thy thoughts shall be established" (KJV). Good counsel for exam week. Yet, I know I grieved the Spirit last night, and my thoughts were not established. Jacob had the right idea, though he seems a hypocrite straight through this chapter, when Esau wanted to journey his way quickly. Lord, don't allow me to follow the man of flesh that my faint and few spiritual possessions be overdriven in one day. I would not even be accompanied by Esau's host. Lead on gently according to the pace of the little children.

JANUARY 29 *Genesis 35*   Lord, I would recenter my spiritual life as Jacob does in this portion. Instead of Beth-el, he centers his experience on El Beth-el—not the house of God but the God of that house. Often I feel compassion for Thy Church, because it is visible and can be physically apprehended, but I would not have that be my concern any longer. Lord, I want to be centering my interest on *Thee*, the God of God's house. Be then revealed to me that my desires might be fixed on the primary thing. Christ, the Son of sorrow (v. 18) has now become the Son of His right hand. Praise God, the Savior is exalted in heaven and there given His deserved place. "As in heaven, so in earth." Even so, *come*, Lord Jesus!

Evening. Had fellowship with Brother Harper in prayer and discussing the things of God. [Harold Harper was one of the leaders of the Plymouth Brethren in Wheaton and started a meeting place and social-activity center called Bethany House.] A happy experience in prayer for the state of God's Church, and He gave confidence of a future work. God, I pray, light these idle sticks of my life and may I burn up for Thee. Consume my life, my God, for it is Thine. I seek not a long life but a full one like Yours, Lord Jesus. As I came out of Harper's study, several were enjoying a social time, and I had thoughts of self-righteousness as I turned away. But God knows my heart. To that soul which has tasted of Christ, the jaunty laugh, the taunting music of mingled voices, and the haunting appeal of smiling eyes—all these lack flavor—and I would drink deeply of Him. Fill me, O Spirit of Christ, with all the fullness of God.

JANUARY 30 *Genesis 36*   Esau left Canaan because his substance was too great for the land. His sojourning by faith is
never enough to support the man of the flesh. He must have
chiefs, princes, and rulers; he must be free to roam as he likes.
No restrictions for him. None of this sojourning near Hebron.
He had enough of such. Lord, keep me willing to be a pilgrim
in the land of promise. To those who refuse the promise there
is nothing to hold them in the land (v. 24). How typical of the
flesh is Anah. Instead of feeding submissive sheep, he is feeding headstrong asses. He is not in green pastures, but in the
wilderness, and he finds not cool waters, but hot springs.
What uselessness. Yet so it is for the sons of Esau—the liber-
tine "wild" man. He has no submission but herds the self-
willed ass. He has no sanctuary but the howling desert. He has
no satisfaction but tepid, repulsive springs whose tasting
drives him further in search of refreshment.

JANUARY 31 *Genesis 37*   Joseph was hated for three causes.
First because it was evident that his father loved him (v. 4).
Then, because of his dreams and his words (v. 8). So with the
Savior. Because the power of God clothed Him with grace
("glory as of an only begotten son" [John 1:14]), they were
moved to envy. His aspirations of a Kingdom built in the
Spirit, wherein all things in heaven (stars) and earth (sheaves)
would be subject to Him, called forth hatred. His reasoning
and words maddened them, so that when He came seeking
them, they plotted to destroy Him. "They could not speak
peaceably to Him" (v. 4). Jesus, like Joseph, was the Son of his
Father's old age. In the realm of supratemporal life before time
began to flow, before matter could be known as either old or
young, the Son Eternal was the object of His Father's affection,
and He alone is cognizant of the experiences of His Father's
"old age." At His revelation the Father clothed Him with the
varitinted character of the God-man, so that we see in Christ's
life such amazing paradoxes—the uniting of power and perfect
love; the fusion of compassionate mercy and consuming truth;
meekness and might; zeal and reticence so that He was mis-

taken for both fire-demanding Elijah and weeping Jeremiah—
the pattern being so much more vivid for the contrasts. It was
this many-colored coat that betrayed Him from afar so that His
brethren could say, "Behold, the heir, let us kill him and the
inheritance shall be ours" (Matt. 21:38; Mark 12:7; Luke 20:14).

FEBRUARY 1 *Genesis 38*   Judah had no patriarchal power,
because he had no covenant with God, but instead chose for
his companions those of the land. There was no thought that
he should go to the land of his fathers to take a wife—anything
he saw that pleased him was well enough. "He saw her and he
took her" (v. 2)—how like Shechem's method with Dinah.
(Gen. 34). And how quick is he that he should not be shamed
himself, though quite willing to burn alive the woman Tamar
who was more just than he. O Father, deliver me from being a
man of the flesh whose associations mark him not as a true son
of Israel. Impart holiness, I ask Thee.

FEBRUARY 2 *Genesis 39*   Thrice in this chapter it is stated of
Joseph that "Jehovah was with him." Not only so, but
Potiphar *saw* that "Jehovah was with him," for whatever this
man put his hand to prospered. Lord, I know Thou art with
me, but I fear that because my life is barren for Thee so much
of the time, that You gain little glory from being with *me*. I pray
Thee, make my way prosperous, not that I achieve high station, but that my life might be an exhibit to the value of knowing God. Vindicate Thyself through me. Joseph's intimacy
with his God would not allow for unholy intimacy with sin—
"he refused even to be *with* her" (v. 10).

FEBRUARY 3 *Genesis 40*   Lord, I confess to Thee that now
that it is well with me I have not remembered Thee aright.
Thou knowest how it is easy to get into service after release
from chains and to be so active that it is possible to forget the
One who ministered when there was no hope of escape. I

would remember Thee, Lord Jesus, because of the seven famine years coming upon earth—the future of the entire peoples depends upon my not forgetting to make mention of Thy Name. Show me, I pray, the difference between budding and blossoming worship and service (the vine) and those "prepared" foods. In worship of the Great King, I would know how to press into Thy hand the fresh juice of living worship, not the hardened dead meat which is only in my head and quickly plucked away by the Plunderer. I would put Thy truth to practice—in the hand; not only have it for display—on the head. Not as the baker, but as the butler. O God, save me from a life of barrenness, following a formal pattern of ethics called Theism and give instead that vital contact of the soul with Thy divine life that fruit may be produced and Life-abundant living may be known again as the final proof for Christ's message and work!

FEBRUARY 4   *Genesis 41*   I cannot but see Christ in Joseph today. He is the young man, thirty years (v. 46), a Hebrew servant (v. 12) who has been long forgotten through whom alone life is sensibly meaningful. And he takes no credit for his wisdom (v. 16) even as Christ declared that He spoke not His own words but those of His Father. None of the wise economists could give Pharaoh an "answer of peace," so today none but the forgotten Hebrew can give nations the true solvent for their impressing fears. Well might kings ask, "Can we find such a man in whom the spirit of God is?" (v. 38). Given His rightful place, Christ blesses a nation; forgotten, there is languishing in a land. "Without me ye can do *nothing*," said the Savior (John 15:5). "Without thee shall no man lift a hand or a foot in all Egypt," says Pharaoh to Joseph (v. 44). And the fruit God gives him is enough to make him forget all his toil and his father's house. So Christ in seeing the travail of His soul is satisfied, forgetting the shame of Calvary for the glory given Him in His people. Only my heavenly Joseph can open all the storehouses of God's wealth; all must go to Him for blessing.

FEBRUARY 5   *Genesis 42*   Pictures of the unsaved are abundant here. Famine stricken, they go to one who loves them but whom they do not know (v. 8). He speaks roughly to them that their repentance might be complete; gives their money back with provender to make them tremble at what God does to them (v. 28). Oh, that men might say of Christ, "We are guilty concerning our brother, we saw the distress of his soul and would not hear" (v. 21). "All these things are against me," said Jacob (v. 36). Little knew he the hand of God, for what seemed to be against him was really working for his salvation. Give me, this day, Lord, fresh confidence that "all things are working for good" (Rom. 8:28).

FEBRUARY 6   *Genesis 43*   Jacob was concerned with little things. With all the storehouses of Egypt so filled that the amount could not be tabulated, Jacob says, "Buy us a *little* food" (v. 2); "Take a little balm, a little honey" (v. 11). His unbelief parallels mine. When "all things are mine," I hesitate to ask for the greatest, though my Master be Lord of all. How that "little" must have delighted Joseph's heart, though. Perhaps he had not known much of the "choice" fruits of his homeland while in Egypt, and this gift would recall a flood of former loved associations. They feared he would "roll upon them" (v. 18 note) and make them bondmen, and if they received what they deserved, he should have. But instead he "rolled himself" upon them for good and they "drank largely" with him. Lord, make me ready to receive all that Thou hast for me. I would make ready what I have to offer since I have been told I shall eat with Thee at Thy House. Tarry not, my Savior. "And Joseph made haste for he yearned . . ." (v. 30).

FEBRUARY 7   *Genesis 44, 45*   Jacob had asked for a "little food." Joseph commanded that they have as much as they could carry. The provisions and wagons were enough to overcome Jacob's unbelief and he declared, "It is enough" (45:28). Unlike the prodigal of Luke 15 who remembered that there was *"enough* and *to spare"* (v. 17) in his father's house. How like my

Father, who has given abundantly; and how like me who only sees that it is enough—forgetting *all* that He gives.

Divining (44:5, 15). It may be that this was an accepted way of determining God's will before the law was given, for it is therein forbidden (Lev. 19:26). Another perhaps of the originally divine means of contact with men which became corrupted through careless use and is ultimately condemned.

In Benjamin, Jacob's life was "bound up" (44:30). So in me God's life is bound up in much the same sense. His nature is given me. His love is jealous for my life. All His attributes are woven into the pattern of my spirit. What a God is this! His life implanted in every child. Thank you, Father, for this. Live through me today.

FEBRUARY 8   Read this morning in R.V. [Revised Version], Weymouth, Conybeare and Greek N.T. all I could find on the fullness of God (John 1:16; Eph. 1:23; 3:19; 4:13; Col. 1:19; 2:9). What is this, that I, partaking of God's fullness, become myself a manifestation of that fullness and thereby am made party to the tremendous scheme of filling all things with God? The purpose of Christ's descent into the grave and His subsequent exaltation to the throne is part of the vast program that God might ultimately be all in all—a "pantheism" of a higher sort than most!

FEBRUARY 9 *Genesis 45*   Lord, for my consistent thoughtlessness and careless neglect of prayer and Bible study, I fear that I shall be as Joseph's brethren in Thy presence. They found themselves afraid, and I wonder if instead of being in great rejoicing at Thy return, I will be "troubled at Thy presence" (v. 3) when You stand alone as my discoverer with "no man with You" (v. 1). Father, give empowering grace to be both faithful and fervent that I be not silent before Thy Son. I thank Thee, Savior, that Thou hast been slain, not because the plans of men succeeded, but because God brought Thee before us all through death to preserve life in the earth. Give us to be in this time of blessing, unified in Thy cause; may we none of us "fall out by the way" (v. 24).

FEBRUARY 10 *Genesis 46* "And Joseph shall put his hand upon thine eyes" (v. 4). "And God shall wipe away all tears from their eyes" (Rev. 7:17). Yes, there will be tears in heaven ("he wept on his neck a good while [v. 29]), but they shall vanish. I thank Thee, Lord, that Thou wilt yet make me forget all my failure. "Soon shall the cup of glory, Wash down earth's bitterest woes!" (from "The Sands of Time," otherwise known as "Rutherford's Hymn," Annie R. Cousin).

FEBRUARY 11 *Genesis 47* Isaiah 55 tells me that the Word of the Lord gives both bread to the eater and seed to the sower. So here with Joseph. The people gave all they possessed—yes themselves also—in order that they might be fed with what Joseph had accumulated. Lord, I, too, would be willing to sell all for the treasures of Thy Word. *Bread:* that which is prepared and ready to be of immediate use for my daily sustenance. *Seed:* that which must be sown that it may die and produce fruit. Seed may speak to me of what God gives to me to be placed in another's heart, or it may be that which I do not at first apprehend but is slowly made effectual in my life after some time having been sown.

FEBRUARY 13 *Genesis 48, 49* Yesterday I was an unbeliever and did not get "seed" from the Lord for sowing among my fellows. I did not spend time enough with God to obtain a blessing. But today He has given plenty. Chapter 48 yields a blessing in verses 20, 15. I will that God bless me as Ephraim (fruitful) and Manasseh (forgetting) (cf. Phil. 3:13). Blessed be the God who has fed me all my life long unto this day. Today, too, in chapter 49 I see exhortations and examples in every one of the sons of Jacob. Reuben, the firstborn, attained not to preeminence because he boiled over as water (cf. Col. 1:18). Christ, who emptied Himself, became preeminent over all. In battle, Lord, teach me to be as Simeon and Levi who strove together as brethren. Let not my anger be as theirs, though. I would be angry but sin not. Judah—the uncrowned ruler, the lion's whelp. He had teeth after drinking milk—so must I, to use the Apostle's figure, become a man, after feeding on milk, to take meat (cf. 1 Cor. 3:2). Zebulun teaches me to be a comfort to those who sail, a haven for those who bear tidings over the water. Issachar is an ass who was strong and willing to be a servant. I would judge as Dan, casting down high things (cf. 2 Cor. 10:5). Gad, by pressing, overcame pressure. Like Asher, I would be God's baker, yielding both for His people and for Himself "royal dainties." Naphtali is freed and can speak goodly things. My right to speak good things is contingent upon my freedom which God has given each believer. Joseph, the persecuted, is more fruitful than all. Make me to be separate then, Lord, for I would have branches that run over the wall—blessing which goes beyond the usual bounds. Benjamin, like me, shall have victory, in the morning.

FEBRUARY 14 *Genesis 50*   Joseph had spoken "roughly" before (42:30), but now when fear leads them to repentance, he speaks "kindly" to their hearts. How like my God, who seemed harsh once but now promises to sustain in spite of all the evil I once intended. The promise of the dying patriarch is one I need today to believe. "Surely God will visit you and bring you up into the land promised" (v. 24). Lord, Thou hast said that the believer should enter a land where he would be as a fountain flowing, a land which is crossed on a narrow way. Lead me on in it I ask, for Jesus' sake.

FEBRUARY 15 *Genesis 49:22–27*   A few minutes' meditation of Jacob's prophecy about Joseph speaks to me of the Heavenly Man. It is Christ whose branches were neither appreciated nor given room inside the restricted bounds of Jehovah's first garden. He is the One who has broken down the middle wall of partition, in Himself abolishing the enmity. His place is by a fountain—the Godhead Himself whose pourings forth have never ceased and will not for eternity. My Savior was hatefully abused—and that without cause—but God strengthened the arms of those outstretched hands at Calvary, yea, God's own hands they were. God was in Christ reconciling the world unto Himself. This God is the Shepherd who guided, abode with, fed, and clothed Jacob as He made covenant (28:20–22). And the stone which was Jacob's resting place became a pillar of testimony. And God has seated Christ at His right hand until He makes all His enemies His footstool—things in heaven and under the earth (49:25). Yes, the blessings which Thy Father is gaining for Thee, Lord, surpass all the blessings of the progenitors—a Greater than Abraham, a Greater than Solomon—blessing which abounds to the extremities of the everlasting hills. Thou art worthy!

FEBRUARY 16 *Exodus 1* Because Israel was fruitful, she was feared. When persecuted, she prospered. The more she was afflicted, the more she went abroad. Their lives were made bitter, but their number still increased. Lord, here at Wheaton we need some affliction to unite us in our purpose, to make us prosper, to scatter us abroad. I pray, then, Lord, for—should I ask for a pharaoh who knows not our Joseph and is antagonistic? Yes, send persecution to me, Lord, that my life might bring forth much fruit. Make me as those Hebrew mothers, lively in childbearing.

FEBRUARY 17 *Exodus 2* From Levi, the fierce-feeling one (Gen. 49:6), whose wrath becomes cruel, God chooses another whose nature seems of the same fiery stuff. Moses, whose impetuosity and strong sense of social justice is here recorded in an incident similar to the affair at Shechem about Dinah, is later termed the meekest man of the earth. From this tribe God chose those who were to be His priests. Their sense of holiness was terrific (they slew three thousand one day in the wilderness) and of this sort God selects men for the service of His house. Lord, give me the spirit that is so offended at evil that it stops at nothing to judge sin. Moses means "drawn out," and how his life illustrated it—drawn out of the Nile, drawn into the wilderness of Midian, out of Egypt, chosen of God to draw out His people. His whole life is one of constant moving away from old sites and pitching on to new ones. Even the firstfruits of his body he called by a name that would ever remind him of the character of his life—a sojourner. Father, choose me as you did Moses; draw me out and away from the entanglements of the Nile; strengthen my arm to carry the pilgrim's staff.

FEBRUARY 18   *Exodus 3*   As the bush burned and was not consumed, so God enters a man and performs a miracle. God is an eternal burning (Isa. 33:14) and when He makes His abode with a man, He allows that man to become a witness to His power without being consumed by His person. John was a "burning and a shining light" (John 5:35). Make me one, Savior. Consume me with that Holy Spirit and fire that were promised for my witness and my purgation. How great is the "I AM." No man can say as God does here, "I AM because I AM"; all men must say, "I am because another begot me." Jehovah is the One whose existence and being are dependent on no other than His own Being.

FEBRUARY 19   *Exodus 4*   I did not get to the Word until this afternoon and only then after a real battle. But how good the Lord is to me, for He shows me truth here in illustration I have not seen before. God was to bear witness to Moses' authenticity as a messenger from Himself by three signs: (1) The rod was to become a serpent; (2) his hand was to become leprous; (3) water taken from the Nile was to become blood. All of these are common things—a rod, a hand, and water—and all of them are changed to representations of violence—a serpent, leprosy, and blood.

These changes were for signs that God had appeared unto and remained with the man of God. The first represents a sublime occupation. What is in your hand—a shepherd's rod? You shall be made a shepherd in the flock of God. A fishing net? I will make you a fisher of men. Art thou rich? I would appoint you to stewardship in the house of God (cf. 1 Cor. 7:20, 24). The second represents a surprising renovation. Hast thou a clean hand? And dost thou trust in thine own works instead of Mine? But place thy hand within upon that wretched heart and see how it changes your hand—leprous and sinful within. You would be nothing without Me. This sign of a purged life, a purified heart, a perfectly clean hand shall witness to the fact that I have appeared to you. But what of the last? The first two were demonstrable to the servant alone to himself as God witnessed to him in private, but the final proof must be done before men, without previewed experiment. This is for significant illustration. Take the world's own waters, dip from her own store of knowledge, and pour out before the eyes of all the redemptive story latent in the smallest bit of truth. "Using the world" for the advantage of God's cause, slaying Goliath with his own sword—this witness they will believe.

FEBRUARY 20   *Exodus 5*   God's first command to the people or person whom He has visited is that they be unbound from those things which held them in sin's power. Lazarus must be loosed and let go. Israel must be freed from her former bondage to go out and sacrifice to her God. This brings immediate conflict with the world, and the opposition is usually characterized by mockery: "Who is Jehovah?" (v. 2); "Ye are idle" (v. 17); "They regard lying words" (v. 9). Then, too, Satan sees to it that the responsibility is increased to discourage the young believer. Before, the enemy gave encouragement in making the treasures of earth, but now that God makes claim, there is no help, but only labor in mundane occupation. Satan's word is "go and work." God said, "Go and sacrifice" (vv. 17, 18).

FEBRUARY 21   *Exodus 6*   When God separates a Christian wholly, the world is not only glad to let him go, it would rid itself of him "with a strong hand" (v. 1). "Away with such a fellow from the earth" (Acts 22:22). The Lord makes known His covenant character to Moses as He had not done to the patriarchs. They had no need to know Him as such. To them He must only be *able* to do what He promised, but because He intended to fulfill His word to the children of Israel now, they must know Him as not only *able* to save but *ready* and *willing* to save. At first God demanded a three-day release, but now the request is for complete liberation—yea, the promise becomes such a demand. But pressure kept the Israelites from belief (v. 9). I enjoy the sevenfold promises of verses 6–8.

"I will bring you out from under"—free from care (worry).

"I will rid you from bondage"—free from sin (wrong-doing).

"I will redeem you with judgments"—free from judgment (wrath).

"I will take you to Me"—(the hope), free to wait.

"I will be to you a God" (cf. Eph. 2:13)—free from idolatry (for worship).

"I will bring you in"—free from wandering.

"I will give the land to you"—free from want for I am Jehovah—the God who keeps His promises.

FEBRUARY 23 *Exodus 7–12*   Yesterday, though I had plenty of time for study and read the seventh chapter faithfully and earnestly sought truth that would be fresh, I cannot say that I really found some. Perhaps I sought too hard. Perhaps I strove with the Spirit and frightened the Dove in my eagerness. Teach me, Lord, how to listen and not always seek to squeeze truth out of Scripture Thou dost not yet choose to open. My study and prayer time is not yet what I would have it. Perfect right attitudes within, I pray that I may grow and bear fruit for Thee, I ask. The plagues of chapter 8 are more clear tonight. Listed, God's wonders in Egypt would appear:

Rod turned to serpent . . . private demonstration (4:2).

River turned to blood . . . all Egypt affected . . . into vessels (7:19).

Frogs from river into the home, bed, oven, trough (8:3, 4).

Dust becomes lice . . . magicians foiled . . . upon man and beast (8:17).

Flies attack . . . Pharaoh touched . . . separation (8:21, 23).

Murrain on cattle . . . cattle die . . . possessions (9:3, 4).

Boils on men . . . on men from *furnace dust* (remains of judgment) (9:8, 9).

Hail ruins land (barley and flax) . . . death upon the un-gathered (9:31).

Locusts upon herbs . . . the remnant judged (10:15).
Darkness (10:22).
Firstborn slain (12:29).

Exodus 9:24: "Since Egypt became a nation." Does this imply there were catastrophes of like nature before Egyptian national solidarity? Perhaps the flood?

Exodus 9:16: "But in very deed for this cause I have made thee to stand to show thee my power, and that my name may be declared throughout all the earth." Wilt Thou say this to me, Lord?

FEBRUARY 24   *Exodus 5, 9*   Turning back to see if every time the Lord said, "Let My people go," He added, "that they may serve Me," the portion at the end of chapter 5 spoke to me. Looking at the state of the assembly at Lombard, yea, and the condition of my brethren and sisters here in Wheaton, I feel like saying to Thee, Lord, "Wherefore hast Thou dealt ill with this people? Why is it Thou hast sent me?" I've been here three years now—the closest years I've yet had with Thee, and yet there has been no apparent deliverance. Lord, why then hast Thou placed me here? Exodus 5:23 fits almost exactly. Lord, make me to be patient like Moses to await Thy great working. Oh, that it might be soon. Don't let us go on longer in our complacency. Rouse us by judgments, I ask.

In Lombard, a small town near Wheaton, Jim regularly attended the struggling Plymouth Brethren assembly.

Exodus 9:8: That which had gone through fire was able to cause the magicians to go from the place of contest. If self-judgment fire would flame in my heart so as to leave nothing but ash, then could the wind of the Spirit cause me to go forth convicting others of judgment. Be it so.

FEBRUARY 25   *Exodus 10*   God hardened Pharaoh's heart for three reasons: (1) that the power of God might be seen in judgment by the Egyptians, (2) that Moses might witness to his sons about the work of God in the deliverance of Israel, (3) that Moses himself might know (be witness to) that the Lord is Jehovah. Pharaoh's servants are awake to the power of God while the great one is still stubborn in his heart. How often the servants apprehend truth before masters. Pharaoh wanted to stipulate how the Israelites should go. "So be Jehovah with you, as I will let you go" (v. 10). So with the world—"Serve your God," say they, "but don't take this into your family; don't bother about the children. They are young and will be all right in Egypt." But God wants all to go—all or none at all. When all Egypt was in darkness, the children of Israel had light in their dwellings. Brickmaking ceased; Israel was at rest. Leave nothing, not a cattle hoof, in Egypt's care, for God wants all I have, and I know not what He shall have of me until I am outside the world system—until it is crucified to me.

FEBRUARY 26 *Exodus 11*   Pharaoh would have a half-hearted Exodus. "Go, but leave the children or the cattle." God's deliverance was complete. Israel was to be separated from Egypt at the command of the Egyptians, with the Egyptians' jewelry, and not a dog was to raise a voice against the departure.

FEBRUARY 28 *Exodus 12*   Yesterday was one of those ἀργόν days—idle, not working in the inner man. Yes, I studied but could not draw anything specific from the chapter to put down here. Strange that I cannot with such a chapter as Exodus 12 find any fresh practical truth. I know it must be there, but my unbelief makes me shortsighted. They ate the passover in haste and readiness to journey—that struck me, but I cannot relate what it said. Also they had their kneading troughs bound on their shoulders—why?

Last night I was reading 2 Corinthians 4, 5 accompanied with the Greek. The verses 4:16, 17 became meaningful, and I could not get back to Exodus this morning.

ὸ ἐσα ἄνθρωτος ("our inner nature") Ephesians 3:16: εἰς τὸν ἔσω ἄνθρωπον ("strengthened with power in . . ."). Romans 7:22: κατὰ τὸν ἔσω ἄνθρωπον ("delight in God's law after . . ."). 2 Corinthians 4:16: make new again day by day . . . .

ἡμέρα καί ἡμέρα ("is being renewed every day") Psalms 68:19: ἡμέραν καθ ἡμέραν (God bears our burden). Genesis 39:10: ἡμέραν ἐξ ἡμέρας (Joseph tempted day by day). 2 Chronicles 24:11: collection made "day by day." 2 Peter 2:8: Lot's soul tormented "day by day." 2 Corinthians 4:16: Inner man made new "day by day."

FEBRUARY 29   *Exodus 12 (again)*   The beginning of months. Redemption marks the new beginning of life. Men do not live at all until they have life eternal. If the household was too little for the lamb, it had to be shared. What man or household is sufficient to take in all that the Lamb of God embodies? None. He must be shared with the neighbors. The flesh was eaten the evening the sacrifice was realized. This is God's order—that those who believe should promptly apprehend all that they can of the slain Christ in their present state of growth. The flesh was to be eaten roasted, with unleavened bread and bitter herbs.

The Christ in His death must be taken hold of by me as a consumed sacrifice—not raw (How many today think only of His death as martyrdom for a cause, without consideration for the fire of God's judgment making Him sin for us?), neither boiled in water (as some would saturate the Cross with human ideas), but with the unleavened bread of sincerity and truth (1 Cor. 5:8) and with bitter herbs (the terrifically forceful demands implicated to my flesh if I am crucified with Christ). It must be eaten in readiness and haste—one must recognize his character as an unwanted pilgrim. That very night the world of Egypt rose up to thrust out those by whose testimony to the protection of blood, condemned the glory (the firstborn) of every house to death. In fact, the Egyptians declared, "We are *all* dead men" (v. 33). "This is that night of Jehovah, much to be observed" (v. 42).

MARCH 2 *Exodus 13*   Yesterday I was in 2 Corinthians again, preparing to take devotions in Greek class. Mostly review thoughts although I had some definite blessing from the study of "as He is." As He was sent, so are we. As He loves us, so we love one another. As He is pure, we are to purify ourselves. As He walked, we ought also to walk. Yea, "as He is, so are we in this world."

This thirteenth chapter of Exodus ordains the holiness of the firstborn among men and beasts. He is worthy of the first and of the best. All that opens the womb is God's and must be redeemed from Him by the blood of a Lamb. Leaven must be put away at the feast of remembrance. "It is because of that which Jehovah did for me when I came forth out of Egypt" (v. 8). Never noticed before why God led them through the desert instead of through the land of Philistia. "Lest peradventure the people repent when they see war and return to Egypt" (v. 17). They were armed and hated the house of bondage enough to leave it, but they had not yet acquired a zeal to enter in where there would be battle. So with the new Christian often. He has to develop a yen to enter the land of sweetness by wandering in a waste wilderness.

MARCH 3 *Exodus 14*   Pharaoh well might say of many Christians, "They are entangled in the land, the wilderness has shut them in" (v. 3). When saints see a path of faith through a lonely waste and when they realize the cross must cut across their path, ofttimes they are willing to become entangled in the old associations. The Red Sea seems typical of the cross in the life of the redeemed—that which protected

Israel (walls on both sides) destroyed Egypt's power. God in the work of the cross shelters the trusting soul but judges the trifling soul—deliverance for one, destruction for the other. Israel's last view of Egypt was their seeing them dead along the shore. The Christian only appreciates his deliverance from Egypt until he has seen the world under judgment as it already is. "Ye shall see them no more again forever" (v. 13). The people saw; they feared; they believed. Lord, I have an Israelite's unbelief, wondering at times if it were not better to have a grave in Egypt than struggle in this wilderness. But You have promised. I believe.

MARCH 4 *Exodus 15*   Much unaccounted-for joy in my soul this afternoon. Surely the Lord is my strength—for the body; and my song—for the emotional soul; and is become my salvation—for the spirit. The God of peace (Phil. 4:9) was one day—and shall yet be again—showing Himself a righteous man of war. The bitter waters of Marah my God has sweetened by showing me a tree which when applied to all my difficulties makes them sweet. Dave taught me a poem of Amy Carmichael's yesterday:

> From subtle love of softening things,
> From easy choices, weakenings,
> Not thus are spirits fortified,
> Not this way went the Crucified,
> From all that dims Thy Calvary,
> O Lamb of God, deliver me.
>   "Make Me Thy Fuel"

Another, by Bishop French:

> I must share if I would keep,
> These blessings from above.
> Ceasing to give I cease to have,
> Such is the law of love.

MARCH 5 *Exodus 16*   To the query, "What shall we drink?" (Christ commanded us not to ask this), God's answer is a tree cast in bitter waters so that they become sweet (15:25). At their murmuring for meat and bread He sends quail and sweet bread. They asked for Egyptian flesh pots. God asked that a pot of manna be placed before the testimony for their remembrance. Every complaint was answered with something better (v. 8)—could one say their concept of Jahweh did not contain mercy and love? The manna:

1. Came after the dew went up—I apprehend Christ after I have sent up to God what "dew" of refreshment He has given me.
2. In the wilderness only, not in Canaan (Num. 11). This morning by morning for the one who has not entered in, but a continual flowing of milk and honey for him who is in the land.
3. Small—Christ in the incarnation became small.
4. Is not easily recognizable as what it is—food.
5. Satisfied every man's need—no lack, nothing over.

MARCH 6 *Exodus 17*   A thirsty tongue is liable to be a murmuring one. When Israel was not satisfied, she tested God with her lips. So with me, and how often I have known this, when I have not been wholly satiated with the water of life in the morning, the tongue is apt to move loosely in criticism of God's children, His ways of leading, His apparent slowness to provide. I confess to Thee, Lord, I have said with genuine wonder, "Is Jahweh among us or not?", thinking I said it with Elisha at Jordan, "Where is the Lord God of Elijah?"

Really, I have been rebellious at Thy guiding, I suppose. Forgive me, I would not tempt Thee more. Thy hatred for Amalek is comparable to Thy hatred of my flesh. Do indeed, as You have sworn, blot out the remembrance of Amalek from under heaven. Yea, rehearse this in the ears of the young warriors (v. 14). The Hebrew note on the last verse is beautiful.

The Lord is my banner—"A hand is upon the throne of Jehovah" (v. 16). Moses' hands, typical of holy hands lifted up in prayer, prevailed so that a hand was laid on God's throne. Today, Christ's hand is upon that throne to entreat, to mediate, my great Intercessor, in this wilderness war against the flesh. "The Lord will have war with Amalek from generation to generation" (v. 16).

MARCH 7   *Exodus 18*   Both these last two chapters show the weakness of any human judge. In chapter seventeen, we see Moses a failure as an intercessor without someone sustaining his hands, and then we hear (v. 16) of the hand upon the throne of God that makes the everlasting war with Amalek a perpetual victory since God swore that this enemy would ultimately be wiped out. Like our battle with Satan—he is already defeated, having lost the power of his woeful instrument, death. So also with Amalek, the flesh. Since God has declared his final doom (17:14) it is easier now for us to battle, knowing the victory is already ours by virtue of God's promise. In chapter 18 Moses fails as a judge—he was wearing away at the little things they brought to him, and the people had to bear part of the burdens themselves (v. 23). Not so with my Judge—He beareth *all* their burdens. "Casting *all* your care upon him" (1 Pet. 5:7).

MARCH 8   *Exodus 19*   Israel doubtless wondered where God was taking them as they were led from wilderness to wilderness—three months of wandering and no sight of the flowing land. Here Jahweh tells them that His real purpose is not in the establishment of a commonwealth in the land, but in the bringing out of a peculiar people which was for Himself. The eagle is the lonely bird, dwelling in inaccessible crags, and its fledglings must learn that when borne on the parent's wings, they are helpless and had best not struggle or endeavor to go on their own power. The best place for the young one is in a place where he must learn dependence and obedience—the success of his life depending on the latter of these (v. 5).

God wished to make of Israel something until now unseen in the earth, a kingdom of priests, but they fell far short of this calling. None apprehended. Lord, is it possible that the Church has missed its calling as far as Israel missed hers?

MARCH 9   *Exodus 20*   Deliverance—both from the place of judgment and the power of sin. "I brought thee out of the land of Egypt"—the world which is condemned already as a place where Satan is prince—"and the house of bondage"—or of bondmen, the people who are slaves to a power they have not power to overthrow (v. 2). Thank You, Father, for delivering me from this world's system, for releasing me from this flesh's evil power to make me do evil.

Knowing that such deliverance is mine, I am committed to an order of things logically demanded, but not grudgingly enforced by my Deliverer. The moral law. His first command is that He alone secure my affections. Nothing tangible can be held dear besides Him. Such a command thrusts me into a walk of faith, following a God, praying to a Father, sacrificing for a Lover I cannot see. "No other Gods . . . Jahweh is jealous for thy love" (v. 5). His Name then becomes sacred property for having first demanded my heart; He cannot but have my lips. And then He would have me rest. The day of His rest becomes my day of rest. "Hitherto my Father worketh, and I work" (John 5:17). And so on. His commands are my delight since His hands wrought my deliverance. Lord, allow me, like Moses, when people stand afar off, to draw near to Thee. Make me one of Thine intimates, Savior. Confide in me. Tell me of Your love for me and for this world. I would draw near, unworthy, but loved and bidden.

MARCH 10   *Exodus 21*   The mark of a bondslave's love was upon his ear. His ear was for his master alone; other voices could never have claim to its obedience. It was bored through at the door so that while the slave suffered the boring through his ear, he was conscious that perfect liberty to go his own way—out the door—was being surrendered. Savior, I know

Thou hast allowed me absolute liberty, to serve Thee or to go my own way. I would serve forever, for I love my Master, I will not go out free. Mark my ear, Lord, that it might respond only to Thy voice.

MARCH 11   *Exodus 22*   The Hebrew seems to confuse the terms *God* and *judge*. Possibly the righteousness intended to be dealt out by the judge was considered to be akin—even the very righteousness of God. As God would judge, so would be the action of the magistrate. "Thou shalt not delay to offer of thy harvest [fullness], and outflow [tear]" (v. 29 note). Blessing and sorrow, joy and labor must immediately be considered before God as coming from Him and going to Him—they are intended to bring Him glory. "And ye shall be holy men unto me" (v. 31).

MARCH 12   *Exodus 23*   Justice to perfection is the law of God for man concerning his fellow. The multitude is not to influence my decision about what is right or wrong; they are not to be followed in wrongdoing. The majority is not always right. Favor is out of the question. The rich man's bribe and the poor man's misery are not to be factors in judgment. The law of treatment for a sojourner (v. 9) is illustrative of what the Savior has done. He knows the heart of a sojourner, for He was one Himself. For that reason I am not oppressed. The work of the guiding angel (v. 20) sounds like the Holy Spirit's description. He is sent before to prepare the situations I must face. He keeps me by the way (Paraclete). He brings me to the prepared place. ("I go to prepare a place for you" [John 14:2].) To Him I must take heed, for He is the Holy Spirit of God ("My name is in him" [v. 20]).

MARCH 13   *Exodus 24*   "They beheld God and did eat and drink" (v. 11). The unchanging purity of the throne of God is signified in the sapphire. Ezekiel (1:26) saw the throne of sapphire; the lover in Canticle of Canticles is seen as ivory encrusted with the stone (Song of Sol. 5:14); Job 28 says though it is valuable, it cannot buy wisdom. Jeremiah in Lamentations allows that its polish is comparable to moral uprightness; the breastplate (center stone, second row) carries it (4:7); the second foundation of the New Jerusalem is covered by it (Rev. 21:19). Its transparency allows for no impurities or flaws; its hardness (second only to diamond) denotes its unchanging character.

Feasting in God's presence is seen accompanied by several things. First the partakers were purged by blood (v. 8). There must be a purging of the leaven before the bread can be eaten in sincerity and truth (cf. 1 Cor. 5:8). The feast is to be partaken of with gladness and singleness of heart (cf. Acts 2:46). It must be eaten in haste, in readiness to move on, in recognition of the eaters' pilgrimage character (Exod. 12:14).

MARCH 14   Further meditation on the above. Lord, may I remember to keep the feast today in all these ways.

MARCH 15   *Exodus 25*   There is no reward offered to the man whose heart made him willing to give an offering (v. 2). The only reason given for all the plans and details, the only reward for all the effort, was that God should dwell among them—and this only if the construction was absolutely in accord with the pattern given on the Mount. Interesting that of the articles prescribed in this chapter, the mercy seat and the lampstand, with all their decoration, were to be of one piece. The blessings of God and all the things I have in connection with Him, my testimony, my place of meeting, the illumination of the Spirit—all that I have is of one piece of pure gold. All gifts in one—Christ. Only of Him are all things.

MARCH 17   *Exodus 26*   Meditation yesterday on the curtains and boards seemed fruitless. I fear I don't have time in a single hour to both pray and study. Lord, awaken me earlier for to spend much time with Thee. Make the *Law,* not only the New Testament, the joy of my heart. Open my eyes to truth packed into Thy word, for Jesus' sake.

MARCH 19   Somehow the study of the tabernacle seems fruitless. I can see no plausible interpretation method. My brethren who are older and much more experienced have been able to draw much from it in type. Lord, I need to have my spirit refreshed with somė new thought from Thy Word. Open my eyes and let me behold some of those "wondrous things" contained in Thy Law. The "tent of meeting," that section of the tabernacle before thė veil, was to have an oil lamp burning continually, the oil for which was to be brought by the people themselves. Does this signify the bringing of oneself, beaten, to the place of fellowship that witness might be given continually to the fact that God meets with His people? But only does He meet with those who comply with the pattern. The lamp is a unity, beaten into shape; the oil is pure, pressed and beaten.

MARCH 20 *Exodus 28*   The garments of the one who ministers to the Lord in the priest's office are for glory and for beauty, or glory and ornament, as Darby says. The ministry is "toward God" (cf. DARBY v. 1) thrice stated, and this doubtless explains to whom the glory refers. Lord, hallow Thy Name in me by keeping me aware of the truth that I am a priest *unto God*. I do thank Thee that Thou hast not made me first a minister to men but first a priest toward Thee, to bring glory to Thee in the sanctuary. There is the truth, too, of priests before men, and this, I think, is in the word *ornament*. First Peter 2:5: a holy priesthood to offer up spiritual sacrifices to God. First Peter 2:9: a royal priesthood to show forth the excellencies of Him who called you. Let your light so shine *before men* (ornament of beauty) . . . that they may glorify God (Matt. 5:16). "Showing all good faith that they may *adorn* the doctrine" (Titus 2:10). The ephod was for a memorial upon Aaron's shoulders. The breastplate was for judgment.

MARCH 21 *Exodus 29*   The religion of those on "the road out." Having ordered the priests' garments with the utmost care for details, choosing only the most wise spirited as to the making of them, insisting upon the quality of the materials used, Jahweh demands that they and those who wear them must be consecrated and sprinkled with blood. To what lengths God went in His persistence to impart the concept of the holiness of His house is seen again here. (Lord, give me a sense of that holiness, a genuine reverential fear at the assembly of Thy priests). The dedication ceremony involved:

1. The clothing of the priests at the tent door.
2. The sin offering: a bullock, blood upon altar horns, innards taken out, burned flesh.
3. The burnt offering: a ram, blood sprinkled about the altar, all burnt.
4. The wave-offering: a ram, blood sprinkled on Aaron and sons, burnt entire with bread, cake, and wafer.

The consecrated ram had a portion for Moses, the breast, and for Aaron and sons, the right thigh, or shoulder. They shall eat those things wherewith atonement was made. So this morning, as I am at the Lord's table, I shall partake of those things wherewith atonement was made. The loaf—the flesh of the ram of consecration. The wine (Old Testament saints partook not of blood, for it was as yet unshed)—that blood which was sprinkled upon and around the altar and upon the ears, thumbs, and toes of the priests. All the inwards went to God. Christ said that He was to be taken by the hands of sinful men—His body. But his inward part—His spirit—that He commended into the hands of His Father.

MARCH 22 *Exodus 30* The altar of incense seems to be representative of my daily offering of worship to God. First, its place—outside the veil wherein the Lord always says (of the ark and mercy seat), "There I will meet with thee." He meets us at the ark today as an assembly inside ("where two or three are gathered, there am I" [Matt. 18:20]), but the incense altar is the place for the individual's offering of worship daily. Second, the time of its use—continually, but especially when, in the morning, the lamps are dressed, and in the evening when they are "caused to ascend." So when I come to God morning and evening, there is the opportunity to place incense before Him. Notice when one's witness is trimmed—morning and evening. Third, its incense—sweet spices, pure and holy, tempered together, beaten very small—was not to be copied for one's own pleasure. Keep me from this, Father. Make me to realize that my individual devotion is not for the pleasure I get out of it, though I cannot help but enjoy its odors, but for Thee. Fourth, no other offering was to come on the altar. Nothing shall occupy my thinking then—not even scriptural things—when I burn incense these mornings.

MARCH 23 *Exodus 31*   Bezalel was "called by name" (v. 1). Interesting, then, must be the meaning of that name. It means "in the shadow of God." This, linked with the meaning of his assistant's name, "the father's tent," and Psalms 91:1 brings an immediate lesson. These names suggest intimacy. One who has remained in God's shadow cannot have been far from God; the man of the "father's tent" is likely the well-loved and familiar son. These men's nearness to God, as suggested by their names, shows that God makes cunning and wise, yet practical builders, those who are in close proximity with Him and are consequently conformed to His will. He that dwelleth in the secret place of the most high (the father's tent) shall abide under the shadow of the almighty (Bezalel). Their ability as builders in God's house rested upon their acquaintance with the Master Builder ("*I* will build my church" [Matt. 16:18], yet Paul claims that he, too, is a master builder [1 Cor. 3:10]). "In the hearts of the wise-hearted I have put wisdom" (v. 6). "To him that hath shall be given" (Matt. 13:12). If I display earnestness for God's work, He will give strength and wisdom to accomplish it.

MARCH 24 *Exodus 32*   "When Moses delayed to come down, the people gathered themselves to Aaron" (v. 1). How like the people of God in my own day. Thinking the Lord delays His coming, they make men their center points for gathering, forgetting that Shiloh is to come and "unto Him shall the gathering of the people be" (Gen. 49:10). They forgot God entirely, saying of Moses that it was he, a man, who brought them out of Egypt. Jahweh takes up their words and speaks to Moses thus: "*Thy* people whom *thou* broughtest up" (v. 7). Moses' argument is strong because he reverses this wording. Why are You angry with *Your* people whom *You* brought forth (v. 11). God's anger is allayed when His servant reminds Him that it is His own Name, His own people, that would be dishonored if He destroyed them.

The "finger of God" (31:18) is an interesting expression. In Luke 11:20 the Lord says He casts out demons by the finger of God. Parallel portions in the other Gospels substitute *Spirit* for finger, thus making *Spirit* equal *finger*. Christ is God's "right arm," but the Holy Spirit is represented by the finger. I can think of three instances where the fingers are instruments used by God, and I think they may correspond to the threefold ministry of the Holy Spirit. He shall convict the world of sin, righteousness, and judgment. Here in Exodus 32 the finger of God writes the law—"that sin might be seen to be sin." In John 8, Jesus writes with His finger, and men are convicted of righteousness. In Belshazzar's feast (Dan. 5), the fingers of a man's hand convict the king of impending judgment.

MARCH 25   *Exodus 33*   Worse than staying in Egypt would be going into Canaan without the Lord. Stiff-necked rebellion provokes the ire of a consuming God as nothing else. Murmuring and unbelief He endures, but the rebellious He consumes when He is with them for a moment. Lord, meet me at Horeb today, that I might strip myself of all ornament (v. 6). Show me myself as I am and lead onward into the flowing land. The tent of meeting was outside the camp. Lead me *outside*, Lord, away from all thought of men and their ways. I would speak with Thee face to face; Lord, make me Thy friend! Give the Spirit of Joshua that I might not depart from the place of meeting. Moses looked for a presence. He asked to see Your ways, and You showed him what the multitude of Israel saw not (Pss. 103:7). Lord, for this Kansas FMF trip, "if thy presence go not up, carry us not up hence" (v. 15).

Jim was an officer in the Wheaton College chapter of the Foreign Missions Fellowship, an arm of the Inter-Varsity Christian Fellowship. They made several trips to raise missionary interest among students on other college campuses.

MARCH 26 *Exodus 34*   Lord, my heart is weak this morning; make it strong in faith. Just as Moses rose early and ascended to the top of Sinai to have You write on the stone tables, I ask that I might rise, apart from others, to have Thee engrave Thy law of love upon the fleshy tables of my heart. Surely Thou knowest this hunger for holiness I now experience, for Thou must have implanted it. Raise me, Jesus, that I may hear the proclamation (v. 6). Take me for Thine inheritance, poorly as I am. I would take heed that my alliance is made with inhabitants of this land, breaking down idols I would learn Thy Name is Jealous. *"In plowing and harvest, thou shalt rest"* (v. 21).

MARCH 27 *Exodus 35*   God grant a willingness on the part of His children that there it might be sufficient to finish the work of His house—yea, too much (36:7). The fear of the Lord is the beginning of wisdom; a man who respects God's demands is wise hearted. To him that hath, even to him shall be given more besides. "In the hearts of all that are wise-hearted I have put wisdom" (31:6). And the wiser one is, the more willing he becomes—and so is the converse true. He who walks this path—beginning with a God-given willingness and proceeding in wise steps until he is willing for anything God sends—that man God uses to build His house. "If any man willeth to do His will, he shall know" (John 7:17; cf. 2 Cor. 8:11, 12).

APRIL 8 *Exodus 36–40—Leviticus 1–6*   I've just come back last night from twelve days missionary-deputation work out among student groups in Kansas. The Lord worked mightily, and I hope His Word may yet be seen effective in the lives of those He touched. It made writing practically impossible, so I'll just jot down outline blessings in the chapters studied.

Exodus 36: Men's hearts stirred them up—not God but the willingness of my own heart (v. 2). Middle bar helps boards to stand and stand together—so the Holy Spirit (v. 33).

Exodus 37: Staves of furniture constantly reminded priests of transient, moveable character of their religion—not so mine!

Exodus 38: Must not have had much exercise—no remembrance.

Exodus 39: The lace of blue (hope of the Coming) held uppermost on the priest's turban and the plate engraved HOLINESS TO THE LORD. So today, His coming purifies my motives and deeds.

Exodus 40: "As the Lord commanded"—Grant I may follow this example.

Leviticus 1: "It shall be accepted for him" (v. 4). So Christ for me.

Leviticus 2: Burn no leaven (hypocrisy, making things seem greater than they are) nor honey (natural sweetness that is not already in the offering—flavor of your own making). Always offer salt—remember the bitterness.

Leviticus 3: Fat is the Lord's, and blood shall not be eaten (vv. 16, 17).

Leviticus 4: Christ, the sacrifice for my ignorance in sin.

Leviticus 5: Applied actually. Sinning in the holy things—worship, witness, prayer—is no uncommon offense (v. 5).

Leviticus 6: I find it hard to maintain a consistent view of interpretation in these offerings. Whether the brazen altar should speak of the cross or simply of God's judgment I cannot say. This I know, that the fire continually thereon is typical of the purgative effects of Calvary, never to be put out, and also of the eternal character of God's judgment (v. 13).

"A fifth part beyond" (v. 5) perhaps this is one of the places where we derive the typical meaning of five as speaking of man's responsibility. Changing garments to carry out ashes shows me the high regard in which God holds His holiness. Father, give me to consider Thy holiness yet more sacred.

APRIL 9 *Leviticus 7*   The priest shall possess the skin of the sacrificed (v. 8). Typically there is here suggested the transaction which is effected when one commits his sin to Christ—he receives the covering of that sacrifice, the righteousness of God. The flesh must be eaten either the first day or the second—if on the third, no sin is atoned for (v. 18). Here is warning for those who wait to partake of Calvary's sacrifice. If you wait until the third day, when all shall believe in Him—your sin will be uncleansed.

APRIL 10 *Leviticus 8*   The sin offering was good neither for God's altar nor Aaron's table. Sin and all it can offer, no matter how appealing or refined, must be burnt outside the camp. The burnt offering goes all to God—laid in order upon the wood. Christ was thus sacrificed—all His life ordered and perfect, His agony, His condemnation, His spirit, and His body. In Him there was no blemish, and God saw it a perfect display offering of His own ideal. It was a sweet savor to my Father. The Ram of Consecration was given to be eaten—that's my part in Calvary, partaking of the sacrifice so that I am cleansed and consecrated by the sacrifice.

APRIL 10   A couple of things came up in evening devotions that I should jot down.

2 Corinthians 1:3: The Father of mercy.
Ephesians 1:17: The Father of glory.
James 1:17: The Father of lights.

Last night I was comparing the Greek with R.V. [American Standard Version] and discovered the change from A.V. [King James Version] in Ephesians 1:11 not "we have obtained an inheritance," but "we are made a heritage"; ἐκληρώθημεν is passive—"we are made a private possession" (cf. Titus 2:14; 1 Pet. 2:9; Eph. 1:14). "Purify for himself a λάον περιούσιαν"—not a "peculiar people," but "a people for his own possession" (Titus 2:14). "But you are a . . . λαος εἰς περιποίησιν"—a people for God's own possession or property. Note play on word χάρις in Ephesians 11:6: "the glory of His grace which He graced us with," and Luke 1:28: "highly favored."

APRIL 11 *Leviticus 9, 10*   Thank You, Father, for showing me the *order* of ministry. Aaron first offers for himself and then for the people. So with me, Lord, I pray that the sin offering might have its full effect upon me before I am concerned with dealing with the sins of Thy people. They brought the burnt offering "piece by piece" (9:13). So would I know the One who stood in my place as a burnt offering to allay the fires of God's judgment. Appear today, Lord, and show Thy presence in power. Be sanctified in them that draw nigh Thee and glorified before all the people (10:3).

APRIL 13 *Leviticus 11*   Aaron had to be told not to drink strong drink so that he could make a distinction between the holy and the common, the unclean and the clean (10:8–11). All these animals are listed one way or another because the people had no discernment in what was clean and what was unclean. It is taken as understood that God's people are to be holy, since He is holy, but how to become so, they do not know apart from His telling them. In the age of the Spirit there are no dietary laws because the believer is indwelt with the πνεῦμα ἅγια— his Holy Conscience which gives him discernment in all things (1 Cor. 2:15). These distinctions seem arbitrary, and Jews would doubtless be dubbed narrow if they adhered to such standards, but God's ways are not arbitrary but purposeful. He makes distinctions on grounds of physical characteristics— hoofs, fins, cuds, scales, eating habits (of birds). To the pure, all things are pure.

APRIL 14 *Leviticus 12, 13*   "I was shapen in iniquity, and in sin did my mother conceive me" (Pss. 51:5 KJV). From the beginning of life my contact has been with the unclean—how then can a man become pure? The atonement blood that cleanses my mother must avail also for me. O Lamb of God, what a sacrifice Thou art! Whose blood could avail like Thine? Goat's blood could not cleanse for animals are nonmoral. My own would not avail for I am immoral. Only Thou art perfectly moral, and only Thy blood could be of any effect.

Leprosy breaks out in several ways and places which may be typical. Leviticus 13:

1. In the skin of the flesh: a rising, a scab, a bright spot (v. 2).
2. Quick raw flesh, an old leprosy (vv. 10, 11).
3. Breaking out of a boil (vv. 18–20).
4. Breaking out in burning with fire (vv. 24, 25).
5. Scall on the head (v. 30).
6. Rising in a bald place (v. 42).
7. In garments (vv. 45–58).

1. A rising of the flesh—the primary root of sin, pride.
2. The reexerted willfulness of the old flesh of Adam's kind.
3. The issue from the flesh—the corruption from the mouth, the evil thoughts proceeding out of the heart.
4. Rising in a burn—rebellion at judgment or justice.
5. Intellectual difficulties—a rising in the head, doubts.
6. Nakedness of a sinner.
7. In the best of our good woven garments of deeds there is impurity.

APRIL 15 *Leviticus 14*   The test for determining cleansing of leprosy whether in flesh, garment, or wall seems to be the law of recurrence. Leave the suspected article for a while, and if there is spreading, there is surely disease. So with the professor. He may not appear diseased but observe him carefully awhile, the eating canker. Sin cannot be covered indefinitely—it will be out in time. Birds and lambs (the free and the innocent) must die for cleansing. Thus was my Savior—as a free heavenly creature sacrificed in an earthen vessel while underlying all this mysterious sacrifice ran the living water, carrying away refuse, refreshing with renewed bounty moment by moment.

APRIL 16 *Leviticus 15* Yesterday Ruth Stam said to me that someone had made this statement about my manner: "We know he is humble, but we wish he would act it." How they can be so certain of the first statement I don't know; my own proud heart is fully aware now of its self-exaltation. Probably I have been a hypocrite clever enough to conceal what really lies there. But the last clause speaks to my heart in powerful tones. Often I have felt this self-exertion coming out and know now that my mode of self-expression must have been, yea, and is, most offensive. I cannot do anything about this, Father. I've tried again and again to be silent and act gravely and soberly as I feel a holy man ought, but to little avail. Either someone asks if I'm sick or my own affable, self-confident nature bubbles over with something that breaks the spell. This is self-effort and is most ineffective.

As I opened the Book just now, the Scripture said, "When any man hath an issue out of his flesh, because of his issue he is unclean . . . . whether his flesh run or whether his flesh be stopped from his issue, it is his uncleanness" (vv. 2, 3). This flesh of mine is constantly issuing something of itself, or perhaps holding it in, "stopping the issue," but it is all uncleanness. And the whole chapter tells how the unclean defiles all it contacts. Lord, Thou must put an end to my fleshly issue. Stop it, Lord. Staunch the flow of this defilement which springs from rotten flesh. Instead, flow Thou through me, today, yea, for seven days, until Thou dost see me to be clean.

Ruth Lois Stam was a student at Wheaton and a member of the Foreign Missions Fellowship along with Jim. She went to Pakistan as a missionary.

APRIL 17 *Leviticus 16* This idea of two offerings (as the two birds for the cleansing of lepers and here the two goats for a sin offering) seems to refer to different aspects of Christ's death. Part of the sacrifice was used as a blood sacrifice within the veil; the other goat had sins laid on its head and is taken by a man appointed unto a solitary place. So Christ's death spoke

before God satisfactorily, as cleansing for men from uncleanness; but it also speaks of the loneliness of the Sin Bearer. This
Sacrifice spoke both where God dwelt and where no man could
dwell—in the wilderness alone. The latter goat was led by an
appointed man—one who was in readiness. How descriptive
of the lonely Man of Sorrows who willingly offered Himself.
Aaron offered blood and incense worship for himself before he
did anything as a service for the people. So must I.

APRIL 18 *Leviticus 17, 18*   The place *is* important. There
was to be no indiscriminate choice of where the sacrifice was
to be slain. Only at the door of the tent of meeting could God
accept the oblation. So today every act of faith which is acceptable is accomplished before Him who said, "I am the door"
and only there. Those who would do their contacting of God
through nature in the open field are not taken into account.
Those who would meet my God must not presume to meet
Him because they have attained the top rung of social or cultural prestige. All faith must be in Christ before it is true faith.
All other persons, places, and principles are false resting
points for faith. The life of the flesh is in the blood. Blood is
given upon the altar and is never to be eaten. He who consumes blood will ever have God's face set against him (17:10).
So with me. If I would save my life blood—forbear to pour it
out as a sacrifice in opposition to the example of my Lord—
then must I feel the flint of the face of God set against my
purpose. Father, take my life, yea, my blood, if Thou wilt, and
consume it with Thine enveloping fire. I would not save it, for
it is not mine to save. Have it, Lord, have it all. Pour out my
life as an oblation for the world. Blood is only of value as it
flows before Thine altars.

Leviticus 18:3: The pattern of my behavior is not set in the
activities of those about me. Don't follow the example of those
you left in the world, or those you find in the church. Rather
the law of God, found in His Word, shall be my standard, and,
as I see it, there are few examples of this sort of living anywhere. God gives commands to abstain from all enormities
and confusion and the reason given—though it is practically

that of not being vomited out of the land—is actually because "I am Jaweh, your God."

APRIL 19 *Leviticus 19*   Because of who it is that commands—because of His holy nature—there is to be holiness among the people. Not for outward show or cultural esteem were the Israelites to conform to law, but because of the nature of their God. Verse 4 reads well in the footnote, "Turn ye not unto things of nought." (Lord, teach me what these be. I fear there are many to which I have turned aside.) "Thou shalt not curse the deaf, nor put a stumbling block before the blind" (v. 14). There can be no taking advantage of others' weaknesses in God's economy.

APRIL 20   *Leviticus 20*

V. 8: I am Jahweh who sanctifieth you.
V. 24: I am Jahweh who separates you from the peoples.
V. 26: I, Jahweh, am holy and have set you apart . . . that you should be mine.

Sanctify yourselves (v. 7) . . . . I sanctify you (v. 8). So I would set myself apart from the customs of the people, to become a peculiar treasure of Thine. Take this life, Lord, that I crave should be Thine, and separate it for Yourself. Purge and cleanse with the fire of Thy Spirit and the water of Thy Word that I might be unto honor.

APRIL 21 *Leviticus 21*   Lord, I pray that I might be holy. These things spoken of—defilement with the dead, pollution with women, inherent blemishes—I've known them all to a degree. Make me conscious, instant by instant, that Thou hast anointed me to do a priest's office by the shedding forth of the Spirit of holiness. These blemishes mentioned must be typical, for You will accept and use those who are thus handicapped today. My fear is that even today, while thinking of definite guidance, I might be blind to the truth Thou wouldst teach me.

And lame—my walk not straightforward, but inconsistent and staggering as one lame. Of my life it can be said, "he hath a blemish" (v. 21). Wilt thou heal me, Lord, that I might be a man who does not defile Thy courts.

APRIL 22 *Leviticus 22*   "I am Jehovah" is repeated nine times in this chapter. It makes a difference who says a command whether or not it should be obeyed. Lord, give me to fear Thee for Thy great Name's sake. Verse 23 states that a perfect offering not only has nothing lacking in all its parts, but there is nothing superfluous, either. Christ was this in a moral sense.

APRIL 24 *Leviticus 23*   I've been thinking of the priests a little this morning. Somehow I find it difficult to understand the picture the Lord has here laid out. Father, Jesus promised Thy Holy Spirit would lead me into all truth. May He show me the truth of Leviticus. I want to get it from Thee for myself. The Israelite gave offerings to the priest, not as a gift to the priest but as if he were actually giving to God. Much of it was used for the priest's own sustenance, though. So in my giving should be this attitude, not as giving to men for their pay in the field, but as giving directly to the Lord. Jehovah accepted or rejected a gift, not the priest. This made Aaron's family live by faith—since they could keep no meat after the second day.

APRIL 25 *Leviticus 24*   I'm impressed with the recurrence of the word *pure*—pure olive oil, pure candlestick, pure table, pure frankincense. The oil and incense are God's supply; the table and candlestick (though also from Him) I am responsible for. These are suggestive of the witness and fellowship. Lord, keep mine pure!

APRIL 27 *Leviticus 26, 27*   The Lord spoke from 26:10 yesterday; it speaks of the Old Testament illuminated and made applicable because of the New. Surely without the New Testament the Old Testament Hebrew Scriptures would mean little to us (cf. Matt. 13:52). That chapter (Lev. 26) surely shows life a vain thing if the Word of the Lord is not heeded: verse 16—ye sow in vain; verse 20—your strength is spent for nothing; verse 26—ye eat and are not satisfied. Give me to value Your precepts, Father, that life might be worthwhile. Chapter 27 seems something added to the rest of the book—a word on tithes and vows that suggests perhaps that the Lord actually was giving Israel a test to see if they held His Word in estimation.

APRIL 29 *Numbers 3* Read 1, 2 yesterday but got nothing definite to set down. Today the comparison of Levi and the rest comes clear. Levi's sons were numbered from a month old and upward (not twenty years as the rest), for they were chosen to be ministers, dedicated to the Lord apart, not fighters. They were taken in place of all the firstborn—22,000 strong. "They were wholly given" (v. 9), or "given, given" (note). So with the saint-priest today—given wholly to God. "Not your own" (1 Cor. 6:19).

APRIL 30 *Numbers 4* I must confess, Father, that these passages are difficult to draw soul food from. Numbers themselves seem to be of little value in spiritual applications—now, that is, for I'm sure it's only my inability to discern that makes these chapters so inscrutable. There are new thoughts, though. Covering all the tabernacle furniture with blue except the altar and putting purple on that is surely of some significance. As they journeyed, the burden of the Kohathites would remind them of their heavenly character—some covered with skins over blue cloth. The ark of witness showed blue outside, the table of showbread was covered with scarlet under skin. The great altar showed purple. These speak of glory veiled in flesh. None may see the thing itself. Incarnation?

MAY 1 *Numbers 5* The law of jealousy may refer to my unfaithfulness to my Bridegroom. How often I must cause the spirit of jealousy to come upon Thee, Lord Jesus, when my heart desires others beside Thee. The holy water mingled with dust put into an earthen bowl in which the curses are blotted (v. 23) speaks of the Word, I'm sure. God's holiness put in words—the water; the dust of the tabernacle floor—the holy men who wrote; the curse blotted in the water—the curses written but removed by faith. This is John's experience when the Book is sweet in his mouth but bitter in his belly (Rev. 10:10).

MAY 2 *Numbers 6*   The Nazarite was holy in three negative ways: (1) he must not touch the grape; (2) he must not cut his hair; (3) he must not touch a dead body. Were I to transpose such consecration into New Testament parallels I suppose this would be the setup:

1. Grapes—the source of natural joy—that which makes glad the heart of man. This is denying oneself the allowable pleasures for the sake of a greater holiness.
2. The long hair of man is his shame. He must let it grow so that he becomes unashamed of shame—reproach bearing for God.
3. Separation from evil men in all their doings—yea, even from family pulls (v. 7).

I know little of any of these.

MAY 3 *Numbers 7, 8*   One thought stands out in Numbers 7:9. The sons of Kohath were to be given no aid in bearing the furniture of the sanctuary. The others were given covered wagons and oxen to pull them. This speaks to me of methods used in doing God's work. Some phases of it—the Gospel testimony, for example—can be carried on with various plans and in different manners, letting the work append on all sorts of things (so long as it was a *covered* wagon so that the holy things were not exposed to common view). But worship, the service of the sanctuary, can have no clever means of execution and transport—it must be upon the individual's shoulders, his personal responsibility.

MAY 4 *Numbers 9*   Perhaps this word about partaking of the feast later when one is defiled or journeying has significance for breaking bread. A man whose contact with the world has been such that he knows he is unclean or one whose heart is wandering from God's people should not cease partaking forever but should wait a month until fellowship and a pleasing state of soul be regained. The time is not essential—the principle seems plain.

Guidance for Israel in wandering was unquestionable. There could be no doubt if God wished them to move—the only question there could be was, were they willing to follow as the cloud moved? Shall my Father be less definite with me? I cannot believe so. Often I doubt for I cannot see, but surely the Spirit will lead as definitely as the pillar of cloud. The question for me is, are my plans flexible enough to be subject to immediate revamping? When the cloud remained long, the people must have wondered why and been restless. I must be as willing to remain as to go. The presence of God determined the whereabouts of His people. "Where I am, there will my servant be also" (John 12:26). At the *command* of Jahweh they encamped, at the command they journeyed (v. 23). Very well, Lord, what of this summer?

MAY 5 *Numbers 10–12*   My daily cry should be that of Moses as the ark moved or rested, "Rise up, Lord." "Return, Lord." Savior, be then quick in what Thou doest. I know Thou wilt soon come to scatter Thine enemies and to unite Thy church (10:35). Rise up to judge Thy people, set captives free. Teach me while You tarry to value Thy leading, Thy feeding, Thy leaders, and Thy burden. The people murmured in dissatisfaction even though the pillar of cloud was witness to the fact of supernatural guidance. I would rely on Thy Spirit and promises—the cloud and ark of witness. Then they complained at the zestless manna—it was too common and simple a fare. Let not my soul be dried away (11:6) but keep me fresh with daily gathering of good things. Deliver me from the lusting after spicy food—thrilling experience, strong meat and lots of it. Give me the Spirit of Moses in wishing all the Lord's

people were prophets and in not being jealous of any where-
ever they are used by the Spirit. I would value the burden
placed on me. Make me feel more still of a concern for Thy
Church. Surely it is too heavy for me alone, so raise up others
who will share in this work of carrying Thy people. O God,
show us the power of Thy holiness lest we find ourselves at
another Kibroth-hattaavah.

MAY 6   *Numbers 13, 14*   The land of promise has been spied
out. Those who come back from there know well its rigors and
its beauties, but it depends upon the Spirit which is in them
how they tell of it (14:24). Verses 18–20 give some things about
the land which also may characterize the Spirit-filled life. What
is the land? A place of rest (Heb. 3, 4), yet a place of struggle
("labor to enter into rest" [Heb. 11:4]); the people there are
strong—but of both sorts. Some are demon-giants—fear,
pride, and so forth—but the Spirit-filled man overcomes these.
The land is rugged but fruitful, and the cities inaccessible
without great faith ladders and courageous weapons. Some
camp there only, others settle down, securely fixed inside
strongholds. It is fat, that land, yet it eats up the people who go
there, consumes them as the zeal canker (13:32). Always there
is joy, though, for it is perpetually the land of first-ripe grapes.
"Let us go up at once"—yes, and remain in our own sight as
grasshoppers. Keep yourself in good perspective. If Jehovah
delight in us, He will bring us in (14:8). The giants there we
shall feed on—reverse Satan's attempts to repulse. If we go not
in, the Egyptians will say that Jahweh was not able to do as He
planned.

MAY 8   *Numbers 17, 18*   "The rod of the man I shall choose
shall bud" (v. 5). This may give hint to a promise of fruit
bearing for one whom God has chosen. Dare I apply this,
Father? If you have chosen me, my life should be budding,
blossoming, and bearing fruit as did Aaron's. But, alas, I see so
little evidence of Your power in my life. What witness dost
Thou give that You have chosen me? Perhaps it is because I

have not yet been long enough before Thee as was the rod. Everyone that comes near to the tabernacle dies (17:13). In one way or another, I would die. Either take me to be with Thee, Savior, or put out the life of this old man as I draw near Thee in the flesh. Consume me, Fiery Lover, as Thou dost choose.

MAY 9   *Numbers 19*   The water of impurity—running water into which the ashes of the heifer were put to be used in sprinkling the unclean for purification. This is the Word and its cleansing power, as it has suspended in its every part the ashes of a slain victim—bits of Christ throughout.

MAY 10   *Numbers 20*   How often I have complained about the place into which God leads me, as these Israelites. At Lombard I feel I'm in wilderness—the place of nonproduction—no seed, figs, vines, or pomegranates (seed corn of wheat dying; figs; fruit not only leaves; vine-abiding; pomegranate—"much fruit." Not even water—to satisfy, to cleanse, to cause to grow). It is time for me to fall upon my face before God for this matter. The rod of power, the scepter of faith, is to be taken but not used violently—take the rod, but speak, don't smite. Act as one in a place of authority (seated together with Him in the heavenly places) but believe God will send refreshing without blows. Moses knew how to pass through Edom. Have nothing to do with the sources of satisfaction there—pass not through field or vineyard and drink not from her wells. Pass through on the king's highway—straight and unwavering. If Edom resist thee, turn aside and meet God at Mount Hor.

The Lombard (Plymouth Brethren) assembly did not measure up (any more than any group of Christians anywhere could possibly) to Jim's expectations. He wanted the immediate and unqualified fulfillment of scriptural promises.

MAY 11   *Numbers 21*   "The soul of the people was shortened because of the way" (v. 4 note). Father, Thou knowest my way of being short in the grain, discouraged so quickly, riled without any warning at all. How I need to be exercising that fruit of the Spirit: μακροθύμια "long-soul-edness." Teach me patience in this waiting time. O God, I crave Thy power. Help me to possess my soul in patience until Thou dost come upon me in might—until entry into the flowing land. It was natural for them to become dissatisfied—no bread but the light stuff of which the soul soon wearies. Lord, I must have something more than this morning-by-morning manna. It must be a more stable food if this soul is to be satisfied. I'm not murmuring against Thee, Lord. My prayer is against my own "short soul." Make me to enjoy the riches of Your land—Christ, Christ, possess me!

MAY 12 *Numbers 22–24*   The error of Balaam—his teachings are condemned in 2 Peter 2:15; Jude 11; Revelation 2:14. There it is seen to be the hire or pay that led the prophet astray and his putting a stumbling block before Israel is condemned in the letter to Pergamum. In 22:7 begins the evil, when princes came to Balaam with the "rewards of divination" in their hands. In verse 32 we are told why his going after the second summons was wrong—he was too eager to go, "thy way is headlong," or *perverse* (note). This is suggested again in the Greek of Jude 11: "They ἐξεχύθησαν (ἐκχέω, 'to pour out') in the wandering [error] of Balaam." They poured themselves out, were lavish in their eagerness for hire—gave way with full force to desire. Nothing would hinder them—note the unwarranted ire of Balaam against his ass. The Lord forced him to prophesy only good things of the people, so it was not his cursing that hindered Israel. It was his counsel to waylay the Israelites with harlotry (31:16). It is this that is condemned in Revelation 2:14, the teaching of Balaam—to cast stumbling blocks in the way of God's people. Balak would build a wall of strong-armed defense to hinder Israel. Balaam knows that is not subtle enough. They must be tripped up unsuspectingly, not with the power of princes but with the plague of wily princes' daughters like Cozbi (25:15).

MAY 13 *Numbers 23*   God met Balaam on a "bare height" (v. 3). Here is what I must learn from Thee, my God, to rise high and get into an open place. It must be if I am to meet with Thee that the realm of the commonplace be left, the meadows of mediocrity, the land of the usual and customary, yea, the altars of kings and the place of princes. Above all these I must go to get alone with Thee. Lord, plant my feet on higher ground. Take me up where I can view things from Thy perspective. And lead me into that *bare* height. Lift me to the top of the bald rocks where there is not any subterfuge, no undergrowth to hinder the searchlight of heaven from examining the depths of my soul. Yea, there is the loneliness of fellowship with Thee that I must revel in. God's people as Balaam speaks of them—"To a people that dwelleth alone, not reckoned among nations" (v. 9). Here is a promise, my soul; guard it. "God is not a man that he should lie . . . hath he spoken and will he not make it good?" (v. 19).

Evening. God speaks peace, and I know joy in the Lord tonight. Have been especially encouraged by reading *Behind the Ranges,* biography of J. Frazer of Lisuland, West China. May God teach me to be as that brother.

MAY 14 *Numbers 25, 26*   When sin was in all the camp, and Jahweh was displeased, He commanded that the chiefs of the people be hanged. So among Christians. If the Church is to be purged, her leaders must first be judged. The money-seeking, heartless, "outstanding" theologians and Bible teachers must first learn holiness before the mass of their followers are to walk rightly. Phinehas, while others wept at the gate of the tent of meeting, carried out God's plan by killing Zimri and Cozbi—prince and princess among their people. God, give me his holy jealousy for Thy Name. Deliver me from simple weeping for sin. Teach me to judge it—in the high places of my own heart.

MAY 18 *Numbers 32*   This chapter has instruction for him who would settle down before God's purpose in possessing is finished. The reason they wanted "this" side of Jordan was because they had seen it and saw it fitted their case. How like many today who never having seen the mission field and having talents and training usable in this country stoutly declare "bring me not over the Jordan" (v. 5). This is a land of cattle, and I have cattle, or this is a place where teachers are sorely needed and ably used, and I think I could be a teacher. "Shall your brethren go forth to war and shall ye sit here?" (v. 6). This very thing brought forty years' wandering and left 603,550 carcasses in the wilderness. "Cursed be he that doeth the work of the Lord negligently and that withholdeth his sword from blood" (Jer. 48:10). The only way to be guiltless is to leave your possessions and little ones and go across to war.

MAY 19 *Numbers 33*   If the Lord were to command me, as He did Moses, to write a list of my journeys (in terms of spiritual experiences) I fear my own history would be as Israel's—"Ye did run well" (from Pi-hahiroth to Migdol and through the sea). But since then it has been unbelief fostering discontent and powerlessness. Before entering all of those who saw graves dug for Egypt's firstborn must perish. When the enemies inside (the fifth column of Adam) are gone, then new enemies in a different land—(real opposition from a God-despising world) must be overcome. Not only the world, either—verse 55 implies enemies that become thorns and pricks if not dealt with. God make me a warrior, I'm weary of this slacker's life of unbelief.

MAY 20 *Numbers 35*   For the manslayer who ventured to trust his own wit to escape the avenger of blood there was no law of protection. This refuge city presents a picture of all the world. I had slain the Innocent unwittingly (". . . they *know* not what they do" [Luke 23:34]. "If the princes of this world *knew*, they would not have crucified the Lord of Glory" [1 Cor. 2:8]), and God has provided the city of the Levites—the holy men—for my safety. There can be no leaving now for my High Priest can never die. He Himself took the wrath of the manslayer, and I am free. Give me to rejoice in this, Lord, may such truth not become stale.

MAY 23 *Deuteronomy 1, 2*   At Horeb God thought Israel ready to possess and said, "Ye have dwelt in this mountain long enough, go up and possess" (1:6–8). Forty years later after devouring those who turned back from going up, He said again, "Ye have compassed this mountain long enough, turn ye . . ." (2:3). After failing to exercise faith in one instance, God may have to deal harshly with me for a long time before giving another fit opportunity for entering into my possession. "The cause that is too hard for you ye shall bring to me and I will hear it" (1:17). So with the ministry of intercession. Bear what you can and do what your understanding allows, but when the case is too hard (as it usually is), take it to the great Intercessor—He will hear. Deuteronomy 1:27 comforted me. They said Jahweh hated them, since things went so badly, but in reality Jahweh loved them—yea, loved them as a father bears his son (1:31) (not as a mother her babe—that is hardly comparable) but they mistook His leading. I know the parallel. "Jahweh heard the voice of your words" (1:34)—not your words but their *voice*, not the syllables but the spirit of rebellion, not the expression but the thought. What's the *tone* of my prayer. "Ye deemed it a light thing to go up" (1:43 note). How often today is exercise of soul—spiritual experience—thought of as a light thing. Not a thing to be forward about but to be cautious over—counting the cost.

MAY 26 *Deuteronomy 5*   Much hunger of soul this morning. Wholly dissatisfied with my present powerlessness. Verse 29 speaks especially as I read. "Oh that there were such a heart in them, that they would fear me, and keep all my commands always . . . ." Oh, that I had such a heart. Commandment keeping is terribly laborious when it doesn't spring from an eager pious heart. ". . . doing the will of God from the heart!" (Eph. 6:6).

MAY 30 *Deuteronomy 8*   I see this morning afresh my God's love for me in His earnest desire to see me prosper. As a father chasteneth his son, so He me. "He suffered thee to hunger that he might prove thee" (vv. 2, 3). His Word is given that I might *live* (1 Pet. 1:23), multiply (John 15:16), and possess (Heb.

10:34). Simply to have life is not all God purposes for me—but I know nothing of multiplication. I am still only a living soul. God make of me a quickening spirit.

MAY 31　*Deuteronomy 9, 10*　　Not for my righteousness nor the uprightness of my heart would the Lord lead me unto Himself, into my promised inheritance ("greater things" [John 14:12]), but for two other reasons (9:5). First to show His righteousness by dispossessing the hordes of Satan, and second, to establish His Word, make good His promise. "Stiffnecked" describes my attitude—slow to bow in submission to commands or in act of prayer and slow to plow, rebellion in the yoke, not eager for service. But, blessed be His Name. He intends to bring me into this promised place regardless! Remember Thy Son, O God, and look not unto the stubbornness of this people! (9:27).

At the place of the water brooks, God set apart Levi (16:8, 9). Three reasons for their separation are given and one result: (1) they were to bear the ark of the covenant—the witness of all God's promises (for me, the Word); (2) standing before Jehovah was their task, waiting as servants for His bidding to minister to Him—note, to *Him* first, not to men; (3) then they were to bless others in His Name. They were Word bearers, worshipers, and workers. Wherefore, Levi hath no "inheritance." Lord, if You will but allow me to take this set-apart place, by Thy grace I shall covet no inheritance. Nothing *but Christ!*

JUNE 1　*Deuteronomy 11*　　My thirst for the blessed land increases as I read Moses. Here I must refresh my dry soul "with the foot," or, I suppose we would say, "by hand." With fleshly effort and striving only is it possible to produce. How I long for the land that *drinks* effortlessly, of the rain of heaven—the land that God cares for and not man! It's that state of the soul that has entered by faith into perfect rest, a broad, open country of hills and valleys, exhilarating heights and mossy cool quiet times—upon which the eyes of God remain continually—not as a puny garden of cooped-up herbs.

JUNE 2 *Deuteronomy 12* "Ye shall rejoice in all that ye put your hand unto" (v. 18). The Levite is not to be forgotten (vv. 12, 18, 19). Who today is the man whose inheritance is the Lord Himself? That one I may not forget. What is right in every man's own eyes is not the Law of Canaan. There it is, "What saith the Lord?" Are you ready for this, my soul? No blood to be eaten. Yet Jesus said, "Unless ye eat my flesh and drink my blood," no life. Many eat His flesh, exult in the perfection of His manhood while disallowing the blood, counting that a light thing.

JUNE 3 *Deuteronomy 13, 14* The dreamer is plain without question because he spoke of turning aside (13:5). God grant thee this power, my soul, to put away *any* evil (this sort even had a religious tang to it) that suggests incomplete following after the Lord. Yea, though thine own brother—or that friend who is as thine own soul, Jim—must not be consented to. Every force of your being must be steeled against the least wavering. The will (thou shalt not consent), the ear (nor hearken), the eye (let it not pity), thy conscience (spare not), thy mouth (conceal him not)—all must be vividly aware of the tendency to departure (13:8).

JUNE 4 *Deuteronomy 15, 16* "Jehovah's release" has been proclaimed—as God for Christ's sake has forgiven you, forgive ye one another. Only of foreigners is pay exacted. So only those alienated in heart must be responsible one day for the great debt owed their Creator. Thus the poor will be eliminated. In God's economy all should be lenders, giving from a joyful heart as He does Himself. To many we should lend— giving as God prospers—but if we do so, God will never suffer us to borrow (15:6). And all giving is to be done (not as unto the Lord, the New Testament method) but in respect of reward and blessing from God—done with an open hand and an ungrieved heart (15:9–11). In it all I must remember I was once a bondman. And constantly thou shalt "appear before Jehovah"—and not empty, either. God's man is to be full so that he may be always giving—ἔχων αὐτάρκειαν (2 Cor. 4:8).

JUNE 4 *Deuteronomy 17*   The ox—or devoted servant—and the lamb—a common follower among the flock—must be without blemish. Romans 12:1 says "holy, acceptable." May there be no blemish of soul, Lord, no impurity of motive, nothing unsightly in my "living sacrifice." The witness of sin is responsible before all else and others to judge sin. Bring forth the offender and stone it whatever the pain or how dear the desire (and must this mean her, Lord?). Judgment is best understood by him who remains in the Lord's presence. Better to be instructed by a simple holy man than by a wise man who has not been where God put His Name (1 Cor. 6:1–8).

Jim and I had one "date"—a missionary meeting at Moody Church in Chicago—in April. We had sat together in Greek classes and often studied our Thucydides assignment together. But on May 31, following an FMF breakfast in a park, he told me that he loved me. He hastened to quell my rising hopes by adding that God had given him no indication whatsoever that he was to marry me or even that he was ever to marry at all. I was going to Africa as a missionary (I thought), and he was headed for South America. We were perplexed as to the proper course to follow. Agreeing that the matter was too big for us to handle, we decided to pray about it separately.

JUNE 8 *Deuteronomy 23, 24*   Seems some time since my last entry. Mind has been muddy about Betty H. lately and have had trouble in concentration. Thankfully God has borne with me and shown me fresh substance this day. Deuteronomy 23:24 says I can take refreshment and encouragement from my neighbor but cannot get substance for my gain from him. Eat what you can but don't put into a vessel or move a sickle on his standing grain. So in spiritual refreshment I can get bits of nourishment along the way from others, but I cannot get abundance—over and above profit from my brethren. I must get from my own labor and study those things which will be gain to me in this soul's building. Deuteronomy 24:5 tells of a man who enters into a new relationship—he is not to go out with the host or be charged with any responsibility. True in the birth of a soul, I think—let the soul become accustomed to its new state before sending it to war. Verse 9 reminds me of two other women which Scripture exhorts me to remember—this one for sin's cleansing. Remember Miriam (Num. 12). Remember Lot's wife (Luke 17:32). A memorial for the woman with the alabaster box (Matt. 26:13). The power of remembrance is known to God. Many times He says to Israel, Remember you were a bondman . . . . Thou shalt not forget to blot out Amalek (25:19). The flesh I must continue to slay. He is attacking me where I lag behind in the least.

JUNE 10 *Deuteronomy 29* Came to an understanding at the Cross with Betty last night. Seemed the Lord made me think of it as laying a sacrifice on the altar. She has put her life there, and I almost felt as if I would lay a hand on it, to retrieve it for myself, but it is not mine—wholly God's. He paid for it and is worthy to do with it what He will. Take it and burn it for Thy pleasure, Lord, and may Thy fire fall on me as well. Meditation is easier now.

You saw the wonders, says Moses, but God has not given you a heart to understand, nor eyes to see, nor ears to hear. Like Jacob, like Jim. I know God's working but fail to perceive or discern what it all means. My eye is not quick enough to know all implications. Give spiritual senses, Lord, that I might know Thy way. "Ye have not eaten, nor drunk that ye may know me—who I am" (v. 6). He suffered them to hunger that they might learn what man lives by (8:3). ἔμαθεν διὰ ὧν ἔπαθεν (Heb. 5:8). Their garments waxed not old (8:4)—God keep things fresh and new, deliver from threadbare Christianity, and keep my shoes whole and in repair, for I tend to walk in rough, out-of-the-way paths.

JUNE 13 *Deuteronomy 32* It was as if the chapter were planned for me today. Last night it seemed as if this matter with B.H. was hard to renounce. I have been so wide awake it will be hard to slumber in God's will immediately—yea, to sleep until He wakes me, if He does, to bring me an Eve. But hard as it may seem (Golgotha's prayers, "Father, if it be possible," went unanswered) the Word comes today as Moses describes it: "rain dropping," "distilling dew," "small rain on tender grass," "showers upon the herb." Thus God would have me grow—though the rain may seem disagreeable, it comes softly and builds me up, giving me what I lack to withstand yet heavier storms (vv. 1–3). The eagle illustration is most apropos. Mine has been to nest while others struggled with temptation, and now I must fall to exercise my delicate wings, must realize how unable to stay aloft I am without the great wings beneath (v. 11). And then, thank God, comes that word in verse 29: "*I wound,* I heal." My wounds are allowed by the Great Physician that He may show me His skill in spiritual therapeutics. "The Lord," said Job, "hath given; the *Lord* taketh away." This is another in that host of πάντα in Romans 8:28.

2

Summer, 1948

Jim attended Wheaton summer school, and in July traveled with a Gospel team under the auspices of the Foreign Missions Fellowship, a branch of Inter-Varsity Christian Fellowship. The other team-members were Roger Lewis, Verd Holsteen, and my brother Dave Howard. He had a brief visit in Portland with his family before returning for his senior year at Wheaton.

JUNE 15 Wept myself to sleep last night after seeing Betty off at the depot. Wistful all day today in spite of outdoor exercise. Feel a concentrated pressure in my throat even now. Homesickness partly—but I never felt it until after I left her. Perhaps God is trying to make me thirst after Him—to find "all my springs" in Christ (Pss. 87:7). Thinking of Moses tonight. He was "drawn out" (his name means this) from the beginning. His mother hid him at birth, and his God hid him in death—forty years of that life were gone in hiding. Loneliness—what I feel now—must have been the keynote of his life. "Yet no prophet like him whom Jehovah knew face to face" (Deut. 34:10). And none with his power, either. "Teach me *to do* thy will" (Pss. 143:10). The Lord gave me this affair with B.H. to try me, to see if I were really in earnest about the life of loneliness He taught me of in Matthew 19. A eunuch for the Kingdom's sake. I believe He has proved me, but I doubt if He was satisfied. I am willing to let her go but only with

struggle. Put upon me the deep sleep of Adam, Lord. My
father gave me Psalms 25:9 for FMF's responsibility this year.
"The meek will he guide in justice; the meek will he teach his
way." Moses again (Num. 12:3).

Following my graduation from Wheaton in 1948, I attended the
Summer Institute of Linguistics at the University of Oklahoma.

JUNE 16 *Joshua 1, 2*   Two things are necessary that one
might do according to the Word: "be strong and courageous"
(1:7); "meditate" (1:8). Boldness in doing God's will combined
with contemplation of the Word to know God's will is the
formula for "good success" whithersoever thou goest. Three
days of preparation were spent: (1) in preparing victuals, (2) in
spying out Jericho. So with any spiritual experience—spy the
land (or in Christ's words, "Count the cost") and prepare
sustenance, spiritual reserve strength for future battles.

JUNE 17 *Joshua 3–5*   Moses and Joshua both came to the
place where they had to remove their shoes—to be a leader for
God, one must take a shoeless (uncovered) stand on holy
ground. A burning bush unconsumed is typical of Moses (no
man can see God and live, but he did) (Exod. 3:5). A man with
a sword as prince of Israel's host is the Spirit of God in Joshua
(5:15).

JUNE 18 *Joshua 5–7*   The heap of stones for a witness to
God's *greatness* must be accompanied by a heap of foreskins to
signify His *holiness*. There can be no lasting testimony without
a corresponding act of obedience (often a painful one) on the
part of the individual. A monumental outward work for God
must not be divorced from a more real, inward, secret dealing
in all persons concerned. "Devoted" things! (6:18)—here is
something for my soul as regards Betty. As far as we both were
concerned, she was "devoted." Not to destruction as was
Jericho, but to God, as a burnt, living sacrifice. Now I agreed to
this with God, allowing that He should have her and me

both—wholly His, devoted. But the subtle danger was in retaining hopes (nice things! "Golden and silver") that He would give her back to me eventually, that our decision to go separately for God would be ultimately revoked by Him and on such fare I survived. But this was just as if I never really "devoted" her at all, for there was still a future claim on her. Now comes this word: ". . . keep yourselves from the devoted thing, lest when ye have devoted it, ye take of the devoted thing and become . . . troubled" (5:18). Ah, how like again—hidden in the tent in secret were those secret longings for something I may not have, gloated on in lonely moments. But the Cross is final. There is no turning now, no halfway stopping place. I must go on asleep until God sees my need of Eve, if such a need ever rises. Fix my heart *wholly*, Lord, to follow *Thee*, in no detail to touch what is not mine.

> And shouldst Thou ask me to resign
> What most I prize—it ne'er was mine,
> I only give Thee what is Thine—
> Thy will be done.
> From *The Little Flock Hymnal*

"They stole and put it among their own stuff" (7:11)—as if it were theirs! And this must all pass through the valley of troubling (7:26).

JUNE 19 *Joshua 7–10*   Ai and Gibeon—the first two setbacks. Ai—thirty-six men lost as a judgment for secret sin and the Name of God put in disrepute. There is also a twinge of self-sufficiency manifest—"Send not all . . . they are but few" (7:3). The moral defeat was terrible as well—"melted hearts, as water" (7:5). Israel fleeing before the "few" she had thought insignificant. Lord, teach me this: in situations where I think myself competent, let me find then my whole sufficiency in Thee. Thou art able to make all sufficiency abound always "*in ALL things*" (2 Cor. 9:8). Then there was Gibeon where the

princes committed themselves with an oath before inquiring at
the mouth of Jehovah. Keep me from hasty decisions, no matter how obvious they may seem. Circumstances (rent and
bound-up wineskins, moldy bread, and so on) may be very
deceptive. It took only three days to discover that the Hivites
were neighbors (9:16). "He that believeth shall not make
haste" (Isa. 28:16). Compare the old garments of the Hivites
with the unaged clothing of Israel's forty-year wanderings
(9:12, 13; Deut. 29:5, 6). Joshua's "speaking the word of faith"
made a day unique in history (10:14). He did not pray; he
simply commanded (*"Say ye to the mountain"* [Mark 11:23]),
and it happened ("Command me concerning the work of my
hands" [Isa. 45:11]).

JUNE 20 *Joshua 11:19*   "There was not a city that made
peace with the children of Israel . . . save Gibeon." So in
spiritual war—no area of the life which Christ is to make conquest of can be at peace with the conquering invader. If one
area struggles not against the coming of Christ into a life but
receives Him peaceably, that area is in treacherous
subtility—Gibeon. "I came not to bring peace, but a sword,"
says my Joshua. Come them, O Conqueror (Rev. 6:2) and war
with my old established strongholds of self-centered habits
and thinking patterns. Destroy, burn, devote that You might
gain Your promised deserts and be satisfied in seeing the
travail of Your soul (Isa. 53:11).

JUNE 22 *Joshua 12–14*   Failure begins: "They drove them
not out" (13:13). Such a slacking will doubtless be followed by
further departure. Oh, that they all had been as Caleb who
wholly followed the Lord. Levi's inheritance is three times
mentioned in this section (13:14; 13:33; 14:3). Nothing but
Jehovah! What a poor tribe, we would say. How will they ever
live? Ah, faith's eyes look up and are satiated with the unseen
possessions in God's person. I would be so—nothing save
God. Satisfy me, O my Heavenly Inheritance.

JUNE 23 *Joshua 15–17*   Israel was victorious in driving out the inhabitants only as long as all tribes worked together. Judah could not drive them out alone (15:63), nor could Joseph's sons (17:12). When they were strong individually, they put them to taskwork but did not drive them out. This illustrates a principle in dealing with the flesh. "It is better to marry than to burn" (1 Cor. 7:9). When a man finds himself unable to completely make a eunuch of himself (Matt. 19:12), then he should marry. When Israel could not rid herself of present troublers within, she used them for the service of the Lord (16:10). So with strong passion: it should be sublimated—its normal direction force rechanneled into the building of God's house (9:27). I would feel compressed as did Joseph's sons—too narrow is the common allotment. I must go out, Lord, into the hills and forests and fight with those who are strong with iron chariots (17:16–18).

JUNE 24 *Joshua 18–21*   Tribal inheritance details interestingly correspond to name meanings and Jacobic prophecies of Genesis 49. Manasseh and Ephraim—forgetting in toil and fruitful in affliction—so runs the Christian's warfare. Their land was too narrow. Dan ("he judged" [Gen. 49:16]) found more than his allotment. Any who judge themselves abound before God. Simeon and Levi were to be scattered for their fierce wrath (19:9; 21:3).

JUNE 28 *Judges 1, 2*   The Lord refused to drive out all the nations "to prove Israel" (2:21, 22) to see if they would walk in the way of their fathers or not. Perhaps this is His plan with me. There dwell yet so many of the "original inhabitants" of my old flesh that I have not been able to drive them out. The Lord wants to see if I will follow Him regardless of civil conflict. He is wise in this. If He emptied me all at once, I would be overcome of emptiness, as the Israelites would have been by beasts—but little by little He drove them out, that the last state of that man be not worse than the first (Exod. 23:29; Luke 11:26).

JULY 1 *Judges 6*   Midian's work was to destroy the people's sustenance. Thus would Christ's enemies today destroy the Christian's food and bring him "very low" (v. 6). Will it take a Gideon to restore the people—one who gets his food at the winepress? Getting food at the place of judgment—that is how I must prosper.

JULY 6 *Judges 8*   Gideon's strength was that he realized and faced openly the fact that God was not *practically* with Israel. So today. This is the sin of Laodicea—she does not realize Christ is outside knocking (Rev. 3:14–22). As water came out of the rock for washing and satisfaction, so fire comes out of the rock to accept the sacrifice of one who will war and overcome God's enemies (6:21). Only men who acted as dogs are used in decisive battles (Caleb)—those who are in a hurry to wholly follow (7:5). How bitterly true is the fact that the spoil (remnants of victory) often becomes a snare (8:27).

JULY 7 *Psalm 104*   Psalms 104:4: "He makes his ministers a flame of fire." Am I ignitible? God deliver me from the dread asbestos of "other things." Saturate me with the oil of the Spirit that I may be a *flame*. But flame is transient, often short-lived. Canst thou bear this, my soul, short life? In me there dwells the Spirit of the Great Short-Lived, whose zeal for God's house consumed Him, and He has promised baptism with the Spirit and with fire. "Make me Thy fuel, flame of God."

JULY 11 *Judges 20*   Kingless Israel is confused Israel. It took horrible sin to unite the people in wrath (20:11). And when they refused to judge the sin of a few in Gibeah, many were slain as a result. Can this be the people of whom Jehovah spoke so highly? Now making images at the slightest chance, while every man did that which was right in his own eyes? Even Israel's judges are deceived. Samson dies for speaking the secrets of a Nazarite.

Evening.   Father, let me be weak that I might lose my clutch on everything temporal. My life, my reputation, my possessions, Lord, let me loose the tension of a grasping hand. Even, Father, would I lose the love of *fondling*—how oft I have released *grasp* only to retain what I prized by "harmless longing," the *fondling* touch. Rather, open my hand to receive the nail of Calvary—as Christ's was opened—that I, releasing all, might be released, unleashed from all that binds me here. He thought heaven—yea, *equality with God*—not a thing to be clutched at . . . so let me release my grasp.

JULY 15   *Ruth*   Naomi had to become empty before God could restore life (1:21; 4:15). The weakness of two widows at the mercy of God He uses to give ancestry to great David and David's "Lord." Naomi's tendency was to become embittered at her loss, not knowing this was God's way to make His and her name remembered (4:11) in Israel. How like Orpah I am— prone to kiss, to display full devotion and turn away; how unlike Ruth, *cleaving* and refusing to part except at death (1:14–17). Eternal Lover, make Thou Thyself inseparable from my unstable soul. Be Thou the object bright and fair to fill and satisfy the heart. My hope to meet Thee in the air, and nevermore from Thee to part!

JULY 17   *1 Samuel 1–3*   Growth is accompanied by corresponding service: weaned (1:24); ministered (2:11); ministry (2:18); growth (2:21;) growth (2:26); ministry (3:1); growth (3:19). These two must come together to maintain balanced godliness. This is surely the day of infrequent vision; the word is rare. God grant me Samuel's heart, that I might not let any of Thy words fall to the ground (3:19).

JULY 22   *1 Samuel 9*   Many days without an entry. Summer school has kept be pressed and not too fruitful in the Word, I fear. First Samuel 9: the selection of Saul. He was on a menial task of obedience when God appointed him king. Be faithful in seeking asses and thou shalt be honored in God's own time.

Have had much struggle of soul lately, doubts as to the truth of God's care for this world, springing, I think, from so little observable evidence of His power in the Gospel. Comforted mightily yesterday morning by realizing the rest of faith is upon fact and that especially in the Resurrection of Christ. If He be not raised, my faith is vain. Today I would "stand still first and hear the word of God" (v. 27).

JULY 24 *John 17* Meditation in the Gospel of John in Greek has been sweet these last few weeks. Never noticed how many things "God had given" Christ before:

V. 2—authority given over all flesh.
V. 2—men given that they might be given eternal life.
V. 4—work given to be done on earth.
V. 8—words given to be given to men.
V. 10—name given that men might be one.
V. 22—glory given that men might receive it and be one.

JULY 28 *1 Samuel 15* Port Huron, Michigan. Keewahdin Conference. The FMF team (Rog Lewis, Verd Holsteen, Dave Howard, and I) left Wheaton last Saturday, came to Winona Lake, Indiana, for Sunday, Gull Lake, Michigan, Monday, and here last night. We had been asking the Lord for openings to speak nights, and so far we've only had one meeting. Last night when we got here, the place seemed so small that we were discouraged, thinking it hardly worth the effort, though we have four meetings today. But the Lord showed us after a prayer session last eve that we must not doubt—we still have seven (empty) days—or waver. God is leading surely, and we are not to despair if things seem "small" or commonplace. Reading 1 Samuel 15 this morning. Samuel's all night crying to God (v. 11) challenged me. I have never done this. "But you need your sleep, you know," counsels the flesh. "Yea," says the Spirit, "but you need something more than sleep!" "Humility before honor," says Samuel (v. 17).

JULY 29 *1 Samuel 16*   Saul was anointed while seeking asses; David while tending sheep. The kings came from things commonplace. "God looketh on the heart" (v. 7). Skill, fine features, pleasing manners—"personality"—can be had by external imposition, and God cares little for such. His eye is on the heart. Now external effects are not bad—David had them: cunning, courageous, clever, and comely. But what was important was that "the Lord was with him" (v. 18). When personality is made from within, it is acceptable.

The holy life of fearless Samuel brought trembling to the elders of Bethlehem. Lord, wilt Thou impart holiness of this sort to me? I can make men laugh; I cannot make them tremble. This chapter illustrates the power of music (v. 23).

JULY 31 *1 Samuel 18*   When the "Lord was with him," David had his closest friends as well as his bitterest enemies. Saul hated him and feared; Saul's family and servants loved him—even the name *David* became precious (18:30). Father, if Thou wilt, give me the spirit of wise behavior (vv. 14, 30). I shall not care for enemies, nor covet any friendship but that of Thyself. Betty's letter to her mother I read when given me by Dave just now. She brought out this thought: "The world cannot hate you,"—so said Jesus to those who were of the world spirit. Oh, that it could! The Lord is not enough "with me" that the world can recognize and hate me for what I am—"not of the world." The world loves its own, and for me it shelters no hatred. Lord, have I wandered so far? Eternal life is to know the "great *alone* God" (John 17) (μόνος θεός) and Jesus Christ whom He has sent. Teach me Thy nature—to be alone more . . . that I might say ultimately with Christ, "Behold, the children Thou hast given me." Not asceticism but fellowship with God. Wordsworth put it thus: "The world is too much with us; late and soon . . . ." But I seek something else beyond what he knew. And I cannot define my craving. Shall one put thirst into words? My soul thirsteth for Thee as the hart panteth after the water brooks. "Oh, let me seek Thee, and, oh, let me find!"

AUGUST 1 *1 Samuel 21–23*   Hallowed bread can only be eaten by holy men—those who have kept themselves from women. What temptations have assailed me in this regard of late only the Spirit can know (1 Cor. 2:11). Father, how Thou canst give holy bread to one whose heart is so divided, I cannot say, but I ask simply for the power that comes from assimilating "holy bread"—that which is not for the common man, though I am so common. The priest wanted that the young men should *keep themselves* from women, suppress base desire, but the *women were kept from them,* David said. So protect me, Lord, I am frail in contending with myself. As David used Goliath's sword, so I would use Satan's own tool to accomplish great things for God. Goliath's death and his sword equals the fear of death and the great beyond. Pressing this is an effective way to prevail, both in God's people and the world. "Knowing the terror of the Lord, we persuade men" (2 Cor. 5:11). "None like that . . ." (21:9). A faithful servant who goes at the king's bidding—or abiding commandment—is honorable in the king's house, at home (22:14).

AUGUST 2 *1 Samuel 25*   "There is that which withholdeth more than is meet, and it tendeth only to penury" (Prov. 11:24). Nabal, having plenty, withheld what he owed and demonstrated that he was well named (v. 25). He would not be spoken to (v. 17), even with powerful pleading, but becomes, in his attitude, a monument of selfishness for all time. "Shall I give to men whom I know not whence they be?" (v. 11). How like the "churlish" church. "I cannot know the African—why should I feel responsibility? He is too distant." And the feasting goes on (v. 36). What can such deserve but "slinging out" (v. 29)—induration—turning of the heart to stone (v. 37). Prosperity (v. 6) without sharing brings barrenness. Realizing that the world is as a servant broken away from his master (v. 10), there is no compassion with Nabal and nothing done for restoration.

AUGUST 6 *2 Samuel 1–7* Have been unable to jot down meditations because of traveling inconveniences—no pen or no notebook. The Lord has given some good illustrations. Disobedience to explicit commands brings barrenness of soul and, worse yet, deafness in heaven (1 Sam. 28:18). Jahweh could not hear Saul, because Saul had not heard Jahweh. The love of David and Jonathan (1:23–26)—felt again today for Bill C. [Bill Cathers, a classmate] upon receipt of a letter from him en route to China. How great shall be our fellowship in heaven! Oh, to spend eternity with such whose spirit quickens my own—makes me throb just to read his soul's surgings. But better still to see there face-to-face the Son of God whose Spirit makes Billy the way he is. How I long for another like him—one whose "love surpasses that of woman" (and who shall weigh what I have known of Bett's?). But kindred spirits are few—not many are willing to bare their souls. If they only knew the joy and cleansing such unashamed confession to one another brings, they would soon strip off the veneer! Lord, give me a *David*, I pray—one whom I can know as David knew Jonathan—"sweet, swifter, stronger" (v. 23).

Then Asahel in chapter 2—the one who was *too* swift. His eagerness prevented him from taking proper preparation—no armor, just speed (v. 21). That is not enough to do God's will. *"Tarry ye"* (Luke 24:49). Father, teach me the speed of eternity. Synchronize my movements with the speed of Thine Own heart—then hasting or halting, I shall be in good time.

Chapter 6 brings two characters into focus—one a lesson on trust, the other on jealousy. Uzzah felt that God's testimony needed the support of a human arm, and thereby halted its going forward three months. When the ark of God is going, when His will is being done, be not thou the fool to trust thine own arm to sustain it. Yes, even when it looks as if shaky and unstable, the unseen arm is enough! And Michal—how shall I mourn her barrenness? She was dissatisfied because her David revealed himself to other handmaids. How often is this the cause of the curse of barrenness. Selfishness—even in our love for the King—is inexcusable. I have known this, though, Lord.

Often I must confess having jealousy, "that only gnaws with jagged tooth," takes hold of me and spoils my meditation when I've seen other young men get more of Christ and His power than I possess. Teach me to rejoice in other's growth and bearing children (v. 23). And David in chapter 7—uncompelled to build for God—was distressed because God's work lagged behind his own. "God has no house but curtains, and I live under cedar" (v. 2). The Lord, not proposing any such project, answers David by promising a house for David—eternal. Let me be consumed with a passion to get Thee a habitation.

AUGUST 7 *2 Samuel 11*   Uriah the Hittite was a man who declined proffered ease because the soldiers of his God dwelt in tents and open fields. This was David's error: "When kings go to battle . . . David tarried at Jerusalem" (v. 2). How often is this the history of Christian failure. The time comes for forward marching, and Christians are lying on beds of self-interest—and in such a context Satan sees to it that a Bathsheba is not far away. And to cover the results of "tarrying" overmuch, Uriah must die, and it cannot "displease" (v. 25) our brethren but, oh, how it must displease our Lord (v. 27). David's waiting meant Uriah's death in the thickest of the fight. Lord, let not this servant be found so reluctant that those besieging enemy walls fall because of my selfishness.

AUGUST 13 *2 Samuel 12–21*   Seems a time since I noted anything. Hard to be a consistent "water drawer" when on the move and constantly searching for "sermon material." Second Samuel 13:4 gives a charge. "Why are you *lean* from day to day seeing you are a king's son?" The reason was because of a misplaced affection—unchecked inordinate desire will make even a king's son sickly. The spirit of Ittai should rest upon me (15:21). Where the king is—in life or in death, joy or sorrow—there will the servant be. I pray that I might not be a counselor like Ahithophel (cf. John 12:26). He gave "*good* counsel." It was as if he had enquired at the oracle of God, but it was brought to foolishness (15:31; 16:23; 17:14). David's heart of love for Absalom compares with Paul's for Israel (18:33; Rom. 9:3) "Would I had died for thee"—only Christ can really say this. He was actually forsaken of God for those He loved. Lord, keep my zeal from being as Saul's—bloody and resulting in famine and death for my own children (21:2).

AUGUST 14 *2 Samuel 23* Good day of stirring and heart searching in Bemidji, Minnesota. Oh, may God revive His work in this country. What weak and rebellious children we are; how unworthy to be given such opportunities. Lord, I want to become pleasing unto Thee (none else), and I pray that You would make of me a minister who is a flaming fire (Pss. 104:4).

Four meetings, and I trust they were conducted in the Spirit. Tonight the Word comes from 2 Samuel 23:2: "The Spirit spake *by* me, because the word was *in* me." Oh, fill me with *Thy Word*, Savior, that the Spirit may have free course in transmitting its message! Let me not be as the sons of Belial, whose thorny ways make them unwieldy to take with the hand (v. 6). Take me, O God, and may my life be yielded that it might be wielded. Yea, I would know wielding the sword myself so that my hand would cleave thereto—wholly helpless without the Word—weary in its use but unrelenting in my clutch of it (v. 10). David reckoned the booty of daring as sacred as the blood of the daring (v. 17). Your fruit is of as much value as yourself (small and insignificant though be the fruit), but only as you sacrifice for its getting.

AUGUST 15 *2 Samuel 23, 24* Morning in Northern Minnesota is beautiful—as bright as in 23:4. But, oh, the sunset last night! It was as if the dying sun sprawled gory riot in the western sky, wallowing in its own bloody throes, warming the folds of the clutching darkness with the heat of its passion, and moving even mute cloud forms to flush crimson with the huge horror of its passing. But clouds are fickle. For it was only an hour or so before they had turned their faces to reflect the grim glory of a ghastly grinning moon. Enough—that sounds overworked, but it's fun writing.

From the Scripture came the words of David with fresh force—"Neither will I offer burnt offerings to the Lord of that which cost me nothing" (24:24).

AUGUST 23   I write on board the train, having just finished *The Growth of a Soul* [the life of Hudson Taylor by Mrs. Howard Taylor]. The month's trip is over, and I trust eternity will reveal fruit for the effort. I have not known before such freedom in ministering. Surely prayer has been heard and answered. What a mystery of grace that God should allow me to take up the sword to battle being such a child. And that (childishness) this day's soul twistings well demonstrate. Boarded at Billings about 5:30 A.M. and slept fitfully till 9:00. Awoke with sense of sex desire and realized I am in Satan's realm still. What with his urging the smolderings of evil within—those which will inflame hell—I struggled over that insane lusting. One woman near me seemed to encourage the red-eyed imp, Desire, and, oh, how base and hateful I think of myself now having prayed and read some of the Word. What *will* hell be like enraged by unslaked lust and made seven times hotter with the vengeance of an outraged God? Oh, to think of these men and women—these happy boys and girls going there. Father, save them I pray; grace only makes me to differ. When will the Spirit's power make me a witness of the things which I have seen and heard?

Slept through the continental divide and woke to find streams running west instead of east. Now a friendly river is ruffled by playful winds. The beauty of the West cannot be written; so high is it, it can hardly be enjoyed in its fullness. The battling of trees for foothold among castle crags, the thunder wars in distant mountains, the casual meadows, and the great rock laminations twisted weirdly and left clutching at the heavens—who can know these but the one who knows the Forger of the Lion and the Enfolder of the Lamb?

Was sensitively touched at reading H. Taylor's love victory. I cannot understand man, even godly man. Having been conquered by a power unseen and willingly owning the sway of the Absolute thus "finding himself" and satiating the ultimate longings of his breast, he can ache with a perfect fury to be subjected still further to the rule of woman's love. Or perhaps it is his desire to possess, having been strangely dispossessed by owning Christ as Lord. And within I feel the very same. Oh, that Christ were all and enough for me. He is supposed to be, and I dare not say, "Why hast Thou made me thus?" Oh, to be swept away in a flood of consuming passion for Jesus that all desire might be sublimated to Him. Copied out a few lines from "Born Crucified" yesterday which I must learn:

> The cross fell like a two-edged sword
> of heavenly temper keen,
> And double were the wounds it made
> Where'er it glanced between.
> Twas death to sin, 'twas life
> To all who mourned for sin.
> It kindled and it silenced strife
> Made war and peace within.
>
> L.E. MAXWELL

AUGUST 25 *2 Kings 3:16, 17* Water from an unseen source—how often is the soul strengthened for battle, succored by no observable circumstance, when we are willing to dig in valley places? But miraculously satisfying thirst is "a light thing" with my God. He wants to make overcomers, victors of those famished hearts. The water came by way of Edom— desert land. How often does God do thus—streams in the desert.

Evening. Father is merciful today. Wept twice in prayer but can't tell why. Thou knowest my motives for asking tears, Lord. Not for tears' sake but for Thy sake, following Your example (Heb. 5:7), and for the promise of Psalms 126:6. God, give me a tender heart. Couple of thoughts that came home real were: Christ the carpenter of Nazareth (Mark 6:3) became the carpenter of Calvary (Col. 2:14). Thank God, He cried, "Why hast Thou forsaken me?" that I should cry, "Why hast Thou accepted me?"

AUGUST 26 *2 Kings 5*   Naaman's sin was pride: unwillingness to do the common thing, "getting down." Gehazi was
courteous: unwilling to do the uncommon thing, "giving up."

AUGUST 27 *2 Kings 7*   Deliver me from the part of the unbelieving lord who died in the gate. How many today would ask
his question (windows in heaven?) if some were to prophesy
an end of the famine of soul. Many appointed gatekeepers (v.
17) would doubtless be overtrodden in the rush for food trying
to hold men back from blessing. Ah, but, condemning them,
have I faith enough to believe God for the "last great push"
before Christ's return? Lord, send soul famine that will be felt
today—men ahunger for the spoils of Christ's victory, and let
no man dare stand in the way!

SEPTEMBER 3   Klamath Falls, Oregon. Kern Hotel, Room 12.
On our way to the Oakland Conference [a Plymouth Brethren
conference]. Thoughts came to me afresh as to "lifting up"
Christ. My preaching last month was on the whole service for
service's sake. Oh, how I thank Thee, Father, for my earthly
father who has seen the truth as to motives for service. It is not
the winning of souls nor the spreading of missions that should
inflame me. Paul said, "I count all loss that I may win (not
souls) but *Christ*" (Phil. 3:8). Oh, that He would be to me as He
was to Zinzendorf, the master passion of life! My heart panteth
after *Thee*, not results or power. From henceforth I would not
seek an experience—a seal or sign—for I have Him as an object. "The bride eyes not her *garment* but her dear bridegroom's face . . . ." (From "Rutherford's Hymn," Annie R.
Cousin.) Occupied not with the tongues of fire; they are incidental to the great transcendental purpose of the Holy Spirit—
to exalt *Christ*.

SEPTEMBER 9 *1 Chronicles 12:8*   A verse stands out this
morning in 1 Chronicles 12:8: Men who wish to do great things
for a rejected king must be "separated," "shielded" (in the
hold), "strong," "skilled," fearless (as a lion in face) and
"swift." This makes a good outline.

3

Senior Year, 1948, 1949

This was the year of the "renaissance," Jim's name for a new spiritual experience in which he felt God liberated him from certain prejudices described in the journals. He completed his college work with a major in Greek and graduated with Highest Honor.

SEPTEMBER 19   My first Sunday in Wheaton after the FMF trip and a little time in Portland. Seems as if I'd always been here and the rest is all a hazy dream. Arrived here Monday and have enjoyed much sweetness in prayers and fellowship, especially with Eleanor Vandevort. Last night we took a sunset walk out into West Wheaton through fields and not well-frequented roads. Our fellowship was wonderfully heavenlike, genuinely Christ centered, with much discourse in the Scriptures. I must pray for her. She is going to Africa as a United Presbyterian missionary. Recognizing the truth of Christ-centered worship, she does not see the issues as to whole separation from the systems of men. Father, make of me a "crisis man." Bring those I contact to decision. Let me not be a milepost on a single road. Make of me a fork, so that men must turn one way or another on facing Christ in me.

Three thoughts on worship came to me this morning. Old verses in new combination. John 4:23, 24: If God were flesh or stone or wood or gold, it would be all right to worship Him in outward ways, with form and pomp and candles. But He is not, so He must be worshiped in the realm of His Being—in Spirit. To worship in truth is not sufficient, that is to worship in true form. There must be exercise of the spirit; the new man must be stirred to action; we must have *spiritual* worship. Philippians 3:3: We have mention of *emotional* worship— rejoicing in soul as well as exercising in spirit. Paul has spoken of rejoicing in the Gospel's furtherance (1:18); in the coming to Philippi (1:26); in the sacrificial privilege (2:17); in the sending of Epaphroditus (2:25), and now he says, "Finally, rejoice in the *Lord*" (3:1). Not in fellowship or in privileges, but in the Lord. "Delight thyself also *in the Lord*" (Pss. 37:4). Then Romans 12:1, 2 gives us rational worship, involving the presentation of our bodies. Yea, Lord, make me a true worshiper!

SEPTEMBER 20   2 *Chronicles 20*   I cannot explain the yearnings of my heart this morning. Cannot bring myself to study or to pray for any length of time. Oh, what a jumble of crosscurrented passions I am—a heart so deceitful it deceives itself. May Christ satisfy my thirst, may the river Rock pour out Himself to me in this desert place. Nothing satisfies—not nature, or fellowship with any, but only my Eternal Lover. Ah, how cold my heart is toward Him. But "our eyes are upon Thee" (v. 12). Possibility of seeing Betty again brings back wistful thoughts. How I hate myself for such weakness! Is not Christ enough, Jim? What need you more—a woman—in His place? Nay, God forbid. I *shall have Thee*, Lord Jesus. Thou didst buy me, now I must buy Thee. Thou knowest how reluctant I am to pay, because I do not value Thee sufficiently. I am Thine at terrible cost to Thyself. Now Thou must become mine—as Thou didst not attend to the price, neither would I.

SEPTEMBER 21   2 *Chronicles 34*   "Because thine heart was tender . . . when thou heardest the word . . . and didst humble thyself . . . and didst weep before me, I have heard thee" (v. 27). Josiah was my age when this took place (v. 3), but he had a heart of a different sort of weeping I know so little—of genuine humility and tenderness I know less. O Spirit of God, rouse me to *feel* these things, I pray.

SEPTEMBER 22   *Ezra 1, 2*   It is amazing to think of the beginnings of all this work of rebuilding. "The Lord stirred the spirit of Cyrus" (v. 1). Then He raised up the spirits of the elders. There is no mention of prayer by the godly for such a stirring. The only reason seems to be that it was God's time (2 Chron. 36:21). O Father, let me tremble to run ahead of Thee! I acknowledge Thy time as best; only give me grace to wait for it. I would not be "self-stirred," but wait for Thy stirring up—be raised up only by Thy Spirit in me. "Except the Lord build the house, they labor in vain" (Pss. 127:1). Tell me of Thy time, Thy concern, Thy interest. Share Thy secrets, Father. Give me childlike graces, that Thou mightest not seem inscrutable. Betty came yesterday on her way to P.B.I. [Prairie Bible Institute, Three Hills, Alberta]. We were out to Saint Michael's again. Oh, that I could understand my heart toward her.

SEPTEMBER 24   *Psalm 73; Ezra 3*   Great struggles of soul last night and this morning, especially over Psalms 73:25: "There is none upon the earth that I desire beside *thee*." This is why he could say, "Thou shalt guide me with thy counsel" (v. 24). Had there been another upon the earth who might have been his counselor, and he desired that one more than his God, no counsel would have been offered him from above. Lord Jesus! Counselor! Mighty God! How could I desire aught upon earth but Thee? Savior, Thou dost know my heart; let me love *Thee*.

> Be *Thou* the object bright and fair
> To fill and satisfy the heart:
> My hope: to meet *Thee* in the air
> And nevermore from *Thee* to part.
> That I may undistracted be
> To follow, serve and wait for Thee.
> From *The Little Flock Hymnal*

Before any building was done for God, there was *sacrifice*— as the duty of the day required (Ezra 3:4).

SEPTEMBER 25   This will be the last entry in this old "Cash Book" of B. Sawyer [an old notebook used for his journal which was given to Jim by a friend, Bob Sawyer, who had written in the front, "Motto: Systematic registration of assets and liabilities pays dividends."], I've just been glancing over some of the things written and am impressed with the fitting aptness of the motto Bob wrote in the front of it as applied to spiritual "accounts." Financial assets and liabilities I have had little interest in, but spiritual gains and deficits are good things to have on record. Betty asked me last night if she could see this thing. I guess it's all right. You are likely to read this, as a matter of fact, so I may as well speak to you directly.

There are a few things I should say about all of this, I suppose. Please excuse the form. I was, at no time that I can recall, writing for an audience, particularly *your* probings, so you will find abundant misspellings, horrors in punctuation, and some of the thoughts are so poorly expressed that they will be wholly meaningless. Remember, too, that I usually wrote with some portion of the Word fresh in my thoughts, giving a background to the entries which a reader cannot fill in without searching every little reference, and this, I think, you will not have time to do.

In spite of what I entered as a prologue regarding the possibility of others reading this, I find on glancing over it that I have been more honest in places than I intended. You will know me as no one else does in reading this. Most of it is a heart cry from a little child to a Father whom I have struggled to get to know. Other parts are surely academic and will do you no good at all. I might say that you were more in my thoughts than these pages suggest. It is not written as a diary of my experiences or feelings but more as a "book of remembrance" to enable me to ask definitely by forcing myself to put yearnings into words. This I have failed miserably in doing, but you asked to read it, and I don't apologize now.

All I have asked has not been given, and the Father's withholding has served only to intensify my desires. He knows that the "hungrier" one is, the more appreciative he becomes of food. And if I have gotten nothing else from this year's experience, He has given a hunger for Himself I never experienced before. He only promises water to the thirsty, satiation to the unsatisfied (I do not say *dis*satisfied), filling to those famished for righteousness. So He has, by His concealing of Himself, given me longings that can only be slaked when Psalms 17:15 is realized.

Betty, we shall behold Him face-to-face, much the same as you and I have looked with longing on one another these last two nights—eye to eye—and He will tell us of His love in those looks as we have never known it here (Isa. 33:17).

> There the red Rose of Sharon
> Unfolds its heartsome bloom,
> And fills the air of heaven
> With ravishing perfume.
> Oh, to behold its Blossom
> While by its fragrance fanned
> Where glory, glory dwelleth—
> In Immanuel's land.
>
> "Rutherford's Hymn"
> ANNIE R. COUSIN

Solomon compares the never-filled maw of hell with the never-satisfied eye of man (Prov. 27:20), but there comes a day when the eyes of the righteous shall find rest, delivered from peering through the glass, catching glimpses dimly . . . "but then face to face"! And His desire is as far above ours as the sun's brightness is above the moon's. "O my dove . . . let me see thy countenance" (Song of Sol. 2:14). He is expecting us . . . and soon (Heb. 10:13). Hallelujah!

He knows our love and is touched from a sympathy within, and I feel He holds us from each other that He might draw us to Himself. Let us pray *individually,* "Draw *me.*" It may be that then we will be allowed to say *together,* "*We* will run after Thee."

And I will wait upon the Lord, that hideth his face from the house of Jacob, and I will look for him (Isa. 8:17) . . . . our eyes are upon thee (2 Chron. 20:12).

SEPTEMBER 28   No entry for two days. Been up late with Betts and feel cramped for time in the mornings. She got here Wednesday. After FMF we were out at Saint Michael's. Thursday—Lagoon moonrising; Friday—long walk to Saint Charles Road: Saturday—Glen Ellyn, Auntie's; Sunday—

Lagoon at Decoration Day rendezvous; Monday—Saint
Michael's. I hope earnestly I have not grieved the Holy Dove in
all this. I really feel quite happy in my soul, yet dare not trust
this treacherous heart. O Father, if I am not pleasing Thee, give
me unrest and deep conviction. I feel now that our love is truly
"in the Spirit," but I would not have false peace, not even if I
got her, Lord! Bare my heart! Search, try, know, see . . . lead!
Felt so definitely spoken to yesterday from Lamentations 3:2:
"He *hath* led me, and brought me into darkness, but not into
light." Because I cannot see, nor even assuredly feel, His satisfaction with me, I cannot doubt the leading simply because of
the dark. The leading is nonetheless real; the pathway has
simply been into a place I didn't expect or ask for.

SEPTEMBER 29 *Acts 5; Nehemiah 1*   Woke this morning with
thoughts from Acts 5 about holding back part of the price.
Ananias and Sapphira were not slain for not giving, but for not
giving everything as they said they did. Holy Ghost! Forbid
that I should lie against Thee, not against man, but *God*. How
can I know my heart as regards Betts? I cannot. Thou dost, my
Father. Reveal myself to me that I may see what Thou dost see.

> My soul is night, my heart is steel
> I cannot see, I cannot feel:
> For light, for life I must appeal
> In simple faith to Jesus.
>
> "In Jesus"
> JAS. PROCTER

Meditation in Nehemiah 1: his preparation, seeing the need
and mourning over it (vv. 3, 4); the plea for God's attention (v.
5); confession of sin—"*I* and my father's house" (vv. 6, 7); the
promise which he reminds God of (v. 8); "Who *delight* to *fear*
thy Name . . ."(v. 11). I don't feel one of that company this
morning. Savior God, be merciful!

SEPTEMBER 30 *Matthew 1*   Received much blessing in
meditation on the Greek of Matthew 1:14–20. Greek word
βούλομαι—intend, be inclined, wish, purpose (from intention, not deliberation) is the same word used in Act 15 when
Paul and Barnabas had their rift over John Mark. First inclina-

tion is never enough to determine God's mind. But "when he thought on these things," ἐνθυμέομαι—"mulled it over," reasoned (Matt. 9:4), deliberated, meditated upon (Acts 10:19), literally "had it in his θύμος (not ἐπι but ἐν cf. Luke 16:21). This is how God will speak to me as regards Betty, I'm sure—not my first inclination (which might be either way) but in my meditation and prayer about this thing. "Search me." "While I was musing, the fire burned; Then spake I with my tongue" (Pss. 39:3).

Morning reading (Neh. 2–4). Feel a tendency to write to be read instead of sincerely noting my feelings. Forgive me, Father, I would seek the praise of God, not of men. I wonder that there is no opposition in our plans to build for God the broken walls. Perhaps these are really not being repaired. Walls equal separation. The Church today has little real conception of what this means. Nehemiah's viewing the ruins secretly at midnight struck me somehow. I've not done much of this pondering of the ruin of the House of God at night. But the work went forward in spite of those nobles of Tekoa (3:5) who would not put their *necks* to the work ("Take my *yoke* upon you"). Opposition only united the builders—perhaps there is a secret here! Nehemiah 4:10 stands out sharply: "Strength decayed for having to get over so much rubble." How often I've known this. Too much clutter in my own life so that confession thieves from intercession and there is weariness in the work.

OCTOBER 1   Flood of peace within this morning as I seek God's face. Have felt a film of uneasiness brooding over my soul since she left, but this very moment it is gone! Woke pondering the holy seasons of last week—those times of nearness which make any distance seem terribly bitter. And this "film," thin as it may have been, was keenly felt. I have confessed much to the Lord but this morning was pressed so that I confessed little things, details, but nonetheless sinful and separative. Then the Scriptures came. First John 1:7–2:2: "*All* sin," "cleansing"; Hebrews 10:14–22: "remembered no more," "draw *near*," "*hearts* sprinkled from an evil conscience; *bodies* washed with pure water"; Ephesians 2:13–18: *"Made nigh,"* "came and preached peace to them that were *far* off." (Oh, how graciously He preached that peace this morning!) Lord Jesus, I thank Thee that Thou didst banish the very *principle* of *distance* on that cross. Thou wast forsaken, thrust away from God, that Thou shouldst bring me near. Grace! All grace. Hymn 136 in *Little Flock*, Hymn 10 just now.

OCTOBER 2   Card from Betty just now (1:00 P.M.) written from Moose Jaw. Got one Wednesday from Saint Paul with just two words, *Miss you,* and today only one, *More.* The second didn't have the nostalgic effect of the first. I am learning, I think, what Billy talks of, the giving out of natural love—it wastes very easily with possession. If ever I am to love her, it must be God's love in me—my own will not last, I know. I fear that the excitement of her presence roused me to an aggressiveness in my ardor that I do not really feel. O Lord, let me deal tenderly with her; lilies are so easily broken and soiled, and my hands are neither steady nor clean. Love her—and all of them—through me, Lord. Give me to know Thy love. Canst Thou really make sons of Abraham from stone? Then You must do it with me. My heart is flint.

OCTOBER 3   *Nehemiah 8*   Much wavering of heart and wandering in thought while praying. The curse of "feelingless-ness" is on me; yet this must be overcome, I know, by faith in the facts. Read Nehemiah 8—people's attitude toward the Lord *before* they read the Law is good to get a lesson from. They stood—awe and reverence, lifted hands empty and clean—all that God requires (v.6). Bowed heads—worship. My cold heart feels little for this this morning. Lord, when wilt Thou come unto me? They read, understood, and wept . . . and had to be exhorted to rejoice. We read, but I fear we do not understand, for we must be exhorted to weep. Imagine a Jew whose heart was not in the Feast of Tabernacles saying, "Why leave your comfortable beds and houses to dwell under tree huts?" And the man of the Spirit replies, "God knows the power of a stirred-up memory, so He tells us to dwell in booths to vividly bring before us our wanderings and His faithfulness." Also day by day, from the first day until the last day, we read in the book of the Law of God. Persistent perusal brings consistent conviction.

OCTOBER 4   Heavy and sorrowful because of my coldness, insincerity, and fruitlessness. Oh, how needy—what emptiness I feel. I am not ready to see the King in His beauty. I should be ashamed to meet Him this night. The Savior's words come tenderly: μακάριοι οἱ πτωχοὶ τῷ πνευματι, ὅτι αὐτῶν ἐστὶν ἡ βασιλεία τῶν οὐρανῶν. "Blessed are those who feel their spiritual need" (Matt. 5:3 GOODSPEED). No possession (in the Kingdom above) is appreciated without knowing first the deep spiritual poverty below. πτωχος equals crouching; cringing, μακάριοι? ¿Como es posible? [Spanish: "How is it possible?"] Yea, for God looks at the end. No comfort is possible where there is no sorrow; no satisfying where there is no hunger nor thirst. Then, Lord, do Thou give poverty, sorrow, meekness, hunger, and the rest. I would know μακάριος.

OCTOBER 9, EVENING   *Romans 15*   "Every hour I need Thee" (v. 13), I claim for these days. My love is faint; my warmth practically nil. Thoughts of His coming flicker and make me tremble. Oh, that I were not so empty-handed. Joy and peace can only come in believing, and that is all I can say to Him tonight—Lord, I believe. I don't love; I don't feel; I don't understand; I can *only believe*. Bring Thou faith to fruition, Great Harvest Lord. Produce in me, I pray. This came today while meditating:

> What is this, Lord Jesus, that Thou shouldst make an end
> Of all that I possess, and give Thyself to me?
> So that there is nothing now to call my own
> Save Thee; Thyself alone my treasure.
> Taking all, Thou givest full measure of Thyself
>   With all things else eternal—
> Things unlike the mouldy pelf by earth possessed.
> But as to life and godliness—all things are mine
> And in God's garments dressed I am
> With Thee, an heir to riches in the spheres divine.

Strange, I say, that suffering loss
I have so gained everything in getting
Me a friend who bore a cross.

I am aware now of writing for an audience somehow. Ever since I let Betty read these notebooks, I have known this feeling of writing to be read instead of writing to be heard of Him to whom my heart now cries, "Lord, make me genuinely pure."

Later. *Job 3–5*   Job 3–5 came as from the Throne after writing the above. I have not been reading and meditating enough. Too much thinking of self and ego searching. Draw me out, Father, that I may flow as Thou dost! Job 3: Job curses his birthday. Mine was yesterday, and verses 20, 23, 26 seemed to be applicable. In Job 4:3–6, Eliphaz spoke to me with conviction. Job 5:17–19 encouraged, and v. 22: ". . . in dearth thou shalt laugh" reminds me of the laugh of faith I had forgotten. Forgive, Father, and restore!

OCTOBER 10   Precious season at the remembrance feast [the breaking of bread meeting in Lombard] this morning swallowed by discouragement tonight. The *Lord's hands* came fresh to me through the Word (cf. John 20:27; Luke 24:50; Job 9:33; Song of Sol. 2:60; 8:3). Blessed be God for the provision of the One who can lay His hand upon us both—the Throne and the child at one reach. He builds (Mark 6:2), blesses children, provides sustenance (Ezra 7:14; 8:18, 22; Neh. 2:8). Prayer and labor in Lombard for fruit in the Gospel seemed frustrated. "Oh, if one soul from Lombard, meet me at God's right hand, my heaven will be two heavens in Immanuel's land" [a paraphrase of a stanza of "Rutherford's Hymn"]. Have been vividly aware of seeking the praise of men today—in visitation, in prayer, and other ways—and tonight the Lord Himself speaks from Matthew 6. O Lord, make me to forget myself. I would not be of those who already have their reward in receiving recognition from me. My God, Thou who dost see ἐν κρύπτῳ, what dost Thou see in me? Purge! Tear off the shell and smash it to bits. Honestly, Father, I do not *now* want to be seen. Hide me in the brighter light of the Son within. And teach me to pray in simplicity as the Lord Jesus illustrated. Concerned with seven things: God's Name, God's Kingdom; God's will, my bread, my debts, my debtors, and deliverance from evil. Singleness, simplicity is required of me. One treasure, a single (ἅπλους) eye, and a sole master.

OCTOBER 12 *Job 26, Matthew 8*   Sweet peace attends His dealings this day. His tenderness is not at all like my method of dealing with my brothers and sisters. Oh, how kind, how loving, Thou hast been, my Shepherd. Truly with loving-kindness hast Thou drawn me. Let me know Thy method, I pray. Verse came for today's meditation from Job 26:13, 14: "By his Spirit the heavens are garnished [the Spirit's work in making us denizens of glory!]; his hand hath pierced the swift serpent [the Son's work in destroying the deeds of the devil]. Lo, these are but the outskirts of his ways: and how small a whisper . . . of his power, who can understand?" What then the fullness; what the thunder of Himself!

Deep longings for the heathen this weekend. I trust it is not false, what I want to do, but real, what He wants done. Intensify my desire to please Thee, Lord. I am cast upon Thee for all just now.

> Our hearts are full of Christ, and long
> Their glorious matter to declare!
> Hymn 220
> From *The Little Flock Hymnal*

Matthew 8 in Greek devotions tonight. To the leper He said, θέλω! To the centurion, "according to your faith." To Simon's mother, "a touch" and fever was gone! Let me know that touch, oh, υἱὲ τοῦ θεοῦ.

OCTOBER 15 *Proverbs 1*   Word is indeed *living* this morning. Am skipping Psalms to read them for noon devotions. Proverbs 1 holds this: Instruction offers a garland of grace for the head, the adornment of a Christlike *mind*, and chains about the neck, picture of a *will* subjected and beautified. "In vain the net is spread in the sight of anything that hath wings" (v.

17). Christ, speaking from Matthew 10, told us we should be ἀκέριους as doves. *Unmired,* guileless, pure-blooded—thus the character of a dove should be mine, single mated. They never have but one mate throughout life. This gives deliverance from the snare (v. 17). "They shall mount up with wings as eagles" (Isa. 40:31). These wings are not so typical of purity as they are of power—strength to live above snares and everything else. Grace to be alone as the eagle. Thanks for wings, Lord. Only let me have eyes to sight the snares and fly. It is not the simplicity of the simple ones that brings their destruction, it is their "turning away." They are "filled with the fruit of their way" (v. 31). Let not *my way* turn me from Thee, Savior. I would "let mine eyes observe *Thy ways.*"

Noon. *Psalm 2*   How terrible the laugh of my God (v. 4). Twice He has told me of this today (Prov. 1:26). Now He mourns over those who will not be gathered. But in that day He shall laugh. Surely in this case "sorrow is better than laughter" (Eccles. 7:3). Herein is Proverbs 14:13 meaningful: "Even in laughter the heart is sorrowful." O Soul Lover, make my emotions coincide with Thine. Now I would weep—"Joy cometh in the morning" (Pss. 30:5).

Night.   How rich still flows the blood of Jacob in the veins of Israel. I cannot think without knowing low motive within. Father, purge me thoroughly—burn, burn. Oh, to be holy! The praise of men setteth off the snare, as the fear of men bringeth it. And this my heart continually smoulders, wanting attention. Lord, Thou hast said of it, "'Tis wicked beyond cure" (Jer. 17:9). Let me know it and pass on.

OCTOBER 17 *Proverbs 4; Psalm 4*   "Thou hast put gladness in my heart, more than they have when their grain and their new wine are increased" (Pss. 4:7). Filled with joy just now (noon) at the amazing riches of the living Word. Just read Psalm 4 in Revised and in Darby. Every note and marginal difference, instead of complicating the meaning, only lends fresh sparkle with the turning of the facet. Blessing springs from every word. Yea, *"no word* of God shall be void of power." Ministered to by the Spirit in Proverbs 4 this morning. Have been wondering if my eagerness to get to the field might not spring from my own desire, and perhaps I am making haste with false motive. Listen: "When thou runnest, thou shalt not stumble" (Prov. 4:12). "They shall run and not be weary" (Isa. 40:31). And Acts 20:16: "Paul had determined . . . for he was *hastening.*" This need not mean I should hurry to Peru, but it does show me that there is nothing inherently wrong in manifest eagerness. Father, if Thou wilt let me go there to Peru with Thee to labor and to die, I ask that Thou wilt let me go soon—nevertheless *not my will.* And his father said: "The path of the righteous is as a dawning light"—it shall be more clear as you travel, pilgrim. Only *weigh carefully* the path of your feet (Prov. 4:18, 26). [Jim's brother Bert was in Peru, and Jim was considering joining him in the work.]

From Betty's last: "Lord, do Thou turn me all into love, and all my love into obedience, and let my obedience be without interruption" (quoted from thirteenth century by Amy Carmichael).

OCTOBER 18 *Proverbs 4, 5; Psalm 5; Hebrews 12* Lord, Thou hast much to do if ever this soul is to be perfected! A letter from dear Billy, one from Mom, and Betty's note enclosing two of her father's letters of this summer left me terribly humbled. Lord, I am not worth Your while, nor do I deserve such friends and lovers as all these Thou hast given. Oh, how Billy brought me to the dust with his description of Irene's love. I know practically nothing of this, so full of *me* I am. Father—Oh! What can I say? That is enough—just *Father*—Abba!

> Being perplexed I say
> Lord, make it right.
> Night is as day to Thee,
> Darkness is light.
> I am afraid to touch
> Things that involve so much—
> My trembling hand may shake
> My skill-less hand may break
> *Thine* can make no mistake.
> ANNA B. WARNER

Recurrent thoughts as to the "straight path" in the Word today have given hope (Prov. 4:26, 5:6, 21; Pss. 5:8; Heb. 12:13). Just as the jeweler carefully levels both weighing pans before decision, so my path is to be leveled, first by the Great Weigher who knows just what it will take to balance my dross. I must be wary of the stranger enticer, whoever *she* may be, for she has not honest scales. And I am not to rush at the decision until He has leveled the scales, and I see the measure is properly balanced. I thank Thee, Father, that Thou wilt not allow a chip who casts himself upon Thy great currents to be lost nor washed wrongly. I cast myself. Do Thou make me sense Thy time.

OCTOBER 21 *Psalms 10, 16*   Lord, Thou hast heard the desire (not the words) of the meek (Pss. 10:17). The wretchedness of unbelief has laid hold on me these last two days. A strange unheated condition which, though deadening enough, does not choke the deep desire for God (never allow that to quench, Father, for it seems all that remains at times). Wednesday I felt like Psalms 10:1: Why afar off, Lord? But now it's as verse 14: The wretched committeth himself to Thee; Thou hast been the helper. I desire constancy, Lord Jesus, stability in our communion. I know other strong tuggings! May I be steadfast, for the testimony of Thy Name (Pss. 16:8).

OCTOBER 22 *Psalm 11*   Sense a deep root of bitterness within. Father, there is very really in me a thing which I must come to hate—that incurably wicked heart which spawns thoughts and words before I even realize it is at work. Ah, gentle Dove of God, be patient with me, I pray, and not too easily affrighted. I must grieve Thee with my rudeness. Oh, be merciful! Forsake me not! Psalm 11: Forbid that I should flee to any rest but that whereunder there is rest for frightened "birds." O Calvary, my wrigglings are away from the spring, from a source other than what I really want. Teach me to perch beneath Thy crossbeams. Savior, I know Thou didst not wriggle suspended on the nails, and verse 7 (DARBY margin) says that "the upright shall see His face," and shall I be one? Yea, the foundation cannot be removed whereon thou dost rest. It is "eternal in the heavens."

OCTOBER 27   Sense a great need of my Father tonight. Have feelings of what Dr. Jaarsma [philosophy professor at Wheaton] calls "autonomous man" in another context. I do not feel *needy* enough. Sufficiency in myself is a persistent thought, though I try to judge it. Lord Jesus, Tender Lover of this brute soul, wilt Thou make me weak? I long to understand Thy sufficiency and my inadequacy, and how can I sense this except in experience? So, Lord, Thou knowest what I am able to bear. Send trouble that I might know peace; send anxiety that I might know rest in Thee. Send hard things that I may learn to rely on Thy dissolving them. Strange askings, and I do not know what I speak, but "my desire is toward Thee"—anything that will intensify and make me tender, Savior. I desire to be like Thee, Thou knowest.

OCTOBER 28   Wonderful season of intercession with Dave tonight. "At thy right hand are pleasures . . ." (Pss. 16:11). Prayed a strange prayer today. I covenanted with my Father that He would do either of two things—either glorify Himself to the utmost in me, or slay me. By His grace I shall not have His second best. For He heard me, I believe, so that now I have nothing to look forward to but a life of sacrificial sonship (that's how thy Savior was glorified, my soul) or heaven soon. Perhaps tomorrow. What a prospect!

NOVEMBER 1   Son of Man, I feel it would be best if I should be taken now to Thy home. I dread causing Thee shame at Thy appearing (Mark 8:38).

NOVEMBER 6   *Psalms 27, 28*   Holy joy in noon prayer just now. What can be said to glorify a God like mine? Father, how shall I praise Thee for the sanctity of this hour? How unreal

men and mountains seem; yet how *actual* the things of Christ
be. Forgive me for being so ordinary while claiming to know
so extraordinary a God. He gives faith to pray for revival
among His people in this country. Psalms 27:8 yesterday
seemed to explain what I have experienced lately of an inner
"answering voice" which laughs at my doubts, argues against
my bickerings with the Spirit. That word says, *"My heart said
for thee . . . ."* I have known this—my own heart speaking
for God, in His place. It calls me "child," "son of my love,"
"Jimmy"—strange and not at all static, but I have sensed it
nonetheless real. Psalms 28:7: "Jehovah is my strength and
shield; my heart confided in him, and I was helped; therefore
my heart exulteth, and with my song will I praise Him."

> I *sought* song inside
> but found a heart of brick unused to singing,
> and the words came very slow. It seemed as if the gentle
> pressure of the Father's finger
> had caused a slight crevasse midst all the hardness,
> and there, down deep, there bubbled up a quiet spring.
> But still no song,
> just risings which never reached above the surface.
> And though there was no singing, somehow there was a
> harmony not often heard among clattering temporalities.
> *Love* was the keynote of the deep spring's song.
> A major key that lent fullness to the pool.
> Peace and joy chimed softly,
> and other little recesses opened in the hardness,
> and gentleness, born of the fractures of sorrow,
> flowed unhindered to fill the rising pool.
> And as the music played, the brick dissolved,
> and my soul was happy, though there were still no words.

NOVEMBER 11 *Psalms 33:6*   "By the *word* of Jehovah were
the heavens made, and all the host of them by the *breath* of his
mouth." The λόγος and the πνευμα. There can be no utterance
without breath. So there could be no Living Word, except by
the power of the Holy Ghost overshadowing the virgin (Luke

1:35). Creation power is through the instrumentality of the *Word* (Heb. 1:2; Col. 1:6) and by the *Spirit* (wind) (Job 26:13; Gen. 1:2). These, working in conjunction with the plan of the "Majesty on high," do God's work in the universe. So let it be with this life, Savior God—thy plans, revealed through the Word and accomplished in me through Thy Spirit's power.

NOVEMBER 9 *Psalm 38*   "To bring to remembrance." I don't know why David put that in the heading, but I certainly feel as though I needed something of the sort. O Lord, how cold I grow; how soon I forget all Thy benefits. Do bring me to remember Thee more often and with more intensity! "The early dew of morning is passed away at noon" [From the hymn "Tell Me the Old, Old Story"]. How descriptive of my life. The joy of the morning's tryst (over Eccles. 4:1) has been muffled with such little time and doing. Lord Jesus, my desire is before Thee, all of it (v. 9). Thou knowest what I want, the good and the bad, the vain and the rich things. Thou knowest them all, and I cannot discern between them. Oh, what dearth of spirit I feel for no apparent reason except that a multiplicity of details (mostly necessary) cloud the low atmosphere. Bring Thou Thy cross before me, Lord—yea, show me Thyself. Naught else can still my throbbings and restore my strength (v. 10). What peace to think of the One who could read Himself into this Psalm. The Son of God "in whose mouth was no reproof" (v. 14), give me Thy quietness, Savior, as Solomon said, "Better is a handful of quietness, than both hands full of labor and pursuit of the wind" (Eccles. 4:6). My hands are so full of labor; there must be some emptyings before the quietness can be held. I need companionship. Oh, that Betty were here, for "how can one be warm alone?"

NOVEMBER 18 *Psalm 39; Ecclesiastes 6*   Two words came to me yesterday. Psalms 39:5: "Thou hast made my days as handbreadths; and my lifetime is nothing before thee." Then in Ecclesiastes 6:12: ". . . all the days of his (man's) vain life he spendeth as a shadow?" I find now the literal truth of these words in my daily round. I watch sunrise silhouette the Tower from my window, and without any sense that day is gone, see gray November deepen into moon mixture. How few, how short, these hours my heart must beat. Then on into the real world where the unseen becomes important. O soul of mine, what shall it be for thee in the day that thou standest before the God who breathed thee? I know thou shalt be destitute of the charm you now seek to impress earth dwellers with—no smiles of friendship when the soul is weighed. Only stark reality. Oh, the mercy of God! Why hast Thouer,u so promised me boldness in that day, what my merit? I find none, Lord. I fear you've made a bad bargain with me.

Evening.   Ὁ κύριος αὐτῶν χρείαν ἔχει (Matt. 21:3). Think of that, my soul! Their lord had need! *Thy* Lord needy! δια ὑμᾶς ἐπτώχευσεν πλούμος ὤν ἵνα ὑμας τῃ ἐκείνου πτωχείᾳ πλουτήσητε. χάρις δη! At His entry to Jerusalem He strips off all the coverings both of humans and of nature, treading on garments and branches. So, when the King of Glory comes in, must all covering be stripped off—no sham then. All things are naked and open to the eyes of Him with whom we have to do. Naked and open! Why cover up then? Better men know thee now for what thou art than to perceive thee then as pretending to be what thou art not—for mark it, ὁ βασιλεύς σου ἔρχεται σοι!

NOVEMBER 24   Just came from the library after about two and a half hours of aimless browsing. Picked up *Ballad Hunter.* Read snatches describing American Negro, particularly prisoners, their songs and sins. Picked pieces of poetry from a new anthology. Found J. G. Holland's "God Give Us Men" for which I've been looking since I left Benson and Karnopp [history teacher and public-speaking-club advisor at Benson, the technical high school Jim attended]. Finally I ran across a sleek volume on Dada and the Surrealists. It startles me to think how I *enjoy* some of that stuff. Much of the same sort of thing finds its way onto my notebook margins and my Hebrew scratch papers. Whatever is there in us that spawns this—so confused, yet so unutterably expressive! My spirit is all aruffle again at the vast, inexplicable complexities of the human kind, and the careless, ineffective manner we fool "fundamentalists" answer the cry of hearts which cannot understand themselves. I don't know what the Ecclesiast meant (3:11) when he said that "God hath *set the world* (or age עֹלָם) in the heart of man," but it might be suggestive of my feelings now. The world with its huge broil of minutiae is within: time with its tempest; space with its apparent infinitude; motion, change—that sense of "something far more deeply interfused," with the psychological and physiological factors—all these and more. Whatever can relate them and bring meaning to this all? Surely not our little church goings and doctrine learnings. It overwhelms me (or can I even class them as *one* by calling all these "it") with its sheer bulk. I would despair indeed were it not for things like this. Καὶ αὐτὸς ἐστιν προ πάντων καὶ τὰ πάντα ἐν αὐτῷ συνέστηκεν, Be still, and know that I am God! (Pss. 46:10).

NOVEMBER 25 Thanksgiving Day.   What I will be doing one year from this day is a complete mystery. Thus far I have told Thee, Lord, that I am willing (hardly "ready") to go to any of the following:

1. Peru—following Bert's example.
2. India—following this inexplicable interest in that land.
3. Europe—following Stacey Woods's [of IVCF] suggestion of working in college camps and teaching Bible. This seems most improbable.
4. Back at Wheaton working on an M.A. in Biblical Literature—this I am the least eager for.
5. Prison or C.O. [conscientious objector] camp—following the simple pilgrims' path of meekness and nonresistance.

Lead on, Lord; if none of these is Your plan, Your revelation must be seen. Only one more possibility—working rural areas in U.S. with Dad—or perhaps a sick bed or a coffin—glory! Any of these would be fine, except the last. That would be immortality, a swallowing up by life. For this I am most anxious!

NOVEMBER 30   *Psalms 51:10–12*   "Create in me a clean heart. Renew a steadfast spirit. Cast me not away from Thy presence. Take not Thy Holy Spirit away. Restore unto me the joy. Let a willing spirit sustain." The result of a clean heart is a steadfast spirit—no wavering. The result of a sense of His presence is the spirit of holiness—no wandering (cast me not away). The result of restored joy is willingness of heart to do all His will—no weakness with a willing spirit. Grant these then, Lord God—a clean heart, a sense of Thy presence, and restored joy.

DECEMBER 4   *Psalm 56*   Much oppressed with vile thoughts these past two days. Sick in bed with too much inactivity. Ah, what a cesspool this heart is if left to bubble up its own production! How well David puts it: *"Man* would swallow me up" (v. 1)—not any particular man, just the principle of man, flesh *per se.* "All the day long fighting he oppresseth me." Persistent as breathing the thoughts are poured full of awful things. Mercy! What would it be with no Spirit to restrain! Thou hast done well, my God, in getting hold of me. I would set this world ablaze with passion didst Thou not possess me. And even now I tremble lest, succumbing to these things, I should openly sin and bring reproach to Thy great Name. Listen, soul: "In that day that I am afraid, I will confide in *Thee.* I will not fear; what can *flesh* do unto me." ". . . thoughts are against me for evil" (v. 5). "Thou countest my wanderings . . ." (v. 8). "Thy vows are upon me . . ." (v. 12). "Thou hast delivered my soul from death, wilt Thou not keep my feet from falling that I may walk before God in the light of the living" (v. 13). Let not him who confides in Thee be cast down, nor slip, Father.

DECEMBER 5   *Isaiah 7*   Deep sense of uselessness this morning. Enjoyed prayer, not for the thrusting out of laborers so much as for their heart preparation in learning to know Christ. What a ragged, shoddy thing Christianity has come to be— honoring man and means and places and crowds. O Lord, deliver me from the spirit of this faithless generation. How I should long to see the simplicity and powerful beauty of the New Testament fellowship reproduced, but no one seems to be similarly exercised here, so I must wait. My brethren with all their talk of New Testament pattern are actually so deceived that they cannot see our mistake in making the "formlessness" a form. O Christ, let me know *Thee;* let me catch glimpses of Thyself, seated and expectant in glory. Let me rest there despite all wrong surging round me. Lead me in the right path, I pray. His Word came clearly just after writing the above. ". . . Take heed, be quiet . . . let not thy heart be faint . . . . If ye will not believe, surely ye will not be established" (vv. 4, 9).

DECEMBER 6   *Isqiah 8*   "This people have refused the waters of Shiloah that go softly . . . the Lord bringeth upon them the waters of the River" (vv. 6, 7). Deliver me from the restless spirit which finds Shiloah's stream too quiet to be attractive, too commonplace or slow. Father, let me be free from the overflowing purge—this great flood of worldliness which sweeps Thy people beyond their depth. Give me to stand firm against it.

DECEMBER 7   Lord makes Himself very near and tender tonight. Spirit of gratefulness and much peace combined with an unworthiness so utter I hardly dare speak of it. War with Japan began seven years ago today. Thankful for peace and confidence within.

DECEMBER 8   *Psalms 60:3*   "Thou hast made (me) drink the wine of bewilderment." Strangely excited with—just the forces of life, I guess. Feel "poured out" over a great many interests with intense desire to do but so little power and time to accomplish. Wrestling—I would love to be on the mat right now, not to be seen as much as just to be struggling, putting out for all I'm worth, and here I kneel at 2:45 P.M. writing! Hebrew—I said last night that I could think of nothing I would like better than to pick a page of the Old Testament and read Hebrew at sight. Greek loses a lot of its challenge when one gets to know a little. Betty—had a letter from her just now. Would long to be with her, or at least sit down and write her right now. So the body, the mind, and the soul I guess are all pretty much awake, and I don't feel at all like doing studies. Perhaps this is the "wine of bewilderment." Father, let me not be dissipated on nonessentials. Bring the Word to me in power; sublimate these huge hungers to the obedience of Christ. Above all these things, I would have holiness—though I covet the "power" of holiness just now. Let me not err in feeling. Teach me the path of faith.

DECEMBER 10 *Psalm 62*   Thankful for two new aspects of truth shown me this morning, Father. Oh, that every day brought something new. Make it so, I pray. Psalms 62:1, 2 and 5, 6: The first describes the rest of the soul's waiting in silence upon God, who is my *salvation*. The second beseeches the soul to rest so upon God, who is my *expectation*. The first is settled; rest in salvation is secure and that is enough. "I shall not be *greatly* moved" (perhaps a little wavering). The second is not completed ever, and I must learn to be *expectant*, waiting only for God, then "I shall not be moved" (at all!). The insertion of *expectation* has removed any question of being moved. "Being confident," Paul could say. Just now I was thinking of separation from the systems of men in their religion. The danger of those of us pretending to be outside the camp is to make a camp out of "camplessness." It is all right for *God* to say, "Come out from among them," but that is not my place to speak. He is outside and above all petty walls. My words to my brethren must be, "Let us go forth unto *Him*," taking my place as one who must go forth, not telling others to come out where *I am*. Teach me what that means, Lord Jesus.

DECEMBER 13 *Psalm 65*   Immanuel! Oh, the glory of a God who can come to those He loves. Struck just now with the tremendous meaning of the incarnation. Think of it, my soul, thy God a wizened, weak babe in a manger of straw. The Almighty Jehovah—all of Him, in swaddling clothes. And there was not the aura in that stable which the artists paint there. No, it was dark and the straw was prickly; the night, chill, God, born of woman! O Jesus, my Immanuel, how grateful I am that Thou art no less with me in common places than in more elevated ones. He who stooped to babyhood in a stable will not defer stooping to abide in this poor, dark, stable-like heart of mine, I know! Ὁ χαρακτηρ τοῦ ὑποστασέως αὐτοῦ. The very character of God's substance, the representation of the invisible God stuff, in Christ. Oh, teach me what it meaneth! "The river of God is full of water" (v. 9). "Praise waiteth for thee [in silence], O God, in Zion; O thou that hearest prayer" (vv. 1, 2).

DECEMBER 22 *Isaiah 40, 6*   Feel within deep latent urges to get things done, to be rising above this slough of unconscious mediocrity that seems to characterize my days. Father, if these strong currents be flesh driven, I pray Thee staunch and slay them, but if they can be sublimated, channeled into courses which will do Thy service, then intensify them, mobilize them, give them direction, for I long—Thou knowest how earnestly—that the bride of Thine own dear Son be made perfect and entire in my day. Yea, Lord, if it cost me my bride in this life, let me have Thy grace and power to bring to the Lamb the reward of his sufferings.

> Were Thy dear house a little fuller, Lord
> For that mine emptier were
> What rich reward
> That guerdon were.

An attempt to quote from memory Amy Carmichael's:

> *If thy dear home be fuller, Lord,*
> *For that a little emptier my house on earth,*
> *What rich reward that guerdon were!*

Strange thought just came from Isaiah 40:6: the call to "cry" came before there was any word as to what cry was made. The message is not given until the messenger is responsive to the command. So with Isaiah 6:8, 9: "Here am I; send me"; then comes the word, Go and tell this people such and such. His announcement was not given him until he expressed his willingness to announce. So Peter at the house of Cornelius. He went, but had no idea what sort of message was to be given the Gentiles. So today one never knows the specific "what" or "where" until he has said the general "yes." "A high mount, say . . ." (40:9).

DECEMBER 23   *Isaiah 41, 42*   This came to me after meditation on Isaiah 41, 42 this morning. There is no good reason why we should have to think of God as One who is still in Palestine, One who must be recalled in a sort of historical dream. The prophet could think of Him in the streets and mountains of Judah. I can think of Him in the bedroom, library, and the Aurora and Elgin depot.

> I sought God in the commonplace,
> And I found Him every day,
> Not in the streets of Jerusalem
> Nor caressed by Galilee's spray;
> But I found God on the sidewalks,
> The backyard, and our upstairs,
> And I walked with Him on Main Street;
> He handled my school affairs.
>
> My Christ stands not in a synagogue
> With a beard and a long white gown,
> But I know Him in the grocery store,
> He rides our car downtown.
> Many smile when I tell them,
> Some say it is not right
> To find the Lord on Broadway
> 'Neath the glow of a neon light.

Great God of the Here and Now,
I pray for that key of Belief
Which unlocks Thee in the daytime,
Which does not wait for grief
To make the Unseen real.
Recalling that word *You* did say,
"I am the God of tomorrow, yesterday
. . . and today."

DECEMBER 28 *Isaiah 46*   Urbana FMF-IVCF Convention [the first of triennial conventions sponsored by IVCF at Urbana, Illinois (FMF is a branch of IVCF)]. "I am the Lord . . . I have made and I will bear . . . I am God and there is none like me . . . My counsel shall stand; I will do all my pleasure . . . yea, I have *spoken,* I will also bring it to pass, I have purposed, I will also do it." This came to me as I wondered for what I should pray as regards this conference. What the Lord has purposed will be accomplished here as surely as this line is written. But what has been His purpose? What has He spoken concerning this people? Lord, show me what Thine intent is regarding these meetings that I might pray according to the will of God. And it seemed the Father said to me, "I will that these should acknowledge My Only Begotten. When He is honored in their lives, there will be time enough to send them forth."

JANUARY 3 *Isaiah 54*   Good season of intercession this morning now followed by the unfailing encouragement of this prophet. *"Spare not,"* he says, "when you enlarge your tent place. Lengthen thy cords; strengthen thy stakes" (v. 2). Lord, I ask Thee to show me wherein I am "sparing," saving my life or substance. Give grace to be unsparing that Thy dwelling place be enlarged. And let me not forget that for all lengthening and expansion there must be a corresponding strengthening and deepening. "Take root downward and bear fruit upward" (Isa. 37:31). I bless Thee, Lord, that Thou who art my Redeemer shall soon be called the God of all the earth (v. 5).

Then verse 13 speaks of all the children being taught of Jahweh. Lord, may it be so among my brothers and me. We would not be human instructed, but have Thy person of the Spirit lead us into all truth. I know that only thus can the peace of the children be "great."

JANUARY 5   *Isaiah 55, 56*   I think there is progression in the commands of 55:1-3. (1) Come—willingness to follow. (2) Buy—no real following without some cost, not monetary but the truth costs (Prov. 23:23). So Christ counseled those who wanted to come after Him to count the cost. (3) Eat—one may have but not possess appreciatively. This speaks of satisfying one's thirst after the buying. (4) Hearken diligently—this is the word for me. I have trouble, having done the first three as best I know, hearing the voice of the Lord. There are so many voices within and without. One must be trained to hear. His Word is both seed to the sower—going out—and bread to the eater—coming in. Isaiah 55:12 makes clear another point. There are two sides to doing anything for God: (1) His sending; (2) your going. "Whom shall I send; who will go?" "Ye shall go with joy, and be led forth with peace." The active and the passive combine to make a perfect walk—full of joy and peace. Isaiah 56:4: O that I might be found as one who chooses those things that please Thee, Lord. And now, as I go to intercede, make me joyful in Thy house of prayer (v. 7). Let me not be the watchman who is compared to the dumb, dreaming dog.

Evening.   Much grace in my soul after a day of defeat with inner sin. Thoughts of His love soon chase fear beyond the horizon. This came as I meditated just now:

O Lord, enfold Thy fledgling in Thy close embrace,
Morning and evening let him know sweet glances at Thy
    face.
Close Thou his eyes at night with soft caress,
And raise from slumber with Thy tenderness.

Thy love—of lovers Thou the first,
O let Thy bloom upon me burst,
That I poor wilting grass
May glory in Thy visage, though my view be through a
    glass.

Soft, quiet looks, that to the lover be
Stronger than duty, let me see.
And all that crowds Thee into the corners of my day
Dissolve to ether by Thy love's wide ray.

JANUARY 6   "Water that I shall give him shall be a
river . . . ." My experience is not thus, Lord. More like a
geyser. There is so much sputtering, sinking, and fainting between exultant bursts. I praise Thee for the times of outflow,
but oh, that I might learn *constancy*. Below ground the geyser
has so many channels—a maze of welling, winding feeders so
that they pour into one another and fail to rise consistently. Be
it not so with me, O Lord. *"Unite* my heart to fear thy name,
then I will praise thee with my whole heart . . ." (Pss. 86:11,
12). Confusion of intake makes for interrupted outflow. Give
me one single delight.

JANUARY 13 *Isaiah 63, 64*   Much stirred in the heart today
at the seeming culmination of a few weeks' meditation on the
display of the Spirit's power among us. I think it began with
Dr. McQuilken [president of Columbia Bible College of South
Carolina] at the conference saying, "We must meet the twentieth century with miracles, not with apologetics." Last night
in FMF Joyce Jones from the British Syrian Mission spoke of a
new work going on in Haifa which is New Testament, entirely
Spirit led, and without any organizational backing. "Missions
are a good thing, but the wine of missionary effort fails, and
the Savior must fill with the New Wine. But missions must fit
into the movements of the Spirit of God." She told of men
being led to conversions through dreams, of purity in the
company, of confession, of healings and miracles of conversions.

And I cry out to God, that now, as at the change of every age, He might make known His power to this generation. And Isaiah—hear him in me, my God: "Why hast thou hardened our hearts to thy fear? . . . Oh that thou wouldst rend the heavens, that thou wouldst come down . . . . That the nations might tremble at thy presence . . . . And we are all become as an unclean thing . . . . Wilt thou refrain thyself in the presence of these [desolations], Jehovah?" (63:17; 64:1, 2, 6, 12). Lord, Lord, what use is it to name Thy Name if I have not Thy power? Where, my God, are those promised "signs" following? Melt out mountains; snap the fetters with which we have so long bound Thee; ride on prosperously, in the might of Thy majesty. Let not the people say any more, "Where is their God?" Let them cry, rather, "Where is our refuge from Him? Rocks, fall on us!" O God, forsake me not until I have proclaimed Thine arm to *this* generation.

JANUARY 15 *Jeremiah 5:7*   "How can I pardon thee?" I sense, Lord, that this must be your attitude about America. Oh, how we resemble the well-fed, blasphemous Judah. There is no fear of God among us. Yea, saint and sinner alike, have lost all thought of reckoning with Thee. O Lord, enlarge the mercy for this people; manifest Thy power so that they at least will have genuine witness to Thee. Arouse the Church; awake the sinners; abundantly pardon. I tremble for these—and me. Their prophets have become wind, but Thou didst make Thy Word in Jeremiah's mouth as *fire* and the people as wood. What can be done with my unclean lips?

JANUARY 17   Stung with a regret that almost brings me to sobbing as I received Betty's letter of the twelfth. I wrote carelessly that I felt God was leading me singly to the field, and it has touched her far more deeply than I supposed. O God, how *can* she desire me? Have I played the part so well that she actually thinks me worthy of woman's love? I tremble, Lord, at what surprises she shall know when all secret thoughts of men shall be manifest. Perhaps then she will believe that I am not worth her while. I felt just now as I suppose an animal would feel when it first discovered that it was an animal in a world of men. So is my flesh—"no good thing . . . ." How hateful and brutish, how dull a thing to house the Spirit, how boorish a thing to be Dove directed. And Psalm 99 came to me—thrice over, "Jehovah is holy . . . ." I have heard of Thee with ear hearing. Oh, that mine eye might see Thee, that I might abhor as I ought.

JANUARY 19   The song of the sorrowful soul:

When I beheld the vanity of my way
My soul withered within me and I was mute.
And in the distance the Holy Dove gave mute answer.*
My sorrow shut out sunlight while something pressed at
     my throat.
"My God," I muttered, "Have I missed Thy way?
Overeager for the journey have I strayed on paths
Which bear not the print of His scarred feet?
Have I lied? Do I not love her as I said,
Is she not the chief sharer of my joys?"
Then said I, "What fool invented words in vain attempt
To put feelings into music? Mine will not be written."
And then there came a word which answered, "Yea,
The discord of disbelief is so inharmonious I have
     decreed
No note of it shall sound in My presence.
Crucify doubt. Go on. It shall be shown thee
What thou must do."

JANUARY 21 *Jeremiah 11, 12*   Exercised about the poor condition of the Church and the mocking of the proud, unbelieving world. How long shall my God stretch out His hand of mercy to this generation? He rises early to offer lovingkindness, but all have hardened themselves against rising

* Heading Psalm 56—Jonath elem rehokim

early. ". . . rising early and *speaking* . . . I called, ye answered not" (7:13). Rising early and *sending*, "they made their
necks stiff" (7:25, 26). "Rising early and *protesting* . . . but
walked everyone in the stubbornness of their own heart"
(11:7). "And Jehovah gave me knowledge of it . . . . I shall
see thy vengeance upon them, for unto thee have I revealed my
cause" (11:18, 20). And this all makes me so aware of the presence of God. Thou knowest me; Thou seest me, and *triest my
heart* toward Thee (12:3). Father, let me be one who lays all this
to heart.

JANUARY 22

> And shall I see Thee, Jesus, face to face?
> Heartrending rapture, crown of all God's grace!
> Face mutilated, form undertrod,
> What shall I feel to see Thee,
> Son of God?

JANUARY 23   *Jeremiah 14*   Much exercised this morning and
this afternoon about the state of the Church and the mockery of
the world at the Name of my God. Jeremiah 14: "the drought"
seemed to picture well the condition of His own. The children
find no water; the plowmen find chapped ground which is too
hard to plow; the creatures of the fields find no forage. Mine is
the day of drought. Babes in the family can find no places of
refreshment; workers in the field find the people too hardened
for the plough. And the world—those creatures of the
wilderness—for them the church offers no food. What can end
all this? The latter rains. "Are there any among the nations that
can cause rain?" (v. 22). O Lord Jesus, how long wilt Thou be
mocked as a mighty man that cannot save? (v. 9). When wilt
Thou act for Thy Name's sake? We have sinned, and we wait
upon Thee. Then for comfort comes Psalm 105: "Give thanks
. . . call . . . make known . . . sing . . . meditate . . . seek
Jehovah and his strength, seek his face continually" (Pss.
105:1–4). "He is ever mindful of His covenant" (v. 8). "He re-

membered his holy word" (v. 42). Lord, we are few, and of small account, but that has not hindered Thee in the past. Oh, that my day would see Thy power. Thou hast promised to make of disciples, witnesses unto the uttermost part of the earth. Remember Thy word, Lord. Answer the moderns with miracles. "Until the time when what he said came about, the *word of Jehovah tried him*" (Pss. 105:19).

JANUARY 29 *Jeremiah 23*   Home for a week for Bert's wedding last night. Find it dreadfully difficult to maintain a time with God in the home context—things move much too fast and the soul must suffer for the care of family things. Dad's talks shame me to silence. I know nothing of the Word, little of God's ways, when I think of how far he has gone into the secret riches of the Father's purposes in Christ. O Lord, let me learn tenderness and silence in my spirit, fruits of Thy knowledge. Burden, burn, break me, Lord (vv. 29, 33).

O God, that goadest me
With hunger-pricks for Thee within.
By stealing from my heart its dearest stays
And staying me with tendrils of Thy love:
A token of friendship from a dear one in Thee,
A word of Holy Writ, a song,
A thousand things of spider-thong
Which lift my heart from seen things, sturdy, strong,
And rest me, relaxed, hung on an unseen stay above,
Wise-goading God, teach me to rest in love.

JANUARY 30 *Psalms 111, 112*   Delightful comparison of yesterday's Psalm and today's, Psalms 111, 112. Both are Hebrew acrostics. Both begin with "Hallelujah." Verse 3 ends the same in both. Verse 8 in both speaks of "maintenance." Psalm 111 speaks of Jehovah and His attributes; 112 of Jehovah's child and his characteristics. The latter is parallel to and dependent upon the former.

JEHOVAH— Psalm 111	HE WHO FEARS JEHOVAH— Psalm 112
V. 1: Jahweh is celebrated.	His son is blessed.
V. 2: Jahweh's works are great.	His son's generation is mighty.
V. 3: His righteousness abides.	His righteousness abides.
V. 4: He is gracious and merciful.	He is gracious, merciful, and right.
V. 5: He hath given meat to	It is well with him.
V. 6: He gives them the heritage of nations.	He is not moved forever.
V. 7: His precepts are faithful.	His heart is fixed.
V. 8: Maintained forever.	His heart is maintained.
V. 9: He sent deliverance.	He scattereth abroad.
V.10: His praise abideth.	The wicked's desire perisheth.

Blessed be the balance of the life whose stay Jehovah is.

JANUARY 31 *Jeremiah 25, 26*   Twenty-three years was Jeremiah pleading with his people—twenty-three years and God still was saying, "Repent and I will turn from the evil I purposed against this city." Oh, the patience of Jehovah and His prophets. Lord, let me learn this grace of Thine, long-suffering. Give me to know Thy full counsel for my generation that I might heed this saying: Diminish not a word (26:2).

Evening.   One does not surrender a life in an instant—that which is lifelong can only be surrendered in a lifetime. Nor is surrender to the will of God (*per se*) adequate to fullness of power in Christ. Maturity is the accomplishment of years, and I can only surrender to the will of God as I know *what that will is.* This may take years to know, hence fullness of the Spirit is not instantaneous but progressive as I attain fullness of the *Word* which reveals the *will.* If men were filled with the Spirit, they would not write books on that subject, but on the Person whom the Spirit has come to reveal. Occupation with Christ is God's object, not fullness of the Spirit. The apostles saw the effects—*Christ exalted*—and noted the cause, which was the blessed working of the Comforter. *Then* they realized and exhorted to fullness, not with fullness as the goal, but merely as the path to that great aim of a Christ-centered soul—drawing attention to its center.

Parable of soils (Luke 8):

Wayside—casual reception . . . by the way . . . "heard" (v. 12).
Stone—quick reception . . . sprang up . . . no depth . . . "received" (v. 13).
With thorns—mixed reception . . . sprang up *with* (v. 14).
Good ground—normal reception . . . buried, slow growth, fruit (v. 15).

FEBRUARY 2   Lord, O my Lover and Light, deliver me from this great dullness!

FEBRUARY 3

> The way is rubble-strewn
> I cannot tell nor see
> Mid all this wandering
> Which is Thy way for me.
> Be this my boon, Jehovah,
> Amid stumblings, this my plea—
> Not virtue, zeal, nor worth
> But my simplicity.

Psalm 116:6: "The Lord keepeth the simple."

FEBRUARY 7 *Jeremiah 33*   Lord, would that the word concerning the Church's restoration were as sure as Thou hast made Thy promise concerning Israel. Somehow I should like to apply all Jeremiah says to the Church—how it needs the restoration of the two chosen families, David and Levi (v. 24). For our rulers today have so little understanding of Thy power;

and the priests—lo, they serve Thee for pay! Canst Thou trust me with the knowledge of the "inaccessible," "unattainable," mighty or "fortified" things of verse 3? O Great Holder of the keys, how I long to know Thy secret workings.

FEBRUARY 8   *Jeremiah 35*   Sons of Rechab cited by God as those faithful to an ancient trust explain more fully Jeremiah 6:16: "Seek the old paths." What of my day? Surely the covenant of simplicity of fellowship and love which we have been commanded has been forsaken. Yea, our pilgrim, sojourning character has disappeared wholly. Lord, call from among Thine own, the sons of Rechab, who would not disobey the old counsels, though a prophet entice them. And Jeremiah—how unlike Jonah who preached judgment and then wept when Ninevah repented. Jeremiah preaches truth and weeps for those of his people whom it is sure to sting.

Relations in Psalm 119:

Wholeheartedness:	brings blessing (v. 2).
	keeps from wanderings (v. 10).
	gotten by understanding (v. 34).
	seeks God's favor with a whole heart (v. 58).
	observes His precepts with a whole heart (v. 69).
My soul:	breaketh with longing (v. 20).
	cleaveth to dust (v. 25).
	melteth for sadness (v. 28).
	fainteth for Thy salvation (v. 81).
Quicken me:	according to Thy word (v. 25); by precepts (v. 93).
	in Thy way (v. 37).
	in Thy righteousness (v. 40).
	according to loving-kindness (v. 88)
According to Thy Word:	quicken (v. 25); Thou hast dealt well (v. 65)
	strengthen (v. 28)
	salvation (v. 41)

FEBRUARY 9 *Jeremiah 37, 38*   God's man accused of seeking his people's hurt and being traitor to the enemy. Not unlike the Christian's intended ministry—a savor of death. Preach judgment, and they will call thee an antiwelfare worker (38:4). Speak of the surety of destruction, and they will term thee traitor (37:13).

FEBRUARY 10 *Psalm 107*   Note that my jotting of a year ago seeks a time when I shall forget all my failures. Brother Armerding's [Dr. Carl Armerding, a leader of the Plymouth Brethren] ministry in Psalm 107 has wrought much peace of heart in this regard. Just today I was thinking of how God loves in spite of all my sin and has promised to bring "them to their desired haven" (v. 30). "He will perform until the day" (Phil. 1:6). What matters then the resident Adam? What care for my bloating pride? What concern for attacking *lust* whose inner fifth column betrays me to that enemy so often? Perfect love casts out fear, and this blessed rest—in knowing *He loves* through all these things—makes them seem too worthless to even be thought upon. I know them. God knows them. I confess them. He forgives them. Oh, that I might praise Him worthily!

FEBRUARY 11 *Jeremiah 42, 43*   For the nation of Judah, Jehovah had commanded going out to the Chaldeans. But to the remnant He said that they should remain. God's word and guidance is not the same at all times as regards *direction*. God sees all circumstance and knows best where I should be at certain times and what my attitude toward outsiders should be always—my part is *obedience*. This both Judah and the remnant fell short in. And their tendency is mine (42:14). Oh, that I might be in a place where the rigors of war are not, where I need not be on the alert for battle trumps, nor want bread. Lord, if Thou callest to war, let me be there to obey.

FEBRUARY 14 *Psalm 119*   Grateful this day for the settled faithfulness of God—that drew me before I sought; that led me before I consciously followed; that instructed me before I had a learner's ear. Psalms 119:89–91: the settled Word in heaven makes for a solid foundation on earth and a safe path for today. Yet I need that "quickening according to thy word." How foolish to imagine a quickening from any other source, or simply from "yielding." Life springs as the ultimate of love, and love expresses itself in the union of the two. With God and man that union is in the Word. Make me, then, Apolloslike, "mighty in the Scriptures," Lover God (Acts 18:24).

FEBRUARY 16 *Jeremiah 51*   Startled with occurrence of remembrance of Jerusalem this morning in Jeremiah 51:50: "Remember Jahweh from far off," and Psalm 122, a prayer for the peace of Jerusalem. Immediately thought of Hebrews 12:22 but thoughts are yet unripe on these passages. Why Jerusalem, *today?* Luke 11:13 brought out a new thought tonight. Ὁ πατηρ ὁ ἐξ οὐρανοῦ. Usually it's ὁ ἐν—"he who is in heaven." But this clearly shows Him as One who has come out or at least designs to work for His own *from* heaven. Luke 11:18: Satan's kingdom not divided. All his subjects are intent on evil. Oh, that it were so of the heavenly citizens conversely! Luke 11:23 comes in as a striking plea for Christian unity when considered in its context. Lord, grant that I may be one of those συνάγων μετ' σου.

FEBRUARY 23 *Ezekiel 8, 9*   Some time since I made any note, I see. Too busy to take time out, and then, too, I haven't been getting fresh things every day. "Too busy"—cursed words, those! I wonder if my studies and activities are not as the "image of jealousy" which so provoked the Lord in Ezekiel's day (8:3). Father, forgive me for being so academic and material in my outlook—so much feeding the mind and the outer man, so little genuine concern for spiritual things. Ah, Lord, "begin at thy sanctuary" (9:6) to purge these abominations which keep us apart. But in wrath remember mercy.

These are the days of Billy's "renaissance." His (and my) thoughts regarding false spiritual standards we FMFers have established among ourselves coincide in that we feel perfect liberty in doing things which we (in our minds) condemned before. Feel I need a balance to keep me from going over backward.

Jim and Bill felt there had been a gap between the "spiritual" students, for example, the members of the Foreign Mission Fellowship, and others who did not consider themselves in that class, such as the football players. Jim and Bill broke across the barrier, began to associate with those who never went to FMF, joined in class social activities and the Junior-Senior rivalry, and called this their "renaissance" experience.

MARCH 3   *Ezekiel 27; Psalm 142*   Must confess the barrenness of a busy life. Seems that too many things press now so that I cannot pray and meditate, either unhurriedly or alert enough to be of much use. Wrestling consumes a good one and a half hours a day so that things may let up in a week or two. Ezekiel 27: Seems that the destroyer of Tyre was to be the sea. That was the means of her living; she trafficked on great waters, but great waters destroyed her. How illustrative of the Word: "I will bring their *own way* upon their heads" (Ezek. 11:21). That wherein lay their trust rose up against them. So in the day of vengeance of our God. Men's sweetest frames of excuse shall witness against them, for God shall be vindicated when He judges. Two words for refuge in Psalms 142:4, 5. There are times when the battle is so pressing one may not find a quiet place to go to and get away from the turmoil. At those times there is a *shelter* (v. 5) in the midst of it all. Remember this, next time.

MARCH 4   *Ezekiel 29*   Egypt—the worldly trust of a backsliding people. But when Israel took hold, "the staff of reed" broke and injured his shoulders; when he leaned upon Egypt in confidence, he was wounded in the loins (v.7). So with me. A fleshly trust only makes for weakness (shoulders—place of strength) and unproductiveness (loins—'at a stand'). Let me find Thy hand my support, Lord God.

Verse 16: Sober exhortation about turning and looking upon Egypt "bringing iniquity to·remembrance." Oh, for pure eyes, that the memory might not call up "mire and dirt."

MARCH 6   What Thou hast declared by Thy *grace,* Thou hast decreed to accomplish by Thy *power.* Lord, grant me an ordered life. Flow in all my hours.

MARCH 8   *Ezekiel 36*   Ah, Lord, would that I had regard for Thy great Name. Ezekiel 36:22, 23 bespeaks Thine own concern for the Name which has been defiled in America *by Thine own.* Be sanctified in me, Lord, and that before their very eyes. I well know the scheming pride and desire for prominence within and know too that only by the grace of the implantation of Thy Spirit can I walk in, keep, and do Thy mandates (v. 27). Not for my sake then, Lord (oh, make this prayer sincere!) but because they should know that Thou art Jehovah. Remember for good Thy wandering sheep.

MARCH 9   Well, it looks as if another page will put this one in the drawer. Seems to me the tone of these things has changed through the months. Not near so much comment on Scripture as prayer now. Perhaps because the Word has not been speaking so clearly as in the early months of last year. Then, too, I'm not near so sure of myself as I was then, and there is much more I feel I must ask for. Wish I could find phrases to express that little *oh* which I see so prevalent in these jottings. It means more than it says. I would make these booklets museums of pressed flowers picked with Him where He is leading me to feed "among the lilies."

MARCH 10   *Ezekiel 40:4*   Cleveland, Ohio. Hotel Commodore, Room 1011. Here for the Case Invitational Wrestling Meet. Don't understand why I'm here, but the Lord told me to be alert in terms of Ezekiel 40:4: "Thou art brought hither that it might be shown unto thee; hear, see, set thy heart."

MARCH 13   What He has shown me seems to be that the world is fading away. All that I have seen and heard, all that my heart has been set upon to know I have found as the Preacher said, "Behold, it is vanity" (Eccles. 12:8). We won second place at the tourney in Cleveland, and we took individual runner-up positions, too—but what is that? Nothing abides. Behold, the Son of God comes! One flash of His burning eye will melt all our polished marble and burnished gold to nothing. One word from His righteous lips will speak destruction to the vast rebellion we call "the human race." One peal of His vengeful laughter will rock the libraries of our wise and bring them crashing to a rubble heap. The wise shall be taken in their own craftiness; mountains shall be brought low. What shall abide that day? Lo, "he that doeth the will of God abideth forever" (1 John 2:17). Church of God, awake to your Bridegroom! Think not to say in your heart, America, "we have upheld the common man; we have the godly for our heritage; we have respect for the religious." I say to you, God is able to raise up righteousness from your pavement stones. You have nothing but awful show before Him who comes. "Oh, that thou wouldst bow the heavens and come down!" (Pss. 144:5). Laodicea, when will you learn that fullness without Him is vacuum? Oh, the awful emptiness of a *full* life when Christ stands yet without.

MARCH 14   *Ezekiel 44:5, 8*   Every egress of the sanctuary was to be noted and "marked well"; God is most jealous for details when it comes to His holy things. How like Israel is Nicolaitine Protestantism whose individuals do not each one care for the sanctuary's details (Rev. 2:6). "Ye have not kept my charge, but ye have set keepers of my charge in my sanctuary for yourselves" (v. 8). I have heard Christians say, "I want to hear someone preach who is trained and authoritative; I cannot be, so I set the preacher in my place to minister holy things." Woe to you, slothful keepers of the sanctuary of thy God.

MARCH 17   *Daniel 1–3*   Those who *purpose* have power in
the day of temptation. Daniel 1:8 and 3:14 give hints as to why
fire and a king's word have no effect upon some men. Every
action was related to previous purpose, and a yielding of body
(3:28) that overruled any circumstance. The railing of the Chaldeans (3:8) turned out for promotion of God's elect, unsus-
pected until the worst had been done. Cast down in the fire
bound, they walked about loosed with the messenger of God
whose superior fires were as a shield about them all. Thou hast
respect unto a purposeful set of one's sail. Give grace to me
that I may set mine wisely, Lord.

MARCH 21   *Daniel 4–6*   Can't get over the character of this
man Daniel, in whom even the heathen recognized the "spirit
of the holy gods." His purposefulness (1:8) caused him to be
granted prudence (2:14) and power to prophesy (4:24, 5 ff.).
Nothing would drive the spirit of prayerfulness from him
(6:10) and the hand of God upon him brought prosperity to his
person (6:28).

MARCH 22   *Psalm 11*   He seemeth distant, saith a whisper
in my soul, "Why, Jehovah, standest Thou far off?" Meditating
just now with my eyes closed it seemed two worlds expressed
themselves in two simple sounds. Outside a cardinal's jaunty,
stereotyped tune told me of nature, my Shepherd's garment
fringe, still waiting, longing with a sort of casual persistence
for the ultimate manifestation. And at my elbow ticked the
clock, measuring these painful things that men call days. Men
say they are all of the same length, but they are wrong, for a
day is not measured by its hours, but by the *content* of its
hours. Hence some are long and some are short, but all are
painful. Painful because they can be measured by a clock;
painful because they deny eternality; painful because they represent that which makes my Shepherd seem unreal, hides Him
all from me except His garment fringe.
   Psalms 11:4: "His eyelids try the children of men." The open
eye brings light to me, His winking only darkness. And I know
now that He is trying me in darkness. O Lord, lift up the light

of Thy countenance upon me; for in Thy light I shall see light, light brighter than *this* day.

This came yesterday:

> I set my love upon thee, Child,
> I knew thee far away
> I wept to see thee wandering, wild,
> I yearned 'til thou didst pray.
> One of a hateful rebel band,
> Strong in thy lust for sin,
> A furtive, fitful, fiery soul,
> I loved; I called thee in,
> Stripped thee of thy grimy pride,
> Laid bare thy secret want,
> Poor vagabond of empty ways
> I sent my Spirit to haunt.
> Now, desert son, the choice is thine:
> My love thou canst forget
> And go to roaming wasteland paths.
> Wilt, willful, wander yet?

MARCH 24   Had a time of real profit with Dave and Bill after hearing Chad Walsh [a professor at Beloit College and an authority on C. S. Lewis] speak in a lecture on the effect of Christianity on the art and literature of the coming Christian future. Stimulating and forced us to do some defining as regards our formation of ideas and growth into maturity. His eschatology and doctrinal thrust is obviously not Pauline, nor does he make any pretensions. He states things well and brings up real problems, though not the most vital ones. Repose upon the Father, cuddling into Daddy's lap, makes all *transienta* [temporal things] as useless as the spices on resurrection morning.

Jotted down a couple of statements that might help some time:

Modern art is depictive of the disintegration of our civilization. Artists are sensitive, they have responded to their environment faster than most of us.

Religion and art have this in common: they are both creative.

Christianity would liberate art by banishing the horror of the commonplace. To the Christian nothing is commonplace; everything is somehow miraculous.

Christianity digs deeper into the mud and rises higher into the clouds than any other psychological system.

We suppress creativity to our psychological peril.

MARCH 25   *Psalms 13, 28, 143*   Sense the joy of Jehovah's salvation restored after some time of distance. Had been harboring unconfessed pride—of face and place. Made it right on Wednesday and knew real blessing in prayer then. How unhappy the saint who has lost contact with his God. Three verses in Psalms describe the child of God becoming like "those who go down into the pit," or "sleep the sleep of death" while living (Pss. 13:3, 28:1, 143:7). If God's face is not seen (143:7), or His voice not heard (28:1), we become orphans, but we are *as* those who are dead toward Him.

> Then keep my soul, Lord Jesus,
> Abiding still with Thee,
> And when I wander, teach me
> Soon back to Thee to flee . . . .
>   Source unknown

MARCH 29   Unconquered land is to be apportioned. Joshua was instructed to divide to Israel their several lots, while they were as yet still in enemy possession (Joshua 13:6). While I remain outside my full inheritance, "Jehovah maintaineth my lot" (Pss. 16:5). He preserves it for me, telling me that its bounds margin "pleasant places" (Pss. 16:6), at the same time telling me it is mine in Christ the Head "in whom I receive now the *portion* of my lot" (Eph. 1:11 CONYBEARE) and in the Spirit who is the *promise* and even the *produce* ("firstfruits" [Romans 8:23]) of the inheritance to come. Not only so, but *His* inheritance (Eph. 1:18) among the holy ones (קְדֹשִׁים) in His delight (Pss. 16:3), even as my possession promised is to me. Practically, He has marked out a line on the earth whereto I am to labor. I would not go beyond it (cf. 2 Cor. 10:13–16).

Night. Psalms 147:17:

> Warm Son of God,
> Who shall endure Thy cold?
> Send forth Thy Word,
> Melt distance, and display
> Thy heart of tenderest mold.
> But not Thy face of flint, for who
> Could stand before such cold?
>
> How faint the touch of peace
> How weak the mercy whispers
> When Thy friendly Dove seems distant,
> And Thy glow of love but glimmers.
> Thy cold . . . .
> Who shall endure?
>
> Let not that earth wind blow
> That bringeth blighting snow
> Upon my tender grasses.
> Thou shining Sun of God,
> Whose love, like summer morn,
> Is vaprous, dewy, warm,
> Cold from Thee . . . .
> How shall it be borne?
>
> And in moon-season, Lord,
> When soft-fingered sleep
> Unravels tangles in a harried mind,
> Spread Thou Thy love upon me,
> Lest, naked in the night,
> I wander from the fold
> Some distance.
> Who shall endure that cold?

APRIL 1 *Psalms 19:7* "The law of Jehovah is perfect, restoring the soul . . . ." Such a law is indeed perfect. Most laws condemn the soul and pronounce sentence, that is all. The result of the law of my God is perfect. It condemns but forgives. It declares unrighteous and guilty, but offers positive justification. It restores—more than abundantly—what it takes away.

APRIL 5 *Hosea 13:6*   "According to their pasture, so they were filled." Israel's satisfaction depended upon and varied with her environment. Was it the "land of great drought"? They complained and were hungry. Was it the "flowing land," then they found fullness and looked not to the hand of God. Heart of mine, when wilt thou learn this lesson, not to be dependent upon thy context for joy, but upon this One who says of all His own, "I will heal . . . I will love them freely" (14:4).

APRIL 6 *John 5*   Strange evening. Bill Deans [Plymouth Brethren missionary from Africa] in FMF on New Testament methods of missions and church government. Wonderful meeting though not all agreed with him, of course. Got to talking to Dave and Art Johnson afterward; got into Stupe [campus snack bar], Bob Blaschke joined. Decided to follow Peg Rodgers and Arlene Swanson home as they came in and decided to have a party at Mortweet House [a girls' dormitory]. [Ed] McCully joined us at the door, and we all went over for pop, ice cream, potato chips, stories, folk dancing, and cutting up generally. Wish my heart were more condemned. I am worse than a social animal; I'm a social fiend—I love to be with a gang. Came home and read the fifth chapter of John. Two phrases outstanding: μηκετε ἁμάρτανε lest a worse thing come to you. What could be worse than thirty-eight years' helplessness before the man was healed? I don't know, but I'm sobered. Then, Christ said God was His Father, and the Jews claimed this made Him equal (ἴσον) with God. Relationship indicates similarity and identity. Does my sonship betray His Fatherhood?

APRIL 8 *Hosea 14:5*   "I will be as the dew unto Israel." It was so this morning. He woke me from a dream in which it was as if He was speaking. And I was roused with gladness and a sweet hunger.

Noon. If God has called Himself Jesus—*savior*—if He has indeed made His Name to be salvation, then He must deliver, for His Name's sake. Is this the meaning of Psalms 25:11, "For thy name's sake thou wilt forgive mine iniquity. O Jahweh, for *it* is great." *What* is great? My sin? Possibly. It may be that the iniquity is so great that no one save God could deal with it, and this is surely true. But the sense seems better if *it* refers to *name* rather than to iniquity. For Thy Name's sake, because Thy Name is great, Thou wilt forgive. "Jehovah is his memorial name" (Hos. 12:5). It reminds Him, that Name of His, what He has set Himself to do, to deliver His chosen. *Jesus* the Name that charms our fears, that bids our sorrows cease, "tis music in this sinner's ears" [From "O for a Thousand Tongues to Sing," Charles Wesley].

APRIL 14   Thursday of spring vacation. Dave H., Ed McCully, Peg Rodgers, Jack Swanson, Ely McKnight, Arlene Swanson, Chuck Holsinger, Marty Gammon and an occasional other are cooking two meals a day at Bethany House. Much stir in Junior-Senior activities. Up at 4:00 A.M. twice this week to try to concrete in solid the Senior Bench. Juniors got it Monday morning after we had gone from an all-night watch at 5:30 A.M. But Seniors found it again on the night of the moon eclipse— Tuesday. [Each year the junior class tried to steal the concrete "Senior Bench" as a part of traditional class rivalry.] Fellowship with the gang is enticing fun. But I feel carried away tonight with soul incitement. Nothing bad, just nothing good. Taken up with Comp. [comprehensive examinations] studies, Robert Service, the old songs that keep ringing in my ears. Strange place, this soul of mine . . . . And I think it is more *place* than *person*. It rings with whatever enters, be it high thoughts of the seated Christ or idle rhymes from any poet. The soul does not seem to mind *what* it is occupied with, but only cares that it be kept occupied. It is passive as to choice. *I* choose; my soul responds, with ringing laughter, emotional incitement, or pure worship. It is a tool, not a craftsman, and must be controlled. It is as amoral as a bed, yet beds can become instruments of illegitimate activity. Son of God, purger of the inner parts, discerner of my sittings down, my risings, wilt Thou hallow this soul of mine? The choice is mine, You say? Ah, yes, the choice is mine.

APRIL 20 *John 9, 10*   This is comprehensive-exam day. Sensed a pride of heart last night which will cause trouble, wrenching my peace away if things go not all right. Awful thing, pride, especially because it makes one believe untruth. Obadiah 3: "The pride of thy heart hath deceived thee." Pride, the devil's first fault, fructifies in deceit, the Devil's first method. As for comps, God knows I have confessed this sense of self-sufficiency, and am now at rest, with no care for a "distinctive" [highest grade for comps].

Thought on Greek of John 9:39 last evening: εἰς κρίμα ἐγω εἰς τὸν κόσμον τοῦτον ἤθον. Christ came into the world for a decision, a *crisis*, a passing of sentence. Oh, that I represented Him thus, pressing His claims upon men in such a way that they were forced to an issue about His person. Then in John 10:3, 4 He uses two words for the guiding of His sheep: ἐξάγω, "I lead them out," and ἐκβάλω, "I thrust them forth." Latter is same as in Matthew 9:38. Would that I sensed both this *leading* and *sending*. The use of τίθημι for "lay down" in John 10:17 is striking. We might say, I *put up* my soul for those sheep, as one would put up surety or wager money. Wonder!

APRIL 23   Dorm party with Florence Kelsy tonight. Got to cutting up again. Oh, when will I ever mature? How I despise myself when I get home here in quiet and think of the noise I've made. This doesn't say what I want, but it says something:

> God of the strangest ways,
> Who silent watches Thy son
> While away rollicking days
> Playing 'til day is done.
> A son who, sobered at silence,
> Loves the sound of a joke
> And drowning the surging quiet,
> Seeks consolation in noise.

How *can* Thy love remain fervent,
Father of this careless child?
How be still in Thine ardor,
A stillness which hankers me wild?
Son of sound-ridden mind,
Question no more of "How?"
Silent or saucy, crowded or lone,
My love rests on Thee now.

APRIL 27   Blessed by Dr. Laurin of Fuller Foundation in Chapel yesterday. Quoted Archimedes and applied to the Christian faith. "Give me a place whereon to stand, a fulcrum strong enough, a lever long enough, and I will move the world." We have it in the Word and the cross.

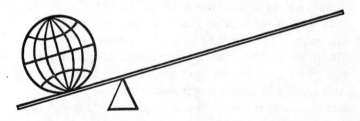

Blessed fellowship with Bill C. at noon—Ephesians 4. Mortweet Party at the cemetery at night. Strange reactions within. Don't know what to feel about such things. The Lord's word for last night was ὃ ἐγω ποιῶ σὺ οὐκ οἶδας ἄρτι, γνώσῃ δὲ μετὰ ταῦτα. What a Savior. When He knew that God had given *all things* into His hands, He took the feet of His loved into those hands and washed them.

APRIL 28 *John 13*   Blessed by a thought in John 13:29. The disciples thought Jesus was speaking to Judas of two matters. What He was accustomed to speak to Judas about was : (1) that something should be bought for the feast in preparation, (2) that something should be given to the poor. These should be two prime concerns with me. "I will sacrifice naught to the Lord of that which cost nothing" (2 Sam. 24:24). And the sacrifice of praise is no less easily bought than a threshing floor. "Only take care of the poor" was Paul's instruction from Jerusalem (Rom. 15:26). Two concerns: worship and service.

MAY 1   Twentieth-century version of Isaiah 58:1–7:

Speak out, spare none, blast forth as a trumpet,
And reveal to my people their error,
Yea, to this "Church of God" their sins.
Oh, they seek Me regularly,
Delighting in the mere knowledge of My ways,
As though they were upright all the while,
And forsook not the principles of their God.
Why, they make bold to ask for justice
And smile as they come to prayer.
"Look, we do good and You reward us not,
Why should we sacrifice since You pay no attention?"
Lo, in their praying they meditate enjoyments;
Their thoughts wander to doing things of more interest.
See, you "go to church" to wrangle about nonessentials,
And to flare in fleshly anger at one another . . . .
Not as you spend Sundays will they become a day of audi-
    ence with the Throne.
Is this indeed the way of power which I have laid down?
A day in which there is much talk and wearing of fine
    dress,
Will you call this "the Lord's Day"?
Shall He accept it?
Rather, is not this the manner I have appointed,
To release yourselves from wicked ways,
To confess pent-up wrong,
To free the heavy spirit,
To sever cooperation with sin?
Is it not to share with the needy
And to invite those unfortunates home to dinner?
And when you see a man who prospers not,
Should you not sell your furniture to clothe him?
And stop covering your own raw sores
With warm suits and closing of your own eyes.

MAY 2   Τὸ πρὸς ἅπαν εὐνετὸν ἐπὶ πᾶν ἄργον. The man who will not act till he knows all will never act at all.

MAY 4 *Habakkuk 3:19*   "He maketh my feet like hinds' feet, And will make me to walk upon my high places." Mine seem so prone to drag, Lord, especially when it comes to walking in my high places—that is when I attempt walking in Thy truth. I have difficulty believing that I am actually *in the heavenlies*, yet it is so. Jehovah *is* in His holy temple. He *did* come forth for the salvation of His people. Forbid that I should make it a lie, Lord.

MAY 5   Doctor Tenney [professor of New Testament at Wheaton], speaking of Mark 16, used a phrase I enjoy. The picking up of serpents—does the future tense imply a command or a *"privilege of faith"*? What privilege God has granted us, taken in faith. Meditation on the forty-fifth Psalm. Three "therefore's": His beauty and grace, *"therefore* God hath blessed thee" (v. 2); His "moral emotion," love of right and hatred of evil, *"therefore* God hath anointed thee (v. 7); the remembrance of His name, *therefore* the peoples praise (v. 17).

MAY 11 *Zephaniah 1, 2*   I sense a dangerous possibility within, Lord. It was in the reading this morning which described three different ways. It's that shoulder-shrugging attitude, that oh-well-so-what idea about sin and wandering. Zephaniah calls it "settling upon one's lees" (1:12), or, as the margin says, "men who are *thickened.*" Then the margin reading of 2:1: "The city that hath no *longing.*" Unimpassioned morality (it was said of my Lord, He *loved* right but *hated* iniquity). Then in 2:15: "careless dwelling." Father, grant moral muscle to this poor child of Thine. He is weak and has but little desire for holiness.

MAY 12 *John 14; Psalm 49*   Two thoughts regarding Christ's character which are assurances of His dwelling in me. First, John 14:19: "Because I live, ye shall live also." His life gives assurance of mine. Death shall not feed on me. Psalms 49:15: "He will receive me." Then, 1 John 4:19: "We *love* [not Him] because He first loved us." My whole life attitude should be one which is responsive to His love, "unmerited, unheeded, and unsought."

MAY 13 *Haggai 1:13, 14*   The realization of Jahweh's presence in the midst of His people had the effect of stirring up their spirit to build. So with Christ's word on abiding. If ye abide in me and I in you, ye shall bear fruit. Let me experience Thy nearness this day, Lord.

MAY 14   Florence Nightingale Banquet at Oak Park Arms Hotel last night. I was asked to go by Elsie Margaret Olson from West Sub [West Suburban Hospital which had a nursing program in conjunction with Wheaton]. Big formal feed . . . but, oh, the emptiness of being full. Everything was perfect, and it should have been a good time, but when it's all over, were it not for a God who does miracles with the commonplace, what's their use? Haggai 1:6: "Ye have sown much but bring in little . . . ." Life is as that "bag with holes."

Evening.   Found this in the library tonight:

I see His blood upon the rose
    And in the stars the glory of His eyes,
His Body gleams amid eternal snows,
    His tears fall from the skies.

I see His face in every flower;
    The thunder and the singing of the birds.
Are but His voice—and carven by His power
    Rocks are His written words.

All pathways by His feet are worn,
    His strong heart stirs the ever-beating sea,
His crown of thorns is twined with every thorn,
    His cross is every tree.

"I See His Blood Upon the Rose"

JOSEPH MARY PLUNKETT

MAY 17   *Psalm 51*

The spirit of the godly is: steadfast (v. 10).
                                 holiness (v. 11).
                                 willing (v. 12).
                                 broken (v. 17).

MAY 18   *Psalm 52*

Uprooted and cast down,
No strength to rise again,
Withered, cold, and dead, behold,
The man who rests in sin.

His roots drank avarice,
His leaven soaked up deceit,
Mischief, sin, he revelled in,
All evil was his meat.

But God, the woodsman came,
And tore him from his place,
Broken down, that gloried crown,
Destruction and disgrace.

And now the godly sees
He trembles first, then blesses
Him his God and laughs aloud
For loving-kindnesses.

MAY 26   Long talk with Billy and Bob Weber in the room here. Renaissance freedom seems a superficial thing to the real issues. Bill read me a letter Betty wrote regarding my getting in with the kids. Why her concern—or rather, why should it come just now, right after the hilarity of sneak time?

Back let them fall from me, my clamorous foes,
Confusions multiplied;
From crowding things of sense I flee, and in Thee hide.
                "O Thou Who Art My Quietness"
                    AMY CARMICHAEL

MAY 26 *Malachi 1*   Struck with the world vision of Malachi 1. Verses 5, 11, 14 declare that God's purposes are not only in Israel. "My name is great among the nations"; "Jehovah is magnified beyond the border of Israel." Let me learn this, Lord, that there is no restriction with Thee in the borders which I feel as limits, whether within the church or without. Thou art capable, yea, great, before those who do not yet acknowledge Thee so. Exercised in prayer this morning about the liberties I have taken in things before adjudged nonessentials, and am cognizant of the losses sustained.

MAY 27   Spoke to Glen Ellyn Bible Church Young People's Group at a high-school banquet tonight. Wonder if fruit is being borne. I experience much liberty, but must commit the Word to God.

MAY 29   The words of my mouth, O God, let them be as Thine arrows. Blunt them not, nor let them fall short of targets viewed in Thy design. Words can be either deadly or deadening, depending on their source. Kind Spirit, own these lips, I pray. Let not my weariness nor weakness mark the words of my mouth but let them be acceptable, O Lord.

> I spoke
> Words fell
> Aimlessly on ears.
> Later
> One said,
> "Your word—
> It helped
> That day."
>
> I turned
> Wondering—
> Forgot I said
> That word.
> Let me speak
> Those words
> Often.
> Helpful words
> That I forget.

JUNE 1 *Psalm 59*   I sense that I am dwelling in a generation to whom nothing is holy. Sacredness is an aspect this people never assumes toward anything. In a rebellious reaction to Victorian prudishness, they revel in bald frankness which enervates moral consciousness. Tragedy is that I feel it affecting me. We have a noncommittal morality. Nothing is so bad, and nothing is so good. Everything is a muddle of both. "Yea, do thou, Jehovah, the God of Hosts, the God of Israel, arise to visit all the nations" (v. 5). "God, whose loving-kindness will come to meet me . . ." (v. 10). At "their strength" the singer is silent (v. 9 DARBY), but "I will sing of thy strength" (v. 16). Let not Thy people forget that power which is Thine, my Lord.

JUNE 2   Doctor Brooks [the dean of students] used a phrase at Student Council Banquet tonight which I should like to experience. He called some folks "love-mastered men." Oh, teach me what *this* means.

JUNE 3   I threw away an evening tonight. Met with Blaschke and Dave to go down to Stafford Studios for the sneak pictures. Came back to campus and went around the front lawn pestering kids studying for exams by asking them how many mosquito bites they had and how many of the brutes they had killed. Talked with Bill Willsen at the Tower entrance awhile. He says Tom [his brother] is plenty sorry he was a perfectionist regarding women when here. It's lonesome in South America. Get that? Met [Barbara] Priddy and Roylene [Alley] and went to the Stupe for a black cow and a bull session. Norm Hoyt and Jim Patterson joined it. Talked till eleven on love and marriage and so on. Walked the girls home, and Dave and I stood on the street in front of his house and talked out our four years here. I just got in; it's ten minutes after one. Feel a little like writing poetry, but have a Hebrew and Greek final on Monday and must get lots of studying in tomorrow.

JUNE 6   Hebrew and Graduate Greek exams today. Feel miserably prepared for both. Kids from Lombard gave me a wallet and a farewell social Saturday night. I wonder how many of them have been really helped by my being here. Spoke at Bethany House last night—entertained, rather. I'm beginning to dislike being asked to preach. Lord, deliver me from showmanship. I cannot impress folk with my cleverness and at the same time minister to their hearts and exalt the Savior. Dropped in to George Shoffer's meeting with some Young Life kids in Celt Hall. Talked about conditions in the Church for some time afterward and was blessed by some close words with Bob Blaschke. I would so like to help, but I just don't seem to have the goods when the time comes. Thought of Moses in Acts 7:20. He was ἀστεῖος τῷ θεῷ—"cultured" or "citified" toward God. He was no rustic from God's point of view, but "knew his way around" in divine circles.

JUNE 7   Diary of Grad Week. Thursday: speech recital; Friday: class night, North Ave.; Saturday: Pottawattomie, Jones Beach; Sunday: lighthouse; Monday: graduation.

4

Summer and Fall, 1949

Following his graduation from Wheaton, Jim traveled with his father, mother, and sister Jane who had driven east from Portland. Since his father was an itinerant Plymouth Brethren preacher, the trip took many weeks. Jim stayed at home for a year, seeking to know the will of God concerning where he was to serve Him, and using the time to help at home, to learn to preach (on street corners, in jails, at the "Brethren" assembly), and to do odd jobs.

JUNE 19 *Psalm 67*   I'm lying in a field in the shade of some little scrub in the north of Grand Rapids, Michigan. Dad, Mom, and Jane came here yesterday from Glen Ellyn. Nice trip through Michigan to Holland where we stopped at Ebelinks's for lunch. Meditation on his front lawn in Psalm 67 was a blessing. The song outlines itself nicely:

Vv. 1, 2: three requests for a single purpose that the knowledge of "His way" be disseminated.

1. God, be gracious unto us—general act of God, principle of grace.
2. God, bless us—specific act of God, practice of goodness.
3. God, cause His face to shine on us—individual relationship, Person of God.

God "has a way about Him," just as we say of some men. The three above-stated methods of His dealing illustrate pretty well what His way is. I like the A.V., "saving health" for "salvation" ($\kappa\alpha\tau\grave{\alpha}$ DARBY) in verse 2.

Verses 3, 4 and 5, 6 parallel each other well. Verses 3, 4 concern themselves with the *peoples* "Ammim" and *nations* "Leumim." First he exhorts both peoples and nations in order to praise and rejoice, then he gives cause for rejoicing in both instances. First, the peoples are to be judged equitably. Far cry from present-day justice, but true, blessedly true. And then the nations, God Himself shall be their guide. Can it be! Nations and politics divinely controlled? Rest, my soul. It shall be! Verses 3 and 5 repeat exactly the same thought. First, let peoples praise, then, with the face of the incremental repetition taking hold, let *all* the peoples praise Thee. The exhortation is followed by prophecy and promise.

> Praise: verse 5.
> Prophecy: the earth shall yield
> Promise: *our* God shall bless.

Am meeting some good kids here: Chum and John Heetderks, Lauren, Verna and Phyllis Dronsink, Tom and Ben Leavenworth, Don Peton, Bob Shea. They asked me to write if I ever get into the Lord's work.

JUNE 23   *Matthew 26:73* $\dot{\eta}$ $\lambda\alpha\lambda\iota\acute{\alpha}$ $\sigma\sigma\upsilon$ $\delta\tilde{\eta}\lambda\acute{o}\nu$ $\sigma\grave{\epsilon}$ $\pi\sigma\iota\epsilon\tilde{\iota}$. Sensed much of the harsh secular tone in my speech lately—idle hillbilly songs springing first to my lips in the morning, slurring remarks come too easily. Out of the fullness of the heart the mouth speaketh.

JUNE 25   Traveling all week. Monday, Gull Lake, Michigan, with the Weebers. Tuesday at Arlene Swanson's in Stillman Valley, Illinois. Wednesday at the Norman Swansons' in Sioux City, South Dakota. Thursday at the Wheaton Science Station outside Rapid City, South Dakota, in the Black Hills. Last night in a hotel in Hardin, southeast of here, and now at Billings for the weekend. Letter from Betty here today makes me feel strange; I cannot tell whether or not I love her, and I tremble to write how shallow a prayer comrade I've been.

JUNE 27 *Acts 20:19* Billings still. We'll be here all week. They have asked Dad to take a week of meetings to attempt to straighten out a festering split in the "church of the air." Must go at it with more prayer than I am used to. Paul's words to the Ephesian elders sobered me last eve. Acts 20:18, 19: "I arrived in Asia as a slave of the Lord with all lowliness and tears . . . ." If I ever lacked any two graces and needed them worse, I don't remember when it was. *Lowliness*—I know not what it means, and *tears*—I haven't shed any for months. This present trouble here in Billings demands a great deal of both. Thou knowest, Lord, my sufficiency is of Thee.

JUNE 30 *Romans 7* I had always supposed that the analogy of the husband and wife in Romans 7:1–4 was changed in verse 3 from what one would suppose the conclusion would be, that is the husband died, the wife was free. But in the analogy, the woman was the one who died. I see it a little different this morning. The truth of the law (the husband) found its fulfillment in Christ's death, hence the binding power of law—the husband—died. I am "made dead," a passive form, by the death of Christ to the law, though I remain quite alive. Christ, the minister of circumcision, therefore becomes the "first husband"—law, and the second—grace, to which now I am married. "Grace *and* truth came by Jesus Christ." Only truth, the law, came by Moses. It is Christ's death, not mine, which frees and in verse 6 the clearance is so complete that I may effectively be said to have died. Actually, my bondage to law was such that it slew me, even before Christ died. So that I was married as dead to the law which effectively held me in death till Christ rose.

JULY 1   Up on the rim rocks of Billings this morning. The Lord is not as near as He must become if I am to minister the Word tonight. Felt great weakness and little manifest blessing in the meeting last night. So different from Tuesday, when the Lord seemed to melt our spirits in joy at the hearing of His Word. Help, Lord, for the godly man faileth!

JULY 5   I won Jane Feely [daughter of a pastor in Montana] as a real sister last eve in the lodge house of Clydhurst on the Boulder.

Evening. Walked in the sunset tonight out west of Thomas's in Bozeman. Only a little stirred in spirit for God. Much impressed by the voice of the birds and the scent of the sweet clover. Thought of God as the Great Upthruster of mountains, and the Great Downthruster of men. Impressed with that verse, "For that thy name is near thy mighty works declare" (Pss. 75:1). Some sweet converse with Christ as I walked.

JULY 6   Bozeman. Blessed in morning reading with the Thomas folks after breakfast. Thinking of *falling*. I was thinking Monday morning as I had devotions on the Boulder River at Clydhurst of three benedictions beginning with τῳ δυναμένῳ. Ephesians 3:20—able to do; Romans 16:25—able to establish; Jude 24—able to keep you from falling. This last thought began a series of thoughts on falling when compared with:

2 Peter 1:10: Doing . . . ye shall never fall—physical deeds.
Galatians 5:4: Separated from Him . . . fallen from grace—mental attitude.
Revelation 2:4, 5: Lost first love . . . remember from whence you fell—misplaced affection.

JULY 8   Home at 7272 at last. Mingled feelings of "not belonging" and thanksgiving for all God's grace these last few days—these past four years, in fact. We stayed in Missoula,

Montana, Wednesday night. Visited Jim and Fran Thomas and Jack Hydes there. They are a warning to me. The cares of this life press hard upon them, and I fear that they have *fallen* as did the Ephesians from *love* (Rev. 2). God, preserve me from living a life which conforms to the general duty and in private thinking, as J. G. Holland puts it. How many Christians will find the character in the poems of Robert Service who left the Arctic:

> . . . Came out with a fortune last fall
> Yet somehow, life's not what I thought it,
> And somehow, the gold isn't all.

How ever shall I learn to represent Thee favorably, my Lord? To whom should I go for counsel for a way of life, to whom for example? To Thee? Yea, I come to Thee.

JULY 9 *1 Corinthians 1*   Reading in 1 Corinthians 1:8 this morning. Struck afresh with the idea that God is going to make me ανεγκλήτους—unimpeachable in the day of Christ. It is absurd, I know, for Satan finds valid occasion for slander in me. But blessed be God. Jude 24 says I shall be brought into the presence of His glory exulting—ἀμώμους! Not that God is going to overlook all my shortcomings and gloss over my inconsistencies. He is going to declare me unblamable and without spot because He sees me in Christ, and Christ becomes for me all that 1 Corinthians 1:30 says.

JULY 10   Folly shot another Sunday evening. Blessing in breaking the bread this morning. Good Gospel and street meeting too. Came home and Bill and Mabel, Mick and Ruth, [Jim's uncles and their wives] and I joked away the blessing. Sorry, Father—dead flies. Restore me in mercy.

JULY 12   Went to Herb Butt's for supper. Long conversation regarding Bible-school programs and unscriptural atmosphere thereof. He teaches his children the Westminister Shorter

Catechism. Men's meeting at the hall. Thrashed out policy of meetings and effectiveness of the assembly. Better understanding of it all, I think.

JULY 15   Went with Stark St. Y.P. [Stark Street Brethren Assembly Young People] to Talbot Park in evening.

JULY 16   All day at the hall, washing and repairing it for painting—maybe next week. Much in exercise about personal holiness which I dreadfully lack. Argued loudly with Mom at supper before the whole family tonight. Wretched ingrate!

JULY 17   *Psalm 84*   Lord's Day. Happy meditation on Psalm 84 this morning. I see two divisions: (1) the heart, (2) the course. It is dangerous to get the cart before the horse, but essential in God's program to get the heart before the course. So we have in verses 1–4 the heart longing for nearness to God's habitation. The tabernacle, courts, altars are named as different aspects of the finally mentioned "house" (v. 4). Then the longing stirs to action, and the man who trusts God, whose heart longed for the courts of God, found that the highways were in his heart. He begins moving, "passing along"; "going from strength to strength." The section is divided at Selah in verse 8 as the first division was at Selah in verse 4. Then comes a testimony as to God's faithfulness in blessing the one of whom the former eight verses are true. Verse 10 mentions the courts and the house again, and verse 11 describes what God is to him who *walks* uprightly. He is a *sun* (for enlargement) and a shield (for the entanglements). A sun for engendering life; a shield when life is endangered. He gives grace for the "going on" of verse 11 and glory at the appearing of verse 11.

JULY 23   Painted part of the hall today. Restless to do other things more directly related to the Lord's work. Longing for a companion, who will be a David to me, and me his Jonathan. Lack spiritual stamina to keep fresh in all this eating and doing. Oh, there is time to read and seek God, but my desire slackens. Lord, uphold Thy lily saint! Stay me, Jahweh, for Thine is a strong right arm, and mine so weak! Saturday night again, and weary from work but seeking something from the Lord now. How shall I build with these weak and slack hands, Lord?

JULY 26   Been a while since I wrote anything. Seem to be pulling out of one of my month-long spiritual-slack spells. Confession of pride—suggested by David Brainerd's diary yesterday—must become an hourly thing with me. How vile and base my thoughts have been lately. Not just unkind or unsympathetic, but rotten, lewd thinking that cannot be overcome by simply *willing* to be rid of them. However dare I minister to God's saints in such a condition. Lord, rebuke my flesh and deliver my heart from evil.

JULY 27   *Acts 20; Galatians 2; Hebrews 10*   "I shrank not from declaring the whole counsel of God . . . whatever was profitable" (Acts 20:27, 20). "Cephas . . . . when they came, shrank back, fearing the circumcision" (Gal. 2:11, 12). ". . . If he shrink back, my soul shall have no pleasure in him . . . We are not of those that shrink back to perdition but of them that have faith to the saving of the soul" (Heb. 10:38, 39). The Word seems to peculiarly apply to the attitude saved Jews took when challenged as to their boldness in Christ. So I judge, any tendency to quiet down the message of free access is a stealthy shrinking back into the darkness of blinded Judaism. Keep me from such legal bondage, O free Spirit of God. Let me live by faith. Faith is opposed by fear. Faith can only work by love. Perfect love casts out fear. Love, then, is the soul's great "Sanforizor"—it keeps the soul from shrinking back—συμφέρω (Acts 20:20). Everything that profited, Paul preached. First Corinthians 6:12—only the profitable was he a doer of.

JULY 28   Comfort from A.C. [Amy Carmichael] this morning. Sobering letter from Bill C. yesterday about Irene's [his wife] inability to respond to spiritual conversation. Moved to pray a little for him, but, oh, how lax my soul's desires. John Winden came out last night, and we talked of the church's condition and lack of life. The Lord has stirred him much to read and take literally His holy Word. He was a challenge to me. A lusting soul makes for a listless spirit.

JULY 29   Seaside with Howard and Helen Elliot, Ruth, Carol, Joan T., Florence D., and Jane and Mom and Dad. Four and one half hours solid in the natatorium.

JULY 30   Painted at the hall. Weary tonight.

JULY 31   Lord's Day. At Zwald's for dinner. Took up John the Baptizer in Y.P. meeting. Trying to get the kids to study on their own. They are slow catching on. Preached on "God, the Father" in Gospel meeting. Not enough time for preparation and prayer. No noticeable response on the street preaching afterward, where John 6:40 was my verse. "This is the will of my Father, that he who *beholds* the Son and *believes* on him has eternal life."

AUGUST 1   *Psalm 94*   Some spiritual stir over reading David Brainerd's diary. If I were honest, my writing here would be more in anguish as is his. But how cold I have grown, and how careless about it all. O Lord, let not my soul be cast away from the knowledge of Thy nearness. Move upon me, Lord, "my foot slippeth" (v. 18).

AUGUST 4   I must confess much leanness of soul today, O Patient Shepherd. How often I have been angered at delay, short spirited (opposite to $\mu\alpha\kappa\rho\delta\theta\nu\mu\sigma\varsigma$), anxious to criticize. I noticed tonight, too, that one does not live for himself in this regard, but that a little leaven of dissatisfied temper will spread through a group and change outlooks. Then, too, meek Savior, I must bring a boisterous tongue, roguish lips to Thee for cleansing. Oh, to be holy! Just to sense for a moment that I have somehow, however small, simulated some measure of Thy character, Lord Jesus. A word from Horatius Bonar spoke to me tonight. "Holiness is not austerity or gloom; these are as alien to it as levity and flippancy; it is the offspring of conscious, present Peace."

AUGUST 9   Paul could say to the Romans (Rom. 1:9), to the Thessalonians (1 Thess. 1:2; 2:13; 5:17) and to Timothy (2 Tim. 1:3) that he made unceasing ἀδιαλείπτως remembrance of them all in his prayers. What can I say in this regard? Nothing. No one is constantly in my mind as these seem to have been in Paul's. O Lord Jesus, my Great Intercessor, give me an assiduous spirit in prayer. My spirit lags these days. Seem to get so little from my morning reading, and what I do get seldom stays in my mind during the day. What a failure I am to claim such devotion and know so little of God in my thoughts. Teach me Thy way, O Lord.

AUGUST 11   *Acts 16; Isaiah 25*   Much comfort and instruction from reading through Acts last night in bewilderment of spirit because of sin. How gracious my Lord is, not to take His Spirit from me but to win me to Himself by the pure motions of that Spirit within. I noticed in Acts 16:7 that it was the *spirit of Jesus* (κατὰ best manuscripts) which hindered Paul from his attempt to enter Bythinia. I think He is only called specifically that once. Why? What did Jesus have particularly to do with hindering? I wonder if it is not the spirit of Jesus as a man, that which hindered him from going to any but the "lost sheep of Israel" that He might do His Father's will when perhaps His natural desire would have been to take His Word to the ends of the earth. He, as Paul, was directed by the Spirit to go where so great a messenger would not be expected to go. Paul desired to go across Asia to Sinim, but, blessed Word, the "spirit of Jesus" turned him westward and thence down through the centuries to my own family and home! How merciful He is! Brainerd says (Feb. 7, 1744), "Oh, methinks if He would punish me for my sins, it would not wound my heart so deep to offend Him; but though I sin continually, yet He continually repeats His kindness to me." Amen. It is so with me.

Blessed just now in studying Isaiah 25 for reading meeting tonight. We have *waited* for Him (v. 9). Three prepositions are prefixed to the New Testament word μένω which are interesting. Acts 1:4: περίμενω, "wait around for the Spirit." First Thessalonians 1:10: ἀνάμενω, "wait up for the coming Christ." Hebrews 10:32: ὑπομένω, "wait under affliction." We shall wait for Him. Found another late tonight. πρόσμενω (Acts 11:23; 13:43), "cleave," continue in—as our "stick at" the grace of God. Go not beyond it, fall not from it—be μένει πρός it. Wait at it!

AUGUST 12   Dale Morgan married tonight, and as usual, I came away soured. Twentieth-century Christian weddings are the vainest, most meaningless forms. There is no vestige of reality. The witnesses dress for a show. The flesh is given all the place. The songs are absurd if one paid any attention to the words, but no one does; they simply listen to *how* it is sung, not what it means. Candles are useless, but expensive trifles. Ushers help no one, but appear very officious, and the ceremony itself is the most meaningless hodgepodge of obsolete grammar and phraseology—sounds like a schoolboy's translation of Cicero. And the stupid form of asking who gives this bride in marriage! Who cares? Everyone knows it's her father or uncle or some such sweating pawn standing before the altar. Talk of Romanism! We fundamentalists are a pack of mood-loving show-offs. I'm sure the minor prophets would have found a subject for correction in this affair. I must read this to myself on my wedding day, if I have one.

Read 1 Corinthians 7 again this morning, and Matthew 19:12 last night!

AUGUST 16   *Isaiah 26*   Blessed last night from reading Isaiah 26: 8, 9: "Yea, Lord, in the way of thy judgments have we waited for thee; to thy name, thy memorial name, is the desire of our soul. With my soul have I desired thee in the night; with my spirit within me I will seek thee earnestly: for when thy judgments are in the earth, the inhabitants of the world learn righteousness." Noticed the distinction between the work of the soul and spirit here. "With my soul I desired thee . . . with my spirit I seek thee earnestly." Often at evening devotions, there is no earnestness to seek the Lord in my spirit, but the soul never fails for *desire* of Him. Desire at night makes for diligence at morn.

AUGUST 19 *Mark 1* Thought last night of the Lord Jesus' way of concealing Himself in Mark 1. A demon's witness He will not allow (vv. 25, 34); the leper's witness He did not need (v. 44), since the Scripture, the Baptist, the Father, the Spirit and His power in healing had already been sufficient witness as to His unique person. He was preaching a new message, or should I say, a fresh one, with a new manner. The Baptist calls Him the "Baptizer in the Holy Spirit," contrasted with the old water baptism. The Capernaum Synagogue goers remarked not only on his method ("with authority, not as the scribes"), but on the message itself "a *new* teaching!" [v. 27]). How different His prayers and the Pharisees' (v. 35). They prayed long in public at the street corner. He was alone in the desert praying. They reveled in the crowds for a following. He was in the desert (v. 45). His words verify His works and vice versa in 2:1–12. "We never saw it on this fashion before" (v. 12). New cloth, new garment, new wine and wineskins, He calls His work. Phenomenal, this is what truth seemed in the day of lies. The truth was "new." Sad commentary, this, on what the Jew had done with the Sacred Writ.

AUGUST 21 *Romans 5* Lord's Day. Reading Romans 5 again this morning I see the recurrence of the word *through*—seems to be the basis of much of Paul's doctrine. Verses 1–12 show us the complete, yea, the abounding work that God has accomplished through Christ.

Through Him we have peace (v. 1).
Through Him we have access (v. 2).
Through Him we have salvation from wrath (v. 9).
Through Him we have reconciliation (v. 11).
Through Him we have our rejoicing in God (v. 11).

The Holy Spirit shed on us is the instrument *through* whom has come the love of God. The last part of the chapter is concerned with the subjection and deliverance of our race *through* two men.

Sin entered *through* Adam (v. 12).
Death entered through sin (v. 12).
Death reigned through one (Adam) (v. 17).

Pivot:

Not as *through* the one that sinned is the gift (v. 16).
Many constituted sinners through one (v. 19).
Many constituted righteous through one (v. 19).

Receivers of the abundant grace reign through Christ (v. 17).
Through one act of trespass came condemnation (v. 18).
Through one act of righteousness came justification (v. 18).

Grace reigns *through* righteousness with a view to life eternal which is *through* Christ.

Struck too with the idea that God is taking very definite attitudes toward men. In Chapter 1 we have extremes: beloved of God (v. 7) and hateful to God—not God haters but hated of God for their deeds (v. 30). The aim of a man should be to become *pleasing* to God (8:8; cf. τοις ἀγαπῶσιν τον θεον, 8:28).

Evening. I sense tonight that my desires to be great are likely to frustrate God's intents for good to be done through me. O Lord, let me pray again with earnest, honest heart. I will not to be great, only, God, grant to me Thy *goodness*.

AUGUST 23 *Isaiah 26* How long will a vile heart corrupt a pure spirit? The peace-keeping, perfect peace, of Isaiah 26:3 is for the steadfast mind, the *stayed* imagination. Lord, how wretched has been my outlook today, how low and flagging my spirit. Went to Herb Butt's with Francis Ball and talked some of the reformers' doctrine of limited atonement, or "effectual redemption," as John Owen calls it. Herb spoke, too, of perseverence of the saints, a subject I had no idea there was much issue on. But how cold are arguments, how blasphemous debate over the pure Word of God. I need warmth, fervency, and meekness these days. But the Word is silent often of late. O Lord, be not silent unto me, lest I become like those that go down to the pit.

Took Bunny Paeth [a close friend of mine whom I had asked Jim to meet] to Trout Creek Camp last night. Striking girl and not so full of talk as to be tedious. Learned yesterday that Betty is coming next week. I will need Thee much, Lord Jesus, to deal justly and kindly by her. It is hard for me to admit that I am wholly unworthy of such a girl. My care for her is so shallow, but her love seems unflagging. Obdurate ingrate that I am, from whence for me shall come salvation? "Through your supplication and the supply of the Spirit of Jesus Christ."

AUGUST 24 *Romans 8* As surely as I experience suffering—and as really—shall I experience glory. I reckon that the suffering of this now-time is not worthy to be placed alongside the glory about to be revealed in us (or "to usward"). Suffering is generally caused by the application of an external force or circumstance to my person. Though it is external, it is no less personal, individual, and in a sense, autonomous. Were it not for human sensibility to experience it, suffering would be unknown. So with τὸ μέλλουσαν δόξαν. I have capacity to reflect glory now that I am in Christ—so much so that I as a reflector may be said to have glory. Hence δοξαν εἰς ὑμας. Glory, not simply shown *to* us, but glory which God shall show to be *in* us—as actually as suffering was shown to be in us, though it is *from* another. Thus the revelation is said to be "*of* the sons of God" (v. 19), and the "liberty of the glory of the children of God" is spoken of (v. 21).

His sons shall come singing into glory
Brought there by that Great Leader of His Band.
The mad, the meek, the glad, the weak,
His own, the called of every land.
   That whimperer—His son?
   The one who could not bear with pressure,
   Can he come thus to glory singing?
He comes and sings,
   That lame, that torn-footed wretch
   Whose head looked not above
   On earth, sings she now?
She sings and follows uprightly.
   That boisterous rowdy,
   Talkative. What does he here
   In unison with these?
He sings with all the rest—and learns harmonious silence.
   That gray-beard old croaker,
   With fetid breath and
   Stamp of death—singing?
Hearken to his harmony, was ever instrument more perfectly in tune?
Nay, all of these must sing—for they have long been under groaning.
The rasping tones of earth have ceased for them.
For list—they have heard the voice of Him who hushed creation's moaning,
Who rests in love, who joys over them with song.

AUGUST 24   *Romans 10*   Study this morning in Romans 10 brought me to regard with care that word in verse 16: "But not all gave submissive ear to the glad word." The tenor of obedience is common in Romans. The epistle closes and opens on identical notes—"obedience to the faith among the nations" (1:5; 16:26). There are two words employed—$\dot{v}\pi\alpha\kappa o\dot{v}\omega$ (all the above) and $\pi\epsilon\iota\theta\dot{\epsilon}\omega$, or its negative. Romans 11:30–32 climaxes the argument by showing both Jew and Gentile in ἀπειθεια—shut up to that disobedience that He might show mercy to all. We are not at liberty to do as we will with the truth of God. It is not optional whether or not we believe and obey. Those who disobey truth get wrath and indignation (2:8). Obedience to the truth is not only pressed upon Gentiles, but is expected also of believers as Galatians 5:7 shows. Enough for πειθω (cf. John 3:36). Now in asking for submissive hearkening, Paul sets Christ before his readers, as ever showing His obedience to be pattern for our own:

5:19: ([cf. Phil. 2:1–12]—obey in his absence).
6:12: The lusts of sin are not to be obeyed.
6:16: Obedience to righteousness commanded.
6:17: Obedience from the heart to the teaching delivered.

Israel is seen as a rejected servant in 10:16, 21 because of disobedience, and 15:18 declares Paul's method among Gentiles was to press obedience to faith upon their consciences. The priests of Acts 6:7 obeyed the faith. Vengeance is over those who disobey the Gospel in 2 Thessalonians 1:8. The first chapter of 1 Peter refers three times to obedience: verse 2 is sanctification for obedience; verse 14, children of obedience; verse 22, purification by obedience to truth. Father, grant this onetime child of disobedience a well-persuaded, hearkening heart to obey.

AUGUST 27   Climbed Mount Hood last night, midnight to 6:00 A.M. Dick F., Dutch, Dave Jannsen, Ron McSkimmings, and Ray Benz went along. Came back for an hour's rest then to the Assembly picnic at Lewisville Park, Washington. Too tired and lapsed into playing rowdy songs on the harmonica. Became critical of everything and despaired of any good. Wasted the evening. Went to bed early.

AUGUST 28   I don't know how the Lord is expected to work miracles in preparing my soul for the breaking of bread this morning. Bill and Nellie McLean are here today.

AUGUST 30   I can conceive of utterly no good in me this morning. I have accomplished nothing, attained nothing in the way of holiness. My worthlessness exalts God's grace to sinners but makes His choice most mysterious. And when I think of what Romans 14:12 means in my case, I tremble. How shall my "account" sound when given to God?

SEPTEMBER 2 *Romans 12, 13*   Challenged at hearing William Gibson report of the work in Jamaica where there is actual evidence that God is among the people. For the first time in a long time, I heard a foreign worker say, "We need no missionaries in Jamaica." Why? Because the believers on the island are doing a work of their own, and outsiders are superfluous except for their teaching ministries. Souls are saved weekly; Bible studies begin at 5:00 A.M. in some places. Christians are beginning their days with as much as three hours of Bible study. God is among them, and the practices of apostolic days are common. O Lord, how great is the sin of brethren. I confess, Lord, my terrible weakness of spirit. How poorly I have represented Thee; how dead my duty-doing of reading and prayer. O Lord Jesus, come to me in power. Revive thy work, O Lord. Perfect that which concerneth me. Deadness, leanness, shallowness—things I have accused fundamentalists of—I now find true of myself.

Study in Romans 12, 13 opened up as a development of the παρακαλος of 12:1, 2. The entire section develops the idea of the "renewed mind" functioning in conformity to the nature of a holy sacrifice in all departments of life. Romans 12:1–13 shows the renewed mind *proving* the acceptable will of God in the assembly of saints. Verses 3–8 are "formal" contact in the Church; 9–13 "informal." The section outlines thus:

The Renewed Mind:
  I. In the Church (vv. 3–13).
     A. The exercise of gifts (vv. 3–8). Wise—or sober thinking—not higher than I ought to think.
     B. The exercise of grace (vv. 9–13). Humble thoughts, preferring one another.

II. Before enemies (vv. 14–21).
   A. Thought for men of low estate (v. 16).
   B. Thought for things honorable (v. 17).
III. Beneath the government (13:1–7). Submissive and orderly arrangement under ordained powers.
   A. Deliverance from outside fear—wrath.
   B. Deliverance from inside accusation—conscience.
IV. In relation to law (vv. 8–10).

The renewed mind is summed up in 13:14: "Put on the Lord Jesus Christ, and make no provision for the flesh . . . ." Betty comes.

SEPTEMBER 6   Conference [Plymouth Brethren Labor Day Bible Conference] over last night. Not at all what I had hoped for by way of searching ministry and challenge. Some warmth of heart in hearing of the Lord's coming again. Even though the stress was not what I prayed for, I believe the Lord carried out His purpose. Psalms 115:3: "But our God is in the heavens: He hath done what he pleased."
Very intimate with Betty in speaking of our relation—Sunday on Rocky Butte, Monday on Mount Tabor. Startled to find ourselves talking about marriage so offhandedly last eve. I noticed that she was pained in hearing of some of the social aspects of this Spring's renaissance. I felt sorry myself for much of it. Of the heart Jeremiah said, "Who can know it?" (17:9). Westwood [one of the Plymouth Brethren preachers] said Sunday, the marvel of divine revelation is that I can know God (John 17:3) but *cannot* know myself.

SEPTEMBER 7   Meditating on the keeping grace of the "Shield and Defender." Much perplexed and vacant in soul from long conversation and some prayer with Betty last evening on the Columbia. "He will not suffer that thy foot be moved" (Pss. 121:3) is a source of great comfort this morning. I.V. [Inter-Varsity] Hymnal songs seven, "Unto the Hills," and nine, "We Rest on Thee, Our Shield and Our Defender," are alive with meaning for me today. Stirred to poesy but no proper words, except to say that I wonder why God hangs onto me? Why does He bother to urge me upward when I would return? "When I said, My foot slippeth; Thy lovingkindness, O Lord, held me up . . . . Thy comforts delight my soul" (Pss. 94:18, 19). Oh, blessed be His name, that He leaves me not but haunts me to follow on, drawing me upward away from earth, with promises of freedom from all entanglement and bondage. Psalms 17:5: "When Thou holdest my going in Thy paths, my footsteps slip not."

SEPTEMBER 9   *1 Corinthians 2*   Swimming yesterday with Betts. Prayer meeting last eve was warming. Betty, on reading these pages, exhorts me to confidence rather than the despairing attitude she senses is prevalent. Reading in 1 Corinthians 2 today. "We have the mind of Christ" (v. 16). This is one of the great things "freely given us of God" (v. 12). "We have received the spirit from God . . . things prepared . . ." (v. 12). Oh, how much has been God's giving! How free and rich! But I fail to apprehend for lack of faith. Betty charges me with this daily. But blessed be God. It is so, and I shall live in the truth of it by grace.

SEPTEMBER 10   Blessed of God yesterday in fellowship with Betts at the beach. Stirred to thanksgiving for her. Heard the Lord's voice in 1 Corinthians 3 this morning. "Take heed how you build" (v. 10). God's garden takes tending that is careful; His building, work that is honorable and worthy of the Foundation.

SEPTEMBER 13   She has been gone just one hour. What thunders of feeling I have known in that short time. I could not read the neon lights as I turned away from the bus, and somehow couldn't face the people as they passed me. My lip kept contorting, and I could not seem to look natural without twisting tight together both my lips. How terrible I sound sobbing. Not like myself at all, but uncontrolled grating, animal sounds—and tears that trickled over my jaw and to my throat. Leaving her is terrible. I remember three times now. The station in Chicago as she walked alone down the tracks next to a Santa Fe train on her way to Wycliffe. Then her face in the back window of the taxi on Washington Street behind the Stupe last September. And now this—her twisted brow, the tragic pain of her glance. And she goes off—still wondering. Teasdale's poem ["Night Song at Amalfi"] came back:

> I asked the heaven of stars
> What I could give my love.
> It answered me with silence,
> Silence above.
>
> I asked the deep green sea
> Down where the fishes go,
> But nothing broke the silence,
> Silence below.
>
> Oh, I could give her weeping,
> Or I could give her a song,
> But how can I give her silence,
> Silence my whole life long?

For it seems each time I see her she wants an answer, some assurance, some little promise for the future. And rightly so. But each time I have no word, only that I must wait. How long? For what? I know not. O God of my bitter moments, Father of Christ who wept, grant me some guidance directly from Thee. May I ask it in Spirit-spawned *faith*, Lord? *Please let us not part again in silence.* I would rather never see her again than have to put her through this "going into silence."

Her uprightness makes it so hard. She loves, I know, but, oh, how bitter is love unexpressed. And she will not let me hold her, hardly touch her, for she says, "I am not mine to give you." If God gave her to me and it were certain, if we dwelt not in *silence* but in assurance that He were granting us to one another, it would be easier. She would relax her vigil, and we might embrace. But she does not, and I know how much she

longs for light and thence for expressed love. This came as I
wept between sunset and moonrising on the side hill beneath
the firs:

> Wheels carried her into silence
> Out of my reach.
> I feared lest darkness, closing round us
> Might gain our souls,
> And we lose sight
> Of real things.
> But nay, the sun that ruled our days
> Has lit the moon to rule our night.

I tried to sing coming home, strange croaking notes, but hear,
my soul, hear:

> Does Jesus care
> When I've said "goodbye"
> To the dearest on earth to me,
> And my sad heart aches
> Till it nearly breaks,
> Is it aught to Him, does He see?
> O yes, He cares,
> I know He cares,
> His heart is touched with my grief . . . .
>   "Does Jesus Care?"
>   FRANK E. GRAEFF

SEPTEMBER 15   *1 Corinthians 7*   Quieted and pressed today
thinking much of Betts. Can't tell why my daily reading should
fall at 1 Corinthians 7. What *is* the Lord teaching me? It is
certainly not my natural gift to be continent in this matter of
sexual relation, and if I ever am privileged to live without a
wife, it will be evidence of great spiritual grace imparted. I
have none of it now.

Betty made a poor impression on the family. Mother calls her
a "boarding-school child." Jane never saw her read her Bible
in the mornings. Dad is much freer now that she is gone and

seems relieved though he says nothing. Apparently none feels she fits me, yet we together alone seem to strike it off wonderfully well. But before others she is aloof. Hazel Berney [a cousin] remarked on it at the conference when she tried to approach Betts. Ah, Lord, this tenderness, this eagerness to defend her against every charge, will it pass again? The weak, half-sobbing feeling when I think of her, will it go? Should I encourage these thoughts or stamp them out? They come regardless. Brief diary of her 11 days here:

Friday night: Prayer meeting for conference. Westwood on foot washing. Sing at Masson's [P.B. assembly members].

Saturday: Conference, three meetings. Sing at Howatts's.

Sunday: Rocky Butte between morning and afternoon meetings.

Monday: Mount Tabor—"the question is whether or not I should marry. Marriage and you are synonymous." Talk of Bob Keller. Trip up Columbia River Highway.

Tuesday: Canoeing. Reading letters on Grass Island in Columbia. Full moon rise. Notice attraction for her face. Not common before. First prayer together.

Wednesday: Overcast. Finish letters on slopes of Tabors. Prayer and tears. Side hill bench.

Thursday: Morning devotions in Matthew 18 on west of Tabor, back of Asbahr Heights. Swimming and sport in Columbia.

Friday: Beach. Spent first money on her in Crab Broiler at Cannon Beach Junction. Sunset at Shortsand. Dead deer over Neahkanie. Cave and sea anemones.

Saturday: To Paeth's for a visit. Zwald's pictures at night.

Sunday: Ted and Lou's [cousins] for dinner. Late talk in car out front. "Rubble" recalled.

Monday: Mountain Hood. Paradise Park. "Oh, this is horrible!" Twin Bridges. Tears.

Tuesday: Repair steps. Downtown for ticket. Herb and Olive for dinner. Tears.

Strange, but oh, such happy days! Were these not of Thee, my God? And wilt Thou deny fruition to such love as we have known? As Thou wilt. But how impossible it seems to wait, to reconcile the family. ". . . but with God . . . ."

SEPTEMBER 16   "If any man love God, the same is known by Him" (1 Cor. 8:3). "But now, knowing God, or rather *known* of Him" (Gal. 4:9). "Depart from me, workers of iniquity. I never *knew* you" (Pss. 6:8). Recognized and known of God in Christ. Not even reckoned with apart from Christ, but now "foreknown." The Lord knoweth the way of the righteous.

4:00 P.M.:

Whence are these deeds of goodness?
Come they from meditation on their doing
Autonomously?
Or do they flare as oily rags
Of unknown combination,
Spontaneously?
Nay, they are born as you and I,
Miraculously.
Their fair mother called Desire
Springs them forth from dwelling close
With vision, their unstable sire.
These two, Want and anxious Willingness-to-See,
Bear children.
It is not sure
On what men's hopes do hive.
They sleep to see in dreams alive? (Isaiah 29:8).
All deeds must come from want that's pure.
Then soul of mine, flame purely
And thou shalt see Desire conceive in thought, surely,
Some hoped-for form.
And from the image shall come forth the act.

SEPTEMBER 19   Returned from Eugene with Dad today. Good, intimate fellowship on the way down. Thought of Shortsand episode with Betts returning tonight. Hence:

The bellow of the tide
From the blue expanding wide
Beyond the roughness of the rocks off Falcon Head
Funneled hugely, vainly tried
To rend our cavern where it died
In quiet cool of sandy bed
Beneath our feet.

We shivered as we stood,
Found no words to fit the mood
Which numbed us silent; we quaffed
Each other's good,
But not knowing then to brood,
Spoke nonsense, laughed
The sea to silence.

The touch of naked shoulder
As each felt his own the colder
Melted other touch-things into dream.
False, every fact I told her—
Lie, that overhanging boulder—
All things that were did only seem
As we knew love.

SEPTEMBER 21 *1 Corinthians 11*   Study this morning in 1 Corinthians 11 on women's covering. The Corinthians are praised for their having held fast to a tradition which is admittedly such. It was given as a *tradition*—delivered to be held as such. There is no reference made to the nature of the thing being local or temporary, so it may be either. It was given that we might recognize the order of God that the head (controller and director) of the man was Christ, of woman, man, of Christ, God. Thus when a man covers his head he dishonors not his own head, but his constituted head, Christ. He, putting a cover on his head, signifies that his true head is in subjection as he prophesies, which ought never to be. The woman, who is the glory of the man, uncovering her head, puts man in a place of authority above what God has ordered. If she be shaved, she destroys a veil that is given to show her subjection at all times, and even that is to be covered when she prophesies. Christ would not cover His head, as man would not cover his, but woman, who is seen as a unit with man (v. 11), must bear the sign of human subjection for the sake of angels, whose sense of divine order is not to be violated.

SEPTEMBER 22 *1 Corinthians 11:19* Blessed be Appeles, "the approved in Christ." Struck with the occurrences of this word δόκιμος in the epistles of Paul while reading 1 Corinthians 11:19: "That the approved may be manifest." The man who serves Christ in properly functioning as a citizen of the Kingdom is "well pleasing to God and *approved* of men" (Rom. 14:18). He that refuses to partake of a party spirit manifests himself as one tried and approved. First Corinthians 11:19: he who is commended of the Lord is approved. Second Corinthians 10:18: the Corinthians sought a proof (δοκιμήν) of Christ in Paul. He tells them to prove themselves (δοκιμάζω) by not doing any evil, as he did not seek his approval to be manifest (2 Corinthians 13:3–7). "Be careful to show yourself approved to God" (not men), Paul tells Timothy (2 Tim. 2:15) and this is accomplished by a proper and direct setting forth of the Word. Paul fears lest he be disapproved (1 Corinthians 9:27). Deacons must first be "proved" (1 Tim. 3:10). Thanks be to God that He has approved us to be entrusted with the Word (1 Thess. 2:4).

SEPTEMBER 23 Felt like "the smoking flax and the broken reed" (Isa. 42:3) last night but found enjoyment in the promise, "He will not quench, He will not crush." Thrice blessed be a Christ so patient, a Lord so merciful, a Savior so loving-kind. Lord Jesus, take all of me, my loves, my longings, all I am and have.

SEPTEMBER 25 I prayed this morning that God would deliver me from a vile heart continually perpetrating foul and wicked intents. This afternoon I have been speaking with Mother regarding Betty, the Lord's will, marriage, and diversity of others. Just now was wondering how much of my path in God's way is self-determined and how much God determined for me. He said, "The bad or ill of man is not given by Me; the good I not only permit but determine." So that if there is any failure, that is my part in my guidance. If there is success and blessing in any measure, this is granted by my God. Brutal, you say? Yes, but just, nevertheless. All good, no bad, comes from Him. All bad, no good, comes from my doing or willing.

SEPTEMBER 26 *1 Corinthians 13*   The gift of tongues may be a gift involving two sorts of speech, κατὰ, 1 Corinthians 13:1: "tongues of men and angels." The first would be that demonstrated in Acts 2 where every man heard "in his own tongue." The latter is suggested in 1 Corinthians 14 where an interpreter is needed when a tongue is used ἐν ἐκκλησία. Heard of Dave's engagement.

SEPTEMBER 27 *1 Corinthians 15*   . . . and the thing displeased the Lord. Problem of 1 Corinthians 15:22 clarified this morning. "As in Adam all die, so in Christ shall all be made alive." Does this indicate universal atonement? No. All *in Adam* die. All *in Christ* shall live. Not that all are in Christ as they are in Adam. One must be born again to gain the status of being *in Christ*. Only these are made alive.

Spent the morning reading Charles Stanley's *First Years of Christianity*. Perplexed at his variance with Horatius Bonar ᐧin *God's Way of Holiness* on the subject of the believer's relation to law. Bonar insists on establishing the Law as a *guide* for the believer's life. C.S. says, Law in Christianity has "leavened all Christendom and brought in the utmost confusion. Sometimes the soul believes God, and then is happy, then seeks to attain to a little more righteousness by *the Law as a rule of life*, and then is almost in despair" (p. 101). To the one, Romans 7 is a believer's experience; to the other, the experience of a soul struggling in darkness under Law. I fail to agree with all C.S. says about the preaching of Peter and that of Paul. He thinks Peter preached what man must do—repent and be baptized;

Paul what Christ must have suffered, without giving anything for a man to do. I fail to see how he can say (p. 106), "Did you ever hear preaching of this kind—not a word about what you must do, but all about what Jesus has done?" and then refer to Acts 17, where Paul says, "God commands all men everywhere to repent . . . ."

"For this cause shall a man leave his father and mother and cleave unto his wife." This most blessedly and mysteriously applies to Christ. He left His Father in the incarnation, and mother in ascension and glorification, that He might institute a brand-new creation which partakes of the life of both His Father and His mother—God-men who constitute His bride.

OCTOBER 6 *2 Corinthians 1* Returned yesterday from a six-day hunting trip with Will Van Dyke, Ray, and Bob. Left September 30; camped near Granite, Oregon, seventy miles northeast of John Day. No deer for the larder but a wholesome, restful experience. Met Jerry and John Vodieaux (Vodeay), Jack Robinson, and others. Hunted Fox district Tuesday and desert around Hampton yesterday. Sense again that happy freedom from "the commonplace which lays its bonds upon us all," as Goethe said. Sorry though that the cadence of hunting, getting up so early, and eating so late, cut out the usual time for Bible study. Therefore I was thankful to get some word from the Spirit this morning. During the trip out, the wide desolation around the John Day country stirred this:

> Thou God of all encouragement
> Who sets the juniper
> To stand alone in wilderness
> Apart from any other tree,
> A resting place for prophets,
> Grant me tenacity.

Two cloud forms that I have noticed seemed to take shape in words. Often after sunset a few lingering fragments will remain catching the sun's departed light: ". . . as shreds of shimmering satin snagged on velvet." Then those masses that often accumulate over a vast area of mountains leaving glimpses of sky above: "flat-bottomed fleets of fleece ceiled off the blue."

On arrival home a letter—my first since her visit—from Betts, charging me with half-hearted repentance for the license I took in the renaissance. Then one from Dave exhorting me to stop stirring up love in her by continuing to write. Have I used fickleness or purposed κατὰ the flesh (2 Cor. 1:17)?

Second Corinthians 1 was my morning meditation. Stirred to sober wonder at what, or rather *who*, shall be *my* glorying in the day of Jesus Christ? O Lord, how little deliverance I have wrought in the earth when compared with all Thy lavish promises of fruit. God grant me effectiveness in life and balance.

Read some Nietzsche this afternoon. He uses constantly the idea of "something over there"—the man beyond—the "ubermensch." Dreadful contrast he makes with my heavenly prophet, but he points up, not in the same direction. This while reading:

> Body is not bad.
> Only to him who thinks it everything,
> To him it is very bad.
> Immanuel, what burden Thine
> To bear a body among men
> Who thought their body all?
>> How long e'er Spirit conquer Body?
>> E'er Body finds its frenzied joy
>> In slavery to Spirit?
> What is this?
> The greatest of Thy giving
> Was not Thy giving
> But Thy taking from us,
> With us, Body,
> Son of Man.
> Without this taking
> There would be no giving.
>> Lo, all our generations say,
>> "Our bodies suffice us not.

> We lack not strong bodies,
> We look not for beautiful, delicate bodies,
> We want control of both."
In Thee, Immanuel,
We spat on Spirit
And petted Body.
And still we drink deep of Body
And love him well; for,
Though he masters us,
As in wine, so in Body
Do we tingle.
> How long e'er Spirit conquer Body,
> E'er Body find its frenzied joy
> In slavery to Spirit?

OCTOBER 7 *Psalm 141*   I realized today that I am on very stiff trial; it is the test of free time. The Lord took away all outward activity. No work, no money to spend, nothing to do. I fear lest I waste such days. Spent this one in writing, reading, and a little prayer. Got halfway through [Kenneth] Wuest's *Practical Use of the Greek New Testament.* It is fair in some points, tedious in others, as for instance, his constant rehearsing in italics the benefits of the study of New Testament Greek. I suppose he is right, but he certainly is repetitive. I do not agree with him on Jude 6, 7 about the fornication of angels and not entirely on Hebrews 12:2. I cannot see why grammarians must be so bluntly dogmatic. I have noticed the same in Robertson [a New Testament grammar book]. Lord, grant me, even in old age, a sober reasonableness and deliver from harping, canting, bullheaded pressing of my own points. Psalms 141:3 at noon today. "Set a watch at the door of my lips" (both for what goes out and what comes in!)

OCTOBER 8
The unveiling of 2 Corinthians 2–4:

"Maketh manifest the savor of his knowledge in every place" (2:14).

"By the manifestation of the truth" (4:2).

"Being made manifest that ye are an epistle of Christ" (3:3).

"To give the light of the knowledge of the glory of God" (4:6).

"The life also of Jesus may be manifest in our body" (4:10).

"We look not at the things which are seen" (4:18).

How blessed that the God who "putteth no trust in his servants and charges his angels with folly" (Job 4:18) should thus open to the world of men and spirits the secrets of His knowledge in us, the earthen vessels.

> Oh, blessed be the Love
> That reckons not reward,
> From merit or from blame,
> But grants rich gifts
> In wise, divine regard
> For His own Name.

OCTOBER 9   *2 Corinthians 2–5*   The good hand of God was upon us today. Thoughts of "Abba" and the Prodigal in breaking of bread. Some interest among the kids on the Gadarene demoniac in Y.P. [young people's] meeting. Spoke on the five manifestations of 2 Corinthians 2–5 in Gospel meeting.

Manifestation of the savor of His knowledge.

Manifestation of the commendation of Paul's letter written on his heart.

Manifestation of the truth in preaching to every man's conscience.

Manifestation of the life of Jesus.

Manifestation of the saints at the Bema [allusion to 2 Corinthians 5:10, the judgment seat (of Christ)].

> Miraculous, this power God gives to me,
> To deal in holy barter
> With the souls of men.

OCTOBER 10   *Romans 7; 1 John 3*   Thought of Romans 7:17 as compared with 1 John 3:9. The former accounts for the sin done, the latter for the good done. Two natures in conflict.

OCTOBER 12   *2 Corinthians 7*   Made glad this morning at the reading of 2 Corinthians 7. It begins with the perfection of holiness as a believer's responsibility in the light of God's promises. Verse 6 speaks of the comfort of lowliness as an added feature of God's grace. The heart of Paul is laid bare so really in his sending Titus to Corinth and his pursuit and finding of him in Macedonia.

2:12: An open door at Troas but no relief of spirit because he found not Titus.

2:1: Determination not to go to Corinth and stir up grief.

1:8: Despairing of life in Asia.

1:16: Purpose to go to Corinth through Macedonia, but not fulfilled because of 2:1.

7:5: Macedonia but no relief of the flesh (cf. 2:12).

How real, how human, how divine it all is! Oh, that I might receive the apostle's passion, caught from vision of Thyself, Lord Jesus. David Brainerd's diary stirs me on to such in prayer.

Sense a need for a voice and a vocabulary that will not only reach the saints—the brethren and the fundamentalists—it must be that I can learn to speak fresh words startlingly enough to rouse them. But for the modernist, I must have terms so well defined and blunt as to maintain the similitude of absolute truth (not mere orthodoxy). While for the world, I must have words common enough, simple enough, yet profound enough, to couch divine things. So that my vocabulary must become complex; primarily it must be *startling* (alive and explosive), exact and simple. I see these things in Nietzsche. But for my generation I must have the oracles of God in fresh terms. May I be given them, Lord? Canst Thou entrust such things to me?

OCTOBER 13 *2 Corinthians 8*   Terrible conflicts with my passions yesterday and last night. "But we trust God who hath delivered, that He will yet deliver" (2 Cor. 9, 10). Blessed be the Lord for giving such grace to the Macedonians, those whose offerings were αὐθαίρετοι, "self-appointed" (2 Cor. 8:4). Their abundance of joy and their deep poverty abounded, not in a plea for help, but in an initial giving up of themselves to God and a subsequent rendering of their means to the apostle for the saints' sake. The Corinthians abounded in faith and ἐν λογῳ in expression. There I feel such a lack. How inarticulate in reaching consciences and hearts I am. Again I pray, Lord, that You will give to me a simple, truth-carrying, explosive vocabulary in order that those about may "hear in his own tongue." I feel as the trumpet which gives an uncertain sound. "Who shall prepare himself for battle?" Paul was careful that no one should find cause of blame in him while he was ministering this bounty of the churches. "For we take thought of things honorable . . . in the sight of men" (v. 21).

OCTOBER 14 *2 Corinthians 9*   Second Corinthians 9 teaches the reasons for distribution, not only for the saints' sake, but for God's sake. The provocative zeal of Corinth was a cause of boasting on their behalf by Paul. And he is making sure here that his boasting is not voided by any carelessness on the part of the Corinthians. The reasons for their giving then are:

1. To make good Paul's boast.
2. To demonstrate the bounty God wrought in them (v. 5).
3. To show why God enriches some—that they might enrich others as God did.
4. To cause thanksgiving.
5. To fill up the measure of the wants of the saints.

Good reason for being an ἱλαρον δοτὴν ("cheerful" or "hilarious" giver).

OCTOBER 16 *2 Corinthians 10*   "Not he who commends himself is approved, but he whom the Lord commends" (v.

12). This speaks soberly to me this morning, for how often have I attempted to gain approbation by the commendation of myself. O Lord, would that I knew Thy commendation. Paul could so boast because he knew that his sufficiency in the ministry and preaching of the Gospel had come from God, that his walk had never been according to the flesh, and that his powers had not been autonomous, but "mighty" $\tau\hat{\omega}$ $\theta\epsilon\hat{\omega}$ to the pulling down of strongholds. The "reasonings" of 2 Corinthians 10:5 refer specifically to the opinions and ideas that others had about Paul, since the verbal form is used in verse 2 and translated "count of us." Again in verse 7, "Let him $\lambda o\gamma\iota\zeta\epsilon\sigma\theta\omega$" account thus of us, and so forth. What a work this is, by demonstration of his work, that it was of God he continually blasted and brought low opinions that had been framed $\kappa\alpha\tau\grave{\alpha}$ $\sigma\grave{\alpha}\rho\kappa\alpha$ and $\tau\grave{\alpha}$ $\kappa\alpha\tau\grave{\alpha}$ $\pi\rho\grave{o}\varsigma\omega\pi o\nu$.

Very happy in the Lord tonight. Sense that I am being tested in the matter of "learning to abound." Everything seems directed to my good. I am free now of all work obligations except what minor affairs living at home entails. My health is perfect. The state of the assembly is happy, and there is evident prosperity in the fellowship though the miraculous is little known among us. Still, there are many burdens to be lifted if I choose the path of sacrifice here at home. Lord Jesus, Lord of the apostle who knew how to abound and to be abased, grant me faithfulness this week. Let me not retrograde.

OCTOBER 18   Moved last night at the joint men's business meeting to think how very little we as brethren know of trust in the Holy Spirit. The attitude of the elders here seems to be that the days of well-taught, Spirit-directed ministry in Bible readings are over and that, because we have made such a failure of them in the past, we cannot hope to retrieve the blessing they then gave. I am aware that Bible readings and prayer meetings and preaching services are vain to restore the warmth of earlier days. Nothing will do for us except a re-awakening, and we must first awaken to *sin*. We need not truth so much as we need tears. And tears shall come, I suppose, by preaching the terror of the Lord and His tenderness. O Lord, restore Thy people. Rouse the elect in Portland. "It is time for Thee to work, Jehovah, for they have made void Thy law."

Stirred in prayer this morning for revival on the West Coast. Last night those great sweeping desires for the glory of God seized on me—season when the thoughts pour ahead of the words in prayer and my attitude is as one heaving great gasps of want. Desire there is aplenty. Words are few at such times and faith, I must admit, is not really great.

> 1 Corinthians 9:15: ἀνεκδιηγητῷ δωρεᾷ, His unspeakable gift. All the details cannot be narrated in full (Acts 15:3)—indescribable.
>
> 2 Corinthians 12:4: ἀρρήτα ῥήματα, unspeakable words. Unsaid because of their sacredness. Not to be put in man's words.
>
> 1 Peter 1:8: χαρᾷ ἀνεκλαλητῷ, unspeakable joy. As secrets that may not be let out or divulged (cf. Acts 23:22), for which words are inadequate.
>
> 1 Corinthians 12:1: δει necessity.
>
> 1 Corinthians 12:1: συμφέρον, expediency.
>
> 1 Corinthians 12:4: ἔξον, lawful, legality.
>
> 1 Corinthians 12:11: ἀναγκάζω, compulsion.

In this recent urge to pray for revival among the Lord's people I have naturally been asking myself, "How?" "What is my part?" Two things have come to mind: the first in Brainerd's account of the Forks of the Delaware awakening (pp. 240–244). The Holy Spirit began evident convincing at a time which surprised Brainerd, for he was sick, discouraged, and cast down, little expecting that God had chosen the hour of his weakness for manifestation of His strength. "I visited these Indians at Crossweeksung, apprehending it was my *indispensable duty* . . . I cannot say I had any hopes of success. I do not know that my hopes respecting the conversion of the Indians were ever reduced to so low an ebb . . . yet this was the very season that God saw fittest to begin His glorious work in! And thus He ordained strength out of weakness . . . *whence I learn that it is good to follow the path of duty, though in the midst of darkness and discouragement.*"

This recalled something Betty wrote (I have just gone through all her letters looking for it, finding it in the one of May 17, her first from Patience [Patience, Alberta, where I spent a summer with the Canadian Sunday School Mission]). She quotes Mrs. Penn Lewis in *Thy Hidden Ones:* "In the Holy Spirit's leading of the soul through the stripping of what may be called 'consecrated self,' and its activity, it is important that there should be a fulfillment of *all outward 'duty'* that the believer may learn to act on a principle rather than on pleasant impulse."

OCTOBER 21 *Galatians 1* "They continued assiduously in fellowship" (Acts 2:42). Noticed for the first time today that I am to be in full fellowship with all three persons of the Godhead. First Corinthians 1:19 says that I am called into the fellowship of the Son. First John 1:3 tells me I am in fellowship with the Father, and 2 Corinthians 13:14 lets me know that I ought to be abiding in the fellowship of the Holy Spirit.

In Galatians 1:4, I see that the work of my salvation involves some tremendous issues. "Jesus Christ who gave himself on behalf of our sins that, as a result, we should be rescued from the existing sinful status of our age, and this is according to the will of God." I see here, first, the free choice of the Son of God in giving Himself as sin for sin. That was not a mere acquiescence to a higher thought. It was the deliberate, conscious, realistic choice of my Savior. I see, too, the substitutionary effect of His sacrifice—not merely the giving of His life to an ideal, but the sacrifice of Himself on the principle of substitution, for our sins. As well, the resultant deliverance from the present cursed system is involved. And all this is done in accordance with the wise and gracious planning of the Father. So I see:

1. The purpose of Christ.
2. The power of His offering.
3. The position of His people.
4. The plan of His Father.

Today I learned the meaning of that word, "For of Him and through Him and unto Him are all things" (Rom. 11:36) as it applies to circumstances. *Every* surrounding factor in my environment is *from* Him. The administration of it to my personality is *through* His doing. The effect of it in me and as my person reverberates the experience is *unto* Him, for His glory. I am not, therefore, called to be a slave of circumstance, for circumstance is His servant on my behalf, doing for me what He would do were He here to do it. In being His servant for my good, circumstance becomes also my servant, and from this time henceforth I shall be a fool for doubting.

OCTOBER 22 *Romans 11:33; Ephesians 4:6*   This day I am struck with the fact of how Christianity unites all the *truths* of all religions into an organic whole. I found the words of Orr in *The Christian View of God and the World* on page twelve extremely helpful. And the sixth verse of Ephesians 4 became real as did the huge triad of Romans 11:33 yesterday. "One God and Father of all, who is over all, through all, and in all." No system survives for long without some connection with truth. In a sense, God is in them all; yet over them, through them, but beyond them. Oh, praise be to the All Wise for His revelation! Happy indeed the case of him to whom His wisdom is more zestful then his daily meat. I see time and history tonight as a tiny one-room schoolhouse—magnificent and complicated, but only one room, wherein are taught to men the vast principles that apply in God's universe. And in eternity we shall hear the words often, I suppose, "Remember that incident?" or "Recall that fact of science? They illustrate this great truth of God which is immutable, part of Himself." Oh, how I want to exalt Him, to put Him where He belongs—above all. I fain would call Him *God*, rather than *Lord* tonight, since He seems to me to be above being but in relation to His lessers, as the word *Lord* must imply. Glory, then, to God Most High! Power, wisdom, worth ascribe to Him, my soul. For the first time I am actually without words because of respect and honor for Him.

OCTOBER 23 *Acts 17; Titus 1*   Wondered this morning at Paul's boldness in the use of the literature of the Greeks to affirm the truth of his preaching. In Acts 17:28, he quotes Aratus, τοῦ γὰρ καὶ γένος ἐσμέν, to affirm the deity of God, that He is not to be worshiped as dead material, because men are His offspring. In 1 Corinthians 15:33 he quotes Menander to prove the moral obligations imposed on a Christian to be separate from evil and not to toy with damning doctrines such as those which suggest no resurrection: φθείρουσιν ἤθη χρηστὰ ὁμιλίαι κακαί. Then in Titus 1:12 he cites Epimenides to prove or support the idea of depraved humanity: κρῆτες ἀεὶ φεῦσται, κακὰ θηρία, γαστέρες ἀργαί. Paul knew his surroundings and used them for argument. Yea, is it too much to say the Holy Spirit used them, for are not these inspired words? And does not this confirm what I discovered last eve that my Father is over all, through all, and in all?

OCTOBER 24 *Hebrews 13*   I sense the value of good Christian biography tonight, as I have been reading Brainerd's *Diary* much today. It stirs me up much to pray and wonder at my nonchalance while I have not power from God. I have considered Hebrews 13:7 just now, regarding the remembrance of certain ones who spoke the Word of God, "*considering the issue of their life*, imitate their faith." I recall now the challenge of [Jonathan] Goforth's *Life* and *By My Spirit*, read in the summer of 1947; the encouragement of *Hudson Taylor's Spiritual Secret* and *Growth of a Soul*. There are incidents which instruct me now from the reading of J. G. Paton's *Biography* in the New Hebrides read last winter, and now this fresh Spirit-quickened history of Brainerd. O Lord, let me be granted grace to "imitate their faith."

OCTOBER 25 *Galatians 1; Acts 11–14*   Thankful to God this morning that His grace has kept me pressing toward Himself and has not allowed me to wander. It was not from doctrines primarily that the Galatians slipped, but they were "removed from Him who called them in the grace of Christ" (Gal. 1:6). So with the Ephesians; they left not their creed, but their primary love. Instances in Acts of the perseverance of the saints came fresh. In Acts 11:23 Barnabas "exhorted them all that with purpose of heart they would *cleave unto the Lord.*" In Acts 13:43 the believers were urged to "continue in the grace of God." In 14:22 the Lystran hearers were exhorted to continue in the faith, since they must enter into the Kingdom of God through many tribulations.

> Keep me, Lord,
> Oh, keep me cleaving
> To Thyself and still believing,
> Till the hour of my receiving
> Promised joys with Thee.
>> "Praise the Savior Ye Who Know Him!"
>>> THOMAS KELLY

OCTOBER 27   "Enjoyed much sweetness" (as he puts it) in the reading of the last months of Brainerd's life. How consonant are his thoughts to my own regarding the "true and false religion of this late day." Saw, in reading him, the value of these notations and was much encouraged to think of a life of godliness in the light of an early death. Have spent these last two days entirely in reading—six to eight hours a day—sometimes with tremendous profit to my soul. Finished C. J. Crain on Galatians yesterday.

Later.   Reading Nietzsche and Orr I have been soberly impressed with the strength of the forces in the human mind. Christianity has been analyzed, decried, refused by some; coolly eyed, submitted to, and its forms followed in by others who call themselves Christian. But alas, what emptiness in both! There is so much knowledge which, like bellows, though it expandeth, yet maketh emptiness so much more vast. I have just now prayed for God's New Revelation—this generation's *real* laying hold of the Old Revelation. The old is become so undefined, so "accepted," so followed in blindness, that when the truth of it is brought to light, it shall be as a *new* revelation. I have prayed for new men, fiery, reckless men, possessed of uncontrollably youthful passion—these lit by the Spirit of God. I have prayed for new words, explosive, direct, simple words. I have prayed for *new miracles*. Explaining old miracles will not do. If God is to be known as the God who does wonders in heaven and earth, then God must *produce* for this generation. Lord, fill preachers and preaching with Thy power. How long dare we go on without tears, without moral passions, hatred and love? Not long, I pray, Lord Jesus, not long . . . .

OCTOBER 28   One of the great blessings of heaven is the appreciation of heaven on earth—Ephesian truth.

He is no fool who gives what he cannot keep to gain that which he cannot lose. Luke 16:9: ". . . that, when it shall fail, they may receive you into everlasting habitations."

Scripture leaves so many stories untold. Think of the calloused heart of the priest who stooped over, squinting in the dimness of the sanctuary, looking for the thirty pieces of silver Judas cast there, pausing to see if he had found all thirty. Too legal to put the money in the treasury since it was blood money, they wax very philanthropic and buy with it a field to bury strangers in. How cold the heart of man! How feelingless and obdurate!

OCTOBER 29   *Ephesians 4–6*   On the reading of Wilfred Tidmarsh's letter to Bert written September 9, I responded to a simple urge within me to offer myself for the work there [in the jungle of east Ecuador]. This morning it struck me as quite a presumptive action, and I covenanted with the Lord quietly that I would not post the letter unless I had some definite word from Him. It seems the situation he is in demands that he abandon the Indian work among the Quichuas because of his wife's illness. He had asked the Christian and Missionary Alliance to take over, but they have given no verdict as yet. The Roman Catholics are waiting to pounce on what was an expensive work.

Doctor Wilfred Tidmarsh of Bury Saint Edmunds, England, who has a Ph.D. in geology, had been working for many years with the jungle Quichua Indians, whom he called "Yumbos." His wife had been injured in a plane crash, so they left the jungle work for several years.

While reading consecutively three chapters in English this morning, I was engaged in Ephesians 4, 5, 6. At 5:16 the words "redeeming the time" struck me as I had exercise [an expression, common among Plymouth Brethren, usually meaning to ponder, to be spiritually stirred] over my diary entry of October 18, 1948, last night. The marginal reading encouraged me even more, "buying up the opportunity." And when I turned to the Greek ἐξαγοραζομενοι τὸν καιρον and turned to the lexicon, I had certainty that I should mail it. Thayer: "to redeem, by payment of a price to recover from the power of another."

OCTOBER 31 *Ephesians 4*   Happy weekend. Bill Paeth [Bunny's brother] and I went to H. Butt's Saturday but missed him—good fellowship walking in the woods. Spoke at George's church on Sunday night. Today I was forcefully reminded of the distinction the New Testament Church made between the breaking of bread and fellowship. We say "I'm in fellowship; I break bread," but they continued in fellowship and in the breaking of bread. I sense we have a multitude of leeches in the church, gaining what they can from all sources, but few "joints of supply" (v. 16). Fellowship is reciprocal— one must give himself to be fed upon if he is to maintain the right to feed on others. Fellowship, I take it, is in building with one another, each essential to the other's profit. Some go everywhere to get, but will go nowhere to give. "It is more blessed to give than to receive," said Christ. "The Son of Man came not to be ministered unto but to minister, and to give his life a ransom for many" (Matt. 20:28). Is the servant greater than His Lord?

NOVEMBER 1 *Ephesians 4, 5*   Ephesians 4:22: ". . . that ye put away, as concerning your former manner of life, the old man, that waxeth corrupt after the lusts of deceit." The old man cannot be put away entirely so that he has no longer force within me, but it is given me by the new man to put him away in certain respects. Here I am able to put him away "as concerning my former manner of life." He remains a rot within, waxing corrupt and corrupting, but he is no longer my chief or ruling stimulus. My life is lived now both externally and internally different from what I knew when the old man was in the saddle. Bless the Lord for this, for it is only the prospect of what shall be known when God claims His inheritance, when not only my "former manner of life" will be put aside, but all my former life itself—the *old man* and *his deeds*.

Thinking again of the "great mystery" of Ephesians 5:22–33, I see that marriage in God's view is intended to be an expensive thing for both parties. Man enjoys headship over woman only at the cost of his own freedom—so Christ and the Church. The woman's body is "saved" (He is the Savior of the Body) by the connection she has with the man; saved from fruitlessness and purposelessness. But a man must give himself up (παραδοκέω) for this. He saves the body and sanctifies it, as 1 Corinthians 7 shows; as the believer "sanctifies" the unbeliever, so Christ set apart for Himself her that was impure by His connection with her.

At this time I fail to see the motive of "loving one's own body" (as Christ did in figure!) when we are so careful to teach buffeting of the body, subjection of it, discipline of it. "No man ever yet hated his own flesh," true, but is it right that it should so be? Evidently it is right that this universal love of the flesh should be God ordained, since Christ is so spoken of as—shall I say it?—selfishly giving Himself for the Church!

NOVEMBER 2 *Ephesians 1–6*   Mark Rumble, Wayne Flora and Gordon Grover stayed here last night. They are quiet, spiritually inclined fellows from Modesto—German Brethren. Pacifists, of course, and one dropped a word that was helpful: "The Scriptures tell us to be subject to the powers, not subjects of the powers that be." Well said.

Thinking just now of Ephesians 3:6 which seems to be the key verse, ". . . the Gentiles are fellow-heirs (1:11, 14, 18; 5:5) and fellow members of the Body (2:15; 4:4; 4:16) and fellow partakers of the promise (2:12, 19, 20) in Christ Jesus through the Gospel. No simple "beliefism" the Apostle preached—see how much detailed doctrine he includes in his Gospel. In spite of (or because of) the fact that we have been *seated* together, we are also besought to *walk* (4:1, 17; 5:2, 15) carefully, the theoretical (seated) becoming practical immediately. Called to a high position, therefore, we must walk worthily. Chapters 1, 2, and 3 describe our privileges: what we were, where we are, and what we are here for. Chapters 4 and 5 deal with our responsibility to walk uprightly (progress, offense), and chapter 6 with our duty to stand steadfastly (defense). The weapons of chapter 6 are, however, both offensive and defensive:

Loins girt with truth (v. 14): defense—protection of the vitals.

Breastplate of righteousness (v. 14): defense—keep thy heart with all diligence.

Feet shod with readiness (v. 15): offense—to preach the Gospel where Christ is not named.

Shield of faith (v. 16): defense—active faith, no shield is stationary.

Helmet of salvation (v. 17): defense—sanctified mind.

Sword of the Spirit (v. 17): offense—ready to give an answer.

NOVEMBER 5 *Psalm 5* I see in the Hebrew more abundant wealth of study than in the Greek, and far more untouched as well. Reading Psalm 5:3 last night, I noticed the "my prayer" in italics and wondered what the word *order* could mean apart from the italicized. It took me until this morning to remember that such a form as אֶעֱרָךְ could be derived from עָרַך. It is the usual Old Testament word for *form* or *frame*. It may also mean "devise," "plot." This fifth Psalm is a morning prayer as the fourth is an evening prayer. The third verse is beautiful in telling of the intimate details of the psalmist's attitude. "O Lord, in the morning you will hear my voice, in the morning I will purpose (עָרַך) in meditation and will look up watchfully to Thee." So let my mornings be a tryst with Thee, Lord; Thou hearing my voice, inditing my meditations, becoming the object of my watch and desire of my waking hours.

NOVEMBER 6   Sweet, sweet grace of God! It was a happy day. Spent with saints and sinners today. Street meeting tonight brought me in contact with a successful man who has an empty heart. How shall I praise God sufficiently for the inexplicable miracle of divine grace in my soul—and how to explain it to others? I have committed this man's soul to God and His Word, expecting to write one day in these pages of his turning to the Lord and finding great peace. You see these words, Lord, and are my judge as to whether they are in faith. Hebrews is ministering to us on the unity and function of the Body of Christ. Blessed in the meeting tonight with the force of the simplicity of it all and more than ever with the grace of the "happy God" who has thus opened His heart to man! What huge distance between the sinner and the saint there is. Lord, let this day be a beginning of great deliverance. Of all the things that comfort me, I think the chief is the knowledge of the fact that I am loved. It took Betty to show me this in the human realm that I might learn it in things divine.

Had thoughts of eternity lately. Eternity shall be at once a great eye-opener and a great mouth shutter. It shall be the Rectifier of all injustice (and how vast is injustice!), the Confirmer of martyrs' blood, the Explainer of years of labor swallowed up in meaningless ruin on earth. Lord, deliver me from sweet doctrinal nothings.

NOVEMBER 7   I finished Bunyan's *Holy War* today with much profit. Lord, keep me walking toward the Diabolonians in my walls! Let Godly Fear ("I sometimes wish he had sole control in Mansoul!") discover the vanities of Carnal Security who wooed Mansoul from Emmanuel. And this Mr. Lustings who has not eyes or ears, who cannot see the end of his desires nor heed the warnings of them that do, wound him near the heart!

NOVEMBER 8   And how cleverly do these Diabolonians change their names! Lord Covetousness soon joins himself to Mr. Mind and calls himself Prudent-Thrift. Lord Lasciviousness soon becomes Mr. Harmless-Mirth and Lord Anger is in a trice Mr. Good-Zeal, an honest servant of Sir Godly-Fear. False-Peace on trial will always call himself Peace, though it be known that he is the pampered son of Mr. Flatterer and Mrs. Sooth-Up. So with Pitiless, when under pressure, he becomes Cheer-Up and swears he could not abide to see Mansoul inclined to melancholy. Mr. Covetousness covers himself with the name of Good-Husbandry; Mr. Pride can, when need is, call himself Mr. Neat, Mr. Handsome, or the like.

I have noticed just now the force of ἐπίσκοπος in Thayer. He is appointed to the "duty of seeing that things done by others are done rightly." It is not that he is the doer of everything in the assembly, but he is the guardian and overseer of those who are doers. And διάκονος does not merely mean doorkeeper. It is used of Paul and Apollos in 1 Corinthians 3:5, "Ministers through whom you believed . . ." implying a verbal ministry. I had just discovered Paul's use of the word καρπον in Galatians, Ephesians, and Philippians, when Mom called me to vacuum the front room. Finishing that, I noticed the table decoration was meager, so went out and cut a couple holly sprigs. That reminded me of the shoots growing under the chestnut tree (from seeds dropped by birds in the tree) that had to be moved if they were to grow. Decided to put a hedge of them around Jane's wing of the house, so removed the azalea that was there to the rockery and put in a dozen holly roots out there. Heigh ho! So goes the Greek for this morning.

Galatians 5:22: καρπον of the Spirit (cf. fruit of flesh).
Ephesians 5:9: καρπον of light (cf. unfruitful works of darkness).
Philippians 1:11: καρπον of righteousness.

NOVEMBER 9   Letter from Fritz (Sunday's entry [November 6]) today. Most encouraging. Lead him on, Lord.

From Gaussen's work *Theopneustia* I have been stimulated to define my view and reasons for inspiration of the Scriptures. Here are jottings: Gaussen defends the Old Testament as inspired first (wholly on New Testament grounds), because he then strengthens his New Testament argument for inspiration by saying that if the first shadows of God's doings be pure and theopneustic, how much more surely inspired the plain exposition of Christ in the New Testament. Now to a man who is merely *logical* (*see* John Herman Randall, *The Making of the Modern Mind* on the J & E theory of Genesis 1 and 2) this makes no sense; you are arguing in a circle. Outwardly, it is true that the doctrine of inspiration can only be proved conclusively to a soul that will assume the basic tenets of Christianity. If I can get a man to believe in a God who raised Jesus Christ from the dead, I have already made him a supernaturalist, and he will take easily the fact that such a God would necessarily protect the records of the Resurrection and preserve the revelation perfect and entire.

So this is my first task, to set before the soul the claims of the Resurrection and expect the Holy Spirit to give the gift of faith to the hearer. This is the inference of Hebrews 1:1. God spoke in times past to the fathers by the prophets (I need not press the prophets' inspiration first), but now He speaks through His Son. So Christ is God's method of opening men's hearts to all truth, and this particular truth of inspiration as well.

But how complex immediately is the proving of it. One scarce can differentiate between the subjective and the objective. The Son speaks through the Word, telling me that the Scriptures are from God—all of them—the Law (which includes Genesis (*see* Galatians 4:22, 23), the Prophets, and the Psalms. Once I accept the Christ of the Scriptures, I am bound to accept the Scriptures of Christ. I stress that inspiration is a doctrine, as clearly taught as justification by faith, and with as much emphasis. The obscurity of revelation is only proof of its divinity, since God fitted it to meet the needs of a race through centuries, whose needs and questionings are ten thousand legion. Wonder that it is not more complicated to accomplish such an all-effective answer.

It's almost midnight. Don't feel like bed somehow. Spent the evening in the Reader's Digest and Wordsworth and Coleridge. Not profitable for sanctifying. Good broadening. Stepped out just now to mail a letter. The moon seems ulcerous, oozing yellow through torn gauze of cloud. Slow-drying pavements, the gutters' sopping rotten leaves, motionless cold whose intensity lies in its quiet qualities, rather than its chill.

NOVEMBER 10   *Romans 7*   It has puzzled me quite often that Paul could say in Romans 7:9 that he "was alive without the law once." What did he mean? Certainly not that he possessed eternal life before the Law brought him to death and thence to Christ. May not Philippians 3:6 have some meaning here? He regarded himself ἀμέμπτος, *blameless* according to that form of outward righteousness which is of the Law. He was alive so long as the commandment was external. But when the "commandment came" (that is, the spiritual force of the Law gripped him), "sin revived and I died." I am coming to believe that Romans 7 is the normal experience of the believer in grace. Herb Butt and *God's Way of Holiness* by Horatius Bonar are the chief factors in the shift.

Why does Paul mention that he is of the tribe of Benjamin? I wonder if this could not refer to Genesis 49:27 in which Benjamin "is as a wolf that raveneth: In the morning he shall devour the prey, And at even he shall divide the spoil." Paul in his natural state in his ferocity toward the Church is well pictured in this.

The gaining of Christ is both an inward reckoning of loss and an outward suffering of it. I have known myself to lose something for Him; yet cherish it in my thoughts. Paul says I not only reckon them scraps fit for the heap, but I have actually undergone the loss of them.

I gain Him—sensing my losses, not losing my senses.
I am found in Him—lost to myself.

I know Him—forgetting Him as One I know after the
flesh.

I experience the power of His Resurrection—positive
force.

I experience the fellowship of His sufferings—natural outcome.

I am conformed to His death—ultimate on earth.

I attain resurrection—ultimate in glory.

NOVEMBER 11 *Philippians; Ephesians*   If the unity of Ephesians is theoretical, the unity of Philippians is practical. The
key preposition of Ephesians is $\epsilon\nu$; of Philippians, $\sigma\upsilon\nu$. The
fellowship of Ephesians is in the Spirit, in the heavenlies, in
the family. In Philippians it is in the confirmation of the Gospel, in finances, in persecutions, in the yoke, on the earth.

Philippians 1:5: Fellowship in the furtherance of the Gospel.

Philippians 2:1: Fellowship in the Spirit . . . be of the
same mind.

Philippians 3:10: Fellowship of His sufferings.

Philippians 4:14: Fellowship with my affliction.

Compare Ephesians 3:6 and Philippians 2:25; 4:3:

fellow-heirs	Epaphroditus	fellow-worker
fellow-members		fellow-soldier
fellow-partakers		true yokefellow

Ephesians tells us of Gentiles united in one Body with Jews.
Philippians tells us of saints united in one effort in the Gospel
(1:27). Ephesians—we share His glory; Philippians—we share
His sufferings. Who is to say which of these is "higher truth"?
Are they not essential complementaries, and do they not come
in order? Ephesians looks at us as called above in the heavenlies; Philippians shows us to be called upward from earth
(3:14). Let me be in balance with these, Lord. Philippians: the
establishing fellowship—"with." Ephesians: the established
union—"in."

Oneness on earth can only be as we recognize our oneness in heaven. Maud, the eager active mare, makes a fine teammate with Major, the stable, plodding workhorse. The first cries, "Do, do, do." The last says, "This, this this!" So we have Philippians (do) and Ephesians (this). "This do" is the whole command.

I am spending this drizzly afternoon reading *The Pilgrim Church* [W. H. Broadbent]. Who can describe the waves of pity, excitement, self-searching, and holy desire that have gone through me as I lift my eyes from the page to stare upon the soaked side yard. I find myself constantly trying to bring these ancient arguments up to date, to apply anabaptism, separation from nominal reform, fasting, Quaker freedom, into my own day. "And Thou, Lord, how long?" I see clearly now that anything—whatever it be—if it be not on the principle of grace, it is not of God. Here shall be my plea in weakness; here shall be my boldness in prayer; here shall be my deliverance in temptation; at last, here shall be my translation. Not of grace? Then not of God. And here, O Lord Most High, shall be Your glory and the honor of Your Son. And the awakening for which I have asked, it shall come in Thy time on this principle by grace, through faith. Perfect my faith then, Lord, that I may learn to trust only in divine grace, that Thy work of holiness might soon begin in Portland.

NOVEMBER 14 *Colossians 1* Pondering this morning what Paul means in Colossians 1:6: "the gospel bears fruit and *grows*. αὐξανω is used thrice in Acts in a similar expression.

1. After the selection of the seven (Acts 6:7), "The word increased; disciples multiplied."
2. After the smiting of Herod (Acts 12:24), "the word of God grew and multiplied."
3. After the burning of books at Ephesus (Acts 19:20), "mightily grew the word of the Lord and multiplied."

This may mean simply: (1) the Word became known to more people, although this is dubious since that would mean useless repetition in Acts 6:7 in which "disciples were added"; (2) it may suggest that the Word became applicable in more situations—God spoke and His Word grew in that it became effective in many contexts; (3) it may refer to the ministry of New Testament prophets who were as the Book to the first-century Church, speaking the Word of God by inspiration while the New Testament was being formed.

NOVEMBER 17 *Colossians 2*   Spent all day yesterday at Vanport College. Will be starting a Bible study there on Wednesday noons in Acts. Ah, Lord, how I should tremble as I rejoice in this privilege. I pray, make it a work of God and not of man. Finished *The Pilgrim Church* yesterday. Noted again the importance of biography and history in learning God's ways. Anthony Norris Groves was a pioneer missionary in India who started work on New Testament lines. I must read his memoirs if I can get them.

Noticed these three dangers in Colossians 2 this morning:

1. Let no man make booty of you (despoil) (v. 8). Philosophy of vain deceit.
2. Let no man judge you (condemn for not following ordinances) (v. 16).
3. Let no man rob you of your prize (v. 18).

NOVEMBER 18   Just finished *Under a Thatched Roof* by Rosemary Cunningham, the story of a five-year term on the Xingo River of Brazil. Stirred for pioneer work again, like the feeling I had on finishing [James] McNair's *Livingstone the Liberator* a couple of years ago. O God, raise up a vanguard of young men to reach the untouched, the untouchables!

NOVEMBER 19 *Colossians 1–4*   *Thanksgiving*—the stressed attitude of the Colossian epistle.

1:3: Giving thanks for believers.
1:12: Giving thanks.
2:7: Giving thanks (abounding in it).
3:15: Giving thanks—being thankful.
3:17: Giving thanks in all activity.
4:2: Giving thanks in prayer.

NOVEMBER 19   Stupefying weakness and dullness in the things of the Lord. Seemed to lack communion in the Holy Spirit for spiritual energy. Show me my failings and goings backward, Lord, for who can understand his faults? Depressed and sensible of uselessness tonight. Satisfied that Fritz Tallifson (see entry for November 6) is in the Lord, a brother. Thanks be to God for his deliverance! Remembering with profit the reading of *Behind the Ranges* [Mrs. Howard Taylor], the story of the pioneer work of James G. Frazer in Lisuland. Also *Livingstone the Liberator* by McNair. These were read three years ago, but I can still recall lessons learned from them . . . "Considering the issue of their life, imitate their faith."

NOVEMBER 21   "It is not for you to know the times and seasons" (Acts 1:7). ". . . seasons of refreshing . . . times of restoration of all things" (Acts 3:19–21). "Elijah indeed comes and shall restore all things" (Mark 9:12). "Wilt thou at this time restore the kingdom to Israel" (Acts 1:6; cf. 1 Thess. 5:1). *Times* seem to refer to Israel's blessing; *seasons* to Gentiles. Christ's last words before death, "It is finished"; before ascension, "the uttermost part of the earth" (it is unfinished!).

NOVEMBER 22   *Hebrews 10, 11*   I see this morning that one may obtain a promise but not receive it. Hebrews 11:33, 34 tells of those who "through faith and longsuffering inherited the promises" (6:12) but did not receive the end of the promise. This is the meaning of 10:36: "For ye have need of patience (ὑπόμενη) *after having done* the will of God, that ye may receive the promise." Old Testament saints saw the promises afar off, greeted them, and confessed a pilgrim character, but did not obtain them (11:13). "God having provided some better thing concerning us, that apart from us they should not be made perfect" (11:40). Practically, this is to be true of me in my prayer life. By faith and patience I am to get promises from God (as recently in the case of Fritz), then to exercise more faith and ὑπόμενη in the receiving of that promise. This is the sphere of Christian *hope*. It is the "patience (ὑπόμενη) of hope" that Paul commends the Thessalonians for. "If we hope for that which we see not then do we with patience wait for it" (Rom. 8:25). This all refers to the ultimate future ends of faith, but practically the principles are daily applicable.

NOVEMBER 24   Lord, give me firmness without hardness; steadfastness without dogmatism; love without weakness.

NOVEMBER 25   I see that a year ago today I was questioning what I would be engaged in today. Of six possibilities then supposed, I have done none. The first two are still the most real exercises of my heart. Still, even in meditating on these, Peru or India, fears seize me and my inadequacy and unpreparedness, my real lack of intensity regarding them, come to me so forcibly that I can hardly believe I am being led in either direction. Yet, I say, "Lead on, O King eternal; I follow *not* with fears."

Enjoyed the truth of "singing in psalms, hymns, and spiritual songs" this morning. Found my prayer list so unstimulating to real prayer that I laid it aside and took the Inter-Varsity Hymnal and sang aloud with much heart warming such songs as seemed to fit my need. This is as decidedly a means of grace as anything given by God to His people, but how little we use it!

NOVEMBER 28   1 *Thessalonians*   Readings have been in 1 Thessalonians lately. Stirred up about one or two things. First, this business of "working with your own hands" for a testimony to those without and a supply for those within. Twice I have been to inquire for work this past week—once to the school board, once to the post office (the latter was not open). And twice has the Lord ministered five dollars unexpectedly from other sources. I will go again to the post office for work during the December rush. Sense now that the Lord is definitely leading me to British Guiana to work with Ray [a cousin] in the lumbering business. The other matter is a point of doctrine regarding the coming of the Lord. J. R. Graham has unsettled my acquiescent repose on the "two comings" of the Lord. Paul speaks of the day of the Lord in 1 Corinthians 3:13 and in Thessalonians as a time of judgment for work done in the Church and the wickedness done in the world—*The Day* as though it were *one* day for both judgments. The "Lord's descending from heaven with a shout (of battle)" as Conybeare has it, is valid Greek, may not the coming of the Lord with and for His saints be a single act? *¿Quien sabe?*

NOVEMBER 29   *1 Thessalonians*   The *calling out* ("election," ἐκλογην) of the Thessalonians (1:4) resulted in the *sounding out* of the Word of the Lord (1:8). These were both determined first by Paul's *entering in* (2:1) among them and the coming among them of the glad tidings in power, the Holy Spirit and much assurance (1:5). Becoming Paul's imitators (1:6), they also became such as could be imitated by all in Macedonia and Greece (1:8). Not only as individuals but as an assembly was this imitation manifest, for (2:14) they became in their persecutions imitators of the churches in Judea, those pressed but progressing saints among the militant dogmatist of Judaism.

The meaning of 1 Thessalonians 4:4 becomes quite practical if one takes Darby's note as not entirely decisive. The word κτάομαι is not just the act of possessing, but of acquiring as well, so that Weymouth's translation "procure" seems to fit very well. How many young men in the church today procure—court and keep—their wives in purity, honor, and not in lustful passion? The sex hungers of the generation are so intense that seldom does an average woman arrive at marriage a virgin, and hardly ever a man—while "neck happy" Christians regard true courtship as going as far as one can outside of marriage. What is this meaning, then, "not in lustful *passion* as the Gentiles who know not God" (4:5)?

And who is my teacher—the world's method? No. John 6:45: "They shall all be taught of God." In relation to brotherly love (4:9), *God* is my teacher. In 1 Corinthians 2:15, I am taught in words of the Holy Spirit's teaching. In 1 Corinthians 11:14, does not *nature* (φύσις) teach me in regard to women's coverings? And 1 John 2:27: "And ye need not that any man teach you." Grace, too, is a great teacher (Titus 2:2), and that not by precept (διδάσκω) but by experiment and practice, too (παιδεύω).

I think there is nothing so startling in all the graces of God as His quietness. When men have raged untruths in His Name, when they have used the assumed authority of the Son of God to put to death His real children, when they have with calloused art twisted the Scriptures into fables and lies, when they have explained the order of His creations in unfounded theories while boasting the support of rational science, when they, using powers He grants them, claim universal autonomy and independence, He, this great silent God, says nothing! His tolerance and love for His creature is such that, having spoken in Christ, in conscience, in code of law, He waits for men to leave off their bawling and turn for a moment to listen to His still, small voice of Spirit. Now, after so long a time of restrained voice, bearing in Almighty meekness the blasphemies of His self-destroying creatures, now, how shall break upon the ears, consciousness, hearts and minds of reprobate men the voice of One so long silent?

It shall thunder with the force of offended righteousness; rage with lightning bolts upon the seared consciences; roar as the long-crouched lion upon dallying prey; leap upon, batter, destroy, and utterly consume the vain reasonings of proud humankind; ring as the battle shout of a strong, triumphant, victory-tasting warrior; strike terror and gravity to souls, more forcefully than tortured screams in the dead of night! O God, what shall be the first tones of Your voice again on earth? And what their effect? Wonder and fear, denizens of dust, for the Lord Himself shall descend from heaven with a battle cry, with the voice of the archangel, and the trumpet blast of God Himself—made more terrible, if that could be, by the long suffering of His silence.

DECEMBER 1 *Psalm 17* "It is not for you to know . . . but you shall receive power . . ." (Acts 1:7, 8). Knowledge, they tell me, *is* power, but the Lord says that power is not determined by knowledge. The Holy Spirit is the source of power for the believer's witness, and though he have all knowledge of apologetics, be settled in a philosophic basis for a Revelational Theism, if he lacks that power of the Holy Spirit, he is ineffective, yea, detrimental as a witness.

Much disturbed at noon today by a report to Dad by Walter Purcell [one of the "brethren"] that "people are talking" about my being unemployed. I trust I have had more exercise than they all in this matter. W. P. thinks I ought to go to work for a year. God knows I am willing. Felt this charge come as a cutting criticism and sensed a strong desire to retaliate by justifying myself before them, telling of my applications for three jobs lately, of my prospect of the B. G. [British Guiana] work with Ray, of my work with Oppel, of the Bible studies, of my reading and work—small indeed—keeping up the place here. But the Word of the Lord Jesus came to me, "Ye are they which *justify* themselves before men . . ." (Luke 16:15).

Not wanting to be found such, I knelt to pray and read the noon psalm for today. It was number 17. Verse 2 smote me: "Let *my sentence* come forth from *thy presence.*" "Thou has tried me . . . my steps have held fast to thy paths (vv. 4, 5) . . . deliver my soul from men *who are thy hand* (v. 14 margin), from men of this world whose portion is in this life . . . they are satisfied with children, but I shall be satisfied, when I awake, with thy form" (v. 15). So, Lord, I am in Thy hand and say now in faith that Thou hast led, searched, exercised, and tried me. If there lacks now that which I should be doing and am not, O Lord, hide it not from Thy servant who would follow Thee.

DECEMBER 2 *Psalms 16, 17, 127*   I have been wondering what the psalmist experienced in 16:7, "Yea, my heart instructeth me in the night seasons"; in 17:3, "Thou hast visited me in the night"; 127:2, "So he giveth to his beloved in sleep." My own nights are dullnesses. No response to anything divine, rather, an awakening often with some frivolity on my mind. Visit me, O Lord, the Spirit in the night, that I may know A. C.'s [Amy Carmichael] prayers:

> My Lord, my Love, my heart's eternal light,
> Shine on Thy lover through the hours of night;
> Shine on my thoughts, my very dreams be found
> About Thy business on some holy ground.
>
> Should friendly angel come to meet me there
> Let me not miss him, deaf and unaware,
> And if I may, one other prayer I bring,
> O Lord, my God, make no long tarrying.
>
> From *Toward Jerusalem*

Again, in "The World is Still," "In Sleep" she speaks of this mystery of impartation in unconsciousness. Be Thou as real to me, Guardian of my midnights.

Evening.   Great God in heaven, I wish I understood what Betty wrote on November 30, 1949.

This letter contained a long discourse on the meaning of the Greek words for love and quotations on the subject from H. C. Trumbull's Friendship the Master Passion; *from Oswald Chambers (for example, "True love is spontaneous, but it must be maintained by discipline."), from Aristotle ("Friendship consists in loving rather than in being loved"), from Emerson ("It is sublime to feel and say of another, 'I need never meet or speak or write to him; we need not reinforce ourselves, or send tokens of remembrance.' "), and from Goethe:*

> *True friendship shows its worth in stern refusal*
> *At the right moment, and a strong love sometimes*
> *Heaps the loved one with ruin, when it serves*
> *The will more than the weal of who demands.*

Excerpts from the letter: "I believe that you and I, Jim, if we are to continue, must know this true friendship, apart from anything else, for it is this alone which continues without consummation, for it is in itself and by its very nature a fulfillment. For a long time, it seems to me, we have gone along, you insisting on claims and evidences, I trying to maintain a relationship that is 'from feeble yearnings freed.' . . . the love that is true friendship is selfless, divine. I am selfish, human. So I have fallen many times. But can you see any evidence of my goal, at least, in our past contacts? ἀγάπη asks nothing more than an object upon which to shine, whether that shining be reflected or even recognized or not . . . ."

No wonder Jim was confused.

DECEMBER 5   ". . . Give attendance to reading . . . ." Finished a short biography of Allan Smith, missionary on the Paraguayan and Amazonian River systems. Stirred for Tidmarsh's work among the Ecuadorian Quichuas again. Prayed to be sent out soon with definite steps of guidance for my path. Took some confidence from Psalms 18:36: "Thou hast enlarged my steps under me, And my feet have not slipped." Having finished Gaussen's *Theopneustia* last week I began S. J. Andrew, *Christianity vs. Anti-Christianity in Their Final Conflict.* Prophetic and clarifying to some big present-day issues.

DECEMBER 12   Much distressed with the corruptions of indwelling sin. How I dare open my mouth as one who speaks the "wisdom which is from above" I cannot know, but I do. Spent this forenoon with Sam Squie visiting high schools for Young Life contacts. Terribly needy field, and the young Christians so awed at what is going on around (and within!) them that they cannot witness well or consistently. Lord, send them help from the sanctuary! This wisdom from above is ἀνυπόκριτος, unfeigned, and I see it is needed for true living. This word ἀνυπόκριτος is used also in Romans 12:9 and 2 Corinthians 6:6 and 1 Peter 1:22 as describing the Christian quality of love. In 1 and 2 Timothy 1:5 it is used of faith unmasked. Let it be known in me, Lord.

DECEMBER 13 *2 Timothy 3:1–5* How χαλεποί these last days. Reading over the list of attributes characteristic of the last days, I can find application in every one for myself, more obviously in others around, because of the blindness of my heart to its own errors. *Love* is not lacking in the last days, as it is a universal tendency in man, but the *objects* of love have reversed.

1. φίλαυτοι: self-lovers. Those whose interest and desire is inward for their own benefit.
2. φιλάργυροι: silver lovers. A variant of number one. An expression of self-love. Notice how neither of these things said to be "loved" can reciprocate with profitable response.
3. ἀλαζόνες: vaunters, vain braggarts.
4. ὑπερήφανοι: eager to show oneself superior, ambitious.
5. βλάσφημοι: derogatory in attitude, despisers.
6. γονεῦσιν ἀπειθεῖς: unwillingness to be guided by constituted authority.
7. ἀχάριστοι: unwillingness to admit dependence on any other, ungrateful.
8. ἀνόσιοι: adverse to pure thinking and acting.
9. ἄστοργοι: lacking *human* qualities of affection.
10. ἄσπονδοι: implacable, cannot be entreated with any form of libation.
11. διάβολοι: intent on talking down what is good; poking holes in everything.
12. ἀκρατεῖς: incontinent, lack of self-mastery, giving way to the base within.
13. ἀνήμεροι: untamed.
14. ἀφιλάγαθοι: not regarding good as a thing to be cherished.
15. προδόται: those who give up, betray: traitorous.
16. προπετεῖς: rash; see Acts 19:36, "falling forward," precipitous.
17. τετυφωμένοι: being filled with smoke; not just "empty pride" but filled with foreign, choking gas.

18. φιλήδονοι: pleasure lovers.
19. ἔχοντες μόρφωσιν: having a form but denying the power.

Evening. I have just finished Sam. J. Andrew's *Christianity and Anti-Christianity in the Final Conflict*. An excellent, almost prophetic, work on the philosophical merges and currents as they relate to the rise of the Antichrist. Contains solemn warnings for the Church for so neglecting her real, personal Head. Unfortunately, it is poorly footnoted and documented, but fairly indexed. Spent the afternoon at Cleveland High making contacts for Young Life. Not really successful. But my hope is in God for them.

DECEMBER 15   Made a brief study of conscience in the New Testament this morning. It is more important for the believer than I had realized. In the unbeliever it accuses and excuses, depending on his attitude. But for the believer the imperative of a healthy, correctly functioning conscience is an essential.

1. A *good* conscience (1 Tim. 1:5, 19) exercised in faith prevents swerving in doctrine.
2. A *pure* conscience (1 Tim. 3:9; 2 Tim. 1:3) is a qualification for the service of a deacon.
3. A *defiled* conscience (Titus 1:15) gives one an impure outlook on all his doings. Overcome, it makes all things pure.
4. A *weak* conscience hinders freedom (1 Cor. 8:7). Strengthened, it gives liberty in partaking of food, and so on.
5. An *evil* conscience (Heb. 10:22) must be gotten rid of before approach to God may be made.
6. A *seared* conscience (1 Tim. 4:2) makes one bold to sin.

DECEMBER 19   *Matthew 5*   "Blessed are the pure in heart, for they shall see God" (v. 8). Purity of heart gives clarity of vision. Oh, to be holy! I see by the Beatitudes that capacity to appreciate the good things of God—comfort, mercy, and so on—can only be developed in a situation where such good things are not predominate. Hence the necessity for conflict in the believer's life. Noted for the first time the distinction in Matthew 5:13, 14:

> Ye are the salt of the earth ($\gamma\widehat{\eta}\varsigma$).
> Ye are the light of the world ($\kappa o\sigma\mu o\widehat{v}$).

Salt	Light
Involves taste.	Involves sight.
Detected by its absence.	Detected by its position (city on a hill).
If it be savorless, it is useless.	If it be covered, it becomes destructive or goes out.
Salt manifests flat, tasteless, poor quality of things about it.	Shining light manifests its own good works.
Unsuccessful, it is cast out and trodden down.	Successful, men glorify God.
Meant for earth as a physical factor.	Meant for the world as an intellectual factor.

Verse 28 speaks of the man "looking on a woman to lust" and declares him guilty of adultery. If such be the case of a man toward a woman, what tremendous force there is in Paul's admonition to *modest* dress in woman. If, by intention, she dress in any way to emphasize her body, so that one may not look on her without lust springing to life, is she not guilty of seduction as really as he is of adultery? I must act in a holy manner, not for reward or appearance, but because of God's nature. The Law continually reminds me that commandments are to be kept, not for their own sake, but for God's sake. I will be righteous, then, because God's nature is such. His character determines my conduct. "This do . . . for I am Jehovah."

Verse 47 strikes home. "What do ye more than others?" How

much does my righteousness "exceed" beyond. Oh, how common the idea "I compare favorably with these." But how Christlike the precept, "What may I *excel* in morally, not simply *pass* in." "Lord, where has gone the *spirit* of that second mile?"

DECEMBER 21   *Hebrews 1*   The surpassing excellence of the Son is set before the Hebrew in two vivid contrasts in this chapter. The Son is set above the most respected of Hebrew ideals: the prophets ("Ye build tombs for the prophets" [Matt. 23:29]), the angels ("worshipping of angels" [Col. 2:18]).

I. The Son surpasses the prophets as a spokesman

A. His method of speaking	The prophets
1. In the last days	1. Of old time
2. To us	2. To the fathers
3. Once for all	3. At differing times
4. Unified, consistent mode	4. In differing manners
B. His right in speaking	
1. Heir of all—promises to Him by God	1. Promises to men through prophets
2. Creator of all—made all things.	2. Created beings
C. His perfection of expression	
1. Produced God's glory (ἀπαύγασμα)	1. Spoke and promised regarding God's glory
2. Expressed God's person (κάρακτηρ)	2. Told of God's person
3. Upheld all by His power	3. Hinted at God's power
D. Effect of His speaking:	
1. Delivered men from sin	1. Denounced sin only
2. Honored by God—His end is glorious	2. Rewarded by God— their end is great

II. The Son surpasses angels
    A. In Name (v. 5)—My messengers versus My son.
    B. In relation (v. 5)—master-slave versus Father-Son.

C. In substance (vv. 6, 7)—*makes* angels wind and fire versus brings first begotten into the world as a man.

D. In honor—anointed above His fellows with gladness because of His moral passion.

E. In power—Creator versus created.

F. In position—My right hand versus sent into earth (v. 14).

G. In occupation—sitting versus ministering.

We see the difference between the worshiped and the worshipers in this connection.

DECEMBER 24 *Hebrews 1, 2* The "more excellent" Head (1:4) insists on a "more earnest heed" (2:1). Chapter 1 speaks of the exaltation of the Son; chapter 2 of His humiliation. Chapter 1 of His contrast to angels as above them; 2 as One who became below them. In 1:8 He is called "O God"; 2:6 shows Him to be a man.

I had not noticed before today the part angels played in the administration of the Law. Hebrews 2:2: "The word spoken by angels." Galatians 3:19: "The law . . . ordained through angels by the hand of a mediator." Acts 7:38: "Moses . . . and the angel that spoke to him on mount Sinai"; and 7:53: ". . . received the law as it was ordained by angels." Interestingly enough, I cannot find any Hebrew Old Testament reference to this teaching. Deuteronomy 33:2 in LXX has ἄγγελος as a translation of קֹדֶשׁ, but the passage is very obscure.

Hebrews 2:1–4: The surpassing Author of salvation demands from us a more sincere attendance upon salvation. Having established the deity of the Messiah from the Old Testament in Chapter 1, the writer proceeds in Chapter 2 to establish the humanity of the Messiah from the Old Testament.

I. Deity and humanity unite their witness
   A. Things heard (v. 1)
      1. From angels (v. 2)
      2. Through the Lord (v. 3)
      3. From those who heard Him (v. 3)

    B. Things confirmed by God
       1. Signs
       2. Wonders
       3. Manifold powers
       4. Distributions of the Holy Spirit
  II. Deity exalts humanity (vv. 5–9)
    A. Things observed
       1. Failure of Adam—we see not now all things subjected to Him
       2. Success of Christ—we behold Him crowned
 III. Deity partakes of humanity
    A. Author of salvation
       1. Constituted such by God (v. 10)
       2. Shares the nature of man (v. 11)
         a. Calls them brethren (v. 11)
         b. Exerts faith with them (v. 13)
         c. Partakes of flesh and blood (v. 14)
         d. Tastes death (v. 9)
    B. Merciful, faithful High Priest
       1. Sufferer
       2. Succorer

DECEMBER 25   Wilma and Gene are in town this vacation. What a surge of regret comes over me just to look at her. Why, oh, why, would I not have been subject to the counsel that should have been given me straight? How many wretched remorses flood into my thinking when I regard how close we were—that proximity which now makes distance so much more tremendous and poignant. Yet I *would* love her in the flesh though all the world had counseled me not to do so. The tugging then was simply undeniable for my flesh, and how I abhor the red passions which led us so close that we might be driven so distant apart. O Lord, Thou who hast patiently instructed me since those wild nights, preserve the many now ensnared in this dreadful mesh. Young innocents—I pray keep them from my present remorse in these things. Yet how shall they be told, and what power but Thine can restrain the early flames? Yea, what power but Thine can lift the later ashes?

Some would infer, from the measure of remorse expressed in this passage, that the sin referred to is fornication. It was not, in the literal sense. Jim had indeed, however, looked on Wilma, a high-school friend, "to lust after her," and had kissed her, he believed, too passionately. This was sin, and to Jim, no sin was a triviality, for all of them, of whatever kind, exact the same price: the death of Jesus on the cross.

It is typical of Jim that on this date no mention is made of Christmas. He, following the example of his father who saw all festivals and ceremonies as pagan, tried to "esteem every day alike" (Rom. 14:5).

> The ghosts of forgotten actions
> Come floating before my sight,
> And the things that I thought were dead things
> Were alive with a terrible might.
> And the vision of all my past life
> Was an awful thing to face
> Alone with my conscience sitting
> In that solemnly silent place.
> . . . And I know of a future Judgment,
> How dreadful soe'er it be,
> To sit alone with my conscience
> Will be judgment enough for me.
>
> C.W. STUBBS

DECEMBER 27 *Ecclesiastes* "The thirst that from the soul doth rise doth ask a drink divine" [From "Drink to Me Only With Thine Eyes"]. Felt very deserted this morning and utterly unable to pray because of the crowded passages within. Too much excitement at the reunion last night. I was reminded of the "rubble" instruction of last fall. Desire for the earthly was increased and enlarged; still I recognized that were it sated, I would not be at rest. *Wandering Thoughts* (Toward Jerusalem, p. 64) was some comfort. Left my Greek to turn to Ecclesiastes which I read partway through. The kindred pessimism helps me some, but I cannot tell why. Passages that seemed to say what I feel stood out.

1:8: "All things are full of weariness; man cannot utter it: the eye is not satisfied with seeing, nor the ear filled with hearing."

2:2: "I said of laughter, It is mad; and of mirth, What doeth it?"

2:17: "So I hated life, because the work that is wrought under the sun was grievous unto me; for all is vanity and a striving after wind."

3:10: "I have seen the travail which God hath given to the sons of men to be exercised therewith."

4:6: "Better is a handful, with quietness, than two handfuls with labor and striving after wind."

4:11: "How can one be warm alone?"

Let me read this page when I get to hungering after civilizations, excitements, and excesses in some lonely place. Take counsel, then, my soul, the whole of life is vanity, and you would be no happier in brighter atmospheres. Woe and loneliness may be miserable but hollow happiness and many in a crowd are much more so. You may say justly of it all, sighingly, "when will it end?"

Shelley's *Ozymandias* fits fairly:

> I met a traveler from an antique land
> Who said: Two vast and trunkless legs of stone
> Stand in the desert. Near them, on the sand,
> Half sunk, a shattered visage lies, whose frown,
> And wrinkled lip, and sneer of cold command,
> Tell that its sculptor well those passions read
> Which yet survive, stamped on these lifeless things,
> The hand that mocked them, and the heart that fed:
> And on the pedestal these words appear:
> "My name is Ozymandias, king of kings:
> Look on my works, ye Mighty, and despair!"
> Nothing beside remains. Round the decay
> Of that colossal wreck, boundless and bare
> The lone and level sands stretch far away

"One moment in Annihilation's Waste . . ." [From *The Rubaiyat of Omar Khayyam*]. O Lord, be not silent unto me, lest I become like those that go down into the pit.

Evening.   Much comforted later, though sinning. Read Hebrews through aloud in English.

DECEMBER 29   *Hebrews 4*   Visited with freshness both in prayer and study today. Reading Hebrews 4—the rest remaining for God's people engaged me. It seems now to me that it can teach nothing else than the perseverance of His people in the boldness of their faith. Massah and Meribah are examples given to show what sort of disobedience and unbelief displease God. It is the disbelief in a past working on the part of God, a doubt that the God who wrought wonders in Egypt is among us. Such a situation can only rise when the day of miracle has ended. Those who know God acted in the past with power and glory to Himself, begin to doubt His ability to act in the present, when God has ceased from His works. This is the act of letting go the boldness, the beginning of our confidence and confession. Such are those in whom faith does not accompany the word preached. Such are those who do not enter rest.

It is a present and continuing act: we who *have* believed *are* entering His rest. But watch lest this deceitfulness of sin should hinder and befool us in regard to God's ability to keep His word. Hence the wording of 4:12, 13, "The word *lives* and *operates* . . . ." How well was it written of Judas and the Judas tendency in me, "He delighted not in blessing" (Pss. 109:17). What manifold appearances of God's blessing were upon the traitor and fence me about, but how seldom does my heart delight in these blessings.

DECEMBER 31   This is New Year's Eve. Lighthearted and empty all day. Moved to sober prayer again after reading Tidmarsh's moving letter of December 26. O Lord, You see the places secret in me; You know all my wanderings and reserves. If You see anything in me that is holding back the clear revelation of Your will about Ecuador, uncover it to me, I pray. Oh, send a helper to that pressed ambassador; send a laborer for his sustenance. Tonight, Lord, tonight. If You find no man near to encourage him, then send an angel, Lord. And if it is Your mind that I should go there, then send me—soon.

5

Waiting on God, 1950

Jim remained at home until he went to the University of Oklahoma in the summer to take a course in descriptive linguistics which would prepare him for work with tribes with unwritten languages. It was there that he made the decision to go to Ecuador. Several months were spent in Oklahoma after he finished the course and in Indiana and Wisconsin, visiting his friends Bill Cathers and Ed McCully who planned to go to Ecuador also. Wherever Jim was, he found opportunities to teach and preach the Gospel and to continue his own study of the Bible. His Plymouth Brethren background made him highly suspicious of formal religious training of any sort, and few with graduate degrees in theology know the Bible better than Jim did. What he lacked in systematic training, he made up for in personal devotion.

JANUARY 1   Liberty in proclaiming the Resurrection with boldness at jail.

JANUARY 2   Mount Hood skiing with Sam, Hilda, May Beth, Gloria, and Florence.

JANUARY 3   *Hebrews 1, 2*   Hebrews is a good place to begin with men. It is so because it brings them into the presence of the *God who speaks*. Many words meaning to say, tell, speak are used, and in several forms:

1:1: λάλήσας: active aorist participle of λαλέω, sound of what is spoken.

1:2: ἐλαλήσεν: active aorist indicative of λαλέω, sound.

1:3: τῷ ῥήματι: instrumental of means, ῥήμα

1:5: εἶπέν: second aorist active (λέγω)

1:6: λέγει: present active of λέγω—substance of what is spoken.

1:7: λέγει: present active of λέγω—substance of what is spoken.

1:13: εἴρηκεν: perfect active indicative, ῥέω.

How effectively has the noise of men silenced the voice of God! Would that He should speak aloud in thunder soon. How gracious of Him to go on speaking in a still, small voice while the nations rage. "Let the earth keep silence before Him," rather than He keep silent at all the wrong of earth. Let the Word run and be glorified, Lord. And if there be an authoritative speaker, there must be a responsible and responsive hearer. So Hebrews 2:1 brings in the necessity of our heeding the Word spoken. The media of God's speaking has varied: prophets, angels, apostles (2:5), and ultimately the Son. But all are to be granted hearing because of the One they speak for. And who has most effectively spoken? Is it not the Christ? Then He must be the most earnestly heeded.

JANUARY 4   I have been musing lately on the extremely dangerous *cumulative* effects of earthly things. One may have good reason, for example, to want a wife, and he may have one legitimately. But with a wife comes Peter's (the pumpkin eater's) proverbial dilemma—he must find a place to keep her, and most wives will not stay on such terms as Peter proposed. So a wife demands a house; a house, in turn, requires curtains, rugs, washing machines, and so on; a house with these things must soon become a home, and children are the intended outcome. The needs multiply as they are met: a car demands a garage; a garage, land; land, a garden; a garden, tools; tools need sharpening! Woe, woe, woe to the man who would live a disentangled life in my century. Second Timothy 2:4 is impossible in the United States, if one insists on a wife. I learn from this that the wisest life is the simplest one, lived in the fulfillment of only the basic requirements of life: shelter, food, covering, and a bed. And even these can become productive of other needs if one does not heed. Be on guard, my soul, of complicating your environment so that you have neither time nor room for growth!

I must not think it strange if God takes in youth those whom I should have kept on earth till they were older. God is peopling eternity, and I must not restrict Him to old men and women.

JANUARY 7   *Exodus 19:15*   I cannot say what led me to read the Law of Moses yesterday, but I was strangely affected by a verse that seemed to leap out of context of itself and apply to my attitude toward marriage. I have been considerably reminded lately of the one-thousand-years-equals-one-day principle of Peter and its application to the length of human history. The third day speaks of Christ's returning to rule (see the "after two days" references in Scripture)—really the seven thousandth year of human history if the conventional reckoning is anywhere near valid. Exodus 19:15 spoke, as I said, of its own force to me, ". . . Be ready against the third day: come not near a woman." This with Matthew 19:12 and 1 Corinthians 7, and, in type, those of Revelation 14:4 present to me a challenge I never heard from any pulpit.

JANUARY 9   *Hebrews 10; Romans 3*   Hebrews 10 got me thinking along lines of the basis of forgiveness of sins this morning, and I was made very thankful for the writings of other saints. Thayer and Trench on πάρεοις of Romans 3:25 and Abbot on ἀφίημι as used in the New Testament are very helpful. How little I have appreciated the actual *sending away* (ἄφεσις) of my sins. Not merely their being passed over, but the purgation of my soul from them. What an act that God should make Christ *sin* for us and be toward Him as He is toward sin. What distance in the words *Eli, lama sabachthani?*—ἐγκατέλιπες as LXX renders it, "to be left behind among" (Thayer), among *what* or *whom?* In the midst of my iniquities, compassed by demons. What *forsakeness* my *forgiveness* entails! What sending away of the Son to send away the sin. What embarrassing distance for Him, that there might be endearing nearness for me. Praise and acclaim, Lord Jesus Christ! I jotted down three forms of αἴρω found in the chapter:

V. 4: ἀφαιρέω—take sin away, cut it off entirely (as Malchus's ear [Matt. 26:51]).

V. 9: ἀναιρέω—take up, lift off the old order (as Moses in the river [Acts 7:21]).

V. 11: περιαιρέω—take from about, uncover the soul of sin (as the veil [2 Cor. 3:16]).

So we have the final deliverance of the soul from sin, the fading distance of the old order, and the effective disentanglement of the soul from its former environs.

If archeology may be trusted in its dating, it is most engaging to assume with the archeologist that Abraham's time was about 1800—2000 B.C. If such be the case, is it not of some moment to realize that we are just as far this side of the fulfillment of Abraham's promise as he was the other side? It took two thousand years to impress Hebrew revelation; it has taken two thousand more to repress it to the status of these last days. The time of the Gentiles is filling up, even as was the time of Jacob filling up when Zacharias stepped into the sanctuary to meet Gabriel. And what of Israel? From 2,000 B.C. to Christ she grew, prospered, multiplied, spread, all in spite of her waywardness. Since her Messiah's time, she has waned, thinned, paled, wasted, because of the hardness of her heart against Him. And what is the pivot point? Is it not that insanely hateful sentence, that pang of resentment which surged through the throats that day in Gabbatha: *"His blood be on us, and on our children!"* In this behold a multitude prophesy their own doom, a nation of prophets to whom God has answered, "Be it so, as you have said."

JANUARY 10   *Hebrews 10*   Began chapel series at the Christian School today. Sadly need the power of the Holy Spirit in my ministry aloud. "Ye shall receive power," He said. I have yet to know the fulfillment of that statement. Spoke on "Signs of Life"—Jairus's daughter, widow's son at Nain, Lazarus raised.

The announcement of Einstein's new theory of gravitation—which I fail to understand in any degree—caused no small stir in the news this week. All I see is the "integration process" at work again, this "one world" idea of Wendell Willkie's. World government, World Council of Churches, unification of ideals, and now the explanation of all phenomena on the basis of a single formula, mark the signs of the end. Social, religious, political, and technical unification they will find. But where will they find a moral integrator—a common denominator for good and evil? There is no unification of those, nor understanding of them apart from the consideration of the Christian God. Hebrews 10 again:

V. 2: No more consciousness of sin—personal, inner effect of Christ's blood.

V. 18: No more offering for sin—historical, objective finality of Christ's blood.

V. 26: No more sacrifice for sin—theological, unique provision of Christ's blood.

JANUARY 11   Spoke on hypocrisy from Luke 12:1–3 at the Christian High School. Its meaning ($\dot{v}\pi o$-$\kappa\rho\dot{\iota}\nu o\mu\alpha\iota$) and its method (leaven). Acts 3 at Vanport Bible study.

JANUARY 12   Importance of the Word at high-school chapel. Its place (in the lives of the godly), its power (ye shall be free indeed [John 8; Heb. 4:12]), its purpose (revelation of God—Word became flesh), and its profit (1 Tim. 3:16, 17). Spoke on the names of a Christian at noon IVCF meeting at Lewis-Clark—believers, disciples, brethren, saints, Christians.

Most encouraging letter from Fritz today. Thank God for the faith to believe for him, that first night. He grows daily, it seems. How faithful my God! [*See* November 6, 9.]

JANUARY 13 *Exodus 1:8; Judges 2:10*   How well has Bunyan's Interpreter spoken: "Things present and our fleshly appetite are such near neighbors one to another; and things to come and carnal sense are such strangers to one another. Therefore it is that the first of these so suddenly fall into *amity* and that distance is so continued between the second." How unlike God I am. When He stretches forth His hand in mercy and forebearing love, I point an accusing legal finger at the sinner He would bless. And when He judges righteously, and slaughters His enemies in stern justice, I whimper for softness. As Israel did not utterly drive out the inhabitants of the land when they were strong, so I am weak to carry through to the letter God's mandates. It is bad when a ruler arises that knows not Joseph (Exod. 1:8), but how much worse does it become when a generation arises that knows not Jehovah! (Judg. 2:10). Spoke on discipleship and sacrifice from Mark 8 at the high school.

JANUARY 15   Spoke on John the Baptist at Stark Street Gospel Meeting. His degree, decrees, decrease, disappointment, and decease.

JANUARY 16   Deserted all morning. Much time on my knees but no fervency or any desire for prayer. No heed or hearkening in study of the Word either. What good is Greek, commentaries, insight, gifts, and all the rest if there is no heart for Christ? Oh, what slackness I feel in me now. Wasted half a day. No school because of snow. Good thing. I had nothing to say to the kids anyhow.

JANUARY 17 *Psalm 103, Hebrews*   Snow continues, no school today at Christian High. Oh, the shame of forgetting!

Psalms 103:2: "Forget not all his benefits." This was the danger in Hebrews, and the encouragement was that God did not, like man, forget (Heb. 6:10). They forgot the exhortation which dealt with them as sons (Heb. 12:5) and were in danger of forgetting their practical responsibility to entertain strangers (Heb. 13:2) and do good and communicate (Heb. 13:16). So also those of the Diaspora are warned by Peter that they should not forget their cleansing from their old sins (2 Pet. 1:9). Peter felt it his business to stir up these Hebrew believers by causing them to remember (2 Pet. 1:13, 15; 3:1). It was remembrance that brought him to his senses after the denial (Matt. 26:75). The distinction between ὑπόμνησις and ἀνάμνησις is good to think of in relation to the Lord's Supper. We do it for an ἀνάμνησις, that is, not by way of another's suggestion, but by our own recalling to mind. It is conscious volition—more seen in our word *recollect* than in *remember* (107:6 TRENCH).

JANUARY 18 *1 John 1:3; 2 Corinthians 13:14; 1 Corinthians 1:9*   Spoke on fellowship with God: the Father (1 John 1:3), for will and purpose; the Son (1 Cor. 1:9), for walk and practice; the Spirit (2 Cor. 13:14), for witness and power. Supposed to be a combined nurses' and med students' meeting up on Markham Hill, but there were only two men besides me, maybe a dozen girls. Felt like I wandered and joked overmuch. I must learn to be more sober, Lord, in such serious matters. How carelessly I handle the Holy Word—how dangerously offhandedly! Help, Lord, let my ministry be Spirit empowered, not put over by my personality. Feel I failed the Lord in too much digging for sermon thoughts and not enough time in letting the Scripture speak to me.

Finished F. W. Krummacher's *The Suffering Savior*. Found it stimulating to my imagination, warming to my heart. The emotional, unwritten backgrounds he interprets from the text are helpful, and encouraging to the use of sanctified, imaginative powers. He lacks accuracy in one or two points of interpretation, it seems to me, but on the whole has written a spiritually edifying work.

JANUARY 20, 21 *Romans 8:4* Four meetings with an OSC-IVCF [OSC—Overseas Student Camp, a proposed missionary-preparatory camp] gang at Jennings Lodge. Spoke on New Testament semantics and "What a Christian Is Called." Believer, disciple, brother, saint, Christian, and the relations they entail. Felt the sustaining power of the Spirit, but, oh! how I need Him. I wonder if Romans 8:4, ". . . that the requirement of the law might be fulfilled in us" might have prophetic implication. I mean that not only are the "thou shalts" of the decalogue commands to us, but prophecies concerning us. That is, "Thou shalt love" of the foremost commandment actually becomes, "We love . . ." in 1 John 4. The same as the Great Commission is not only a charge and a challenge, it is a prophecy concerning the future. Oh, blessed Spirit who makes the Law of God my life, its commands, my practice, hold not Thyself from me, nor me from Thee! Thou shalt love the Lord thy God with all thine affection, with all thine emotion, with all thy cogitation, with every action.

JANUARY 23 Disheartened tonight because of my lack of discipline. How dare I be so careless and preach as I do? "To him that knoweth to do good (as I have been taught and taught others to be hard on ourselves) to him it is sin!" Sinned, by being intemperate in working all day at my stamps, and while keeping up a rationalization that I should quit any minute. Oh, what hypocrisy! What a heart of sin, and how it deceives! Father, forgive it, and let not those who put their trust in Thee for tomorrow's high-school chapel be ashamed *on my account.* Deliver me from this strong "conscience of sins"; let it not have dominion. Give the Spirit of forgiveness, I pray.

Spoke on love for God: the *precept*, "Thou shalt love the Lord . . ."; the *power*, "The love of God is shed abroad"; the *practice*, "We love because He first loved us."

JANUARY 24 *James 1–3* Delightful time substituting in the Christian school as a seventh-eighth-grade teacher. Spoke at high school on love for one's neighbor, the second being like the first, "Who is my neighbor?" (Good Samaritan) and "How do I love him?" (No man ever yet hated his own flesh!)

Pondering what the τροχὸν τῆς γενέσεως of James 3:6 can mean. Obviously, it is something bad as he condemns the tongue for igniting it. It may be those springs of inner response unleashed by a careless word, either said or heard. That *natural* cycle (γενέσεως) having this meaning in James 1:23) which is not to be provoked without some evil issue. How often I have sat "thinking, I betook myself to linking fancy unto fancy" (as Poe's *Raven*) over some word uttered which gyrated downward and landed me in vile-thought acts. If this be so and the world of iniquity in my tongue so potent, how important that it be kept, as a watch set at one's lips. I have considered that this whole passage (3:1–12) refers specifically to *public* preaching, that communication of teachers which is so formative to a listener. As one has said, "The sins of teachers be the teachers of sins."

Ah, tolerant generation, who pays the prophets and fondles them who are sent unto you—woe. How much better had it been for you and for them if only they had found death at your hands! Cursed be your Judas embrace. Damned be your friendliness—it speaks not well for you; it lays shattering condemnation on your prophets. Ah, generation that hears, but feels not, listens but aches not, harks, but knows not pain nor the pleasurable healing balm thereof. Tell me, does all fire extinguish save in hell? Damned be this cool tepidity. Have we no fire to hate? Does no flame seize our prophets? Show me *one* burning heart. Let me see a single worldling afire with true passion, one heavenling consumed with his God's eternal burning. In them I would find excuse for you, my cheating, shamming, joyless generation. Well has your own poet said, you live and die "ox-like, limp and leaden-eyed."

JANUARY 25   Taught the seventh and eighth grades again. Had to apply discipline a little more than yesterday. The kids like me too easily, and I soon became "Jim" instead of "Mr. Elliot." But how I need wisdom from the Lord for them. What they shall be in ten years startles me.

Spoke again on the "Christian attitude" at the high-school chapel. "Thou shalt love *as* you love yourself." "Love as brethren." "Love *as* I have loved you." Particularly was I moved to stress Christian comradeship as Billy C., and I have known it, as being more blessed for unmarried believers within the sex than between the sexes. Some kids want to talk, but mostly girls, and I would reach young men for God. Give me subtlety, sanity, and strength to catch them alive for Thee, Lord Jesus!

JANUARY 26   Touched on "Sex Life for the Saint" at the high school: (1) the divine plan for sex (Gen. 1:27); (2) the dangerous pressure of our century (Song of Sol. 2:7); (3) the devilish plot in our social setup. *Purity* seems to be the missing passion in the high-school kids.

JANUARY 27 *James, 1 Peter*   School closed again today because of four inches of sifting snow which fell overnight and until noon today. Read some in James and 1 Peter. Wrote Rowland Hill and Wilfred Tidmarsh. Picked up Bret Harte for novelty—not much edified.

But a phrase in A.C.'s [Amy Carmichael's] *Gold Cord* struck me as I read this evening. Speaking of men in the Services of India who helped in the work of rescuing children from the temples she says (p. 137), ". . . being known to be on the side of the angels." I must consider this strongly. Carelessly, I suppose, I have left these ministering spirits to themselves. But Peter warned me this morning that I had obtained a salvation into which angels desired to look. There must be more care about my talk on their account, since they are to be instructed by me. I must develop an awareness of them and see them work, since one day I must judge them. I must learn reverence before them (women wear hats for angels' sake [allusion to 1 Corinthians 11:10]); they know my God's holiness better than I. So we shall teach one another, my spirit friends. We are both servants of God, both His creatures, and we must learn cooperation. May I be found worthy of this compact that I make with you tonight, comrades angelical. Let us together honor God, to whom be dominion, the right and power to reign, both now and forevermore. Amen.

JANUARY 28   *1 Peter 1; James 1; John 3*   Is it not significant that our term *born again* comes only from three authors of the New Testament (Paul uses it in a different sense in 1 Corinthians 4:15 and Galatians 4:19 in which he pictures himself as the one who was author of their Christian lives), and that these three are those three who were most closely associated with Christ while on earth? (Correction: this James was probably James, the Lord's brother, not the son of Zebedee so prominent in the Gospel narratives.) They all use different expressions and with slightly different thrusts.

Peter	James	John
ἀναγεννάω (1:3, 23)	ἀποκύω (1:18)	γεννάω ἀνῶθεν (3:3, 7)
This is to bring birth afresh. Stresses the change and difference between the two lives.	This is to be delivered from the womb. Stresses the will of God working in rebirth (as though His will were the pregnant womb).	This is to be begotten from above. Stresses the divine character and source of the new life.
Great mercy shown in resurrection effects the change (1:3). The incorruptible *Word* gives a lasting effect to our lives.	Purpose of God takes effect through the truth of the Word (contrasts to sin bearing fruit in our desires [1:15]).	Water and Spirit— the effective means of our partaking of this life.

FEBRUARY 2   No school all this week. Studying 1 Peter but find my thoughts badly scattered by confusion in the house and lack of concentration within. Jim Cochrane and wife from Vancouver, B.C., came through last night en route to Dominican Republic. Asked for ten or a dozen young men at the assembly to do evangelistic work, and have consistent prayer and study with. It is a big "ask" but the Lord Jesus said "whatsoever."

FEBRUARY 3 *1 Peter 5* Here's a degree for the great ones of earth; one they cannot simulate or confer. It is FGAR, spoken of by Peter in the first epistle 5:1: ὁ τῆς μελλούσης ἀποκαλύπτεσθαι δόξης κοίνωνος equals A Fellow of the Glory About to be Revealed. Better than any fellowship yet granted among men, it is at once present and perpetual; possessed, yet promised; a prospect of promptitude.

I like the attitude elders are to have for their work, not as though they were forced to it, but ἑκουσίως κατά θέον, "a willingness that befits one commissioned of God." It is not compulsion; yet it is certainly constraint, and describes an attitude that should be general in all God's work. It is a self-imposed imperative executed with a will responding to God's overlordship. The doing of God's work is a balance of autonomous zeal and desire spurred and strengthened by the recognition of God's being concerned with it and partaking actively in it.

This balance excludes two extremes I have observed. First, that careless disregard for the souls of men, characteristic of those who profess God's sovereignty in His work, saying, "God will take care of it, don't worry too much." Actually, they have no experience of God's working in them as is evident by their unconcern. The second is that overzealous action of the flesh which acts as if God were neglecting His work and needed my stirring to accomplish things. Lord, grant to me this spontaneous willingness which is prompted by the true inward motions of the Spirit, and let me not be slack to respond, that my eagerness might be "according to God."

FEBRUARY 4 *1 Peter 1:1-4* Difficulty getting anything from the Word at all. No fervency in prayer. Disturbance in the house, cold weather, and occasional headaches have made spiritual things less precious this whole week. I find I must drive myself to study, following the "ought" of conscience to gain anything at all from the Word—lacking any desire at all sometimes. It is important to learn respect and obedience to the "inner *must*" if godliness is to be a state of soul with me. I may no longer depend on pleasant impulses to bring me before the Lord. I must rather respond to principles I know to be right, whether I feel them to be enjoyable or not.

First Peter 1:1–4 has been puzzling me for several minutes. It seems very involved, and I think making my own translation is a help.

> Simon Peter, both slave and apostle of Jesus Christ, writes to those who in the righteousness of our God and Savior Jesus Christ have been granted by divine allotment a faith of equal value to ours. Grace and peace be multiplied on your part in the knowledge of God and Jesus our Lord, even as through the knowledge of that One who called you in and unto His own glory and virtue you have been given all the things which make for a full life and godliness—the giving itself being in divine power. Through these things (the total effect of your knowing Him, I mean) priceless and profound promises have been given as well, in order that by their use (your claiming and exercising faith in these promises) you should demonstrate your partaking of the nature of God, as those having escaped the corruption permeating the world in its lust.

This much has been done by God. He, by power, made His knowledge to come to us, offering promises, providing in Himself all things that are necessary for the life of godliness. Now, in verses 5–11, we see the believer's part in apprehending those things for which he was apprehended. Utmost diligence is required in the putting of this virtue (given of God [v. 3]) into my faith (given [v. 1]) and to that increasing knowledge (given [vv. 2, 3]). This knowledge of God makes me responsible to learn self-control, steadfastness, and so on. Those who are faithful in the fulfillment of this responsibility are in turn promised life without stumbling and a rich entrance into the Kingdom at the end of it. The spiritual myope of verse 9 can see neither far behind (forgetting his cleansing from those old sins), nor far ahead (disregarding the entrance into the Kingdom). Peter in this epistle stirs them to remember both, what is past and what is future.

I have this minute finished Amy Carmichael's *Gold Cord*.

How can I write the effect it has upon me? Ah, what a sham I am carrying on in the name of spirituality! No scar? No scar. No tear? No tear. But I hear you talk so well! Yes, I talk well. O God of the thorny crown, please, in Thy tender mercy, privilege me to walk Thy path of royalty. Urged to prayer, I asked—falteringly, I fear—for young men to "live the life of Jesus" in Portland. Words are waste here. My feelings are at once too complicated, too simple to be written.

I do not understand why I have never seen in America what missionaries write of—that sense of swords being drawn, the smell of war with demon powers. Corresponding is the unity among Christians, forced by the onslaught of a very real foe. Satan is not real, though we talk much of belief in a "personal devil." As a result, our warfare takes on this sham fight with shadows, a cold war of weary words. There is no sense of shouting, rather of yawning. Laughter long ago stifled sobs in our assemblings together. Woe, woe, woe unto us for we have not submitted to sacrifice. We have not guessed the power of the calling to which God has called—its power to ruin and to revise, its strength to slay. Service's *Law of the Yukon* has some words—utterly out of context—yet secularly applicable to the life to which I think God is calling.

> Send not your foolish and feeble; send me your strong and
>   your sane,
> Strong for the red-rage of battle; sane for I harry them
>   sore.
> Send me men girt for the combat, men who are grit to the
>   core,
> Swift as the panther in triumph, fierce as the bear in de-
>   feat,
> Sired of a bulldog parent, steeled in the furnace of
>   heat . . .
> And I wait for the men who will win me—and I will not be
>   won in a day,
> And I will not be won by weaklings, subtle and suave and
>   mild,

But by men with the hearts of Vikings and the simple faith
of a child,
Desperate, strong and resistless, unthrottled by fear or
defeat,
Them will I gild with my treasure, them will I glut with my
meat.

Teach me to count the cost, O God, most expensively won!

FEBRUARY 6   Well might the eyes of the Lord weary themselves searching the crannied corners of earth, running to and
fro, to find the heart that is *perfect* toward Him. Perfection
lacks in all things human, but most sadly does it lack in the
human heart. Lord who desirest truth in the inward parts,
reset my heart. How vacuous, how vain the *inner* part. Spoke
on Adam's helpmeet, Adam's deep sleep (committal), and his
lesson for the believer in getting a partner. High school resumed. Teaching seventh and eighth grade this week.

FEBRUARY 7 *1 Peter 2; Psalm 37*   Spoke on *desire*—the
Christian's inner drive. Its inception: the soul evacuated of the
world, commanded 1 Peter 2:1–3. Its increase: Psalm 37: Delight thyself . . . give desires.

FEBRUARY 8   Spoke on effect of sin in a Christian (Isa. 59:1,
2). Makes God seem distant, deaf. In the body, sin saps animation (Pss. 37:20) as cancer. In the soul, sin stifles the affections,
as corrosion (Matt. 24:12). In the spirit, sin solidifies the attitudes, as callous (Heb. 3:12, 13).
    Much distraught with encumbrances of teaching, but glad
that God has given the task.

FEBRUARY 9   Touched today in high-school chapel on the
three occurrences of Paul's word *be ambitious. Study* to be
quiet; ambitious to be well pleasing to Him; have ambition to
preach Christ not where He is named.

FEBRUARY 10   Finished the chapel services at Christian High with a conversational word on how to study the Bible, making practical suggestions as to time, place, notation after study, meditation, and so on. I felt as though it was ineffective. After these meetings, I feel something like a cow must feel who has been milked—relieved but with an emptiness. Yet, I know that just as the bovine is ready for another milking by feeding, resting, and digesting; so, thank God, reading, meditating, and assimilating will restore to me the spiritual supply I now lack. Forbid, Lord, that any of those to whom I minister should be so foolish as to take *my* word as though it were Thine; or so daring to set aside Thy Word as though it were mine.

FEBRUARY 11   I see tonight that in spiritual work, if nowhere else, the character of the worker decides the quality of the work. Shelley and Byron may be moral free-lancers and still write good poetry. Wagner may be lecherous as a man and still produce fine music, but it cannot be so in any work for God. Paul could refer to his own character and manner of living for proof of what he was saying to the Thessalonians. Nine times over in the first epistle he says, "you know," referring to the Thessalonians's firsthand observation of Paul's private as well as public life. Paul went to Thessalonica and lived a life that more than illustrated what he preached; it went beyond illustration to convincing proof. No wonder so much work in the Kingdom today be shoddy; look at the moral character of the worker. In 1 Corinthians Paul has to ask several times, "Know ye not?" as though they had not rightly apprehended his meaning. In 1 John, it is "We know," where the knowledge is based on firsthand individual experience. In Revelation, Christ speaks saying, "I know." Oh, happy state when hearer and speaker may prove each other true. "Knowing, beloved, your election."

FEBRUARY 13   Spoke tonight at the quarterly meeting of the Christian School Association. Touched on demon forces in the classroom ("We wrestle not against flesh and blood . . .") and of the institutionalization of the child, the ability we get to develop good deportment without having godly devotion, scholarship without spirituality, sincere, pure minds without spiritual, powerful motives. Felt clumsy in expressing myself and not too sure all I said was of use. Oh, for the lips of Samuel, from which the Lord let not drop to the ground a single word!

FEBRUARY 18   *1 John 2:1–3*   Teaching seventh and eighth all this week. The board wants me to decide soon about what I am to be doing in the fall. They want me to teach for a year in the high school. O God, so many turns, so many ways, so many pits! Help me, Lord, to see all Thy way for me—and to do it without consideration of any man. If I refuse Inter-Varsity work, I offend Dave; refuse the school board and offend them; go to India and discourage Brother Tidmarsh in Ecuador. How am I to know, my Father? It looks like I must make a decision soon, but I can make no decision unless I hear Thee speak, O Lord. Be not silent unto me.

I was shocked today to look into the eyes of a sightless man. What is more pitiable than the wild woe that shines in open but sightless eyes? There is something peculiarly tragic about blindness of this sort, for it seems the instruments of sight are so near for use, but the seeing is a different matter. And if it is true in the body, how much more tragically true in the soul. "Eyes . . . but see not, ears but hear not" (Mark 8:18).

I have been reading tonight Sir Robert Anderson's *Human Destiny.* Helpful in many passages, particularly 1 John 2:1–3: "The propitiation for the sins of the whole world." This word *propitiation* does not mean that the whole world is reconciled to God. It is as Romans 3:25, Christ is as a mercy seat set up whereat, and only whereat, God may meet the sinner. This leaves grace free to choose which of the sinners He wills to reconcile. If Christ were not the propitiation for the whole world, then grace would be bound to effect salvation only for those elect. But grace is free now, because Christ is set up as a propitiation for the sins of the whole world, to act in accord with its own wise principles. God could not frustrate his own grace by making propitiation for just a few.

FEBRUARY 20   Realize how little I have really understood of the truth of the basic teachings of the faith of Christ. The implications of substitutionary atonement, its universal meanings—how barely I have touched them. They've asked me to preach four Gospel sermons to unsaved college kids in March, and I greatly fear that I shall be wordless. I am no evangelist. But blessed be God, one may *know* God's work for his soul without understanding it all. He that grasps God intellectually, grips Him coolly. Let the heart be warm at all costs to the head in the getting of Christianity. Put head and heart to balance for the apprehending of it all.

FEBRUARY 22   Still teaching seventh and eighth. Little time for recording, though experiences are varied and blessed. Got my first paycheck today for three days work in January— $29.70.

Blessed studying Exodus 18 in Jethro's council to Moses, verses 13–27. First the principle of *sharing* God's work in verse 14, "Why sit alone?" and verse 18, "Thou wilt surely wear away . . . this thing is too heavy for thee." Then the *standards* for God's workmen in verses 21, 22: "Able men, such as fear God, men of truth, hating covetousness . . . they shall bear the burden . . . ." Finally, the *strength* to do God's work in verse 23: "If God command thee so . . . thou shalt be able to endure."

FEBRUARY 25   Spoke last evening to the junior class at Multnomah School of the Bible on 2 Timothy 2:4—the war with spirit forces, disentanglement and something of the call to service. What a mockery. I felt as though little or nothing was accomplished as I was jocular and not sober enough to speak on any such themes. Forgive me, Father, for this semideceitful handling of the Word! The Lord has been distant most of this week, and I have found myself too weary and sinful to draw near to Him. Desire seemed to fail, and my soul lies faint, lapping at its own stale dregs.

I have pondered for some days 1 John 2:7–10. Why the new and the old commandment; how is it true in me and in Him? I wonder if in this translation is not the meaning: "Beloved, I am not writing a new commandment to you but an old commandment which you have held from the start; the word which you have heard is this old commandment. Still, I am writing it as a new commandment (the command being in a real sense both old and new, and this as respects yourselves and as respects Christ, your having gotten it previously, His having given it previously; your getting it now afresh, His giving it now afresh) because the darkness passes along and the true light shines on." This last meaning, I think, that the command to love one another becomes increasingly diversified in its application. That is, as I gain more light and the darkness that formerly characterized all my living is removed progressively, the command to love takes on fresh meaning and is to be applied more and more as my knowledge of its implications grows.

FEBRUARY 26   Spoke at Sellwood Baptist Church with the singing groups of the Christian High School. Touched on 2 Kings 6, 7. Outlined thus:

Plague of famine: hunger, hardness to sin, horror
Promise of feasting: Elisha's word was precise, prompt, painful (for doubter)
Plight of the Four: wretched realists, keen perception— death; key position—outside city
Plenty found and hid
Proposition framed: we do not well
Precise fulfillment

I discovered their pastor, Ernest Mallyn, came from what he called "P. B. [Plymouth Brethren] background" in Sault Sainte Marie. He wants to talk with me sometime about this "background." I suspect he is a compromiser enmeshed in denominationalism which is burdensome to him. Mr. Jones asked me afterward if I would preach for a group which is thinking of pulling out of Evangel Baptist. All are quite impressed with my "preaching." Asked to give up the breaking of bread for a "service" next Sunday morning. What folly. Ah, for the spirit of Rutherford:

> E'en Ainworth were not heaven
> E'en *preaching* were not Christ . . . .
>   "Rutherford's Hymn"
>   ANNIE R. COUSIN

How can one explain without bringing offense? I offended in refusing, but, oh, the Lord was real tonight out underneath the moon. A February night, it is, pregnant with spring.

> . . . Too many devious paths lead down the land
> And I shall need in that strange, vast unknown
> Thy hand upon my hand.

MARCH 6   My exercises in the Word have been few these busy days. Dave was here last weekend and will return on Thursday. He wants some answer about IVCF-FMF work. I see several restrictions, the primary one being the compromises I would be called upon to live under in recommending mission boards, while knowing that the way of God is so far from organized methods that none with whom I would deal would be able to see the consistency of my own attitude and the things I would have to recommend. Further, this leaping from place to place, here a night, there a day, has been shown in the summer of 1948 to be ineffective, lacking the substantial quality of settled local building. My exercise seems to be undergoing crucial fires just now. I sensed afresh last evening the truth of Paul's word, "How shall they preach, except they be sent?" O God, here I am, *send* me. Let me not miss my path in running ahead. Send me, oh, *send* me afield!

MARCH 13   Mary Seater resumed her teaching this morning, so I was free to spend the day with Dave. We went to Multnomah to contact their SMO [Student Mission Organization] heads for FMF affiliation. Norman Douty from Seattle is here with stimulating and Christ-exalting ministry, taking up Hebrews.

Tonight I see how God had reason to permit evil. He allows nothing but what is for good ultimately. The satanic angels have no joy, find no profit in doing and in inspiring evil. Evil is no reward; it is purely negative, and the only motive for it is the will to destroy and defame. In itself it does utterly no good, not to men, to God, nor to Satan. Still, God in His wisdom and decretal permission allows it to be sustained in His universe, though it seems a useless, unproductive, damaging, and parasitic element in God's vast society. Still, though in its essence or in its sustenance there is no profit; yet in its end there shall be seen a vast amount of good springing from it. Already the fruits of God's wisdom in allowing it are manifest, for it was evil which was the effective factor in the death of Christ; sin that led me to hate sin; wrong that inspired crusades against itself. Just as all passion must have hindrance to become puissant and strong, so good must be opposed that I may know *moral* passion for goodness.

MARCH 15   *1 John 2; Jude 5, 6*   The statements of 1 John 2:20 and Jude 5 regarding the knowledge of the saints refer only to the basic doctrines of the faith. John, contending for the truth of the person and work of Christ, refers to that knowledge intuitive in all saints. This is that universal testimony of creedal Christianity, that basic agreement on the saving work and divine character of the Son of God. Not all agree on lesser doctrines, but these doctrines of salvation are so essential and universal to Christianity. Augustine says that in these we must have *unity*; in lesser doctrines let us have *liberty*; while in all things we must maintain *charity*.

Jude 5 and 6 shows two sins that are the Charybdes and Halcyon [Scylla] on the saint's path. The children of Israel went not where they were told to go (that is, into the land when God had them at Kadesh); the angels remained not in the position where they were put by God. It seems to me, Lord, that You have reenforced this lesson time and again. How am I to know when to go, when to remain? There is great sin in either failing to believe when Thou art speaking for me to go, or in anxiously leaving a place when I am set there by Thee.

Jude 8 refers to them that in Jude 4 crept in privately, who defile themselves in *dreaming*. How often have I know this! To see one's thoughts on a degrading theme and by the simple force of sin in those thoughts actually let myself fall into defilement!

It seems strange to me that Wuest is so adamant on the phrase, "these in like manner," pressing for the reference to angels in the previous verse (*Practical Use of the Greek New Testament*) and supposing the reference to mean that angels actually fell into lust for humans (as some have interpreted Genesis 6:2). This seems contrary to what Christ taught in the temple about the quality of angelic beings, not capable of either death or marriage. Obviously the phrase in verse 8 ("in like manner these also") does not refer to angels, since they have not flesh to defile as we know it. Both phrases (vv. 7, 8) refer to those cited in verse 4, the evil men corrupting the Christian community.

Evening. *Genesis 24.* In Genesis 24 Abraham warns his servant of two things: (1) not to take Isaac a wife from Canaan's daughters; (2) not to take Isaac back to Ur. In the first instance there was something inherently wrong with the daughters. Hereditarily, they were idolaters. Second, it was the environment of idolatry which made for the danger. A Chaldean in Canaan would suit, but not a Chaldean in Chaldea, nor a Canaanite in Canaan. In this sense the believer is a displaced person. He loses the controlling features of both environment and heredity.

MARCH 16 *Jude 11* The false men of this passage are seen as beginning quietly in a wrong way and ending violently at its end.

They proceeded in the path of Cain—murder.
They poured themselves out ($\dot{\epsilon}\kappa\chi\dot{\epsilon}\omega$) for the pay of Balaam—false witness.
They perished in the perversity of Korah—rebellion.

MARCH 18 *Revelation 2:1–7* Ephesus was intolerant of evil men. That church could not bear the evil workers who sought to settle among them. But that mere intolerance of evil did not make Ephesus what Christ wanted her to be. Intolerance of evil is, or can be, a negative attitude, and if it lacks the moral backing of positive love for God, it will quickly degenerate into bigotry and narrowness. This is for me, for though I pretend zealously to have hatred for wickedness, often it is not from a knowledge of and love for righteousness, but from mere external, social, and environmental feelings.

MARCH 21 Paid by school for February and March. Total of $200—$23.20 was withheld for income tax. Letter from Tidmarsh telling of his proposal to leave Shandia to the C & MA. Lord, give light! [The Christian and Missionary Alliance had the two mission stations nearest to Shandia. If no replacement came, Dr. Tidmarsh was going to ask C & MA to take over.]

MARCH 22 John calls the Lord Jesus "the faithful witness." There are three things about faithful witnessing to which I must comply, with Christ as my example:

I. A witness must be thoroughly acquainted with all the details of the matter whereof he speaks.
   A. Illustration: Ahimaaz the son of Zadok (2 Sam. 18:19–30) failed in this. He had the will to run (v. 23), great things were expected (v. 27) of him, but he hadn't the facts straight (v. 29).
   B. Demonstration: Christ told Nicodemus heavenly things and earthly things, but things He had personally seen and knew (John 3:11).
   C. Verification: "No one knows the Father save the Son" (Matt. 11:27). "I know him because I am from him and he sent me" (John 7:29). ". . . the things I heard from him, these speak I unto the world . . . as the Father hath taught me, I speak these things" (John 8:26–29). "He hath given me a commandment what I should say, and what I should speak [in detail]" (John 12:49).

II. A *faithful* witness must render the whole of what he knows clearly to his listeners.

A. Illustration: Ananias and Sapphira failed in this. A lie to men meant unfaithfulness to God the Spirit.

B. Demonstration: Christ told the disciples all that was necessary for them, even going so far as to say, "if it were *not so* I would have told you." He left them with no false hopes, but all well-established and real hopes.

C. Verification: ". . . the words which thou gavest me I have given to them . . . I have accomplished the work which thou hast given me to do [in relation to fully preparing the twelve]" (John 17:4–8). Here Christ renders up account honestly to His Father.

III. A faithful witness must maintain this single purpose in all vicissitudes—proper setting forth of truth regardless of personal feelings or public favor:

A. Illustration:

1. Both Abram and Isaac lied in Egypt and before Abimelech concerning the true character of their wives. Their *personal safety* (regardless of Sarah's and Rebekah's) was put above the truth. A plague opened Pharaoh's eyes (Gen. 12:17); a vision Abimelech's (Gen. 20:3); Isaac broke Abraham's vow in Genesis 21:23–25, deceiving as his father had done, Abimelech the second's eyes being opened by Isaac "sporting" with his wife.

2. Herod failed herein, not considering his own state only, but the nobles with him (Matt. 14:9). Public favor made for compromise of what he knew to be the truth.

B. Demonstration: Christ never did so. When the crowd would crown Him, He desisted, knowing that the voice of the people was not the voice of God. Or when Caiaphas made Him know that confession meant personal suffering, the truth came unhesitatingly to His lips.

C. Verification: John 3:32: "What he hath seen and heard he beareth witness and no man receiveth that witness." Simply because the truth is opposed does not mean the truth is deposed. "We can do nothing against the truth" (2 Cor. 13:8). Here is the faithful witness giving His own testimony in court: "To this end have I been born, and to this end have I come into the world, that *I should bear witness unto the truth*" (John 18:37).

MARCH 23 *Revelation 2*   The letter to the messenger of Ephesus (Notice: to the *messenger* of that church, not to the church. The letters are addressed to any messenger in all time who finds himself in the midst of a situation comparable to that existing in any of these churches) is divided into groups and series which are all knit together:

I know thy works. . .

Thy toil . . . hast not grown weary
Thy patience . . . bore up for my name
Canst not bear evil men . . . hast patience
Tried the self-named apostles . . . found them false (v. 2)
but . . .

Thou didst leave thy first love (v. 4) (This should have been at the peak of the ascending series of commendations. But they fell at the very *peak*.)
Remember thy fall! (v. 5)

Just where their works should have been matched by a subjective activity of love (as column 2 above corresponds to column 1), God links the loss of first *works* (v. 5) with the loss of first love. In all, the commendations would have numbered ten, the number of full responsibility, but the Ephesians miss perfection by a hair which God constitutes a total fall. Verse 6: where they lacked love, they did have holy hate.

Ephesus was plagued with inner decay. Smyrna was persecuted with outer destruction.

MARCH 26 *Psalm 65*   Came down to Grant's Pass by bus Friday night; met Phares Huggins and drove with him down to Williams. Gospel meetings begin today for two and one half weeks, God willing.

Psalms 65:1: "Praise waiteth for thee, O God." Why should *praise* wait? I must learn not to approach God incautiously with words, even words of praise. Since it is He who "causest me to approach" (v. 4). I must wait for divine impulsion and inspiration to praise Him properly. He in grace receives praise, but when He sovereignly deigns to do so. I must remember this in breaking of the bread with saints. God can only be glorified in praise when He is the true source and end of it. My rushing to *words* of praise can only be vain and empty until He is in readiness to accept them.

For the meetings Psalms 65:5 is hoped. I hardly dare to believe for it, since my own soul is in such a state that I cannot find faith to lay hold on God prevailingly. "By terrible things wilt thou answer us in righteousness, O God of our salvation, Thou that art the confidence of all the earth."

MARCH 26 Evening.   Spoke this morning on the triumphal entry: the approach (following long road to Jerusalem, raising of Lazarus, Zephaniah's prophecy); the attitudes (multitudes, Pharisees, disciples, Christ); the answers (multitude); His descent (son of David); His nationality (Nazareth); ability (prophet, disciples); His dignity (Lord has need); nobility (King). Some freedom but much unnecessary shouting. Text Matthew 21:10, "Who is this?"

The question, "What think you of Christ—whose son?" Psalm 110: The day of power, the day of wrath. Jehovah speaks regarding Christ's position. Jehovah sends forth regarding Christ's power (rod). Jehovah swears regarding Christ's priesthood.

MARCH 27 *Mark 14:2–10*   Spoke on Mark 14:2–10 on the worship by Mary: the occasion of the Supper, the occupation of the woman; the opposition of the disciples, the defense of the Savior. Stressing the urgency of sacrificial appreciation of the *person* of Christ as more important than work for Christ. Felt deserted, though much prayer had ascended for the meeting. Only two sinners out. Much humbled in heart afterward.

MARCH 28   *Revelation 1*   I see some beauty in the order of John's phrasing in Revelation 1 this morning:

V. 3:   *Read*, but one may do that without hearing the words;

Hear, but one may do that without keeping what is written;

Keep, and one must both read and heed to do this.

Vv. 4, 5: The Trinity—grace and peace from them all:

Him who is, was, and is coming

The seven spirits

Jesus Christ:

I am:

Alpha: who was—faithful witness (His life on earth)

Alpha: who is—firstborn of the dead (His resurrection life)

Omega: who is coming—Ruler of kings (His ascension life)

Vv. 5, 6: "Unto Him who *loves* us":

He must love us before He can loose us from our sin.

He must loose us before He can link us into the kingdom.

He must make us priests before we can fittingly bespeak His glory and dominion.

Of the seven churches, five are addressed ("I know thy works"), even Laodicea. Smyrna is reminded that though she was pressed by tribulation, the First and the Last took not account of what works she could not do, but of the faithfulness she had in trial. Not all may do works, but all are called upon to be faithful unto death. Pergamum had degenerated from a working church to a teaching church. He who neglects practical effort for God when he has opportunity (as Smyrna had not) soon is sterile and in error—teaching false doctrines. Tragic when the Church, untaught herself of the Spirit, goes on teaching.

MARCH 28 *Mark 14*   Spent this afternoon visiting with Phares about the country. Some stir—a certain "sound of a going" there seems to be up the valley—but no conviction generally among the people. O God, soften sinners and save them to Thine eternal glory! Much prayer among the saints but few sinners apparent in the meetings, though the believers go about inviting and have joy in doing it. I feel God has prepared this place but that I failed in not being more in prayer over it sooner with more fervor. Spoke with joy and freedom on Judas from Mark 14:

> Deceived by silver—"how much?"
> Darkened by Satan—Satan entered him.
> Distressed in spirit—"Rabbi, is it I?" Weeping and repentance.
> Damned by the Son—Woe, it were good had he not been born.
> Died by suicide—sent himself to "his own place."

Conviction is not enough for conversion. Sorrow is not a substitute for salvation. Christ said there is a state worse than not being. It is *being after death*, when one has "given up" Christ.

MARCH 29 *Revelation*   The seven churches assuredly represent the universal Church, and the individual letters describe conditions existing throughout the whole Church in history. If otherwise, why are there only seven stars, seven candlesticks, and so on? Surely, there are more than seven obscure congregations seen here. The glorified Christ has a broader interest than Asia Minor. Further, in letters which are seemingly addressed to local conditions, there comes the challenge to hear what the Spirit is saying to the *churches*, as though he spoke to one as a representative of many.

The first three churches are given promises at the very end of the letter concerning the reward of a victor in the specific situation. *Preceding* this comes the word to hear what the Spirit says. The last four reverse this order giving the promise first and then the challenge to hear. Could it be that the first three, Ephesus, Smyrna, and Pergamum refer to situations not universal in history, but at one time existing in different places? Where, for instance, if there is a church now like Ephesus, with the single failure of lost love, or like Smyrna, against whom nothing is said of evil, or like Pergamum, who though she dwells in Satan's throne, holds fast His name?

Whereas Thyatira is to be exemplary to all the churches peculiarly (2:23). From her some are to go into great tribulation. The universal failure of Sardis (3:2) and call to remembrance seems universally needful. Philadelphia is specifically promised deliverance from the hour of trial coming late upon the whole earth—not yet having transpired and showing that Philadelphian conditions prevail to the end. Of the present application of this universal meaning of the Laodicean church I need make no comment. Thus the challenge to hear the Spirit in the last four comes finally and applies to all time wherein the Church exists. The first three have their call to hear and their promise of reward seals their letters.

Meditation on John's use of the Prince of this World (12:31; 14:30; 16:11). Christ and/or Satan. All may refer to Satan. One and three may refer to Christ. No real light yet. Notice the food at Passover time in John, chapter 2: Water changed to wine—a qualitative change. Chapter 6: Bread and fish changed to feed a multitude—a quantitative change. Chapter 13: Bread and wine changed to signify body and blood, a symbolic change.

MARCH 30 *Psalms 104:15; John 6; Revelation*   Spoke last evening on the institution of the Lord's Supper. Bread and wine representing strength and cheer. (Pss. 104:15). Then to John 6. Many unsaved out, I believe. Some adventists who must have been called there by the Lord as I spoke on working the work of God, believing on Him whom He hath sent. Still claiming a deeper work of conviction from the Lord. Noticed that all the churches had boasts, saying things which the Spirit decreed:

Ephesus: Some say they are apostles
Smyrna: Some say they are Jews
Pergamum: No boasts but false teaching held
Thyatira: Jezebel says she is a prophet
Sardis: Has a name that it is alive
Philadelphia: Some say they are Jews
Laodicea: Whole Church said they were rich and had no
     need

MARCH 31   Spoke on Gethsemane. How the Savior suffered in the sinner's place: the horror of death; horror at demonic atmosphere. What tormented Him in time menaces the sinner for eternity. Went into the meeting with a shaking at the horror of sin. Conviction sensed, but the souls of man were not shaken with trembling as we had been hoping. Came home questioning the Father's goodness and was rebuked with two answers. First, God is not frustrating our prayers. He has heard and in wisdom withheld an unusual work. The wisdom of God seemed a good thing to ponder, though I could not understand it. God withholds blessing only in wisdom, never in spite or aloofness. Second, then James's word about asking came: (1) I had not been asking definitely enough—Ye have not because ye ask not; (2) I had not been asking purely enough—Ye ask and have not because ye ask amiss that you might consume it upon your pleasures. I still had my own concerns, my own name connected with the work, and had God granted hitherto, I would have consumed the answer in my pride and selfishness.

APRIL 1   Azel Blodgett came in this morning after breakfast with his wife and the Huggins. Ida and Lester were still in the house. Azel has been waked several times in the night this week and now has been given faith that God shall do this work of reviving saints (prior to a work for sinners) tomorrow morning. He talks of taking out the benches, opening the windows, and doing all sorts of things to accommodate the crowds that are coming. I confess it seemed absurd to me and was forced to examine my heart in the matter. The verse came to me while he was here, "Blessed is she that believed, for there shall be a performance of the things which have been spoken to her of the Lord" (Luke 1:45). His faith rebuked and silenced me. But if Mary could believe for the birth of the Christ child, so Azel can be granted grace to believe for the rebirth of Christ in this whole country. And by God's good grace, I shall believe.

APRIL 5   Preaching every night. Good interest, and the Spirit has some success here, though not the control of me I should wish. Spoke on Jesus or Barabbas last night.

  I. The Symbol—the people's choice
     Satan—a murderer, a rebel, a robber
     Man—betraying what *He* is by whom he chooses
 II. The Substitute—The prisoner's chance
     Jesus and Barabbas change places:
     A. What the exchange provides
       Bondage—Liberty
       Condemnation—Innocence
       Curse—Blessing
     B. What the exchange should produce
       Action
       Appreciation

Lacked power to concentrate this afternoon. This came, half as a poem, half as a dream, though I was wide awake.

I saw the Race wallow as one great man,
Gigantic in aspect, thick-set through the shoulders
But thin through the thighs
And very weak-kneed.

I say He wallowed; meaning that He would not stand
Or perhaps could not find place to stand
Within the slough He lived;
A slough of Blood and Beer and Sweat and Sperm,
Through which darted peculiar little fish.

Methought the muddiness was thick enough to float the mon-
   ster,
But He would swim, and thrashed with stroke
Both artless and without aim.
The more He strove the more the mixture choked him
And blinded His red eye—
(Which He did blink and focus every way about to see
On some horizon, an end of Blood and Beer and Sweat
And tepid Sperm. But naught He saw.)

He got Him strength by gulping up great fistfuls
Of the darting fish about Him. But I saw the strength He got
But craved His exercise in thrashing in His wallow
And snatching more small fish.

Now and again He would look up, and the mixture would
   drain off
His stinging lids and run into His ears.
So He would shake His head, convulse and go again
At thrashing in the slough. For what He saw
When He looked up He could not hear for the rushing in His
   ears.
I heard Him swear His eyes befooled Him, and noticed then
He looked aloft but less and less.

I liked Him, somehow, liked too the smell of that vast wallow,
But when I tasted at it, could but vomit slime.
And so there came to me a flickering love therefore.
And feeble hate of all the things I saw.

APRIL 6 *Revelation*   The seven Spirits of God. This must be
representative of the single Spirit, since He seems to be
mentioned in 1:4 as a single source of grace and peace like the
Father and the Son. He takes on one aspect before the throne

(4:5) and another when sent forth into the world. Seven represents fullness and perfection.

> Seven Spirits—perfect invisibility
> Before the throne—prominent locality
> Burning lamps of fire—brilliant luminosity
> Before the crystal sea—eternal reflectivity
> Seven horns—perfect potentiality
> Seven eyes—perfect perceptivity
> Sent into all the earth—unlimited locality

Revelation 4 shows the creatures recognizing the Creator as they ought. The lion, calf, man, and eagle with full powers of perception (eyes within and round) shall honor God worthily. Each represents the creature in different aspects as related to the Creator:

Lion: The (seeming) self-sufficiency of creation
   (Independent and not to be identified *as* God)
Calf: The sacrificial character of creation
   (Devoted entirely to God, for His pleasure and use)
Man: The sagacity of creation and sovereignty thereof
   (Created to be self-governed by his own will)
Eagle: The heavenly relations of creation
   (Linked with the skies and characterized by its gravitation upward, as originally formed)

When the creatures ("nature") own the glory of God, men are prompted to worship (three times in two chapters men in the glory of maturity "fall down" [4:10; 5:8; 5:14]) and honor Him first as worthy for His creational will. But creation cannot be fully rectified without judgment and so the sealed book comes promptly to view. Why cannot the One upon the throne open the book? See John 5:22, 27.

The Father has given all judgment to the Son, first in order that the Son may be honored as the Father, and, second, practically, because He is a Son of man and thereby a more competent judge, in matters relating to men. This latter of course, not

by the Father's disability to judge, but because of His decree to
have it done by the Son. His possession of the spirits (3:1) as
they are *sent forth in all the earth* (5:6) gives Him power to
convict (horns) and to perceive (eyes). The song of the redeemed creatures expands and affects the angels which in turn
cause the entire creation, in heaven, earth, and under earth to
praise the Lamb. The living creatures say "come" to a rider
related to their own character. The Lion says "come" to the
conquering horseman (slayer). The Calf to the slaying horseman (slain). The Man to the judging horseman with the balance (sage). The Eagle to the horseman related to supernatural
realities (death and Hades).

APRIL 12 *Hebrews 3*   The Lord swore in His wrath in Hebrews 3 that the people should not enter into His rest. But He
swore in His righteousness in chapter 7 that Christ should
enter into an eternal priesthood.

APRIL 16 *Acts 10; Psalm 110; Revelation 3, 4*   Finished meetings at Williams [Oregon] on Wednesday night. IVCF conference at Jennings Lodge over this weekend. Spoke three times
from Peter's initial sermon to the Gentiles in Acts 10 as typical
of primitive preaching. Sunday morning spoke on Psalms
110:1, its use and meaning in the New Testament. Met Jane
Hollingsworth at conference. Tremendous impression of her
experience with God. She should have been the main speaker.
John Paterson here as well. Mingled experience of power and
weakness. Exercised regarding IVCF staff work. No leading
regarding foreign field.

Back to the Greek this morning after three weeks out of it for
all practical study. The door opened before the Philadelphians
(3:8) is not, as I had supposed, referring to opportunity, but to
the door of 4:1, the promise of an opened door into heaven.
Immediate transference from earth upward. John's living creatures differ from Ezekiel's. The third is a calf rather than an ox.
John's have six wings; Ezekiel's four. John's eagle flies;

Ezekiel's no. Ezekiel—wheels and feet and hands; John—wings only. John—on a level with the crystalline sea; Ezekiel—crystal over their heads. Does it represent the heavenly and earthly distinctions of the revelations? Isaiah says "whole *earth* full of glory." John implies the truth in heaven.

APRIL 17   Turned down Vancouver school board's offer to complete the school year as a seventh-eighth-grade teacher. Found some difficulty in discerning the Lord's will, but believe He has guided. It is easy to be swayed by minor (or even major) points when one comes to make decisions if one cannot hark to *principles* of guidance. I have learned two recently which make a fair beginning at a code. One, remember always that God has taught you the importance of a *building* ministry. Staying in one group for some period of time stressing emphases consistently is the best way to accomplish lasting work for God. Two, do not put yourself in a position to any man or group so that *they* and not you direct policies which you know must be decided on the individual's exercise before God. Never let any organization dictate the will of God. A move which does so ensnare cannot be of God for me.

Mount Hood loop trip with Ray Larsen, John Paterson, and Sam Squire. Later: Another principle. Three, whenever the choice is between the doing of spiritual work—whatever sort—and a secular job—again of whatever sort—the choice for me must be the former regardless of financial conditions.

APRIL 18   *Revelation 4, 5*   Round about the throne (4:3) is, first, the rainbow. Other things surround that rainbow, but it is mentioned directly after the One sitting on the throne. The bow set in the cloud was the token of the *covenant.* So God is known as Jehovah, the God in relation to His creatures by covenant promise. God must act *through* His own promises, so that anything proceeding from the throne comes through the perfect rainbow encircling the throne (seen only as part of a circle, a bow, on earth). He may not act otherwise than through His covenants. Praise, praise be to that name Jehovah, His memorial name, which reminds both Himself and His people that He acts consistent with what He has spoken. The *circling* rainbow suggests:

1. The neccessity of His working by covenant (to be consistent in Himself).
2. The perfection of His working by covenant (we need no more than His promises).

The impossibility of opening the book (need for power) and looking thereon (need for purity and perfection in the eye) in 5:3 is answered in the seven horns (power) and seven eyes (perception) of 5:6, possessed only by the Lamb. We always say when one on earth judges another, "What right have you to judge; look at your own faults." Because that is universally applicable to all creatures, no one can open the book of final judgment, except the Blessed Lamb who had no faults. He is worthy to judge because: (1) He is a son of man and can be fair and sympathetic (John 5:27); (2) He is perfect in righteousness and has Himself no one to judge Him. He is thus the only one able to judge the world.

APRIL 19   Sir Robert Anderson's *Human Destiny* roused me this afternoon to some serious thinking. Who shall be held guilty for the death of Christ? It is trivial to smite a fellow man, heinous to smite a parent, treason to smite a king. What must it be to murder the Creator? Those shall be held guilty of that murder who, hearing that He is Creator, take no positive stand against the act by believing in Him. This, I think, is the virtue in *repentance*. It is the shift from a noncommittal position concerning the dying of the Son of God, to that positive assertion of belief in the miraculous imputation powers of that dying.

Destruction: the act of unfitting a thing permanently for the purpose for which it was intended.

Evening, Isaiah 42.   Seeking a promise of God's acceptance of my trust in Him for guidance in the next one and a half months, I got this encouragement from Isaiah 42:16. "I will bring the blind by a way that they know not; in paths that they know not will I lead them; I will make darkness light before them, and crooked places straight. These things will I do, and I will not forsake them." I fulfill the qualifications for once, Lord. Most surely, I am blind.

APRIL 20   I asked earnestly last night for some token of guidance to be shown me today concerning my going to Wycliffe. I got none. It is clear to me tonight that I can do quite well without guidance concerning Wycliffe. I see that God is going to give me specific leading, not when I ask for it, but when I need it, and not until.

APRIL 25   I have been tremendously helped these last two days in the reading of Roland Allen's *Missionary Methods: St. Paul's or Ours*. I see now one reason why God did not send me afield before this: I did not know what this book had to say. The Lord stirred me in various ways while reading it: thanksgiving for the apostle's example; prayer for grace to follow it; boldness to stand out against the generation's attitude in such matters. It must be one of the textbooks for the young man. I have prayed to be given fellowship with in the work of reevangelization. Such truth, applied to the U.S. in 1950, would revolutionize the entire church. Written by a churchman, it carries that much more weight on the side of simplicity and autonomous assembly development.

APRIL 26   *Revelation 21, 22*   Perplexed at the reading of Revelation 22 to find the repetition "I am Alpha, Omega, first and last, beginning and end." Why the seeming repetition if every word is to mean something different and these all seem to imply the same thing? (So Thayer relates Alpha and Omega with first and last as synonymous ideas.) There is seeming repetition so familiar to the psalms. In studying Alpha and Omega in its other occurrences there is light.

Revelation 1:8: I am *Alpha* and *Omega,* saith the *Lord God* (Jehovah Elohim). (Critical deletion of "first and last" valid. Even Tischendorf refuses to follow ℵ* in omitting phrase. Insertion of "God" after Lord has every manuscript authority.)

This shows the Revealer in three relations (What He *is*):

I. Covenantal—as Jehovah, God in His relations to Israel and man
   A. Beginning and end of a series of twenty-four Greek letters A-Ω (Who is)
   B. Center of a circle of *twenty-four* elders (Rev. 4) (Who is to come)
   C. Subject of *twelve* tribes' history and prophecy (Who was)

   Subject of *twelve* apostles' history and prophecy
   Revelation opens in showing its subject to be the God previously known in the whole of the Book in His dispensational dealing. This relation peculiarly applies to the *spirit* of man; his thinking is suggested in the reference to alphabetical teaching.

II. Creatorial—Elohim—the Almighty. Revelation 21:6: I am Alpha and Omega, the *Beginning* and the *End,* saith God (21:2, 3, 7; 1 Cor. 15:28). This shows the Revealer in His *causal* relations (What He gives)
   A. Beginning ("how cause")—the prime mover, Instigator of the universe.
   B. End ("why cause")—the prime motive, Integrator, end and purpose of the Universe.

   Peculiar relation to the *soul* of man (desire of Pss. 42:1, 2; Isa. 26), "To him that is athirst . . . ."

III. Temporal—Revelation 22:13: I am Alpha and Omega, the *first* and the *last,* the beginning and the end, saith *Jesus.* This shows the Revealer in His *temporal* relations (What He *does*). (Listed second rather than third, indicating Son's position.) Peculiar relation to *body;* robes and works mentioned.

APRIL 28   Reaped the deadly fruits of undisciplined think-ing this morning. What destructive power in careless thoughts! How quickly do they spring into my fingers and feet! How long before I learn to bring every thought into cap-tivity to the obedience of Christ? God help me!

Evening. Finished Samuel Zwemer's biography of *Raymond Lull*. Much stirred to thanksgiving and wonder at the man's capacities and ideals, so violently opposed to those of his period. Sensed the hero-worship feeling again and had to judge the vain longing to be one of these biographied "heroes" of the mission field. Felt overcome with the deceit of my own pride and was convicted of my abysmal lack of fresh love for Christ, the thing which possessed Lull. "He that is forgiven much loveth much. He that is forgiven little loveth little." Ah, how poorly I understand my debt to Christ and to all men! "He who loveth not liveth not; and he who lives by the Life cannot die." R. Lull.

APRIL 29   Consider what reversals the day of wrath and revelation shall produce. Man, who now mocks God in pride, shall then mourn in pain. God, who now loves in sorrow for the creature, shall then laugh at the sorrow of men. Awful day, *dies irae!*

MAY 1 *Revelation*   Spoke with Christian High School Choir at Evangelical Methodist and (following) at Friends gatherings in the city. Went afterward to a Singspiration at Hinsen Baptist. Sensed a terrible spirit of criticism and asked the Lord for love for His church. Poor, poor Laodicea! How I would that I had heart to help her. Ignorance is widespread and few concerned. The Church is in shambling ruins and sadly needs awakening to her calling. And where shall an overcomer be found? Alas, they all witness that there is no need for overcoming. What a day when smug Laodicea is spewed from the Lord's mouth, her tepidity witnessing against her, for the Lord shall judge His people. Many, and myself included, are as John was in Revelation 1 with our backs to the testimony, while we look for other resources to encourage us. But Christ was among the churches, *behind* John. The tarnish of the lampstand did not send Him away from them; He is still in their midst. Ah, turn me, Lord Jesus, to see Thee in Thy concern for Thy witness and let me *write, publish,* and *send* to the Church what things I see, being turned.

MAY 2   Sacred Head of Christ! Wondered to think that the Head of the Church had undergone the suffering for the Body. In Gethsemane the Lord Jesus sweat great drops of blood, as A.C. [Amy Carmichael] puts it:

> And never, never can his heart forget
> That Head with hair all wet
> With the red dews of Love's extremity
> Those eyes from which fountains of Love did flow
> There in the Garden of Gethsemane.
>   "The Fellowship of His Sufferings"
>   *Toward Jerusalem*

Even as Masefield saw more to write of in "the men with the broken heads and the blood running into their eyes" than in the elite of earth, so for me the broken Christ is more than all the heroes of fame. Think, my soul, His hair was all red with *thy* suffering, and now is turned all white for thy sanctification. "Though your sins be as scarlet, they shall be as white as snow; though they be red like crimson, they shall be as wool" (Isa. 1:18). So God in the Revelation has shown His servants that Christ's head, once bloody, is now a crown of pristine and glorious whiteness. If God has so broken the Head and healed it with glory, what shall be the beauty of the Body when it takes on the beauty of the Head?

MAY 4 *Revelation*   I am restudying the Revelation with Walter Scott's *Exposition of the Revelation of Jesus Christ* to stimulate my meditation. Noticed again this morning how the letters are written to representatives of the churches, those whose responsibility it is on earth to see to the moral state of the Church ("which God gave to Him to show to His servants"). The fault is found with *the servant himself*, and if the leaders (represented as one star, controlled by Christ to shine as a unified voice publicly) be found wanting, so will the followers. "The sins of teachers are the teachers of sins." Restore a godly elderhood and you will in the same measure find the household of faith respond.

Christ, showing Himself to Ephesus in power (holding seven stars) and in His presence (walking in midst), insists that what is done be done with proper motive, strangely omitting the bases for work (faith), labor (love), and patience (hope) in recounting her virtues. Throughout the series of messages the stress is laid upon individual responsibility—the overcomer is to understand that he is one man against the world.

MAY 5 *Revelation*   Christ is ever applicable to the situation and needs of His own. Are they tending to lose heart for Himself, becoming distant, carrying on labor for Him without a sense of His sponsorship? Then Ephesus must be reminded that Christ is still central (in the midst) and still in control, holding the seven stars in the hand of power. Or are they in difficulty, facing prison, tribulation, poverty, and death? Then Smyrna must hear the voice of the Christ who in time reckoned on eternity, knowing that *final* judgment (God's) would more than right all wrongs. He is seen as the One who lives beyond death, recalling vividly all the horrors known while passing through it and that it hath an end (ten days). The beauty of the Christian's future is that the thing he most dreads on earth shall be the things he is most conscious of having escaped in heaven. "The overcomer shall not be hurt of the second death" (2:11). Those who die for Christ's sake in suffering shall glorify Him when He puts the men who tormented them to death to the second death.

The conflict of science and religion is one between the errors in both camps. Truth cannot contradict itself.

The only way to escape guilt in the matter of the death of

Jesus Christ for which the race is liable is to take God's view of it and believe in the resurrection.

The plea of Christ in the Gospel is, "If any man have ears to hear, let him hear." In Revelation, "he that hath an ear . . . ." The former in a physical relation speaks to a man who might be passing. The latter supposes a listening attitude in the inner man. The former for conversion; the latter for grasping secrets after conversion.

MAY 9 *Revelation 3* Down at Williams again with Sam for a week or so. Word came to me from the letter to Sardis this morning: Christ is seen as (1) the supply of animation ("having the seven spirits"), (2) the source of authority ("having the seven stars"). The trouble in Sardis is that there is false confession. "Thou hast a *name* that thou livest, and art dead" (v. 1). "Thou hast a few names . . . that did not defile their garments" (v. 4). "The overcomer . . . I shall not blot out his *name* from the book of life. I will confess his name before my Father" (v. 5). So true of so many here (and the spirit within me!) that the name is on them but the life that goes with the name lacks. Only Christ can give life ("It is the Spirit that giveth life . . ." [2 Cor. 3:6]. "If any be born of water and of the *Spirit* . . ." [John 3:5]).

MAY 10 *Psalms 90, 89* Psalm 90 (with 89:47) brought me before God. My brevity and His longevity are the most obvious differences between us this morning. *Thou art God,* says Moses and implies that my return to dust is a vindication of that fact. A millennium to Him is as a past yesterday, a night watch; years are carried as wisps on the flood of His eternity, as a sleep, as a grass on a mowing day. And not *alone* is His lastingness, but it assures an eternal holiness. My sin makes me that much more short-lived; His holiness provides a lasting quality to His person. His holiness lengthens His life (theoretically) and shortens mine. Days and years consume my substance; His substance consumes days and years. I labor, struggle, sorrow, and fly away; He controls, rejoices, abides. Ah,

Lord God, sate me with Thy loving-kindness *every* morning that *all* my days may be spent in gladness. Give me the spirit of "numbered days," a spirit of wisdom and sense of destiny. Let Thy work appear to Thy servant . . . Thy beauty be upon me . . . establish Thou *my work.*

MAY 12 *Revelation 3:10* Philadelphia kept the word of Christ's patience. This implies two matters much abused and debased today. The first is the literal possession of a patient, steadfast, and enduring spirit in the individual's upholding of the truth. Christ was patient in His ministry, as none has been to this day, and it is the maintenance of this word of patience for which these are commended. The second matter is the stout maintenance of the testimony to the long-suffering of God. Christ's continued expectancy, His waiting for the time of earth's blessing in the millennium, upheld amid taunts as to His coming again is commendable in the Philadelphians. Christ's patience is the answer to the continued allowance of the existence of evil and the prolongation of my age. I must firmly stand for this word of His patience if I am to account myself worthy to be numbered among them, "Kept from the hour of trial."

The corruption of the best thing is the worst of all corruptions. Woe to Laodicea!

MAY 14 To believe is to *act* as though a thing were so. Mere saying a thing is so is no proof of my believing it.

MAY 15 *Revelation 4* The throne is the first and greatest thing viewed in the entrance to heaven.

The throne *set* in heaven (v. 2)
One *seated* on the throne (v. 2)
Rainbow round the throne (v.3)
Thrones around the throne (v. 4)
Lightnings, voices, thunders from out the throne (v. 5)
Seven lamps of fire before the throne (v. 5)

Glass and crystal sea before the throne (v. 6)
Four creatures in midst and round about the throne (v. 6)
Glory given to occupant of the throne (vv. 9, 10)
Crowns cast before the throne (v. 10)

MAY 17   *Revelation 5*   Without tears the Revelation was not written and not without tears can it be understood (v. 4).

MAY 18   Took up and finished a hasty browsing of the life of William Farel, a reformer of note but not well known. It was three hours before I returned to the Scriptures and prayer. I trust I learned a lesson, for it took special concentration and considerable difficulty to begin to feel the power of the Word. Anything, good as it may be, put before my study of the true and living Word, becomes a snare, and I must assiduously avoid all such if the Word is to be my fresh meat every morning.

Last night I went for a walk around the hill. Found myself again dedicating my clay, asking for God's presence to be sensed more continually. Analyzed afresh and repudiated my base desire to *do* something for God in the sight of men, rather than to *be* something, though no great results were seen. The clouds scudding over the west hills seemed to speak to me, "What is your life? It is even as a vapor." I saw myself as a wisp of vapor being drawn upward from the vast ocean by the sun's great power and sent landward by the winds. The shedding of blessing upon earth must be as the rain, drawn up first by God, borne along by His Spirit, poured out by His own means and in His place, and running down to the sea again. "As water poured out." So my weakness shall be God's opportunity to refresh earth. I would that it should be as He has shown.

MAY 19   Much discouraged tonight as I thought over my past ten months with the younger folks in the assembly. My prayers of college days for Chuck, Tom, Berney, Rick, and Oscar have seemed futile because I failed to follow on in per-

sonal work with them. Strange feelings of futility and, somewhat, of frustration sensed as I spoke to Osk, Rich, Flo, Joan,
and Helen tonight. O great God of power, grant to them each
one the spirit of an overcomer.

MAY 22   Traveled to Spokane with Jordans.

MAY 23   Billings again.

MAY 24   *Genesis 1*   Noticed that God's creative work in the
first of Genesis is, to a large degree, a work of dividing—light
from dark, air from water, water from land, day from night,
and so on. So in all He does, He is most careful to draw fine
distinctions. And does not the perfecting of the new creation
consist in this very thing: learning how particular He is and
discovering the things He has separated? "Woe to them that
confuse good and evil, light and darkness, bitter and sweet"
(Isa. 5:20). "Love abounding in discernment, distinguishing
things that differ" (Phil. 1:9). "Rightly dividing . . ." (Heb.
4:12; 2 Tim. 2:15).

MAY 27   *2 Peter 3:8; Psalm 90*   I have been considering the
greatness of God this morning and am quite amazed that my
thoughts of Him have been so human heretofore. Particularly
am I impressed with the eternality of the Godhead. When
Peter says that one day is a thousand years to the Lord, he does
not mean that God is on a slower time scale than we are; that
is, that 365,000 years of man's time would equal 365 days or
one year of God's time. He means only that in relation to men,
He represents Himself as One with whom the passage of time
is of no import or effect. "A thousand years are in thy sight as
yesterday when it is past, and as a watch in the night" (Pss.
90:4).

The real significance is that God is timeless in His relations
with the universe. Eternality is not the length of passing
myriad of ages; it is above, beyond, and utterly unrelated to

measurement. This settles much talk of foreknowledge and election. God does not think a thing, then do it. He can think nothing but what is done instantaneously.

Further, there is no succession in His mind. To Him eternity is a *single act*, having no cycles, starts, or ends. What God has become in Christ, *God is* from everlasting. It is not that God stooped to become a man and decried to remain such in Christ. God created man in the image He Himself already sustained and this is meaningless unless I believe that God does not *become* anything. I AM. That settles all change. God can neither reverse, go beyond, or step beneath His eternal mode of being. Thus, none can frustrate His design, for His designing is part of His eternal doing and those are forever occurring because of His eternal being.

"Known unto God are all His works from the beginning" (Acts 15:18). But God can speak of beginning only because He has set time in the mind of man, much as Kant has described it, I suppose. I may not think timelessness because I am not so constituted in my thinking. No less can God think time or succession, except He be man to have it set in His mind. What God shall be, Lord of all, all in all, glorified of all, recognized for all, He already *is*; just as what He is now, He ever has been. There can be no *tense* to God, as succession is not known to Him. Why, then, these ravings about "foreknown," "elected," "given choice," "responsibility," and "sovereignty"? God's being determines His thinking and His acting, that they be timeless. God did not elect because He foreknew some man would believe. He elected (and glorified) because He in His one act of eternal being, is cognizant *at once* of the idea within Himself and its final accomplishment beyond all the working out of it. He begins, sustains, carries out, and fulfills His every decree—from *our* point of view. In Him, however, it is a single act, even as though all my life were a single breath.

MAY 28 *Genesis 1* Speaking daily on the radio here in Billings. Taking up the subjects as suggested in the first of Genesis concerning the work of God:

1. God speaks—His Word to us through Christ (John 12:50).
2. God creates—His work in us through the new birth (John, Peter, James). Begotten by the Spirit, the Word and the will of God.
3. God separates—holiness; definition between light and dark, heaven and earth, sea and land.

MAY 29 *Romans 1; Acts 17* Sunday morning: evidence of the resurrection. Eve: the resurrection—so what? Christ declared to be the Son of God (Rom. 1:3). Begotten to a living hope (1 Pet. 1:3). Christ declared to be the Judge (Acts 17:31). All this by the resurrection.

MAY 30 Not all disciples are Christians. Judas was disciple enough, but certainly not the "disciple indeed" that Christ insists we show ourselves to be by continuance in His Word. Nor are all Christians disciples. Theoretically they are, for one may not commit himself to a following of Christ without understanding that he is to follow on to know. But the "disciple indeed" of John 8 is a rare one today.

MAY 31 *Genesis 1* Each of the animal realms of creation are said to be created "after their kind." I assume this means that the species have a unique character and immobile limits which nothing may cross. They are peculiarly fixed in these classes of kind, having no developable potential toward any other or any different "kind." Man was not made according to his own kind; however, he is unique in that he, of all the creation, had a previous pattern for his nature. "Let us make man, in our image" (v. 26)—after the "kind" that God is. His limits, capacities, and potentialities are derived from nothing previous as concerns their "style" and mode of being. Hence they have fixed earthly destiny which may perish as the "kind" perish. Men may not do so because of the nature of their creation.

JUNE 1   Spoke of the worship of God at Mid-Week meeting [Wednesday Bible study] last night, taking John 4:19–24 as a basis. Mentioned how the Father seeks a certain sort of worshipers, those true worshipers. Worship in the Spirit includes:

1. Worship of God as a spirit, immaterial and invisible (idolatry).
2. Worship of God in my spirit, sincerely (1 Cor. 5:9, 10) (not formally only).
3. Worship of God by the Holy Spirit (Phil. 3:3). Priestly function controlled by His influence ($\lambda\alpha\tau\rho\epsilon\acute{u}\omega$).

In truth includes:

1. Matter of my speaking—what I say must correspond with what actually is. For this I must have learned the divine perfections to some degree.
2. Form of my worship: Function as a priest presenting offerings at the table of the Lord.

There is no crime in beauty. Genesis 2:9 says that God made trees "pleasant to the eyes," and "good for food." These two things became evil to Eve because she desired one thing further, to better herself in understanding sin ("to be desired to make me wise" [3:6]), or it actually turned out to be a lie— such "betterment" I mean. Sensations of pleasure, whether in the eyes or on the palate are not in themselves evil, neither are they blessings from the Creator. It is when their enjoyment takes on a covetous nature (Eve is not satisfied in her original innocent ignorance of evil), when they are desired and indulged in with a view to supposed bettering my state contrary to the command of God, that they form links with evil.

JUNE 2   Glen Ellyn. Drove with Les Tomkins and Bill Perry from Billings to here yesterday. Staying at Eileen's. Dinner tonight at Nelson's smorgasbord with the engaged Johnson brothers and Bud Young and wife; Roy Alley included. Long talk with Roy after on the will of God. Impressed with Ephesians 5:17: ". . . understanding what the will of the Lord is" and Romans 12:2: ". . . Proving what is the . . . will of God." Every moment I may be conscious and rejoice in the knowledge of God's will. Obedience to every command puts me on the track and keeps me there. Decisions, of course, must be made, but as in railroad, so in life; a block signal—a crisis—is lighted only where there is special need. I may not always be in sight of a "go" light, but sticking to the tracks will take me where the next one is. Understanding the will of the Lord is believing Him, that He will in all situations where I have obeyed, make that way His own way, effectual for eternity.

JUNE 3   *Exodus 14:31; 15:1*   The order of Exodus 14:31; 15:1 is instructive.

1. Israel saw the great work which Jehovah did.
2. The people feared Jehovah.
3. They believed in Jehovah.
4. Then sang Moses and the children of Israel:

> Jehovah is my strength.
> He it is empow'rs me
> Through journey's length.
>
> He only is my song:
> Music, might, and majesty
> To Him belong.
>
> Yea, become salvation too.
> He my soul protects and leads
> All trial through.
>
> Then sing exultantly
> None like Him deserving praise.
> My God is He.

Paul in 2 Corinthians 3, begins by defending his work done in Corinth. He needed no letters from elsewhere to commend him to that city, nor from that city to be commended elsewhere. In Corinth the saints themselves were witness to his work, that it was God appointed. Elsewhere, it was manifest that Paul's heart bore deeply engraved the marks of his work in Corinth. This was boldness to speak of it simply as though it was manifest in Paul; so he reminds them that it was God who filled him and made him sufficient for this work. Then he changes key to say that not only had God fitted him for ministry in their midst, but for the administration of a better covenant—which was "with glory." And that for these reasons. In form, the new covenant exceeded the older:

1. Letter slaying	1. Spirit-giving life
2. Written in stone	2. Written on hearts
3. Condemnation effected	3. Righteousness effected
4. Passed away	4. Remained

With the great confidence that God had granted such a surpassing administration to him, he defends his private boldness toward them and all men. If he could speak so with boldness when he first came, he could maintain that boldness now not as Moses, whose face fading in its glory, had to be covered so that the people might not see the diminishing character of his administration. That veil covered the weakness of the old economy, and so long as Jews insist on being under the old covenant, the veil must remain. When they return to the Lord (as Moses did, and uncovered his face) the veil will be removed.

But turning to the Lord means turning from the letter to the Spirit. "The Lord is the Spirit." That is, the "spiritual interpretation" of the Law, as Christ interpreted it in its types and metaphors of Himself, would set them at liberty. Not only me, as an administrator, Paul can say, but we all with unveiled faces, having the Spirit to show us the glory are transformed in likeness to what we behold. But where is this glory? Practically, where can one find the transforming glory? That is what all would want to know.

Ah, says Paul, this knowledge is God given, and this glory is in the face of Jesus Christ (4:6). "The Lord is the Spirit." And who is the Lord? ". . . Jesus Christ as Lord . . . ." The very God who said, "Let there be light," shines in hearts to give them the knowledge that the glory of God is seen only in the face—or person—of Jesus Christ.

JUNE 7 *Genesis*   Noting several firsts in the beginning of Genesis:

The first time God spoke: "Let there be light."
The first command of God to man: "Be fruitful and multiply."
The first question: "Yea, hath God said . . . ?"

"Woe to them! for they went in the way of Cain" (Jude 11). Certain men in the group to whom Jude wrote had turned the grace of God into loose living, denying the only Master and Lord, Jesus Christ. This was written for my day: For today I hear of men preaching that *grace* means freedom to live unrestrained lives apart from any standard of moral purity, declaring "we are not under law, we are under grace." Grace turned into ἀσέλγεια! Combined with this is the twentieth-century heresy that Christ is Savior only by right, Lord by "option" of the "believer." This is denial of the only Master and Lord, preaching only half of His person, declaring only partially the truth as it is in Jesus Christ must be preached with the full apprehension of who He is, the demanding Lord as well as the delivering Savior.

Jude calls this failure "the way of Cain." First John 3:12 shows that Cain's real failure was in the evil nature of his works, not in the form of his worship. Hebrews 11:4 stresses Abel's righteousness as seen in his offering. Genesis 4 is plain enough. "If thou doest not well, sin coucheth at the door; and unto thee shall be its desire; but do thou rule over it" (v. 7).

Here is a warning that Cain should have taken to heart. First, he disobeyed in the *nature* of his sacrifice, bringing the fruit of the cursed ground, rather than the slain lamb required. Unaccepted, he became angered. This is nothing other than saying, "God's standards are not unflinching. He requires a lamb, but what I have will do." Denial of the lordship of the Lord. *That* is disobedience which in any way makes pliable the requirement of God, for it makes God not God (this is Jude's charge, "ungodly"). From this comes sin lying in wait to snare the disobedient. But, comes the encouragement, "Rule thou over it."

JUNE 8   *Genesis 5, 6*   In developing a biblical terminology the Scriptures must be the guide. Here is an illustration of Bible psychology. Genesis 6:5: "Every imagination of the thoughts of his heart was . . . evil." The source of all ideas is the "heart," the man inside. The activity in which he is engaged is "thought," distinguishing the actor (heart) from action (thought), while the resulting idea is termed "imagination," distinguishing the motion of thought from its result.

Some excuse themselves from whole-hearted devotion to God because their family problems are weighty. Hear the testimony born to Enoch, my soul, "Enoch walked with God . . . and begat sons and daughters" (5:22), and Noah, "perfect *in his generations* . . ." (6:9). All that emanated from him—words, deeds, children, thoughts—"perfect!"

Evening   *Job 26; Revelation 2*   I see tonight that God's affairs in the universe are understandable in three steps: First, I see God's *work.* What God does is the first thing that presents itself to the human mind, whether in creation or atonement or in any of His multitudinous faithful works in the universe. I am first impressed with the fact that God does things in power. Job 26:7, 13: "He stretcheth the north over an empty place, hanging the earth upon nothing . . . by his Spirit the heavens are garnished." But God wants us only to marvel at the works and go behind them to His *ways.* "These are but the outskirts of his *ways*" (Job 26:14).

The wonder of His work should cause me next to consider *how* He does it. Yet even this is not the end. Moses saw God's *ways* where Israel only saw God's *works*, but God would have led further (Pss. 103:7; cf. Exod. 33:12–23). If His work tells me that He acts, His ways tell me how He acts; but His *worship* is the consideration of *why* He acts. For all God's work is done, not for man's benefit primarily, nor because God needs something to do to pass eternity with, but because He wants to reveal Himself. The end then of every act is His glory, that the creature should regard it and be awed before it.

Now, having gotten at the root and seeing that God Himself is the end and the purpose of all that is, I turn and find that the *way* to accomplish His purpose is in *His own* manner. And doing God's will (worship in action) in God's way I get God's work done in a much better way than I would have if I had only been amazed at the size of it and pitched in without seeing the end of it. Help me then, Lord God Most High, to consider well Thyself and Thy pattern before I make any attempt to effect Thy purpose. The Ephesians of Revelation 2 did work, perhaps in God's way, but they had lacked true worship—love for His person. A study of His person reveals His purpose; of His plan, reveals His pattern. His pattern makes for effective production.

JUNE 9 *Genesis 9:27–11:32*   "For all that Japheth be enlarged in his offspring he still dwells in the tents of Shem." The Gentile hordes of the western world find their frame of reference is Semitic. We dwell under Eastern light, governed by principles laid down in Jewish law, admittedly tracing our spiritual heritage to Moses and Jesus Christ. I mean this generally, not that we wholly conform to their ideals but in the broad sense of continuously harking to them we dwell "in the tents of Shem."

Jones Woods Beach with '49ers last night. Via Leslie's for breakfast this morning.

Significant names in the geneology of Shem are Eber (from which I assume comes the word *Hebrew*), Peleg, and Aram. Eber was living still when Abram was born, dying about the fortieth year of Abram's life, assuming Abram was born in Terah's seventieth year. He outlived some of his sons and would likely be reckoned the head of the patriarchal clan bearing his name. In the days of Peleg the earth was divided, referring (1) to the definite drop in life span from his day onward, and (2) the Babel incident. He died in Abram's thirty-eighth year. Genesis 11 implies that Terah was alive when Abram left Haran. Abram was born in Terah's seventieth year. He was seventy-five when he left Haran, making Terah one-hundred and forty-five years old, having fifty years of life after Abram left for the land of Canaan.

This is contradicted by Stephen in Acts 7:4 which says that Terah was dead when Abram left Haran. No one contradicted Stephen on the point, and the original will bear no other interpretation. I must assume then (1) an error in Stephen's understanding of the Hebrew text, (2) an error in the text itself, (3) an omission in the text of details surrounding the births of the three sons of Terah. I reject the first because: (a) the Jews let the remark pass; (b) the Holy Spirit does not use falsehood in convicting of the truth. I reject the second a priori. I find in the third an element of explanation. Genesis 11:26 names all three sons born in Terah's seventieth year. An impossibility through one wife apart from triplets which is not implied.

Terah may have begun bearing in a phenomenal manner in his old age (the others mentioned just before him have sons at twenty-nine to thirty-two years). Thus the beginning of Terah's productivity is set as a wonderful thing at his seventieth year. The three sons were then perhaps born over a period of fifty years; Abram being taken as a twenty-five-year-old to Haran in the one hundred forty-fifth year of Terah's life. For fifty years the command from Ur lay unobeyed in Abram's conscience.

JUNE 10, 11　*John 4*　Weekend at Milwaukee with the Mc-Cullys. Spoke on John 4:20–26 again with freedom. Needed word for me and seemed to be received by some—but worship is not taught from the pulpit. It must be learned in the heart.

JUNE 12　*Genesis 12*　Will be leaving from Wheaton for Oklahoma after commencement exercises. Bad dose of poison sumac from Jones Woods Beach get-together last Thursday. Seeking to take it as a discipline from the Lord.

Abraham was a slow learner. Commanded to leave his family, he took Lot—probably as a kindly gesture, but disobedience all the same. His leaving of the family to God is common among the called (cf. James, John, and Zebedee). And any disobedience soon leads to doubt and dallying. Famine drove Abraham from Beth-el to Egypt where compromise with truth brought him no good. He had to get back to Beth-el (place of fellowship) to be able to get rid of Lot. Meanwhile he prospered materially. Earthly blessing is no sign of heavenly favor. Behold how many wicked prosper. But I have heard believers say, "This must be of God, for see how I've prospered!" Little do we guess how much money Satan disposes to thus blind the citizens of heaven. Mark it, my soul!

Jim attended the course offered at the University of Oklahoma by the Summer Institute of Linguistics (Wycliffe Bible Translators). This is a ten-week session which prepares the student to reduce an unwritten language to writing.

JUNE 15 *Genesis 15; Revelation 2; Psalms 97:10; Ephesians 2:2* Norman, Oklahoma. Pondering the sign of the promise made to Abraham in Genesis 15. It may be that the three animals represent the divisions of the seed of the three patriarchs. Abraham divided into Ismael and Isaac; Isaac into Jacob and Esau; Jacob into Joseph and his brethren; while the two birds speak of Joseph's offspring, Ephraim and Manasseh. The birds of prey would fall upon the offspring of Abraham but should be driven off, then, if the figure be a fair one. The *furnace* and *torch* passing between the pieces speak of God's refining Israel in Egypt for *testimony* to His own Name. Note, Abraham believed the promise, *then* saw the sign.

Psalms 97:10: the Ephesians in the Apocalypse hated evil yet loved not Christ. This is not an uncommon condition where there is concern for outward form and little care for inward affection. But here is a word for those who love the Lord yet have somehow misapprehended that they must of necessity in such high loving do some hating. "O ye that love Jehovah, hate evil!" "Light is sown for the righteous" (v. 11)—not merely scattered before and upon them but *sown*, I think, in the sense that it is put secretly about and within them, so that it springs gradually up to lead them as their need arises. So also "gladness" in the next phrase springs unexpected to encourage along the path of the upright.

Ephesians 2:2: the walk of the unregenerate is according to the age of this world—meaning partially, I think, that a man without Christ has his roots only in his own times, and his fruits as well. He has nothing to tie him to eternity, nothing to link him vitally either to past centuries or future hopes. He is a man who has nothing beyond his own day. Whereas, the believer is in actual union with the great traditions of the true Church through the centuries and linked with a priceless norm-forming and wise-patterned heritage in the Hebrew people.

JUNE 16 *Genesis 14–17*   Genesis 14–17 give three separate names for the Godhead: *El Elyon, El Roi, El Shaddai*. The first is to teach Abraham sovereignty, dignity, and power.

> *El Elyon* indicates *position* (most high), dominion (posses-
> sion of heaven and earth and things on it)
> *El Roi* indicates *perception* (Thou seest), deliverance
> *El Shaddai* indicates *perfection* (be perfect), supply

God's sovereignty and dominion have dual effect upon the inhabitants of earth. Psalms 97:1: "Jehovah reigns; let the earth be glad; let the isles rejoice." Psalms 99:1: "Jehovah reigns; let the people tremble."

JUNE 17 *2 Peter 2:9*   Why did God not allow the populace of the cities of the plain to be carried away by Chedorlaomer's hosts? Certainly they deserved that. But hear Peter (2 Pet. 2:9). "The Lord knows how to . . . keeps the unjust until the day of judgment to be punished." A most peculiar idea, but how glorifying to the holiness of God!

JUNE 20 *Genesis 13:16; 15:5; 26:4; 28:14; Galatians 4* Abraham had two promises made to him in figure by the Lord. Genesis 13:16 makes his seed as the dust of the earth in number; 15:5 makes it as numerous as the stars of heaven. Isaac is promised the latter (26:4); Jacob, the former (28:14). These figures speak of two peoples, an earthly and a heavenly (cf. Galatians 4).

JUNE 22 *Genesis 31:3; 28:15* I see those matters of encouragement concerning Jacob: (1) the promise of God to do him good; (2) the presence of God (31:3; 28:15), (3) the persistence of Jacob. "I will not let thee go except thou bless me." Oh, for all these things this day, my Lord: confidence in Thy promise to perform all that Thou hast spoken to me of, the sense of Thy presence, and the desire to get blessing from Thee. Would that I had the "limp" of one who prevailed with thee!

JUNE 24 *2 Thessalonians 2:11* This is just such a day as it shall be when the Son of Man is revealed. Evidently, the removal of the bride will have little effect upon the thinking of the world. It may be that *the* lie of 2 Thessalonians 2:11 will be the son of perdition's explanation of where or why he has gone. Business, social affairs, domestic responsibility will be going on as they are today when His lightning shall split the heavens and the sword of His mouth cleave brother from brother in bed and neighbor from neighbor at the mill. There will be no arguments as to whether or not it is He. No discussions or panels will be convened as to the import of certain events and their implications. But suddenly with but slight warning shall the inhabitants of the earth know the Lord's Christ.

260   *The Journals of Jim Elliot*

John 12:20–43; 1 Peter 1, 4, 5   Suffering and glory—God's
way of Life. John 12:20–43 and 1 Peter 1, 4, 5 demonstrate
something of God's purpose in this.

1. Suffering and glory are shared:
   Suffering—Except a corn of wheat fall and die . . . if
   any would serve, let him follow" (John: 12:25, 26). "Inasmuch as ye are partakers of Christ's sufferings" (1
   Pet. 4:13). "Know . . . the fellowship of his sufferings"
   (Phil. 3:10). Glory—". . . him will the father honor"
   (John 12:26; 17:22). "A partaker of the glory about to be
   revealed" (1 Pet. 5:1).
2. Suffering and glory witnessed:
   Suffering—Galatians 3:1: ". . . before whose very
   eyes . . . ." First Peter 5:1: "Witness of the sufferings
   of Christ." Glory—John 17:24: "That they may behold
   my glory." First Peter 5:10: ". . . called unto eternal
   glory."
3. Suffering and glory order reversed by Satan:
   First Peter 1:11: "Sufferings and glory that should follow." John 12:24: ". . . if it die, it beareth much fruit."
4. Suffering and glory duration:
   Suffering—"a little while"; glory—"eternal" (1 Pet.
   5:10).

I shall not reign; I have not suffered.
Heard Art Mittler in Oklahoma City tonight speak on the
cities of refuge.

Kadesh: Holy place—a fount for the unclean
Shechem: Shoulder—a resting place for the weary
Hebron: Fellowship—a shelter for the homeless
Bezor: Stronghold—a refuge for the helpless
Yolan: Joy—a refuge for the tempted
All sunshine makes a desert: Arabic

Shared meeting with Art. Spoke on suffering and glory.

JUNE 29   *Genesis 46:34*   "For every shepherd is an abomination to the Egyptians." This may have reference to Hyksos rule in Egypt, but it seems to have typical significance. Egypt and the world have little care for those whose business is sheep tending. Association with slow and stupid sheep marks one as "simple" or poor. So in my day does the generation sneer at the poor shepherds of God's flock. Untrained, uncultured, and with little other ability, they concern themselves with the flock of God to the peril of their reputation. But what consideration is that to the one who has been himself guided, led, and provided for by that Great Shepherd of the sheep. Genesis 46:4: "Joseph shall put his hand upon thine eyes." Peculiar custom recorded for my encouragement. For I will upon entrance to my "Joseph's" country be enlightened by the touch of his finger. Further, God shall wipe away all tears from their eyes.

JULY 1   *Genesis 28:15*   Drove to Chicago from Wycliffe with Bill C. and Bob W. and Dot Lightrock and Irene D. (their fiancées) for Dave's wedding. Warned of the Lord by Genesis 49 concerning Reuben's loss of prestige because of his volatile nature. "Boiling over as water thou shall not have the pre-eminence" (49:4). My own volatility was manifest after the wedding and my loss of spiritual potency as well. Warned, I did not watch and fell into folly. Saw Betty again with joy and refreshment. The Lord is at work in her. She was faithful in rebuking me for my loss of dignity and manifest crudeness. I am most grateful to Thee for her, Lord Jesus. The Lord gave Genesis 28:15 as a "confidence verse" before making the trip. He means what He says!

JULY 4   Spent most of the day writing letters. At noon we sat with Dave Cooper who has worked among Quichua Indians in Ecuador. He mentioned casually the Tidmarsh abandonment of Shandia. Bill and Bob and I all seemed somewhat moved by what he said and came home to pray together. If God wants us there, we have presented ourselves to Him to pray three times daily for ten days concerning our next move—whether we should write Tidmarsh of our exercise. We will say nothing to each other and try to keep from influencing one another in this matter. July 15 we shall see what God has done in our hearts individually. Make my path sure, O Lord. Establish my go-ings. Send me when and where You will and manifest to all that Thou art my guide.

JULY 5   Billy and I had supper with Nida [Dr. Eugene Nida, then of the Summer Institute of Linguistics]. He describes the highland Quichuas as one of the neediest works he knows of. Says there are 800,000 with five missionaries—"only two worth shooting." Peoples oppressed by Romanism, patron system, drink, and vice.

JULY 6   Spent the evening with Dave Cooper who described the Quichua uplands as the neediest, roughest place in Ecuador. He has worked with Tidmarsh on the Shandia sta-tion, is burdened for the yet unreached Ecuadorians, Aucas, Cofanes, Sionas. Gave us sketch map of the area describing need.

JULY 8   These are days of vision for me—days wherein are revealed to me those great "oughts" which must be if Christ is to have glory. Partly they are revealed in what I see around me by way of departure from the Word of God in practice. Partly they are known in the reading of the Scripture as I see the ideal and its beauty in days past. Oh, what manner of men we *ought* to be in light of what shall soon be on us! What fervent prayer, what diligent witness, what intense concern ought to occupy us in the light of what is now on us! Lord, Thou hast spoken once and again to my soul. What ought to be can be—and I believe. Vindicate Thy Name, Thy Word, Thy pattern by ac-complishing these many "oughts" I see but afar off.

JULY 9   Spoke on Exodus 33:12–23 and John 26 on "show me thy ways"; "show me thy glory." God's work revealing His ways and leading to His worship. See entry for June 8.

JULY 10   Heard a word today from George Cowan [an executive of Wycliffe Bible Translators] in chapel that I liked. "I am just trying to deliver familiar truth from the oblivion of general acceptance." First letter (with Tweed! [cologne]) from Betts since April. Cheered by her spirit.

JULY 11   *Mark 9*   Stirred to confess carelessness and lack of concern in prayer after hearing Bill Patterson [of Scottish Plymouth Brethren] speak on Mark 9 in Oklahoma City. "Why could not we cast him out?" (v. 28). The causes of spiritual impotency seen in the chapter are obvious. Lack of faith (all things possible . . . O faithless generation), lack of prayer (this kind cometh not out but by prayer), lack of humility (argument regarding who is greatest), lack of love (he follows not us).

JULY 14   *Exodus 23*   "Righteousness— regardless." Thus it seems to me is the holiness of God expressed briefly in the Law. "Thou shalt not follow a multitude to do evil . . . neither shalt thou favor a poor man in his cause" (v. 2). Even if the power of the populace be persuasive, if it wrests justice, the mass must be repudiated. And if a man be wrong, his poverty shall not move to pity to work unrighteousness. Justice must be as unflinching as the face of God.

". . . And hate thine enemy" is not a quote from Leviticus 19:18. Love your neighbor is there, and it is exemplified in Exodus 23:4 that the enemy is to be loved. Christ may have been quoting traditional interpretation when He added this in Matthew 5:43.

I asked for some word from God ten days ago which would encourage me in going to Ecuador. It came this morning in an unexpected place. I was reading casually in Exodus 23 (above notes) when verses 20 and 21 came out vividly. "Behold, I send an angel before thee, to keep thee by the way, and to bring thee into the place which I have prepared. Take heed before him . . . ." Coming as it did (plainly out of context) with such preceding feelings and such simple believing for some promise, I take this as leading from God that I should write Tidmarsh telling him that I should come to Ecuador in the will of God.

JULY 15   Bill and I wrote Tidmarsh and Portland and Wheaton elders regarding exercise concerning Shandia. God is sending me there.

JULY 17   Never noted before today the faith Moses was called upon to exercise when God told him to build with gold, silver, and precious stones while as yet he possessed none of them. So with me, here in the mount of preparatory vision, see that God would have a quality of work I do not have means now to produce. But I believe, Lord, that the pattern showed shall be followed by provision supplied, though now I see none of it.

JULY 18 *Exodus 27*   God, in describing the tabernacle, began at the ark and mercy seat and proceeded outward to the linen hangings about the court. Man, entering, must come from the opposite direction. Men cannot appreciate the mercy seat until they have understood the righteousness symbolized in the fine-twined linen, the judgment of the brazen altar, the forgiveness of the laver. It is not intended that his understanding should stop with these externals, however. He wants men to appreciate fully His covenant, grace, presence, holiness—all seen in the ark—but most of all Himself there in the comparative emptiness of the Holy of Holies.

JULY 20 *Exodus 28*   Exodus 28 says that the high priest bore upon him three separate burdens: (1) the names of the children of Israel upon his shoulders for a memorial (v. 12); (2) the judgment of the children of Israel upon his heart continually (v. 30); (3) the iniquity of the holy things offered by Israel (v. 38). The significance of these I do not now thoroughly see, but sense that somehow they must now be applied to Christ. The affections (heart), strength (shoulders), and thoughts (forehead) were involved in this bearing things before God in the sanctuary, broadly represented by the soul, body, and spirit. What Christ's present priestly ministry is to His people is symbolized here. Bearing their names, He is their official representative in the sanctuary above. Bearing their judgment, He is their perfect substitute there. And bearing the iniquity of the things hallowed by their offering them to God, He is their perfecting mediator before God.

JULY 21 *Exodus 32*   The real sin of Israel below the mount was that they forgot just *who* led them out of Egypt (vv. 1, 4). Thinking that the glory of the incorruptible God who really led them out (29:46) could be debased to representation as the man Moses, it was easy to make the next step of representing their god as a calf. God being out of sight, Moses was their god; and Moses being out of sight, the molten calf becomes their god.

Moses' intercession was of such potential that God said of him (before he pleaded one word!), *"Let me alone,* that my wrath might wax hot" (v. 10). Notice, too, that Moses argued, not from the people's standpoint in this prayer, but from the honor of God's Name before the Egyptians and from the promise of God (vv. 11–14).

JULY 23   Preached on the sanctuary of God. God in the midst of His people (Eph. 2:19–22). "The presence."

JULY 25   Heard Dr. E. A. Nida say some things in chapel today that stirred me much and convinced me more in the idea that our present need is for a miraculous Christianity. Some quotes of value:

A man unwilling to go to the field is unfit to stay in the homeland.
Not called, but compelled.
In the eighteenth century, philosophy challenged Christianity.
In the nineteenth century science challenged Christianity.

In the twentieth century history challenged Christianity.
Communists are confident of success and willing to pay
the price.

JULY 30   Preached in Okie City Chapel on Melchizedek,
Genesis 14, Psalm 110, and Hebrews 7. Felt helped of God. Bill
Reyburn had an emergency appendectomy. Spent afternoon
and evening with him. Reading in Leviticus. Difficult to understand typology.

AUGUST 1   *Acts 9*   It is good to think of the first days of the
Church on earth when Christianity was not called merely a
religion, or thought of only as a code of doctrine, but regarded
as a "way" (v. 2). Those believers had a manner, carriage,
observable direction that so-called Christians today do not
have. For a "way" is a display of patterned behavior—and
what a display! Nothing any had was his own; all in *one* place
with one accord while a spirit of love, responsibility, and conviction of truth possessed the whole. God send us *one* of those
days, to vindicate Thy truth, glorify Thy Name, dispense the
knowledge of Thy Son.

AUGUST 3   *1 Corinthians 11*   Doctor Pike [Dr. Kenneth L.
Pike, an executive of Wycliffe Bible Translators] lectured us in
chapel yesterday about culture pattern and its force in the believer's manner of living. "Nature," he says in 1 Corinthians
11:14 can be interpreted as *culture* and, therefore, where culture does not agree with the Pauline teaching as it did in
Corinth by happenstance, the argument of Paul from "nature"
is not valid, and it is all right to unveil the women.

However, he fails to see that this supporting evidence from
the nature of the Corinthians (whether that is "culture" or
innate a priori sense) is only substantive, not basic. The true
reason for a man's having short hair and a woman's long is in
the *order* which God has established in the universe of His
headship through Christ and the man's over the woman which
the Church is to demonstrate to angels. The passage opened up

so clearly today that I think I will crystallize my thinking on it by setting down a commentary:

In verse 2 "the traditions" refer specifically to the things Paul had brought to Corinth to deliver to them, here described as the place of the woman demonstrated in her coverings (vv. 2–16), and the Lord's Supper (vv. 17–34). Doubtless there were other traditions (2 Thess. 2:15; 3:6) but here Paul enters upon discussion of Church order, and it is significant that he begins with the symbolism of tactical underheadship which the Church in *traditions* was to manifest to all the universe. This implies that the wearing of veils in company with a given group was *not* in the culture pattern of the Corinthians until Paul instituted it as a tradition. It was not the *coverings* principle that the Corinthians knew "by nature," but the having long hair for a woman, shaved heads being shameful to them (v. 6).

This is generally true in American culture. Shaven men we see daily with but one and a half inches or so of hair on them, and regard it as quite fitting. But women seldom if ever shave their heads or crop them. This argument about how long hair should be to be long is irrational. No woman wears her hair as short as most men, and few men wear their hair as long as most women. While this is true in America, it is not true in New Guinea, where the men have long queues and the women crop their hair. How explain it? Was Paul wrong in saying *nature* teaches all men so? But he does not say nature teaches all men so. Having stated his principles of the woman being given hair for glory, he happens to find that the general feeling of the Corinthians supports these principles and substantiates his tradition by that attitude in them. Doubtless he would have written to New Guinea believers the same tradition of coverings and hair lengths, but would not have included the mention of their natural feeling. If nature may support a scriptural, eternal verity, argue from nature. If somehow men do contrary to the natural use originally intended (as the changing of a woman's function in Romans 1:26, 27), then argue against "nature." Nature is not the determiner, but it may be the supporter of the truth of God.

"The head" idea is not uncommon in Pauline writings. Colossians 2:18, 19 speaks of those, out of preference to angels, disregarding the head. Actually the head is to be "held" for the sake of angels (1 Cor. 11:10). A man with his physical head covered dishonors Christ by figuratively covering his "real" Head. A woman dishonors Christ in not covering her head (man), since, in symbol, her hair represents the glory of her head (man), and when she speaks to God or man before others about eternal things, she must declare by her covering (sign of authority) that she recognizes (1) her own subjection to her head, man; (2) the subjection of man to his head (Christ); (3) the subjection of Christ to God.

In places where it is no shame for a woman to be shaved or shorn, this principle would have to be carefully delineated and over a long period of time pressed upon the Christian community. When it did become natural feeling for them, then the argument from nature would be understood. Verse 6 implies conversely that where it is no shame for a woman to be shorn, she should shave her head to do away with what angels see as "her glory." Man (the woman's head) must somehow be shown in symbol to be in subjection, shorn of glory. If hair in some culture is a glory to a woman, then the hair must be covered. If it is no shame for a woman to be shorn, then the hair must be shorn in demonstration of the principle of over-headship.

Verse 7: "Man the image and glory of God." Man is but a symbol of what exists in the Godhead. God, the Head, Christ, the Body, doing what the Head directs is symbolized in man whose head directs his body (ideally). Woman is peculiarly more directed by her feelings, her body, her heart, than by her head. Man the image of God should declare by an uncovered head the glory (independence, sovereignty, insubjection, autonomy, self-reliance, and so on) of God. God, the Head, is covered by none, but controlling Christ. Man, the image of God, is covered by nothing, controlling the woman. Woman, the glory of man, is covered, controlled by man, as man should be by Christ, as Christ *is* by God. Woman has her source in man and her existence on man's account. "For this cause ought the woman to have authority on her head, because of the angels" (v. 10). But the one is not independent of the other, just as Christ is not independent of God.

AUGUST 6   Spoke in Bible class on the twentieth of Exodus, what the high priest bears, on his shoulders, on his heart, on his forehead.
Evening, Psalms 110:1:

Luke 20: My Lord.
Acts 2: My right hand.
1 Corinthians 15:25: *Until* I make . . . .
Hebrews 1:13: *I* make enemies.
Hebrews 10:12: Sit down.

AUGUST 7   Received word today from brothers Gill and Doane [leading brethren of the Portland assembly] that I should feel the assembly is behind me 100 percent in my going to Ecuador. God has set His seal.

AUGUST 9 *Acts 27*   I have just heard Cameron Townsend [one of the founders of Wycliffe] tell of God's raising up the Wycliffe Translators work. From Acts 27:22, 31 he showed how Paul's faith in God coincided with his insistence on man's obedience and action. In the first verse, Paul declares that every man will be saved; in the other, he insists that the men stay aboard or they will perish. From this, Townsend deduced that we must link vision and action, prayer and policy, spirit and flesh. The Word stirred me much. God just now gave me faith to ask for another young man to go with Bill and me. Perhaps not this fall, but soon, to join ranks in the lowlands of eastern Ecuador. There we must learn: (1) Spanish and Quichua, (2) each other, (3) the jungle and independence, (4) God and God's way of approach to the highland Quichua. From thence, by His great hand, we must move to the Ecuadorean highlands with several young Indians each and begin work among the 800,000 highlanders. If God tarries, the na-

tives must be taught to spread southward with the message of
the reigning Christ, establishing New Testament groups as
they go. Thence the Word must go south into Peru and Bolivia.
The Quichuas must be reached for God! Enough for policy.
Now for prayer and practice.

AUGUST 15 *Leviticus 18–22*   There are no stipulations in
Leviticus about the character of the man who does the offering.
But all other things that have to do with the sacrifice are carefully insisted upon, that they are holy. First the thing sacrificed. It could have nothing superfluous nor anything which
lacked. It must be a male without blemish, having all its parts.
Otherwise it would not be accepted for the offer. "It shall be
perfect to be accepted" (22:21). Then, too, the priest must be
hallowed, having no uncleanness, or associated with anything
unclean, or lacking any of his parts, or having anything superfluous.

These two things are insisted upon because of the nature of
the *object* of their offering, "I am Jehovah." This phrase repeated no less than forty times in chapters 18–22. He is the
sanctifier of all that is hallowed in the service of the tabernacle.
It is His nature, not His arbitrary commands, that insists upon
the holiness of those things and men which are associated with
His worship. This is not so of other religions. How well Christ
answered this insistence, since He offered *Himself*, perfection
presenting perfection in the offering of the Son of God. Teach
me holiness, Jehovah God.

> Depart from me, ye rivals of my God.
>   ABRAHAM BOOTH

AUGUST 24 *Acts 13*   This is the last night of schoolwork at
Camp Wycliffe. Morphology-Syntax test tomorrow morning
and that concludes a full summer. Never have I known one to
pass so quickly. I feel now that the Lord must still teach me the
old lessons of personal discipline, temperance in eating, sleeping, and less fruitless conversation. Bill and I spent too much

time together, I think. We should rather have concentrated on getting to know others more intimately, so that now we would have built a sense of prayer responsibility into others. But it is gone, and I must save this observation for other days of practice. Lord, grant that I will not forget what You have taught me by this failure. And restore, restore in coming weeks, those co-workers in prayer I feel that I did not gain here as I ought.

Noted two words in Acts 13 which are helpful as respects the work of God. Acts 13:2: λειτουργέω, the word basically means "to work publicly" and is peculiarly linked here with τῷ κυρίῳ. The public ministry of the prophets and teachers was not for the public's sake primarily but "unto the Lord." This is significant because it shows the true attitude of New Testament believers toward preaching. It was a service *for God* to men, not for men by God's goodness, at least basically not that. Two phases of their ministry is obvious: public and private— *fasting*. Perhaps the present fact of this in my own life has affected the Spirit's words in quenching His voice to the group, I mean. N.B. λειτουργέω also means serve at one's own expense.

In Acts 13:2 the word προσκαλέω is one which should affect my attitude toward the work. The Spirit said to the group, "Separate to *me* . . . ." And προσκαλέω is fitly used, since it means "to summon." See verse 7 where Sergius summons Paul and Silas, using the same term. But to what was the summons? To the work? No. In respect to the work they were summoned to the *person*. Here is the cause for my recent dullness in devotion and Bible study. I have been thinking overmuch of my summons to the work and disregarding the primary, essential and basic summons to the Spirit. Forgive, Father, and restore the Dove.

AUGUST 28 *Numbers 11* Went with Carleton Jones yesterday to Henryetta, Oklahoma. Met the Bill Thomasons, Laurence Londons, Porter Hursts, Jim Bryce, Buck and Essie. Precious breaking of bread in the dining room of London's little place at Shulter. Ministered in the evening at Ryal Schoolhouse on "The Man with All Power": power to forgive sins (Mark 2:1–10); power over life, death, and hell (Luke 12:5), "keys of death and Hades" (Rev. 1:18), "Prince of life" (Acts 3:15); power to execute judgment (John 5:20–30). Felt freedom in the preaching, and there were unsaved, but none seemed to understand. Darkness is hard to penetrate. Perhaps I am expecting men to leap to life when I should be patient to see them swell slowly to birth.

Numbers 11:23: "Is Jehovah's hand waxed short? now shalt thou see whether my Word shall come to pass unto thee or not." Wondering just now why the Lord led Bill and me to stay here at Norman. Nothing much seems to have come up by way of ministry for the next two weeks, but the above verse gives me confidence this morning. I expect to see thee *proving* that good and acceptable and perfect will of thine, Lord.

AUGUST 29   *Numbers 14*   God's power is not only seen in the working of His mighty acts, but also in the restraining of His punishments (v. 17). Moses' prayer is that the *power* of God may be great. And when he begins to elucidate, he describes the greatness of Jehovah's power in its restraint of the wholesale slaying of Israel. So God's *patience* is His *power* over Himself. Great is that God who, having all power, yet keeps all power subject to Himself.

Numbers 15:32–41   Having made arrangements for the unwitting sin of Israel and the sin done with a "high hand" in disregard for the commandments of the Lord, the Lord illustrates with the death of one who sins after the latter manner. The man gathering sticks on the Sabbath does so in flagrant unconcern for the spoken edicts of God. He is cut off from the congregation in accordance with verse 31. But to remedy unwitting sin, God commands borders of blue for the garments of Israel. When a man bent his knees to work, as to pick up sticks, for instance, he would see the blue hem and be reminded that something from heaven, the commandments of Jehovah, was incumbent upon him. This is in order that they should "not follow their own heart and their own eyes" (v. 39) but heed the perfect standard of God's revelation. Grant me these remembrancers when my head drops to earth, Holy Spirit of God. Cause me to reflect on that world while engaged practically in this one.

SEPTEMBER 1   *2 Peter 2:15; Jude 11; Revelation 2:14; Numbers 23*   Balaam, son of Beor—2 Peter 2:15: "Forsaking the right way they went astray, having followed the *way of Balaam* the son of Beor, who loved the hire of wrong-doing; but he was rebuked for his own transgression: a dumb ass spake with a man's voice and stayed the madness of the prophet." Jude 11: "They ran riotously in the *error of Balaam* for hire." Revelation 2:14: "I have against thee; thou hast some who hold the *teaching of Balaam* who taught Balak to cast a stumbling block before the children of Israel, to eat things sacrificed to idols, and to commit fornication."

Balaam's sin was in his love of hire, primarily. When God gave him liberty to go he ran "headlong" (Num. 22:32, margin), without telling the princes of Midian the stipulation of his going. Thrice the angel of the Lord turned him aside, once in a field, once in crushing his foot, once in halting his ass altogether. Balaam's impatience at these delays displays where his heart is set—on the reward of wrongdoing. Piously, he says he cannot go beyond the word of Jehovah, but thrice he divines to see if Jehovah might not change His purpose. Balak spoke true when he said that the Lord held him back from honor. Certainly Balaam did not hold himself back, for he would have gladly cursed Israel for the reward.

Covetousness, then, will blind a prophet. Perverse haste will crush a prophet's foot. These failing to bring reproach upon Israel, Balaam gave instruction in religious syncretism, and Israel fell in the matter of Baal-Peor. Where the enemy could not curse, he confused, and Israel was yoked with Moab in its idolatry. God grant to me the spirit of Phinehas, the man who was jealous with God's jealousy and stayed the plague by his zeal for purity in the matter of Cozbi.

Numbers 23:19:

God is not a man, that he should lie, Neither the son of man, that he should repent: Hath he said and will he not do it? Or hath he spoken and will he not make it good?

For consideration: the unwritten wars of the Lord (Numbers 21:14).

SEPTEMBER 4   Weekend in Oklahoma City: Friday with Peggy and Warren Bennet; Saturday, Turner Falls, night, Ralph and Dessa Burrs; Sunday night, Jim and Lela Nelson. Ministered Lord's day morning on "The Father" and "The Worship of God" from John 4.

Every recorded prayer of Christ's is addressed to the Father except the one which began, "My God, why . . . ?"

Matthew 6:9: "Our Father, who art in heaven . . . ."
Matthew 11:25; Luke 10:21–24: "I thank thee, Father, Lord of heaven and earth."
Matthew 26:39: "My Father, if it be possible . . . ."
Luke 23:46: "Father, into thy hands I commend my spirit."
John 11:41: "Father, I thank thee that thou hearest me."
John 17:1, 5, 11, 21, 24, 25: "Holy Father . . . righteous Father."

SEPTEMBER 6 *Numbers 27*   Bill and I were much exercised last night about Huntington, Indiana, where his brother-in-law was recently saved and his sister restored. We had asked before that an assembly be started there, but now it seems there are several souls ripe for gathering.

The Lord spoke to me from Numbers 27:12–19 where Moses, being warned of his departure, prayed: "Let the Lord, the God of the spirits of all flesh, appoint a man over the congregation, who may go out before them and who may come in before them, and who may lead them out, and bring them in; *that the congregation of Jehovah be not as sheep which have no shepherd.*" (vv. 16, 17).

It looks as if God is not going to let us lead our own people into the flowing land; we are departing to another place, as was Moses. But here is an ungathered congregation, an uncemented heap of unorganized stones, a flock without shepherd. The Lord provided Joshua for Moses—but where have we a Joshua? We could hope Bob Weeber were sufficiently persuaded of God concerning the New Testament church that we could send him there, but he is not yet gripped of the truth, I fear. Others we have thought of are "scheduled" for such a long time in advance that none would be free. But God cannot leave them shepherdless! Lord, send one who can "lead them out" of all the forms of Christendom and "bring them in" to the clear light of being gathered to Christ.

Principles of guidance: (1) never allow plans to be so "scheduled" that you find it difficult to respond to the Spirit's working. Let your walk be flexible; (2) work where God is working. Don't hammer at unprepared soil when there is ready ground nearby.

SEPTEMBER 7   *Psalms 31; 139*   These are waiting days for Bill and me. We had hoped by now to have secured passport and begun work on collecting supplies, but God has had other things in mind. We have worked when the opportunity came, waiting for word from Wheaton regarding commendation [a term used by Plymouth Brethren to denote their consent to a member's becoming a missionary] for many weeks. Tomorrow John Massey returns, and we must leave his apartment, but where should we go? The Lord definitely led Bill away from O.C.U. [Oklahoma City University] yesterday when he went there to enroll. Norman is a good place to work but finding a place to live and cook is not easy. Psalms 31:15 was a blessing: "My times are in thy hands." Psalms 139:16: "In thy book they were all written, even the *days that were ordained for me.*" "Ordained days" then, whether spent in waiting, working, or whatever. We have asked guidance, been obedient where we understood what was to be done, and now wait word for the next step.

As further proof that fullness of the Spirit is fullness of the Word, witness those men who are said to be filled with the Spirit and then their speech is quoted.

Zacharias (Luke 1:67–79): Allusions (in quotes) to at least ten Old Testament passages.

The Baptist (Isa. 40:3ff.).

Christ (Luke 4:18, 19): Answers Satan, addresses synagogue from Old Testament.

Peter at Pentecost (Acts 2:14–36): Three long quotes from prophets.

Peter on trial (Acts 4:8–12): Psalms 118:22.

Stephen (Acts 7:1–53): Sermon of approximately 900 words—350 are quoted from Septuagint. More than one third Scripture.

Paul (Acts 13:10): quotes Hosea 14:9 in rebuking Elymas.

Exception: Elizabeth in Luke 1:41, 42.

SEPTEMBER 8   Will be going to Goldsby's to sleep tonight. Still no word from Wheaton. Bill thinks he should endeavor to exert faith in God to seek commendation from Oklahoma City [the Plymouth Brethren Assembly there]. Lord, let me know the ground between unbelief and brave presumption (Deut. 1:32, 43).

SEPTEMBER 10   Preached on John 17 in Bible class at Oklahoma City. "Now the son of man *should* be glorified."

Father, *glorify* thy name.

I have *glorified* it and will *glorify* it again.

Isaiah said this because he saw his *glory*.

They loved the *glory* of men rather than that which is of God.

Evening.   Three things God cannot do:

Titus 1:2: Cannot lie.

2 Timothy 2:13: Cannot deny himself.

Habakkuk 1:13: Cannot look upon iniquity.

SEPTEMBER 11 *Exodus 20; Deuteronomy 5*   In Exodus 20:11 the Israelites learned that the sabbath was kept because God had rested thereon after six days of labor. But in Deuteronomy

5:15 they are told another reason: "Remember that you were slaves in Egypt." God had given them leisure from taskwork they could not bear. So the rest of God is viewed first from His aspect, then from ours. His labor ended, so ours, too, has ceased.

SEPTEMBER 17 *Genesis 1*   Heard John Massey on "Man, the Creation of God for His Glory." Blessed by the word. He mentioned the threefold use of *create* in Genesis 1. The great gaps of the evolutionary theory are filled by this word.

1. The great unexplainable first cause: "God created heaven and earth."
2. The gap between plant and animal life.
3. The gap between lower animals and man.

Stirred to believe God again for a genuine work of His Spirit in the assembly. Praying for an assembly in Norman and on the northwest side of town in the City.

SEPTEMBER 21 *Deuteronomy 20*   Often I've heard it insisted that because war was allowed in the Old Testament, Christians had an okay to fight. But what of aggressive war? In Deuteronomy 20:10–18 the Israelites are instructed in besieging a city far off from them. If war is allowable, then so is aggression. Few of the Christian militarists for defensive reasons will follow here, I doubt. The situation is only explicable on the basis that war is valid for *nations,* and as a nation, Israel had the privilege of making war. But since the Church and the believer do not constitute a nation (other than a holy one, with no boundaries, or organized heads) war of any sort, in defense against evil or in aggression for good, is not allowable.

SEPTEMBER 22 *Deuteronomy 22–23*   Observations on the Law. Deuteronomy 22:5: Man's apparel was not to be worn by women and vice versa. But it is wrongly understood if applied to present-day Christian behavior. Else I am bound to other laws such as wearing skirt garments with fringes (22:12). I may not honestly apply the laws of Israel in defense of some pattern I might like to see observed in this present culture. It is invalid to choose one above another; either I am free from ordinances which were Israel's or I am not free, and he that would keep one part is responsible for all.

Deuteronomy 23:3: I have often heard it said that Ruth should not have entered the assembly of Israel because she was a Moabite, but the law required only ten generations from the possession of the land until a Moabite could be admitted. From 1400 B.C. to the time of David's grandfather Boaz might have been just about precisely that length of time. The law was then fulfilled in her case. (Corrected by Nehemiah 13:1, December 28, 1950.)

Deuteronomy 23:18: A sodomite is called a dog. It may be that this hints at the later idea of Scripture, "Gentile dogs"—whose sex perversion is well known, particularly among the Greeks.

SEPTEMBER 24   Maxims:

1. Answer to the Rudder, or answer to the rocks.
2. Wherever you are, be *all* there. Live to the hilt every situation you believe to be the will of God.
3. Determination, not desire, determines destiny.

Weekend at El Har, Young Life leadership camp. Met Bob McLaren, Dean Nelson, Bill Poston at Dallas Seminary.

SEPTEMBER 25   He who maketh Ease his god, Sufficiency his altar, Pleasure his priest, and Time his offering knows not what man is born for.

SEPTEMBER 27   Levi was not chosen arbitrarily for the office of caretaker to the holy things. From the beginning, he is seen as unique in Israel. His name means "joined," as Leah hoped for a knitting between herself and Jacob at his birth. Born to unite, he lived to divide and make distinctions. It was he and Simeon (Gen. 34) who slew Hamor and Shechem in righteous vengeance for Dinah's defilement. Of them Jacob said their anger was fierce, cruel, and that they should be *divided* in Israel. Exodus 32:27–29 shows Levi's passion for holiness, and Deuteronomy 33:9–11 commends him for that show of righteous indignation and relates his work in the religious matters with it. Who shall find his inheritance in the Lord, who instruct others in His ways? That man who binds himself to all compromise with sin and makes righteousness his passion. Would I were as Levi, Lord, so given over utterly to the maintenance of right.

SEPTEMBER 28 *Joshua 3* At the Jordan crossing, the ark of the covenant served where the rod of judgment did at the Red Sea. At the Red Sea it was deliverance *from* Egypt; at Jordan it was preservation unto Canaan. In neither case was it the goodness of Israel that procured the working of God. At Jordan each man was not judged by his merits as he passed over, rather the ark stood in the river bottom, and it was the *covenant* sign which held back the waters. One man among them may have been rebellious or a murmurer, but God respected His covenant, not the state of Israel. Happy that people who know a God that "keepeth covenant." For with believers as with Israel, God acts in accordance with the set of His purpose, not with the state of His people. As long as the ark remained in the river bed, the people were safe, preserved from *flood waters* (v. 15).

SEPTEMBER 29 Word came from Ed McCully today regarding his exercise before the Lord to quit school and begin looking for open doors for a sold-out life. How I praised God to hear! Even wept as I read of the Lord's dealings, for my desire for him and the spiritual exercise of his gifts has been much enlarged. Now I wonder if he may not be the man God would send with Bill and me to Ecuador. I have prayed for one more for the work and perhaps God will answer thus. Grateful if so, Lord, very grateful.

OCTOBER 5   *Joshua 9*   There is danger in success. Joshua's
favor with the people, his leading them over Jordan, his razing
of Jericho and, after sin had been put away in the matter of
Achan, his conquest of Ai. It was then that the Hivites of
Gibeon "did work wilily" (v. 4), and Joshua was befooled by
them and the plausibility of their case. His confidence in what
seemed robbed him of his sense of dependence on God, and he
forgot to ask counsel at the mouth of the Lord (v. 14). Consequently he overstepped God's plan and bound his future
liberty by his own mouth and oaths. Lord of Joshua's battles,
let me learn this lesson in these days, for my advance this past
three months has been rapid and successful because of the
counsel. Grant me to outwit him who works wilily with plausible stories by hearing the words of Thy mouth.

OCTOBER 7   I have just come from the O.U. [Oklahoma Uni-
versity] versus Texas A&M football game, one of the best, I
suppose, I shall ever see. A&M led out, and the score record
read 7–0, 7–7, 14–7, 14–14, 21–14, 21–21, 28–21 until the third
quarter. Then O.U. failed the conversion which put the score
at 28–27 with 1:55 to go. Within one minute of the end of the
game, O.U. produced a touchdown, setting the final score at
28–34. Crowd reaction was interesting to watch.

Ah, what will it be when, not 40,000 but myriad people rivet
their excited attentions upon the Son of God. No need for
cheerleaders and coaxing, no need for telling people to stand,
for all shall mourn over Him, bowing in one stroke to His
sway. Wonderful day! O Jesus, Master and Center and End of
all, how long before that glory is Thine which has so long
waited Thee. Now there is no thought of Thee among men,
then there shall be thought for nothing else. Now other men
are praised, then none shall care for any other's merits. Hasten, hasten, Glory of the Heavens, take Thy crown, subdue
Thy Kingdoms, enthrall Thy creatures.

OCTOBER 8   Ponca City and Guthrie with M. W. Gibbs.
Badly in need of a shakedown and some new life. How long
will you tolerate such mean things to be called by your name,

Lord God? Oh, that You would bow the heavens and come down and rouse your people to life and power!

Spoke on the evidences of resurrection, Psalm 95 and Hebrews 3, the apostle and high priest, at Ponca. Christ Jesus:

Apostle	**High Priest**
Sent from God to men	Gone from men to God
To represent God as He is	To represent man as he is
for the Father (John 17:4–8)	for the sons (Heb. 2)
to preach	to plead
to shed blood	to show blood

At Guthrie last week I preached on "The Just Living by Faith" from Habakkuk 2; Romans 1; Galatians 3; Hebrews 10, and on the faithful witness of the Apocalypse and John's Gospel. Today on Hebrews 3. My works, my ways, my wrath, my rest.

OCTOBER 15 [Bill] Patterson meetings began in the City. Went with Graw to tiny Baptist church near Noble. Patterson spoke of 1 Corinthians 5 this morning:

   I. Death—a past condition
     A. In trespasses and sins ("Ephesian orgies")
     B. In pleasure ("she . . . is dead while living")
     C. In religion ("thou hast a name to live, but art dead")
   II. Life—a present opportunity ("live unto Him")
  III. Love—a potent incentive.

I spoke in the breaking of the bread on "I am my beloved's," three times in the Song of Songs.

Tremendously stimulating talk with Graw on the recent changes in physics: the theological implications of the intimate relation of space and time; the overthrow of the indestructibility of matter and energy; the frame of thinking now in vogue that light and matter are not respectively ray and particle but that either is both at the same time—all these somehow let us in on secrets of the Most High, He who is at once seen and invisible. Mass *is* energy, as are heat and light. *Immobility* is in motion. I must hear more of this.

OCTOBER 18 *Judges 6*   Considered again the story of Gideon, the men who forced Baal to contend for himself. What a strange mixture of valor and cowardice this man is. His faith must be bolstered thrice by signs and once by a dream. But Jehovah shows no discouragement with him. God had set Himself to overthrow Midian and none, not even His chosen leader, would stay His purpose. Gideon's work began in calling his own village from idolatry, but ended in snaring all Israel with the ephod in Ophrah. His "might" was his dissatisfaction with surrounding conditions (vv. 13, 14) and desire to see God's work. His army, diminished from 32,000 to 300, left no room for self-trust and frightened Midian with trumpets, shouts, and torches, not with swords. Their valor was seen in endurance ("faint, yet pursuing" [8:4]), not in the initial charge.

Evening.   Patterson's meetings started Sunday in the City with no evidence of a real breaking for sin on the part of us saints. He is ministering this week on Leviticus 1—the burnt offering:

   I. The offering
      A. Financially: bull, sheep, goat, dove.
      B. Typically: strength, submission, readiness, tenderness.
      C. Temperamentally
         1. Choleric (passionate bull)
         2. Phlegmatic (dispassionate sheep)
         3. Enthusiastic (eager goat)
         4. Melancholy (brooding dove)
  II. The order—well-ordered life of Christ
 III. The offerer.

I am sorry that the word he preaches, though good, is cold and worn through much preaching, try as he does to make it live and dramatic. O Lord, refresh the minister of Thine to an apprehension of the reality of the truth he teaches! Let not habit and form possess him, Lord. Move him to the fullness of the Spirit that the believers be refreshed. For Thy *Name's* sake!

I leave, God willing, tomorrow for Wheaton, though I cannot now see why. Things are so needy here. The meetings require much, much more prayer than we are giving them; visitation *must* be done. There are several recent contacts on the university campus that should be followed up with personal meetings. John Massey is being drafted, and there are calls for painting jobs, yet undone. Yet I feel constrained to go to Milwaukee to seek Ed McCully, much the same as Barnabas went to Tarsus to seek Saul long ago. Lord, I have trust in Thee with all my heart and now confess that I have no understanding upon which I can lean. Grant that my way may be prepared before me, at Homecoming in Milwaukee, and in Huntington, Indiana—O God, in Huntington! Do the first work there of knitting Ed and me, opening the believers' hearts to the truth of the New Sanctuary! Waste not my hours of travel, Lord. Flood my pathway with light and give me grace to walk therein pleasing.

OCTOBER 24   Milwaukee, Wisconsin, Ed McCully's home. Came here after an interesting time of reminiscence at Homecoming. Praying for guidance for Ed regarding the Lord's work in Ecuador. I feel it would be good to get away from all the encouragement here and learn the exercise of faith in a context where things are somewhat more rigorous. Painting McCully's house now, so will be here for a little time. Lord, let me not miss my signs this day. I sense crisis for Ed and the danger of influencing him wrongly, so grant me wisdom in all that I say among the family here. The field seems desperately far away tonight, and I feel quite dull about the whole matter of the future. God has not yet come upon me in power; His Name is not yet feared in Portland, Lombard, Norman. How far away, how long, the road back to the beginning—even to

that lookout place where one can glimpse the pattern of the
first days. Lord, leave me not alone in my *fears for Thy cause!*
Strike terror to men's hearts, awed, respectful fear to my own.

OCTOBER 29

I. God is Spirit (John 4:24); eternal (Heb. 9:14); Father of
   spirits (Heb. 12:9)
II. God is light (1 John 1:5); Immutable: angels and men
    may have change in their spirits, "leave their first
    state" or "be made perfect." Never so God. We have
    beginning as spirits. He is the same.
III. God is love (1 John 4:8).
   A. As Spirit: *The Spirit*
      1. Invisible
         "Now to the king eternal, immortal, invisible,
         the only God" (1 Tim. 1:17).
         "Who is the image of the invisible God" (Col.
         1:15).
         "He endured, as seeing him who is invisible"
         (Heb. 11:27).
         "No man hath seen God at any time" (John
         1:18).
         "Whom no man hath seen, nor can see" (1 Tim.
         6:16).
      2. Incorporeal
         "Dwells not in temples . . . not far from each
         one of us" (Acts 17:24, 27).
         "The heaven is my throne, the earth my
         footstool" (Acts 7:49).
      3. Omnipresent
         1 Kings 8:27; Psalms 139:7
      4. Incorruptible
         Unchangeable and indestructible (Rom. 1:23).
   B. As Light: *The Son*
      1. Apprehensible
         Wave *and* particle (John 1:5).
      2. Having source and coming upon objects (John
         8:12; 9:5; 12:35, 36).

C. As Love: *The Father*
1. Personal (1 John 3:1; John 16:26, 27; 3:16; 2 Cor. 13:14).
2. Social—if God is love, He must *forever* love, even before John 3:16 could apply. Hence He must be plural in nature, having subject and object within Himself.

OCTOBER 29   Preaching on discipleship at Young People's meeting in Good News Chapel. The price of discipleship, the progress, the practice.

Tonight.   The progress, from John 8:31:

"If you abide"—life of constancy.
"You shall know"—life of discovery.
"Truth shall set you free"—life of liberty.

R. F. Bayles preaching morning and evening. Traditional. Oversimplification of the resurrection of the body from 2 Corinthians 5 this morning. Ah, Lord, our preachers need vitality. Their words come crawling to our ears, rather than striking, assailing, insisting as would Thy true oracles. The ministry of the Gospel is little regarded as a holy ordination and is carried on quite carelessly. With what power, care, simplicity, earnestness, intensity ought one to present the truth from heaven. We rattle words and beat on monotonic ideas, like an all-drum orchestra. There is no beauty, appeal, harmony, cohesiveness, nor crisis to our evangelism. Lord, raise up laborers who will heed the pattern of the apostolate. I believe Thou art raising Ed.

These are days of exercise over Herb Gundelach and Bill Wilbur. They came last Sunday and were startled by the claims of the resurrection. Both men stirred and responsive. Spent eight hours in their smoke-filled apartments yesterday. Ah, it is a privilege to speak of the honor of Christ while choking on tobacco smoke. Glory to God for the example of Him who sat with sinners. I trust Thee to verify the words You have been teaching, Lord, and to make these men and their wives "disciples indeed."

1 Corinthians

1 Corinthians 1:9: God is faithful—to maintain conditions
of fellowship
1 Corinthians 10:13: God is faithful—to deliver in temptation
2 Thessalonians 3:3: God is faithful—to establish and
guard.

Preached today at Emmaus Bible School from 1 Corinthians 3:10–15 on Paul the Architect:

1. The existence of a method—pattern
2. The sufficiency of that pattern
3. The obligatory nature of the pattern

Last night at Don Weber's Hi-C Club the word came from 1 Corinthians 16:22: "If any man love not our Lord, let him be anathema." I am some help to souls here in Milwaukee, at least for a time they appear stirred. But my own spirit so much lacks reality. I cannot see why or how God adds His blessing to my words. It was because of God's presence that none of Samuel's words fell to the ground (1 Sam. 3:19), and I have felt a dreadful lack of the nearness. "The Lord was *with* him . . . ." What a testimony!

NOVEMBER 6 *Psalm 110* The seated Christ:

As Savior: for sinner, "Prince and Savior" (Acts 5:31)
Work finished.
As Sovereign: over the entire universe
Unchallenged control
As Priest: for saint
Offering done

The modern ideal in America of "daintiness" in the female is nothing short of flimsiness, I fear. If only youth *knew* and age could *do*, what a wonderful place this would be.

NOVEMBER 8   Romans 5:6–10 describes the past state of the believers:

I. Weakness (in their persons):
  A. Physically (Acts 3) the impotent man: never got inside the temple until the Name healed him
    1. Lame from birth—stood, walked, leaped
    2. Carried to temple—"held" Peter and John
    3. Laid at the gate
  B. Morally—Samson (Judg. 13:16) "the flesh is weak . . ."
    1. Subject to whims
    2. Mastered by passions ($\delta\acute{u}\nu\alpha\mu\iota\varsigma$)
    3. Blinded by a woman
  C. Socially—Pontius Pilate. "Thou couldst have no power except it were given thee by God . . ."
    1. $\dot{\epsilon}\xi ou\sigma\acute{\iota}\alpha$ Good intentions—marvelled at Jesus
    2. High position—"I have power . . ."
    3. Men-pleaser (powerlessness of politics):

      powerless to persuade multitude
      powerless to maintain nonimplication
      powerless to gain innocence

II. Irreligion ($\dot{\alpha}\sigma\epsilon\beta\tilde{\omega}\nu$) (in their thoughts):
  Pharaoh: "Who is Jehovah . . ." (Exod. 5:2). "I know Him not . . ." "God not in all their thoughts"

III. Sinners (in their deeds): Manasseh (2 Chron. 33) wickedness beyond nations around

  Son of good Hezekiah   Warned and heedless
                        Chained in war

IV. Enemies (in relation to God): Saul of Tarsus
  Persecuted Christ—as men today persecute Christians

1 Samuel 15: Saul's rejection

Plain request from God
Partial response by Saul
Powerful rebuke by Samuel
Pitiful rejection by God

NOVEMBER 9   The fact that Christ left earth implies that God has rejected earth. Earth rejected Him; heaven accepted Him: heaven and earth are inconsolably at odds.

NOVEMBER 10   *2 Samuel 7*   How fearful is the sovereignty of God! He disposes His favors at His own intention, men being no party in the matter. Of Saul He says (v. 15), "I took my lovingkindness from him." Fearful are the Lord's dealings among men; none can move His decree.

NOVEMBER 11   Reading and studying all day. Snow flurries forced me inside and continued cold will keep me from finishing the painting of McCully's house. I have prayed otherwise—that I might complete the job to the glory of the Great Craftsman, but no warm weather comes.

Drummond's *Natural Law in the Spiritual World* has an engaging chapter on eternal life, comparing these two definitions:

> Perfect correspondence would be perfect life, were there no changes in the environment, but such as the organism had adapted changes to meet, and were it never to fail in the efficiency with which it met them, there would be eternal existence and eternal knowledge.
>
> HERBERT SPENSER

This is life eternal, that they might know thee, the only true God, and Jesus Christ whom thou hast sent.

JESUS CHRIST

The natural correspondences to the spiritual are helpful in many cases, but somehow inconclusive. They are stimulating but not establishing.

NOVEMBER 13   Luke's account of Judas's death superficially conflicts with the other gospelers. In Acts 1:18, Judas fell down and "burst asunder" in the midst. In Matthew he hangs himself. I wonder if there was not something rather in the method of hanging which accounts for this. Two Samuel 21:9 gives an account of Gibeon's revenge upon the house of Saul. The stated method of punishment was "hang them up" (v. 6) but the account says "they fell all seven together." A slipknot of some sort may have been used or it may be that the body was cut down after hanging since no body was to remain exposed hanging overnight in Israel. In any case the position of hanging is potentially a falling one, and the two may have customarily been associated.

Preached at Good News Chapel yesterday on Psalms 110:1 and Matthew 22. "The Lord said to my Lord, sit down . . . ."

1. To whom was it said?
2. Why was it said?
3. What advantage or meaning for us?

NOVEMBER 14   Herb Gundelach greeted me tonight with "Willie got saved Sunday night." Thanks, dear Lord, for these two. I am trusting Thee for their wives soon and for their maturity in the Life. Do give the brothers and sisters here wisdom in raising these babes for Thee. I feel it is time to go on to Wheaton and Huntington and hate to leave them struggling alone. Thanks, too, for the clear weather yesterday and today so that I could finish painting McCully's house. "As for God, his way is perfect; the word of the Lord is proved. He is a shield to all that put their trust in him" (2 Sam. 22:31).

NOVEMBER 16   *1 Kings 2*   The establishment of Solomon's kingdom came only after three deaths occurred (v. 46). First

Adonijah, requesting Abishag brazenly after challenging Solomon's throne, is slain. Then Joab, the warrior of blood who slew the king's soldiers, and finally Shimei, the curser of David. Here is illustration of the Man of Peace, Christ, in His enthronement. His enemies, now in political control of His inheritance, desiring part of the heritage, shall be slain as was Adonijah by Benaiah. His military opponents, tolerated by His Father, shall be slain without mercy, as was Joab at the altar of God. And all those "little men," put on conditional footing in the New Kingdom, shall be slain instantly as they trespass, as was Shimei son of Gera. Then, too, shall the faithless priesthood, whose allegiance was not to the Man of Peace, be banished from their place, and Zadok, the righteous, shall fill it as he filled Abiathar's.

NOVEMBER 17   Came from Milwaukee with Louis Borghardt to Chicago in his new "Henry J." Louis has not learned that the "fruit of righteousness is sown in peace by them that make peace." Lord, deliver me from such a death of wearisome words.

Met Bill Patterson in Chicago, Nora, and Kay, her sister. Much stirred again by contact with him. His ways and conversation move me to believe God. "You've a great God, Jim; prove Him; try Him out; try Him. *Try Him!* Pray, boy, pray . . . God will move them . . . whole nights in prayer . . . do God's work, man, get on with the Gospel! They need a John Knox, a Martin Luther . . . the world has yet to see what God can do with a man fully surrendered." On and on in that clipped, Scottish way, with his searching eyes and hollow voice. O God, let me be in such a spirit, let me be such a man. Grant me the spirit of a minor prophet!

This morning at 6:45 again Gideon's encouragements: "The Lord is with thee," "Go in this, thy might," and Solomon's dream, "Ask what I shall give thee." Moved me to ask, but, oh, so falteringly, coldly, heartlessly.

NOVEMBER 19   My soul is exceedingly filled with contempt this Lord's day morning. Passions plagued me all day yesterday and lashed me this morning again. Oh, wretched man, *when* shall I be rid of you? How long must flesh quench spirit, drown devotion, and silence prayer? My God, deliver me from myself. Such awful upsurges of pride attend my conversation these days and the abomination of a self-filled heart wells uncalled to my lips. Sin shall not have dominion . . . let it be, Lord. Though it rage and tear within as the awful traitor to my spirit, let it be a rebel, not a Lord.

NOVEMBER 20   *1 Kings 13*   Jeroboam's understanding of the drawing and gathering power of the house of God in Jerusalem was clear. If he had failed to provide orthodox blood altars in Dan and Beth-el, the return of the ten tribes to Jerusalem would soon have knit the nation again. But foolishly his own pride and position blinded him to the good of a united people, and the golden calves were erected. Not unlike today, I sense, where the power of one gathering center is evident, Christ Himself being the magnetic force capable of uniting a divided Church.

Yet, men will, to defend their place in the religious society existing, gather men to other altars, of other names, and teach God's people adherence to human "communions." And there are "old prophets" defending these eccentric altars today, as there were then (v. 11). Woe be to the young man who, sent of God to reprove the altars of division, harks to the voice of venerable ancients in opposition to the voice of God. His bones shall testify to his God's intensity. "Whosoever will" is all right for the Gospel. It certainly does not apply to those who will be ministering priests at God's public altars (v. 33). "Whosoever would" were anointed by Jeroboam, but God's ministers must be called, gifted, ordained by God to be fit ministers. "No man taketh this office to himself" (Num. 18:6, 7).

NOVEMBER 22   *1 Kings 19*   Huntington, Indiana. Came here yesterday forenoon with Robert and Vera Willey, having a profitable time on the road. Bible study at Cathers's last night, taking up the study of the church in Ephesians. There are a number of malcontents from denominations who may be ripe for assembly truth, but it is all brand new to them. This morning 1 Kings 19:9 moved me to prayer. "What doest thou here, Elijah?" I had to confess that I didn't know but was anxious to find out just what *I am doing here*. All I know is that I have been strengthened by God to come here; He must show me my work.

Ravens and widows—Elijah's supporters in famine. Not too substantial when you think of it, but the promise was that God had commanded them to feed him *there*. If he had not gone *there*, he would not have had the benefits God commanded for him. Ah, Lord, I have been commanded to come *here*. It has not been my desire. I am confident of Thy provision, not only for food, but for that true "jar of meal" and "cruse of oil," that bread and meat afforded for the spirit. I need wisdom here, Lord, and power. These people are weary of men. They have need of Thee. Let me see souls here brought to knowledge of Christ, as in Milwaukee. Give opportunity to preach. Build an assembly in Huntington.

NOVEMBER 23 Thanksgiving Day. Precious privilege to open the Scriptures to Bill's folks this morning. Arminianism has made its devilish inroads upon all their minds, and it comes with such freshness and liberating force to their souls to know the great truths of election, acceptance in Christ, and ultimate rest. Lord, open my mouth in wisdom. Enlarge the truth, and let many hear and be delivered. Exalt Thy Name. Magnify Christ's work and person.

NOVEMBER 24 *1 Kings 18–21* The mystery about Elijah. Much stirred in the restudy of the moody Tishbite this morning. There are some fascinating symbols connected with him which have prophetic significance, but which I cannot see clearly now. First, his peculiar approach to his people. His severe austerity and awesome person mark him as a prophet sent to bring judgment on his generation. As such, he predicts the ministry of John and the witnesses of Revelation. All preach condemnation to *prepare* for something. Elijah for Elisha, John for Christ, and the witnesses for the Coming. He was a man of the wilderness feared by the soft-living royalty. First, generally Ahab says of him, "Oh *mine* enemy" (21:20). There is relief from conviction of sin at the death of all these—Herodias's slaying John to stop his conscience, rousing voice; the peoples of earth greatly rejoicing when the witnesses are overcome in Revelation 11:10.

Elijah was the prophet who controlled water (rain and the Jordan) and fire (Baal's contest and the slaying of the companies of fifty). John baptized with water and predicted the baptism of fire by Christ. The witnesses of Revelation 11 slew with fire from their mouths, and shut off the rains as they chose. In Elijah's vision at Horeb the wind (controlling the rain, the whirlwind of his ascension), and the fire (consuming the sacrifice, destroying his enemies) have illustrations in his own day, but not so the earthquake. The witnesses of Revelation 11 leave seven thousand men dead at their ascension by an *earthquake,* however. But the Lord was in none of these. John is not recorded as having done a single miracle of the wind, fire, earthquake order. It was the *voice* which found its counterpart in John (Isa. 40:3), hence:

Elijah—the wind and fire
John—the still, small voice
The witnesses—the fire and earthquake.

Christ, in Matthew 11, gives the illustration of the children in the marketplace. They pretended to lead a dance by piping, and John failed to comply with their make-believe by refusing to eat and drink and make merry. They pretended to weep and fast, and Jesus refused to cooperate with their religious faking by eating and drinking and gaining the reputation of a glutton, whereas John had been regarded as demon mad. The links are striking:

Elijah and Elisha—the slayer and the restorer
John and Jesus—the austere and the friendly
The two witnesses—the burning lamps and the olive
trees.

Give me the spirit of discernment in all these mysterious leads, Lord. Spirit of the Word, interpret the dark things and let me see clearly all this implies. Make of me the sort of a child who shall justify wisdom in my own generation.

NOVEMBER 25   Much fervency and warmth in prayer with Cathers. Dale: "Lord, keep us all in Thy big corral." Ethel: "I exhort you; we don't do enough of it." Amen. God took us to the place of faith for many things.

NOVEMBER 27 *Matthew 7*   Heard U.B. [United Brethren] evangelist speak on "the will of God," as the condition for entrance into the Kingdom last night. "We are not being saved unless we are doing the full will of God." But these Arminians involve themselves in hopeless inconsistencies. For if I must ever do the perfect will of God to be saved, then I may never sin, for sin is not God's will. And if we say that we have no sin, we deceive ourselves. Further, if one deviation from the will of God expels me from salvation, then salvation, after all, depends on me and my doing, and "works" is my hope, not Christ's work at all. And still, if I did leave my saved estate by some small deviation from the will of God and became lost again, the Scripture plainly states that it would be impossible to renew me again to repentance.

What this man failed to see in Matthew 7, where the Lord Jesus enunciates that solemn and searching truth, "Not all who say to me 'Lord, Lord' shall enter the kingdom of heaven, but those who *do the will* of my Father," is that the will of God is done in my believing and thereby obeying or doing His Word concerning Christ. Otherwise salvation is an external *doing* proposition. The will of God must be assented to for the whole life at the initial conversion point, and in this he stressed a needed point. But what gets me into the Kingdom, from

Christ's own statement, is not saying "Lord, Lord" but *acting* "Lord, Lord." The contrast is not one between faith and works, as the Arminian would teach, stressing works for entrance, but between true committal of life to do God's will and only saying so—a prevalent point of confusion.

Read part of W. S. Maugham's *Of Human Bondage*. Materialistic psychological explanation of things, but stimulating. "She loved him with a new love, because he had made her suffer."

NOVEMBER 30   Perilous days in international affairs. Red menace in Korea and Red diplomats in Lake Success have the sterile capitalists of the Western powers trembling. What children we soft, ease-loving Westerners appear in the face of the craft and steel-hearted purpose of the Red East. American impotency is in her homes where pleasure and money have vitiated patriotic principles and moral stamina. We have lived too long under the idealistic flag of Plenty, while the masses of Asia have learned hardness and intensity of feeling under the bitter ensign of Want. America refused to share her surplus; now she is forced to give account to the multitudes whose drawn cheeks paled as American food splashed to rot into the seas and rivers. It is only just. Would that the threat were terrifying enough to make realists of us! So that we would feel the helplessness of Hezekiah before the defiant Rabshakeh and turn to God for consolation, rather than to our industry! It is a time for weeping and repentance, not diplomacy. O God, turn my people. Send a spirit of breaking and contrition to her leaders, tremor and humiliation to the false pride of her people.

DECEMBER 1   *1 Chronicles 4; Acts 17; 1 Chronicles 5; 2 Kings 22*   Dreadful conflict with the flesh this morning. Unwillingness to accept God's "way of escape" from temptation frightens me—what a rebel yet resides within. How traitorous to a man is his own self, preying upon an idle mind to destroy peace and confidence. Sex urges are terribly strong at times, and it is good to have a store of past prayer preserving me when the onslaught comes. "Lead us not into temptation" is one of the best preservatives of inward integrity I know. Thanks be to God for deliverance in conflict. Loneliness, independence, distance from home combine to fan recklessness on to ruin. Illicit relations, often spun into the fabric of thought, are, when considered, vain and frustrating, inharmonious to the true need. There is no deliverance apart from marriage or the supply of the grace of God, quenching in quietness the burnings within. It is better to marry than to burn, but it is better still not to burn.

Jabez, the *more honorable*, conceived in sorrow, prayed a prayer I, too, have prayed this morning. "He called on the God of Israel saying, Oh that thou wouldest bless me indeed, and enlarge my border, and that thy hand might be with me, and that thou wouldest keep me from evil, that it be not to my sorrow" (1 Chron. 4:10). "And God granted him that which he requested" (v. 11).

Beroeans, *more noble* than the Thessalonians, showed their honor by searching the Scriptures to see if the things they heard were so (Acts 17:11). Grant me this *nobility*, Lord, to be as Jabez who *asked* and as Beroea who *examined*.

First Chronicles 5:22 shows a war that was of God. First, it made His people pray. Second, it brought glory to His Name. Third, it slew the evil Hagrites. It may be that the present Korean problem could be of God, if His people would pray and their confidence in His Name bring honor to Him in bringing it to a successful close. Still, I have the feeling that this is the beginning of the fall of Western might. Avarice (called colonialism and capitalism) has corrupted the entire nation, and it is time for the judgment of God. "Great is the wrath of Jehovah that is kindled against us, because our fathers have not hearkened unto the words of this book, to do according to all that which is written concerning us" (2 Kings 22:13).

DECEMBER 4   *1 Chronicles 25*   Considering this morning the work of prophets. Surprised to find in 1 Chronicles 25:1 that some were set aside to "prophesy with harps." This is explained in verse 3 where they are said to prophesy in "giving thanks and praising the Lord." In all, it shows the wide scope of work included in the biblical idea of prophecy. There seem to be no restrictions as to who may prophesy—women (Miriam, Deborah, Huldah, Philip's daughters) or men, evil or good (Balaam, Saul, Caiaphas), young or old (1 Kings 13:11; Acts 2:17).

In the New Testament assembly the gift of prophecy was granted to build up, exhort, and comfort (1 Cor. 14:3) or teach (1 Cor. 14:19). It was for believers' help (1 Cor. 14:22), although an unbeliever may have been convinced by it. Tongues were to signify God's seal to unbelievers outside the church gathering, or if within, then an interpreter had to be on hand so that believers were edified.

The two verbs used of prophesyings and tongues in 1 Corinthians 13:8 signify that prophesyings would come to an end (perhaps of the sort Agabus was prognosticating), but tongues were to cease ($\pi\alpha\acute{u}\omega$). The prophetic gift of edification was not to *cease*, but to "come to nothing"—as has happened in that none today prophesy the future events as occurred in the Acts. Women's prophecy was restricted to believers then, if the gift was for them only, and since women were not allowed to teach men, restricted to believing women—a nice distinction if it will stand.

DECEMBER 5 *1 Chronicles 28, 29*   First Chronicles 28, 29 came at an opportune time this morning. I have had such conflict of mind lately with unsettlement by sin, and discouragement in this Huntington situation that the very idea of there being "pattern principles" upon which to build for God seemed absurd. Who cares these days if things are done according to Pauline method? Get on with the Gospel; we haven't time to bicker over how the work is to be established. It seems like I hear this on all hands, though no one really says it.

First came the encouragement of 28:9: ". . . my son, *know* thou the God of thy father, and *serve* him with a perfect heart and with a willing mind; for Jehovah searcheth all hearts, and understandeth all the imaginations of the thoughts. If thou seek him, he will be found of thee; but if thou forsake him, he will cast thee off forever. Take heed now; for the Lord hath chosen thee to build a house for the sanctuary; be strong, and do it." (Merciful God, but speak this to *me*, actually make this apply with all its power, promise of good, and warning of evil.)

Just following this in verses 11, 12, 19 the "pattern" is delivered. God never built anything among men without first delivering to them a pattern: Moses (Exod. 25:40), David (loc. cit.), or Paul (1 Cor. 4:6). David's pattern to Solomon was, first, (v. 11) *delivered* (traditionally passed on as a heritage [2 Thess. 2:15; 3:6; 1 Cor. 11:2]), second, *revealed* by the Spirit (v. 12; Eph. 3:3), and third, *recorded* in writing (v. 19; 1 Cor. 4:6).

Noted, too, that Solomon was *twice* made king of Israel (29:22). First by his father (23:1), then by all the people. So God's anointed, now enthroned by the father while the usurper, Adonijahlike, draws the people after himself, soon to be recognized by the people as his father's choice. Arise, Greater than Solomon, to take the throne of Thy Father David, establish the Kingdom in Thine own hand.

Noted, too, in that remarkable praise prayer of David's, his addressing Jehovah as "our Father" (29:10). This expression and some of that prayer may have been in Christ's mind in the disciples' prayer.

DECEMBER 7   Reading daily from Maugham's *Of Human Bondage*. I cannot explain the power he has over me. Partly, I know, and mostly, it is the drama of story which draws me, but not entirely. I find myself rereading a phrase that is charged, or noticing the effect of a sequence's series in a sentence. It thrills me, and I could do nothing else all day but read those wretched novels! Oh, the power of words! They stir in me, charge me with some sort of emotional ferocity, so that I enjoy a slapping wind when coming home from the library. It animates things, too. I find myself trying to fit apt, cryptic words into the description of a tree, a street lamp, a passerby. What is in it? Why should absorption in printed words so change attitudes? It cannot be the words alone, but the whole effect of transmitted idea. My God, if such can be the force of uninspired literature, what shall be the force of truth charged with divine impetus in divinely framed order? Let me speak, write, preach as the wizened Tarsun [Paul], not in word only, but in power.

DECEMBER 13   First trip to Chester [Illinois]. Feel that God is surely leading Ed and me there. Asking for: (1) the turning of Gentiles to Christ, (2) the establishment of an assembly, (3) radio, medical, educational experience. Absurd to ask now for these things, as far as any outward possibility is concerned, but I think God is to be glorified by asking the impossible of Him.

DECEMBER 16   Back at work in the post office at Huntington. Slow going with souls here, but there are encouraging signs. Men unsound in doctrine complicate the issue by "sanctification" experiences. Ah, for a place where the Scriptures have not been twisted! Lord, send me to Ecuador!

Reading *Of Human Bondage* stirred me again to *feel* today. This is one thing I see of value in a novel; it stirs me from apathy, moves me to love, hate, think. I should like to write one on the peculiarities of modern fundamentalism from a member of a denominational church and call it *Shadow of the Spire*. What inconsistencies to be parodied to show the saints their narrowness! A very real possibility of ministering church truth perhaps. Maybe some time in the penitentiary . . . . But, as W. S. Maugham says, "Life is to be lived, rather than to be written about." Other notable quips:

From old habit he unconsciously thanked God that he no longer believed in Him.
These old folk had done nothing, and when they died, it would be just as if they had never been.
God, deliver me.

Outline for a sermon sometime:

Lovers of the Lord: 1 Corinthians 16:22
Lovers of pleasure, self: 2 Timothy 3:2, 4 (cf. Lovers of His
    appearing [2 Tim. 4:8]).
Lovers of earth: 2 Timothy 4:10 (Demas)
Lovers of preeminence: 3 John 9 (Diotrephes)

DECEMBER 26   Spent a quiet Christmas at Cathers's high-
lighted by conversation with Bill regarding ideas faced since
we were in Norman. Thanks be to Thee, Lord, for a friend who
can share, following even into the abstract vagaries, the
thoughts of my heart.

The Moon Is Round!

*This refers to an experience which Jim told me about years later.
He had been depressed, doubting the sovereignty of God. The moon
seemed to show him that there is wholeness, that all things are
complete in Christ, even when they appear to be partially
shadowed.*

Noticed this morning the effect bondage and change of
locale had on the Hebrew idea of God. Abraham in Genesis 24
first calls Jahweh the God of heaven. From then on, through
the patriarchs, judges, prophets, and kings, He is the God *in*
heaven, possessing heaven, seeing from heaven, and the rest,
but He is characteristically the God of Israel. This carries
through noticeably until the captivity where, in Ezra and
Nehemiah, the recurrent expression God of heaven is restored
a significant number of times. Their aspect of God changed,
enlarged, returned to Abramic proportions when the national
conscience was shamed. It was no longer a credit to God to be
known as "of Israel." Now their God fit for the nations as well,
not just for the nations.
   So with Paul—not only "my God," but the God of our Lord
Jesus Christ, the God of the Son of Man, whose extensions are
to the corners of heaven and to the core of earth. Never "God of
the Church," but always Father and Lord of all.

DECEMBER 28 *Psalm 15*   The man who is to sojourn in
Jahweh's tabernacle, dwell in His holy hill (v. 1) shall find
establishment; he shall never be moved (v. 5). It seems slightly
incongruous that the description of this man (who may be said
to be living in the presence of the Lord) should be so mundane. Nevertheless, is it not so, that the man who knows the
presence of God sojourns, dwells with Him, is one who is in
right relation to his fellows? The presence of God fits me to live
uprightly in the presence of men. If I would know fellowship
with God, I must maintain uprightness, integrity with men.
The two condition each other; falling out with men for evil
causes eclipses my being in with God; and being in with God,
enables me to live properly before men.

Studying Nehemiah these days I am impressed with the
fitting illustrations he records for present-day conditions in the
church. First, it is the record of *restoration, opposition, confusion.*

1. Restoration
   a. Ruin of Jerusalem
   b. Repentance of people (ch. 9)
   c. Renewal of covenant (10:29)
   d. Rebuilding of the wall (ch. 3) (everybody involved)

2. Opposition
   a. By enemies without: railing (4:3); ridicule of leaders;
      intimidation (6:9); fraud (6:8).
   b. By associates within: deception (6:10–14); betrayal
      (13:4); relationships (13:28).
   c. By conditions about (4:10).
3. Confusion
   a. Foreign marriages (13:1–3, 23).
   b. Forsaken Sabbath (13:15)
   c. Forgotten responsibilities (13:10)

6

Homework, 1951

Half of this year was spent working in Chester, Illinois, with Ed McCully as home missionaries. They conducted Bible classes for children, preached in every possible place, and had a radio broadcast, "The March of Truth," supporting themselves with various kinds of jobs as they found opportunity. The rest of the year was spent preparing to leave for Ecuador. This included a speaking itinerary in the East, where the Brethren wanted to become acquainted with them in order to support their missionary work.

JANUARY 6 *Psalms 90, 20*   Chester, Illinois. Ed McCully and I came here on Thursday and were prospered in our way by the Sovereign—protected, provided for, and encouraged. We are seeking His face now with the prayer of Psalms 90:16, 17: "Let thy work appear unto thy servants . . . establish the work of our hands." We want, first of all, to see His approach to this area, discover His method, and then see it established in our hands. Sense a high privilege as a truth bearer here and want much grace to present the Word in power.

Encouraged last eve by Psalm 20:

V. 1: Personal deliverance by the *Name* of the God of *Jacob*.
V. 5: Public demonstration of the *Name* of our God.
V. 8: Persistent devotion to the *Name* of Jehovah our God.

Yea, Lord, for Thy Name's sake, work a new work in Chester.

JANUARY 9 *Job*   Last night Ed and I went with Powley to Saint Louis for a profitable visit with the aged Dr. Morey and the young men of the Saint Louis assemblies. Lord, the potential for work there is tremendous. Work among them, Spirit of God; deliver their souls from the conventional tediums, terms, and traditions. Raise up some men of God from the group.

Meditation upon Job has been helpful. Satan is called one of the sons of God—in much the same way as apostate theology has called all men His sons. True, all men were in the mind of God as all bodies were in the matter of Adam, and in that sense we are sons of God as a race, inasmuch as was Adam himself (Luke 3:38). But it is one thing to be a son through Adam and another to be a son through Christ. In Adam all die; in Christ all shall be made alive. Seeded in Adam; selected in Christ, from before the foundation of the world.

The Book of Job was written to demonstrate that there are higher principles operating in the earth than those of wrong leading to retribution and/or right leading to reward. Job maintained that his experience violated that latter; his friends concluded that it demonstrated the former. Neither explanation is the true one. Men are actors on the stage of earth, whose footlights cut off the view of the vast audience of spirits. There history and life are seen as the drama of the universe, where Satan challenges God to maintain His power in men by faith while he requisitions material forces to bring against them. True reward and retribution for righteousness and evil are only hinted at on this stage; the day will come when the curtain falls and the cast appears before the Critic for praise or blame. It will make an interesting study in dating the book to sometime list the cultural features known to Job and his friends. Some are: seals stamped in clay (38:14); feet put in stocks (13:27).

JANUARY 10 *Job* There is evil peculiar to youth. Unique in that it is engendered of youthful lusts (2 Tim. 2:22), requires special penitence (Pss. 25:7), and receives separate retribution (Job 13:26). For youth there is special wretchedness, for then the powers within conflict most bluntly with the powers about. Restraint is most galling; release most desired. To compensate for these, youth has special powers. "I have written unto you young men, because you are *strong*, the word of God *abides* in you; you have overcome the wicked one" (1 John 2:14). Unusual strength is a premium for youth; acuteness and retentive powers are more real in youth; victory sweetest in youth. Lord, let me live it to the hilt, exerting all its force, loosing all its fire. In Solomonic wisdom I would *rejoice* in youth, yet *remember* my Creator.

"The *friendship* ('secret, counsel,' margin) of Jehovah is with them that fear him; And he will show them his covenant" (Pss. 25:14). Friendship has its scriptural basis in *intimacy*, not *acquaintanceship*. Not what another knows of me measures his friendship, but what he has *shared* with me. "I have not called you servants; because a servant knoweth not what his Lord doeth: but I have called you friends, for all things that I have heard of my Father I have made known unto you" (John 15:15). Is not this the testimony of the friend of God, Abraham (James 2:23; Isa. 41:8)? Did not Jehovah inquire "Shall I hide from Abraham that which I do?" (Gen. 18:17).

JANUARY 11 *Proverbs* Social values are not the only standards of good. Modern philosophy instills the good of the group as the great end of doing well, and the loss of group's good as the worst ill. But there is a distinction made in the Proverbs of Solomon which shows there is at least one other valid reason for being wise and doing good. Surprisingly, it is for *one's own* good.

9:12: "If thou art wise, thou art wise for thyself."
14:14: "The good man shall be satisfied from himself."
Job 22:2: Eliphaz: "He that is wise is profitable unto himself."

This demonstrates the balancing powers of Scripture upon a man's thought. For, while it is true that no man lives or dies "unto himself," and that they who live ought to live for Him who died for them and rose again, *the benefits* of such living are not only or entirely altruistic, but very personal. The reward of wisdom is at once upward, outward, inward. Conversely, the evil that a man does is not only to himself. He reaps the fruit of his own doings, receiving *in himself* that recompense of his error, which is right, but not only in himself. Ignorance, folly, stupidity—things which we attribute to be *personal* traits— have powerful social influences. I risk endangering not only myself by being willfully ignorant, I poison my acquaintances, and demean my Creator. *All* things are tremendously significant that relate to a man; nothing he can do will make life or any of its parts inconsequential. This is a happy fact for the righteous; it is a terrible one for a sinner. To say of a deed, a thought, an experience, "It is nothing," would be to say, "It is not."

JANUARY 12 *Proverbs 10* Proverbs 10 has something to say of the lips of the righteous and the wicked. I have been praying this morning for the proper words to be preached publicly in Chester, and these verses came for encouragement and warning.

- V. 11: The mouth of the righteous is a fountain of life— violence covers the wicked mouth.
- V. 13: In the lips of him that hath discernment wisdom is found.
- V. 19: In the multitude of words there wanteth not transgression; But he that refraineth his lips doeth wisely.
- V. 20: The tongue of the righteous is as choice silver.
- V. 21: The lips of the righteous feed many.
- V. 31: The mouth of the righteous bringeth forth wisdom.
- V. 32: The lips of the righteous know what is acceptable.

These seven notices of a good mouth are contrasted with seven other mentions of a wicked man's converse:

V. 8: The foolish of lips (margin) shall fall.

V. 10: The foolish of lips (margin) shall fall.

V. 11: Violence covers the mouth of the wicked.

V. 14: The mouth of fools is a present destruction.

V. 18: He that hideth hatred is of lying lips; And he that uttereth a slander is a fool.

V. 31: The perverse tongue shall be cut off.

V. 32: The mouth of the wicked speaketh perverseness.

This section of the book might well be termed the "Speech Section." From it I learn briefly, that the mouth of a righteous man genders life (v. 11), discloses wisdom (v. 13), knows some silence (v. 19), enriches (v. 20), feeds (v. 21), *buddeth* wisdom (v. 31, margin), suggesting that a wise mouth can utter things in concise forms which will later open up to beautiful display, and frames acceptable speech. (v. 32). On the other hand, the man who has no heart (v. 21, margin), the foolish lipped, shall fall (vv. 8, 10), conceals or engenders violence (v. 11), makes for present ruin (v. 14), conceals hatred, utters slander, lies (v. 18), shall lose his tongue (v. 31), speaks perversity (v. 32).

Very well, my wisdom-uttering Lord, I shall expect Thee to do these good things with these lips which are not my own, and to preserve me from a fool's lips.

JANUARY 13   *Proverbs 11*   Proverbs 11:24–27: The principle of getting by spending (cf. Prov. 13:7):

I. Illustrated by the actions of God

"He had *yet one*, a beloved son: He sent him last" (Mark. 12:6).

"He giveth not the Spirit by measure" (John 3:34).

"He spared not his own Son" (Rom. 8:32).

"He emptied himself" (Phil. 2:7).

Is heaven the poorer for this spending? Nay, both heaven and earth are enriched by it. Who dare not follow God's example?

II. Enjoined in the teachings of Christ

"There is no man that hath left house, brethren, sisters, mother, father, children or lands for my sake and for the gospel's sake, but he shall receive a hundredfold now in this time . . . and in the world to come eternal life" (Mark 10:29, 30).

"It is more blessed to give than to receive" (Acts 20:35).

"Except a grain of wheat fall to the ground and die, it abideth alone; but if it die, it bringeth forth much fruit" (John 12:24).

"Give, and it shall be given unto you; good measure, pressed down, shaken together, running over, shall they give into your bosom" (Luke 6:38).

III. Practiced in the days of the early church

"Neither was there any among them that lacked . . . distribution was made to each . . ." (Acts 4:34, 35).

"An equality . . ." (2 Cor. 8:14).

"He that soweth bountifully shall also reap bountifully" (2 Cor. 9:6).

Proverbs 11:24: What this principle does to a man's store.
Proverbs 11:25: What this principle does to a man's soul.
Proverbs 11:26: What this principle does to a man's society.

JANUARY 15   There is that restlessness, that itching, urging discontent in me again this morning. The milk of the Word curdles before me or seems to sour within. Hatefulness and rebellion against all restraint is not far from the surface; and it is good that I am not alone here. "Lead me not into temptation, but deliver me from evil . . . ."

JANUARY 16   Feel that I must write something tonight in praise of the God of delights. The day passed slowly with little affairs; two conferences for Hytool sales [a job Jim hoped to get], the contract signing for a radio program, some poor script writing, all with a sense of waiting on God for His time, His H-Hour. [Jim and Ed started a program called "The March of Truth" for which they took turns as M.C. and preacher.]

All day the sun dropped hints of spring, and at dusk, returning from the shop, I exulted in the distinct wall of purple—the Ozark foothills—close guarded by the unblinking Venus. The night spread black and blossomed brilliantly with stars. I walked out to the hill just now. It is exalting, delicious. To stand embraced by the shadows of a friendly tree with the wind tugging at your coattail and the heavens hailing your heart, to gaze and glory and to give oneself again to God, what more could a man ask? Oh, the fullness, pleasure, sheer excitement of knowing God on earth. I care not if I never raise my voice again for Him, if only I may love Him, please Him. Mayhap, in mercy, He shall give me a host of children that I may lead through the vast star fields to explore His delicacies whose fingers' ends set them to burning. But if not, if only I may see Him, smell His garments, and smile into my Lover's eyes, ah, then, not stars, nor children, shall matter—only Himself.

Jesus, Thou art now my end;
Thou my starting, too, hast been,
Oh, be Thou my present friend,
I would walk and on Thee lean.

JANUARY 17 *Proverbs 15* The fifteenth of Proverbs records some of the "domestic" effects of righteousness and wisdom:

True treasure—

"In the house of the righteous there is much treasure
But in the revenues of the wicked is trouble" (v. 6).

Simple sufficiency—

"Better is a little, with the fear of Jehovah,
Than great treasure and trouble therewith" (v. 16).

Love—

> "Better is a dinner of herbs where love is,
> Than a stalled ox and hatred therewith" (v. 17).

Security—

> "Jehovah will root up the house of the proud;
> But He will establish the border of the widow" (v. 25).

There are three "abominations" listed in this chapter:

V. 8: "The sacrifice of the wicked is an abomination to the Lord."

V. 9: "The way of the wicked is an abomination to the Lord."

V. 26: "The thoughts of the wicked are an abomination to the Lord."

How vain are the thoughts of sinners that the Lord will receive their offerings or hear their prayers. Solomon has told us in 15:8, 21:27, and in 28:9 that both his sacrifices and his prayers are an evil deed in the sight of God. But the prayer of the upright is His delight (15:8).

Evening.

> There is One whose Ear,
> Unlike our own
> Harks not to sound;
> That needs no atmosphere
> To bear a pitch through distance,
> Vacuum, mountain walls of stone,
> Titanic weight of water.
> It is more quick to hear
> The quiet currents of a tear
> Than oceans' roar;
> The rushings of a sigh
> Than thund'rings more.

To it
More vocal vacant silence
Is, charged with wondering,
Than plaudant shout.
There is an eye
No distance dims
Nor dark impairs;
On light rely
It does not.
More visual conscience
To it is than
High horizons.
The instant dramas of
Imagination, scarce
Glimpsed by our own mind,
And foreign to our aptest lip
To be described,
That mighty optic
Scans with ease;
Deciphering the colors
Twists, the flying mists,
Yea whirling shapes
That scheme and wreck
Those dramas e'er
We realize
The curtain's up.

Sight and hearing.
These two be in God
Not like in man.
We hear what's heard;
He lists where hearing is not,
Views where eye
In all her pilgrimages long
And probings sharp
Has not yet guessed
That being is.

JANUARY 18   *Proverbs 16–18*   Seems like long wait to get the work started in Chester. No sales or income thus far, just draining resources, and those will not last more than another week. I have had hopes of laying by some money for the field, but selling is not going to be able to do that at our present rate [a margin note, written later, says: "Little did I know! Saved nearly $500 by June!]. Desired to share in the work of financing the radio here and other evangelical efforts otherwise, but God has hemmed me in to nothing, that I may have nothing, do nothing, want nothing, save Himself. Lord, Thou seest the impossibility of my hopes, and I expect deliverance from Thee in some days.

Will be speaking with believers in Sparta tonight and in Saint Louis over the weekend. To sober me for this, Proverbs 18:21 came just now: "Death and life are in the power of the tongue; And they that love it (the power of the tongue) shall eat the fruit thereof." Am expecting then that the Lord will grant the fruit of life from our lips. I can plan, but only God can make what I have planned to be fruit unto life. "The plans of the heart belong to man; But the answer of the tongue is from Jehovah" (16:1).

JANUARY 20   *Psalm 30*   "Discovered" a psalm this morning. Often the Hebrew poet will elude interpretation for months of reading, until one day we at last see a clue to the spiritual secret of his psalm. Psalm 30 is the song of resurrection, sung by the Lord Jesus on that first "Lord's day" of His resurrected life. It was a song composed to be sung at the dedication of the House and suits well the founding of the Church, the spiritual house of God. For what else is the basis of anything Christian if it be not that Christ is raised? He sings to the Father, giving thanks for having been "drawn up" (v. 1). He had experienced in life that strong confidence of faith and said, "I shall never be moved." This was not a boast, but the natural outcome of relying on such promises as are quoted of Christ in Acts 2:25. "He is on my right hand, that I should not be moved." But by the mere hiding of the Father's face while He hung alone at Golgotha. . . . "I was troubled" (v. 7). And the pleadings of

Gethsemane may be reflected in verse 9, "What profit is there in my blood when I go down to the pit?" Paul agrees hereto in saying, "If Christ be not risen, your faith is vain" (1 Cor. 15:14). Not the death, but the resurrection makes the blood of profit.

JANUARY 25 *Haggai and Zechariah* Cut first half-hour radio program last night with the brethren in Saint Louis.

Enjoyed the reading of the prophecies of Haggai and Zechariah this morning. They must be understood first in their historical setting before one can hope to see their still future significance. As we draw lessons from past history, taking a microcosm, say of Athens or Rome, and enlarging it to fit a vast national scope, so God, in history, which He sees as a whole, takes the most significant items of future history and distills them into a tiny situation in the history of the Jews. We may interpret present American fears of Russian aggression in terms of Habakkuk's story of Israel and Chaldea—a wicked nation used to correct and punish a nation less wicked than itself. What we see in the present, God has seen in the future and left us the illustration in prophecy. What He has seen in the future on a grand scale, He has condensed to fit some small incident in Israel and preserved for our instruction. This makes prophecy at once wonderful, complex, and pertinent. I must learn it, Lord.

JANUARY 30 *Song of Solomon* Spent a long time deciphering the converse of the Canticles this morning. I see the likelihood of there being many ways to interpret passages in it, as being spoken by one of several characters; but this morning the following seemed the simplest:

The bride, not yet known as that, begins her song as one of a group of virgins, speaking first to her maiden friends and then in asides to him. "Let him kiss me . . ." (1:2). He makes no response, and it seems as though the whole of the first six verses are spoken to the maidens. She rejoices at being brought among them into the chambers of the king (1:4). Then she makes a plea for closer intimacy, not loving to be veiled among his many companions (1:7) but desiring midday for fellowship with him.

He responds rather coolly, but with invitation to draw near (1:8) by the shepherds' tents. The scene is a simple pastoral one with the shepherdess desiring acquaintance with the shepherd king. She praises him and declares her affection (1:9–14), desire dreams crowding into her praise of him.

He suddenly wakes to the realization of her beauty (1:15–17): "*Behold,* thou art fair . . . ." This he repeats three times as though just discovering her. Then he looks about on their dwelling; it is the forest—cedar rafters, grassy rugs. She acknowledges her insignificance—a mere field flower, a lily among many lilies. He sees her as choice among the lilies; none of the daughters compare with her. She is a lily among thorns when classed with them.

Their first love scene (2:3–6). She sits down beneath his shadow as beneath an apple tree, enjoying his fruits. She is brought into the house of wine, and declares she needs his love meats to heal her lovesickness. He embraces her, and she sleeps. It is always *his* charge to the daughters not to rouse *her* from sleep. The Hebrew pronouns in this section will allow most any interpretation, but it seems to me consistent with the story to have him give the adjuration not to wake her. Besides, in the interpretation of the New Testament, where she must be the bride of Christ, the Church, and He must be the Beloved of God, it would never do to have Him sleep while she wakes. Is it not always that she is put to rest by His embrace and then He is given charge for her safekeeping until she wakes?

He wakes her with his arrival in the morning and rouses her to follow him to his land where spring is eternally awake. She readies herself and invites him to return at dawn—probably of the following day since he has gone to herd his flock. That night she has not his embrace to put her to rest, and she seeks him at midnight and finds him after encountering the watchman. She holds him fast until he is persuaded to go with her to her own house where his embrace again puts her to sleep, and she rests. He charges the daughters not to rouse her until she pleases.

It is his own troop that rouses her, and she describes him now as the king, not the shepherd. Her charge to the attendants is to behold him. She lapses into silence as he praises her, answering that she must get away (alone, I conjecture) to her mountains of sweet solitude until dawn. He invites her to leave the mountains and come to be his bride. She is praised, then cajoled to open her fountain, unlock her garden to him. She calls on the winds to waft her fragrance to him, but does not give him all that he asks. He declares that she is his garden and that he has come in to gather her fruits, having already tasted of it.

She is roused by him at night, asking entrance to her chamber, but she has not on any garment and would not defile her feet. While she dallies, he withdraws, and her lovesickness returns.

The daughters require an answer of why to her charge that they find him, and she responds with a description of her beloved. They are willing to seek him with her (according to her own desire in 1:4). Having been drawn herself, she is now able to point others to him. They are obliged to find him as she found him (1:8) as a shepherd, not as a king.

He returns with a suddenness that is surprising when she has praised him and spoken to others of him and praises her more highly than ever, though she is still "behind her veil" (4:3; 6:7). She has not been entirely uncovered by him, and it is plain that he desires it. But again she goes off, this time in her imagination to her own people; the warning given brides in Psalms 45:10 she heeds not and must hear the pleadings of "Return, return, O Shulammite" (6:13). Then it sounds as if the daughters of Jerusalem wonder why Solomon would be so patient and desirous of this dark, comely one.

She obeys, and the consummation of love is found by them both; they break into each other's song (7:1–9). It is at this point that the repetition of the peculiar little chorus "I am my beloved's" finds its proper order.

At 2:16 her possession of the beloved is foremost. She has him and seems satisfied.

At 6:3 her possession is put second, his first.

At 7:10 her possession is forgotten entirely. She is finally and wholly possessed of her beloved. Independence can be no more. All her stores are his, her vineyards, her love, her savings all now are given him (8:12).

The final episode of love is culminated in her sleeping in his arms. His final charge is that she should not be waked. From here on, they are one; she is leaning upon her beloved. No separation, only sweet, intimate counsel together.

The epilogue is for the reader's benefit. It recalls the desire of intimacy for the distant one. The symbols are all so refreshingly simple as regards the believer and her beloved that to state the allegory would be to put a fly in the ointment.

FEBRUARY 5 *Isaiah*   It remains a puzzle to me that the Old Testament prophets are quoted so "loosely" by New Testament writers concerning Messiah. This list is intended to enumerate the prophecies and perhaps clarify their relationships in the historical setting so that a better understanding of the principles of New Testament hermeneutics may be achieved. Since I am reading now in Isaiah, I will begin there. The list will not be complete, but will contain obvious allusions and quoted portions familiar to me. Help, Lord.

Isaiah 7:14: "Therefore the Lord himself will give you a sign: behold, a virgin shall conceive, and bear a son, and shall call his name Immanuel." Taken by itself the prophecy is obvious as Matthew relates it to the events of Messiah's birth (Matt. 1:23). But in historical context the child is to be born for Ahaz's sake, as a sign to him, and before the babe would become accountable, Syria and Samaria were to have gone under (7:16). This is then accomplished in the birth and growth of Maher-shalal-hash-baz (8:4), not Immanuel. The land is called Immanuel's (8:8), and the nations are to be halted because "immanu El."

FEBRUARY 6 *Isaiah 7–9*   The prophetess of 8:3 is from all appearances Isaiah's wife—already the mother of Shear-jashub (7:3)—and therefore will not fit the virginal, or maiden, character of the prophetic mother of Immanuel. The only resemblance of the two, Immanuel and Maher, is that they are a sign for Ahaz, that Damascus and Samaria will fall before the child is grown (7:16; 8:4). Isaiah 8:18 gives a clue. "Behold *I*" says Isaiah, "and the children whom Jehovah hast given me are for signs and wonders . . . ." With this we see that Isaiah himself became typical, and this explains the citation of Hebrews 2 where the author, establishing the oneness of Christ and men, uses 8:18 as proof.

Isaiah 8:14 remains a difficulty. Paul's "careless" quoting of it in Romans 9:33, where it is jumbled with 28:16, is understandable there, but I do not see the relations in Isaiah. Peter's use of it (1 Pet. 2:8) is obvious, for he uses the same interpretation as Paul, that Israel was made to stumble at the rock laid among them, but how they associated this from Isaiah 8 is a mystery.

Isaiah 9:1, 2 is used by Matthew (Matt. 4:15, 16) to describe Jesus' change of address when He moved from Nazareth to Capernaum. The more obvious passage to us (9:6, 7) is not even quoted by New Testament writers, though its ideas are certainly part of the messianic hopes. It may be that the content of these latter verses obtains in the millennial kingdom and that for this reason the New Testament writers were guided in bypassing them. Messianic hopes of a physical rule were already unduly distended, and there was no cause to aggravate by promises what was not for that generation.

FEBRUARY 9 *Isaiah 11*   It may be that there is a key to prophetic interpretation throughout Isaiah in this phrase, "In that day." Each time this recurs, so far as I have seen to date, the subject matter reverts to things either fulfilled in Christ's ministry or yet to be fulfilled in millennial time. The events of his own day are mere illustrations or settings for "that day" of far-future fulfillment. This must be checked. There is plainly a reference to the law of double fulfillment in 11:11 where Israel is gathered a second time—seen scattered and knit in a day beyond Nehemiah's.

FEBRUARY 24 *Isaiah 41–43* Was much cast down in spirit last evening. Ed and I have been here in Chester six weeks and with so little evident blessing from God that the questions which plagued the psalmist have come to us persistently: "Where is thy God?" and "Who will show us any good?" There has been no real work started here, and we have only this confidence: God sent us. It is Jahweh who has said, "*I will work*, and who can hinder it?" (43:13).

But the great Helper of weakness brought sustenance to me this morning in prayer. I think I have obtained the promise for Chester by faith in the purpose and power of God in our coming here. The margin of Isaiah 41:10 reads, "Fear thou not, for I am with thee; *look not around thee* . . . ." This has been my trouble. I have searched all the crannies round about me for help and encouragement for a seal of God's will, but I found none. Where then should I look? The answer is so trite and common I am ashamed to have to have it remind me: ". . . looking off unto Jesus . . . who endured . . ." (Heb. 12:2). This endurance of the Lord as a servant came forcibly from the prophecy of Isaiah 42:4: "He (my servant—not Israel, or Cyrus, or me, but Christ) will not fail *nor be discouraged* till he have set justice in the earth . . . ." The expectancy of Christ, His unflagging patience in the face of powerful foes—here is my strength. Oh, the joy of knowing the God-Man! How perfectly He suits my case today. Triumph, Nazarene, ride on prosperously in behalf of truth.

FEBRUARY 28 *Isaiah 62, 63* Isaiah 62:6. Would to God that I had the spirit of a watchman of Zion, one who was constant day and night (like Paul) in calling God's mind to his work. "Jehovah's remembrancers," how small a battalion that is! But Lord, You are the Director of the watchman. Set me as a remembrancer to give You no rest, and to take no rest myself until You have glorified Your Name. I think Powley is a re-membrancer for he often roused in the night to cry out to God and to meditate upon the holy things—but I find no such watchfulness in me. Send sleeplessness, Lord, and make me watch and pray.

How like Isaiah's is my own case here in Chester. Well can I ask of God, "Where is your zeal and your mighty acts?" (63:15). The land was possessed but a little while (63:18) as was the true sanctuary of Christ on earth. Now enemies tread it down. "Oh, that thou wouldest rend the heavens and come down" (64:1)!

MARCH 5   Started "River Rat" [name the slum children gave themselves] Sunday school yesterday—seventeen out. Encouraged. I am learning the vanity of words. If God does not speak through me, as it is plain He does not through most preachers today, I had better leave off trying to preach. Have been praying the prayer of Psalms 51:15, "O Lord, open *thou* my lips . . ." and trusting that promise made first to Jeremiah (Jer. 5:14), "Behold, I will make thy words in thy mouth fire, and this people wood . . . ." Mere declaration, no matter how eloquent or impelling, will never kindle the fire God's word, spoken by God's man, will kindle. Lord, give me *Thy* word for this people!

Evening. Too weak even to demonstrate weakness. Have come to such a state that I must desire to desire! The tears of my heart are frozen in the cold of my intellect . . . .

MARCH 7 *Jeremiah 15*   The constant prodding and encouragement which Jeremiah required is a helpful matter. From the vision of the almond branch and its attendant promise, "I will watch over my word to perform it" (Jer. 1:12) right through all the sorrow and opposition which crowded upon him, I find strength. Today it was from 15:19: ". . . If thou take forth the precious from the vile, then thou shalt be as my mouth." This is what I have prayed; that I might speak in every word the

oracle of God. Alas, what a prostitution I have lent my tongue
to! The vile must be separated from the precious, the clean
from the unclean, for the word of God is *pure* (Psalms 19:8),
and the wisdom which is from above is first *pure* (James 3:17).
Therefore, he who would speak God's Word must be impas-
sioned for purity—and how far it is from me!

MARCH 17   Sterile days. The past few days have been very
trying and difficult. First, I suppose, because I have not been
fresh in prayer or quickened in devotional reading. Have had
thirty-two nights of "Youth Rallies" in Sparta with fifty to
sixty-five out in the public-school gymnasium. There is little
interest, and very few young people are reached in this way,
I'm beginning to see. This problem of meeting a culture with
truth from God is the most difficult kind of thing. One comes
as a renovator, a conditioner of society, and society is in no
mood to be conditioned. Each man has his fixed concepts and
supposes that he has arrived at them originally, giving himself
the credit of thinking by insisting, "Here's the way I look at
it." Then he proceeds to say what his teachers, parents, and
friends have taught him, who, in turn, repeated what their
teachers, parents, and friends have taught them. The *fixedness*
of the mind is as the walls of Jericho to Gospel preaching. God
must shake, or there will be no shaking.

There has been a sense of discouragement and doubt come
over me through this. I prayed, simply, earnestly, believingly,
insofar as I knew how, and did not receive what I asked for,
namely, 150 people and six conversions. I know all the old
reasons for not being heard and getting better answers, and so
on, and I am resting in them now, but all that does not solve
the difficulty.

Christ's promises are *so* simple, with conditions so plain,
that it makes it hard to think the reasons for not receiving are
as we say they are. I mean, it is damned easy to think that God
is playing a practical joke on one—like Philip Carey in *Of
Human Bondage* when his clubfoot was not restored. There is a
strong pull to the philosophy that "chaos created this lump of
clay in its own image," and to let fall the whole gamut of

theological arguments. Again, I'm held by the resurrection. Were it not that I believed that Jesus was seen of men and proved Himself to be supernatural in outwitting death, I would throw the whole system back to the troubled skies and take a raft down the Mississippi today. But the fact is founding, settling, establishing; it holds as nothing else, and gives the sense that there are answers not yet discovered for which I must wait.

MARCH 22 *Ezekiel 1–3*   Spent the last two days in Des Moines, Iowa. Ed's cousin, Clarice Livingstone and Bill Green, were married on the twentieth, and Ed was best man. Met and dated Roberta (Birdie) Wright of Denver, whom I regard with some affection at present.

Stirred again in the reading of C. T. Studd's biography. Oh, that God would clothe me with the spirit of that gaunt, bearded giant with the fiery words and ringing laugh. Felt assured again that the Lord is sending me to Ecuador, having no more place in the States since so many possess so much truth here. Began work on passport last week.

Reading Ezekiel now. Noted yesterday his call to prophesy. First came visions of God (1:1), which gave him a sense of the consuming, moving, invincible, and balanced nature of the purposes and works of Jehovah.

The beasts: The complexity of His revelation—fourfold
    features. The invincibility of His going forth.
The wheels: The balance and wisdom of His purposes.
The throne: The majesty of His glory.
The fire: The consuming nature of His person.

Having discovered the awful majesty of his God, there comes the revelation through the book (2:9). Vision must be conditioned by understanding, hence Ezekiel must read. Then comes the strengthening (3:9) and warning (3:16–21). God has been pricking me with this latter passage. The prayer of David in Psalms 51:41: "Deliver me from bloodguiltiness," has for me only one meaning, namely, make me to deliver the warning to the wicked, else I become responsible for their blood. Yet, I find such a fear to accost men about their souls' condition. My name is Timorous. Lord, give me strength to deliver my soul!

MARCH 23   Enjoyed thinking of my brothers and sisters who circle the globe in witnessing for the Lord Jesus. It is encouraging to remember God is at work the world around. This is prayer answered. I have been led to pray for nearly all of these before they were thrust forth. See how God hears! England: John Paterson; Belgium: John Winston; France: Priscilla Hoy, Lorraine Woodson; Switzerland: Hans Bürki; Italy: Art Weins, Nick Kalivoda; Israel: Harry Medrow; Sudan: Charlie Guth, Ely Vandevort; Congo: Monty Sholund; India: Ruth L. Stam; Australia: Jan Cunningham; China: Hap and Madra, Rosa Lung, Andrew; Japan: Barb Dean; Parape: Marge and Chet; Mexico: Ron Harris, Vera Alleman, Jim Wroughton, Grimes. What am I doing *here?*

MARCH 24   *Ezekiel 14*   There are men whom God admits to have power with Him above others. Jeremiah found an inexorable spirit in Jehovah when He declared, "Though *Moses* and *Samuel* stood before me, yet my mind would not be toward this people . . ." (Jer. 15:1). Moses had pleaded for Israel when the nation rebelled in the wilderness, and prevailed both at Sinai, when the golden calf roused God to threaten them with destruction, and at Kadesh Barnea, where they despised His good land (Pss. 106:23, 24; Num. 14:13–20; Exod. 32:11). Samuel, too, when Israel was in defeat before the Philistines because of their idolatry (1 Sam. 7) and when they rebelled by asking for a king (1 Sam. 12), stood in the breach to intercede and prevailed for the people.

In Ezekiel the Spirit selects three men who, if any could prevail, would be God's choice. *Noah,* the preacher of righteousness to a scoffing world, *Daniel,* a contemporary figure of powerful effect in the Babylonian court, and *Job,* the man who could be trusted in the hands of Satan to vindicate God's name (14:14). So bad had become the state of the Israelites that the *combined* righteousness of these three giants of God would serve only to deliver themselves and would have no effect on the nation. Thus God finds no remedy for the national evil but its full punishment. Ezekiel's visions and Jeremiah's tears reach no further than to warn the people, not to turn them.

I wonder how God feels about my own day. Would a Noah bring this generation to repentance? Could Moses plead their guilt? Might not Daniel deliver them? Something is there which says no. My generation is doomed to condemnation—would that I could wash their guilt with tears! Lord, remember mercy.

MARCH 25 *Ezekiel 12–24* The parabolic nature of Ezekiel's ministry got for him the title "a speaker of proverbs." Not only did he interpret his situation by the use of extended prophetic parables (namely, the eagles of 17:3, cauldron of 24:3, and so on) but also by short cryptic sayings taken from the vernacular of the captivity:

12:22: The days are prolonged and every vision fails, or the days are at hand and fulfillment of every vision.
16:44: As is the mother, so is her daughter.
18:2: The fathers have eaten sour grapes, and the children's teeth are set on edge.

MARCH 25 *Revelation* Spoke in Maplewood Hall, Saint Louis, in a special parents' night Gospel meeting. Took from Revelation 1:18, "Behold, I am alive," three instructions:

1. Enlightenment about the person of Christ
   I am; I became; I have.
2. Encouragement in the presence of death
   I fell as one dead: I became dead; I have keys of death.
3. Instruction in the "problems of life"
   a. Insured of a promise of afterlife: "Because I live" (John 14:19).
   b. Insured of perseverance in this life: "He is able to" (Heb. 7:25).

c. Insured of being saved to the uttermost: "Seeing he ever lives" (Heb. 7:25).
d. Insured of punishment for this life.
e. "As I live" (Rom. 14:11).
f. Given assurance in that He raised Him (Acts 17:31).

Spoke there before on Matthew 11:28 and in South Side once on 1 Corinthians 15: *vanity* of faith, preaching, labor, and so on.

When it comes time to die, make sure that all you have to do is die!

APRIL 1   *Ezekiel 46*   I have not broken bread with believers since the Sunday before Thanksgiving, at Lombard, I believe. I feel no outward change, due to the lack of this means of grace, but sense a desire, an inner want, need, to break bread. This is the longest period I have missed it, and cannot help but feel somehow that the stimulus of worship has a powerful influence in introducing the mind to fresh truth about Christ. The period has been one of waiting and working, and I see that I have not been fertile in enunciating to myself new truth. How often in those worship times I have been unaffected, unmoved by the grandeur of the sacrifice! Lord, forgive. I would remember Thee, in the way You prescribed.

Noted for the first time the manner of entry and exit commanded in the future temple (vv. 9, 10). When one entered by the way of the south gate, he was to leave by the north gate. The instruction is plain, "He shall not return by way of the gate whereby he came in." How often I have done this in the remembrance feast, approaching the sacrifice and then turning my back on it as I left. The nature of the feast is such that one who has truly partaken cannot go away in the same way he has come in—even as in the temple of the city "Jehovah-shammah."

APRIL 2   I have been thinking for some time of the degrees of punishment suited to degrees of disobedience. In the cases cited, it appears that punishment becomes greater as knowledge (of God's truth) increases, but is not brought into correspondence with life.

Luke 10:12–15: "It shall be *more tolerable* in that day for Sodom, than for that city" (which rejects the sent disciple) (cf. Matt. 10:15; 11:24).

Luke 12:47, 48: "And that servant, who knew his lord's will, and made not ready, shall be beaten with many stripes, but he that knew not, and did things worthy of stripes, shall be beaten with few stripes." Much required of him to whom much is given.

John 19:11: "Thou wouldst have no power against me, except it were given thee from above: therefore, he that delivered me to thee (Caiaphas?) hath *greater* sin."

James 3:1: Be not many *teachers*, knowing that he shall receive the *greater* condemnation.

Mark 12:40: Scribes . . . shall receive the greater (περισσότερος) damnation.

Noted three occurrences of faith, hope, and love in separate contexts which stress one of these above the others:

1 Corinthians 13:13: "Now abideth faith, hope, and love: and the greatest of these is *love*"—in relation to church operation.

Colossians 1:4, 5: ". . . having heard of your faith in Christ Jesus, and the love which ye have for all the saints, because of the *hope* which is laid up for you in the heavens . . . ."
". . . not moved away from the hope" (v. 23).
". . . Christ in you the hope of glory" (v. 27).

1 Thessalonians 1:3: "Remembering your work of *faith* and labor of love and patience of hope . . . ."
". . . in every place your *faith* is gone forth" (v. 8).

C. S. Lewis (in *Out of the Silent Planet*) says: Body is movement (not matter in three elements—solids, liquids, and gases). The faster a thing moves, the more nearly is it in two places at once. Increase movement to infinity, absolute speed, and you have omnipresence, something everywhere at once. The fastest thing we perceive is light and now science is telling us that light is particle (matter) and wave (motion) at once. Interesting again to toy with John's definition: "God is light."

APRIL 9   Preached last night for the first time in the Sparta Chapel. About forty-five out, and there seemed a new warmth among the saints, especially from those who at first opposed our breaking bread because we had no letter. Thank God for their melting; I trust it is a sign of blessing to come. Ed ministered the resurrection from Paul's preaching at Athens, before the Sanhedrin, and before Felix. Best I've heard him. Keep him moving, Lord; loose his tongue.

I preached on *The Chosen One:*

1. The Selected Servant ($\alpha i \rho \epsilon \tau i \zeta \omega$ [Matt. 12:18]; cf. $\alpha i \rho \epsilon \omega$ [Heb. 11:25]) God's *preference* ("choosing rather").
   Chosen servant above the others termed "my servants" in Isaiah 41–53. Christ stands in contrast to the others (cf. 42:1–5).
   a. Israel: failing servant (42:19).
   b. Isaiah: discouraged servant (49:4).
   c. Cyrus: striving servant (44:28).
   God needed an executor to finish a work. (When I look, there is no man [41:28]). God needed an example—to begin a work.
2. The Marked-out Magistrate $\dot{o}\rho i \zeta \omega$ (Acts 10:42; 17:3; cf. Rom. 1:4 "declared"). God's *publishing* of His choice.
   Chosen a judge because He alone suited
   a. No man deserved the honor (John 5:23).
   b. No angel has the right to judge a man.
   c. No devil could have God's glory at heart.
3. The Appointed Heir $\tau i \theta \eta \mu \iota$ "to choose with establishing finality, to constitute, set." The *permanence* of God's choice.

Christ is worthy to inherit God's creation.
Christ is able to handle God's estate.

Sense a fresh zest in prophecy these days. I can remember when Ezekiel and Daniel were tedious, now I find them challenging and stimulating. Behold, how my Shepherd feeds me with food convenient for me! I feel a need to understand the visions, sensing somehow that the sealing up is over and the revelation of the last times is upon my generation. Lord, grant light in these marvels. "Open *thou* mine eyes, that I may behold wondrous things . . ." (Pss. 119:18).

APRIL 11   Ed and I have quite gone the rounds on the true meaning of "the Kingdom." I have not been able to reconcile the traditional view of Scofield and early English Brethren to the simple presentation of the Kingdom given by the Lord Jesus and Paul. The Kingdom of God exists forever, and in the present church age, there is no relinquishment of it.

In history: Daniel 4:35; 6:26—the kingdom seen as unchangeable. Psalms 9:7—Jahweh sits as a king forever. The Kingdom of God has existed from everlasting, and it will never be otherwise. This is the *actual* governing power in the universe. Authority has been delegated to men who in turn relinquished it to Satan. When Christ came, He came presenting a new phase of the Kingdom with Himself as the King—God's plan to restore the rulership of earth to a *man*, its intended governor. Entering the Kingdom now consists in recognizing the *actual* Governor, instead of obeying the rebels (men) and the usurper (Satan). The laws of that Kingdom supersede all custom and ordinance of men, and should there be a conflict, the latter must be disregarded.

In prophecy: When Christ said the Kingdom of God was at hand, and that some standing there would see it come in power, He meant what He said and never withdrew those statements. This business of offering Israel an earthly Kingdom, and then withholding it because of their unbelief is nonsense. If Christ would have set up an earthly rule, how should prophecy have had its fulfillment regarding His death and resurrection? The Kingdom came in power when the King took His throne, and the recognition of Him as living King, substantiated by obedience to His words, makes me a member of His Kingdom.

In the days of Daniel, when the Kingdom had been wrested from Israel, and Gentile powers passed their authority from one to another, it is encouraging to see the contrast of the Kingdom of the Most High.

2:44: "In the days of those kings shall the God of heaven set up a kingdom that shall never be destroyed, nor shall the sovereignty thereof be left to another people . . . it shall stand forever." Destroying all, none destroys that Kingdom.

4:34: "His dominion is an everlasting dominion and his kingdom from generation to generation."

5:21: "The Most High God rules in the kingdom of men and he sets up over it whomsoever he will."

6:26: "His kingdom shall not be destroyed; and his dominion shall be even unto the end.

7:14: "The Son of Man . . . unto him was given dominion, glory, and a kingdom that all the peoples, nations, and languages should serve him: his dominion is an everlasting dominion which shall not pass away, and his kingdom that which shall not be destroyed."

7:27: "And the kingdom and the dominion, and the greatness of the kingdoms under the whole heaven, shall be given to the people of the saints of the Most High: his kingdom is an everlasting kingdom, and all dominions shall serve and obey him."

APRIL 14, 15   Visited Barb Priddy in Memphis with Jim Rust [Wheaton classmates]. Blessed by the trip, weather, and fellowship there. Spoke some with Rust about Ecuador. Study of the Word is not fresh these days. Lord, restore me that I might receive.

APRIL 17 *Joel*   Joel, the prophet, opened up this morning in an understandable sequence. The more I read the prophets, the further I am convinced of the historico-futurist principle of hermeneutics. The prophet must be heard in his historical environment and understood there. Then one must look at what he himself perhaps did not see—the body of prophetic truth which cast its shadow around him, but actually was far ahead of his day.

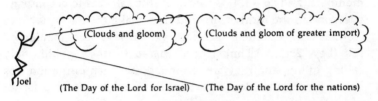

(Clouds and gloom)   (Clouds and gloom of greater import)

Joel

(The Day of the Lord for Israel)   (The Day of the Lord for the nations)

The phrase "the day of the Lord" is the key to the entire prophecy. Divisions:

1. The day of the Lord at hand for Zion (1:15; 2:1; 2:11)
    Devastation of the land (1:1–20)
    Description of the army (2:1–11)
    Declaration of repentance (2:12–17)
2. The deliverance of the Lord promised
    Removal of destroyers (2:18–20)
    Restoration of Zion (2:21–27)
    Results for all flesh and a remnant of Israel (2:28–32)
        verse 31 leads to spiritual blessing
3. The day of the Lord near for the nations (3:14)
    Recompense upon nations (3:1–17)
    Reward for Zion (3:18–21), leads to physical blessing

There is nothing which hints at Joel's having apprehended a personal Messiah, either coming or ruling.

APRIL 22   *Mark 8*   Sensed great liberty declaring the Gospel at South Side Chapel in Saint Louis. Spoke on "the leaven of Herod" (Mark 8:15), showing the growth and permeating effect of unforsaken sin. God warned Herod in John, and reminded him through Jesus, but when he silenced both of these voices in his conscience, God left him, and when Herod faced Christ, Christ had no more to say to him.

APRIL 26 *Mark 9*   Pondering some the puzzle of salt in Mark 9:49, 50. The context indicates that salt in verse 49 means purgative trial and conflict—the overcoming of offending members, and so on. It is said that this salt was to accompany everyone in the form of fire and thus make each acceptable to God, as Old Testament sacrifices were always accompanied by salt (Lev. 2:13). All must be prepared to undergo this fiery salting in life, and they are reminded that such purgation was better by far than to be cast into hell where the fire is not quenched, the sting never subsides (v. 50). Salt is good; such difficulties profit a soul if they have their intended effect, that is, purge, preserve, and season the soul. But if the salt lose its saltiness—that is, if the trial does not accomplish its purging, preserving, and maturing purposes—how can *anything* be done for the soul or the salt? Therefore, let salt do its work in you; have it in yourselves and the result will be the peaceful preservation of unity. They had begun with this in verse 34 where the oneness of the group had been shaken.

MAY 9 *Habakkuk 3*   Sense the indistinctness of lost fellowship again these days. It's awful to have no joy in reading the Word and no fervor in prayer. The causes of vacillation are hard to define. But I feel a certain amount of unbelief to be principal. The Word has left us without marked blessing here so far, though we have done what we could as we knew how to do it. The taunt of "thickened" men who are at ease comes easy. "Jehovah will not do good, neither will he do evil" (Zeph. 1:12). I have a tendency to project my unimpassioned, powerless life to the Most High—I do no good or evil and assume that *He* is the cause for it! Base, wretched rebel that I am! O Lord, let me have the spirit of Habakkuk, confident and exultant.

Though the fig tree flourish not
Though the vine-fruit be forgot;
Though the olive effort fail,
Desolation the fields assail
Though the flock from the fold should fall,
And the herd be vanished from its stall,
Yet in the Lord will I be glad,
For God's salvation with joy be clad.
The Lord Jehovah my strength shall be,
He makes my feet like the hind's to flee
Uplifted in lofty hills!

Habakkuk 3:17–19

Preached last Sunday in Sparta on the Glory of God (John 12:12–14; 13:31. The hour of it (John 12:16, 23, 27, 28; 13:31)

Delayed—Son of Man's glory; preferred—Father's glory.
Deliberate—I will glorify it again.

The power of it:

1. To work through evil (John 13:31). I, if I be lifted up, will *draw all* men.
2. To reach Gentiles in spite of Jewish unbelief (Rom. 9:23; Exod. 33; Isaiah 52; 53:1, 6)—whole earth full of glory.

MAY 12 *Haggai*   Three separate prophecies in the second year of Darius:

First day, sixth month (1:1–12)—plea for rebuilding (vv. 12–15, promise of response "I am with thee," twenty-fourth day, sixth month).

Twenty-first day, seventh month (2:1–9)—promise of restoration.

Twenty-fourth day, ninth month (2:10–20)—powerless people; profitless land. Twenty-fourth day, ninth month (2:21)—promise to Zerubbabel.

Consider!

1. Your ways (1:5, 7).
2. This day (2:15, 18).

Struck with the impotency of the people in the two queries put to the priests in 2:12–14. They could make nothing holy by contact with it, but they could defile. So it is with me. I have no potency to influence for good in the "things that are touched," but am capable of influencing for evil. The holy flesh carried about could not sanctify contacts, but the defilement of death could be passed along. This is a strange principle—rot will encourage rot, but one ripe piece of fruit will not allay rottenness in another. Surely righteousness has the power to make righteous, if it be found in strong enough proportions; but in Israel it was not so. God was not satisfied with their carelessness regarding His house and made their work profitless (1:6) and their worship powerless (2:14).

MAY 21   *2 Timothy 3*   Began tent meetings the nineteenth, Saturday night. Encouraged with about sixty, then had about eighty to ninety last night. Do not feel sufficiently burdened to carry on much effective work, although the opportunity is very good and unsaved are coming out. Lord, lay the souls of men heavily upon me; grant me passion that I might labor impelled by the Spirit.

Spoke on 2 Timothy 3:1–10: lovers of self, money, pleasure, and God on Saturday. Last night on Judas the man with:

1. An unrespected reputation.
2. An unappreciated relationship.
3. Unlimited opportunity.
4. Unused reward—lost his bargain.
5. Useless repentance.
6. Untold retribution—better were it for him if he had not been born.

MAY 23   Bill Cathers dropped in at noon and stayed for tent meeting to preach. Enjoyed fellowship with Ed and him together for the first time. Believe now that God is going to lead us into work together in Ecuador, and trust His grace to knit us and make us compatible. The Lord has answered, rather is answering, my prayer of August 9, 1950, for another man. Father, preserve Ed and Marilou for the Yumbo [the Quichua Indians of Ecuador's jungle]; preserve Bill and Irene; preserve me and prepare us all for Thy work in Ecuador. Many, many thanks for our leading to this moment. Lead on, O King Eternal . . . .

Noted entrance requirements for the Kingdom yesterday:

1. Must be born again (John 3:3).
2. Must be as a little child (Matt. 18:3).
3. Must exceed scribes and Pharisees in righteousness (Matt. 5:20).

Preached on Thomas, Tuesday:

Didymus—your twin and mine (John 11:16).
Daring in words (John 11:16).
Dubious—how can we know? (John 14:5). Except I see and touch (John 20:25).

Discovered another hint of the Trinity in Matthew 23:8–10:

Be not called Rabbi (Bible teacher!). One is your teacher—
the Spirit (cf. John 14:26; 16:13; 1 John 2:27).
Call none father—One is your Father.
Be not called masters—One is your Master, Christ.

The judgment of the sheep and goat nations of Matthew 25:31–46 is not merely for a millennium. The punishment for not aiding Christ's destitute brethren is eternal; and the reward for assisting them is not merely millennial blessing on earth, but eternal life (25:46).

JUNE 6   Completing eighteen days of tent meetings in Chester tonight. Interest good. Should continue, but must go home, though I may one day be sorry for it. Two girls want to be baptized, but I cannot even do that, I fear. Every weekend taken up in June.

It is solemn enough to think of El Elyon taking an oath; but how much more so to consider whereby He swears!

Genesis 22:16: I swear by Myself—none greater—to Abraham.
Psalms 89:35: I have sworn by My holiness—none purer—to David.
Psalms 95:11: I swore in my wrath (or by it)—none more fearful—to Israel.

JUNE 7   Continued meetings because of crowd last night. Winters and Walter will take over for the weekend while Ed and I are in Michigan; then we'll carry on until next Thursday.

JUNE 8–10   Weekend with young people from First Baptist Church in Pontiac at La Peer, Michigan. Spoke on "Intensity and Discipleship." Well received. Met the Holboths; drove up and back with J. Rust from Springfield.

JUNE 11   Ed in Pontiac. Returned to a small tent crowd. Needs advertising and power. Why, oh, why, are the forces of God so few and feeble while the Enemy counts multitudes on his side? Lord, how long will You hide Yourself, concealing Your power and letting men think low thoughts of You? Begin to move, Lord, for the sake of the *Name!* Move me, as well, and let me know the fullness of the Spirit.

JUNE 12   Stirred last night in the reading of a condensation of Elinor Lipper's autobiographical *Eleven Years in Soviet Prison Camps.* Found my prayer this morning tinted with doubt at the goodness of God in allowing apparent innocents to suffer. What an awful place earth is—and how little we Americans know about life as it is lived by Asiatics. "May heaven preserve man from enduring what man is able to endure." This line speaks grimly of an attitude only one who has suffered at the hands of fellow creatures can develop sincerely. The wretchedness of the living death even now being undergone—as I write this morning—by hundreds of thousands of unfortunates—who can say what it means?

Often in this kind of reading I will run across a date on which something particularly horrible occurred. Never does it fail to strike me as I think what *I* was doing that day. While an emaciated woman was raped in the smelly hold of a prison ship by a skinny brute who hadn't seen a woman in seven years, I was complaisantly riding a bicycle on Mount Tabor, toying at model ships, studying simple algebra. And evil has not ceased; for even as I write this, somewhere man is proving the beastliness of his heart, accrediting the worst of the doctrine of total depravity. How I can be unmoved and how God can stay His hand—I don't know. What power must possess a man to obey the word of Christ, "Resist not evil" (Matt. 5:39).

Psalm 37 came as help in this dilemma. "Fret not thyself because of evil-doers . . . they shall soon [oh, how long the years!] be cut down . . . Delight thyself in the Lord . . . wait patiently for him . . . cease from anger, and forsake wrath . . . For yet a *little while,* and the wicked shall not be, yea, thou shalt diligently consider his place, he shall not be."

JUNE 14   Finished tent meetings in Chester, preaching from Acts 1:11: "This Jesus shall so come . . . ." Impossible to register the good God has done in Chester. I can see several reasons for coming now that I did not see in January. Surely the Lord has led. Still nothing "big" or extraordinary in the work of the Gospel, and this I judge to be only because I lacked intensity and perseverance in prayer. Lift me to heights of desire, Lord, and teach me to pray!

JUNE 15–17   Young People's Retreat at Wil Brunk's Arcadia Valley Bible Camp, Ironton, Missouri. Ministered on John 8:31:

Discipleship: Its meaning (learning, following)
                Its marks (progress, problems, power)
                Its maintenance

JUNE 18   Memphis by bus from Chester. Met Bill Ramer, a prospective missionary for whom I must pray. Peggy and Barb are here. Good times of converse with them both. Barb is very responsive to New Testament church principles. God is doing things for her in this polio trial, and Peggy, too, is enlarging in her spirit. Be near them, Lord, and give them godly husbands, men worthy of them.

JUNE 20–23   Oklahoma City. Flying visit with assembly folks here. Growth evident in most, though there are laggers. Spoke Thursday eve on 1 Corinthians 1–3:

Christ the Enricher (1:5)
The Holy Spirit—the Enlightener (2:9–11)
God—the Enlarger (Increaser) (3:7, 23)

JUNE 24   Bill's wedding in Wichita. Preached in hall on John 8:31.

JUNE 26, 27   Huntington. Brief visit with believers. Work there, Lord, work miracles!

JUNE 28, 29   Detroit and Pontiac for Ed's wedding. Happy fellowship with 49ers, back to Wheaton.

JULY 1   At Finchford Community Church with G. Griebenow.

JULY 2, 3   Denver with Birdie. Star Ranch and home via DC-6. First plane ride. Thrilled at the wonders of the air.

JULY 12   Waiting on God for work and guidance these days. Arrived home from Denver with $1.20 in my pocket. Worked one day last week stripping concrete forms. Staub Memorial Church invited me to speak at their Young People's Retreat. Friday and Saturday at Welches on the Salmon River. Ministered with joy and liberty from John 20: 21, 22: "As my Father has sent me, even so send I you . . . receive ye the Holy Spirit."

The Lord gave liberty at Prescott on Sunday from John 12:24: "Who Is This Son of Man," touching on the humanity of Christ and something of the meaning of the incarnation.

Lack funds in hand to buy equipment now. Folks are not wholeheartedly for my going to Ecuador. Want me to be a preacher in the States, I fear, or else to join Bert in Peru.

JULY 13   *John 12–14*   Got help tonight on that puzzling sequence of John 12:31 and 14:30. "The prince of this world is cast out"; "The prince of this world cometh." I have recently felt that the first of these may refer to Christ—that perhaps there were two princes of the world—Christ the rejected One, and Satan, the one who comes chosen as it were by the rejection of the Prince from heaven.

However, Neil Frazer [a Plymouth Brethren preacher] suggested that in the first instance, the place from whence the prince was cast out was not earth, but heaven. It may be that the triumph of Christ at Calvary unseated Satan's position of Job 1 and 2, among the sons of God before the throne. Being therefore cast out of heaven, he is described as "coming" (14:30). With this seems to agree Revelation 12:9, 13 where the cast-out dragon persecutes the Jews—Jerusalem's being destroyed forty years after the resurrection. Supporting this also is Romans 8:33: "Who shall bring anything to the charge of God's elect?" Satan now has no grounds of criticism, and it may be that since the Advocate is seated, Satan cannot accuse the brethren as before the work at Calvary. Still, he is called the "accuser" and the defensive aspects of Christ's office as advocate imply interference (in the heavens) with the cause of the saints. How little do I see!

JULY 13
Intensity

  1 Timothy 4:15: ἐν τούτοις ἴσθι.
  Philippians 1:21: τὸ ζῆν Χριστὸς ἐμοί.

The Christian is a qualitatively different sort of man (1 Cor. 3:3; 2 Pet. 3:11).

  Belongs to another race (1 Pet. 2:9).
  Draws from another source of life (John 7:37, 38; 4:14).
  Lives according to different motives and customs (2 Cor.
      5:15; Phil. 3:20).

Need
Yet must lack
  Desire for this life.
  Drive to pursue it.
  Direction to attain it.

Direction
We must
  Give up . . . "*one* thing thou lackest" (Mark 10:21).
  Sit down . . . "*one* thing is needful" (Luke 10:42).
  Get on . . . "*one* thing I do" (Phil. 3:13).

"*Unite* my heart to fear thy name" (Pss. 86:11).
  Singleness of heart (Acts 2:46), no double motives.
  Singleness of eye (Matt. 6:22), no divided attentions.

Motivation
Nazariteship—the *special* vow—the overcomer.
  Three Nazarites: The sons of barren women—God's
      power comes from weakness.

Vows regarding: Samuel—first of the prophets (Acts 3:24; 13:20) (last of judges).

Wine—my rights.

Hair—the customs. Samson—strongest of the judges (power depends on purity).

Dead bodies—sin: John the Baptist—last of the prophets and greatest (Luke 7:28; Matt. 11:13).

The study of the Scriptures must be done:

1. With desire
2. Daily
3. Devotedly
4. Doggedly

(*Determination* not *desire* decides destiny.)

The truth makes me free from:

1. Satan's delusions
2. Sin's deceptions
3. Self's deprivations

JULY 15   Neil Frazer at Bible study:

Faith that delivers—Sarah's before Isaac's birth.

Faith that defies—Moses' parents, after Moses' birth.

Faith that decides—Moses' choice, as a man.

Faith that discerns—Jacob's hands on his grandson in old age.

Faith that desires—Joseph's bones, hoped for another country as he died.

The "Son of Man"—because He is *man*—has leaped racial barriers. No more is He a "Jew." He has put Jew and Gentile at peace with one another. "He who has made Jew and Gentile one, and *in His own human nature* has broken down the hostile dividing wall . . ." (Eph. 2:14 WEYMOUTH).

JULY 26   Marveling lately on the words of Scripture concerning likeness to Christ. What a job God has undertaken to do this in me—renew me unto an εἰκὼν of Christ! I see now:

1. Eternal purpose (Rom. 8:28, 29).
2. The present accomplishment (2 Cor. 3:18; 1 Cor. 2:16).
3. The actual fulfillment (1 Cor. 15:49; Phil. 3:21).

Take hold, God of Eternal Counsel! Carry on Your great purpose in me. You have certainly set a task for Yourself!

AUGUST 21   *1 Thessalonians 1:4*   Ocean Park, Washington, "Collison Cottage" [the home of Jim's relatives]. Reading 1 Thessalonians 1:4. Paul *knew* the election of the Thessalonians, not before he went there (and therefore went), but after he had been there and seen: (1) the way the Word was preached, (2) the manner of the apostles' lives, and (3) the result in the believers. Election is known only to God prior to its operation. But *as it* operates, it is demonstrable, and Paul was thankful *knowing* their election by the manner and results of the preached message. These are the proofs of election—the Gospel preached:

1. "In word" (not *only* "in word," but "in word" nonetheless, that is, with careful adherence to the factual details and implications of the Gospel). *Paul's part.*
2. "In power," that is, with accompanying signs and wonders (Rom. 15:19); ". . . in the word of truth, in the power of God" (2 Cor. 6:7). No signs are recorded at Thessalonica, however, and it may be that this reference to power is identical with that of Romans 1:16, "the power of God for salvation," that is, the Word preached wrought deliverance in the hearers, a sign of its being preached in power (*Any observer's observation*).
3. "In the Holy Spirit," the unseen force of the Word preached. The explanation of the power observed is that of the divine Mover in the Word (*God's part*).

4. "In much assurance." The settled persuasion of those who believed in that city (Acts 17:4) (*Thessalonians' experience*).

These four proofs made Paul know of certainty the election of the Thessalonians. This is why he could leave them shortly (three sabbaths?) to God's care. He was positive as to their election. Why we do not see these things operating, I cannot tell, but, Lord, make *election* operate!

AUGUST 28   *1 Timothy*   Helped this morning in seeing the recurrence of the word *charge* in 1 Timothy.

In 1:13, Timothy was left with a "charge" at Ephesus. It was to warn certain men not to teach another doctrine. (Incidentally, not only is "other doctrine" contrary to sound Christian instruction, but evil living is contrary to it as well. Ungodliness in all its phases and "any other thing contrary to sound doctrine" [v. 10]). The purpose of it was to attain a household governorship of God (v. 4) with the practical personal results of love, a good conscience, and unfeigned faith (v. 5).

In verse 18 the charge is committed to him again, to confirm by letter as it were, a directive first transmitted by word of mouth. In this I recognize a very real control factor which Paul exercised over Timothy. He was not only making suggestions as to the movements of certain brethren (that is, Apollos [1 Cor. 16:12]), but seemed to exercise an authority over the movements of younger men. Titus (2 Corinthians 8:17, 18, 22: "he accepted indeed our exhortation; but being himself very earnest, he went forth unto you of his own accord") and the other "brother" *sent* with him to Corinth, and Timothy sent to Thessalonica, seem to move at the express directions of Paul (1 Thess. 3:2). This authority may be exclusive to the apostle, given especially to build up the churches (2 Cor. 13:10), but nowhere is such expressly stated.

Does it not seem likely that this is the pattern—method, rather? Should not the leading evangelist or missionary have the same right and honor to, in one sense, arrange the affairs relating to churches he has established? The word *charge* παραγγέλιον is used as a military term for "command" or "direct" in Xenophon. Paul's reference to military relations (fellow soldier, a good soldier of Jesus Christ, and so on) may be enlarged to include the military tactic of subordination to God-appointed leaders in the battlefield. This of course must be modified to conform to Paul's situation. It does not imply mission boards, nor ecclesiastical overlordship. It merely suggests that senior, experienced warriors who are familiar with the whole area of conflict and *are themselves active* in it, have right and responsibility to, within limits, ask younger men to make moves profitable to the overall advance of the effort.

SEPTEMBER 14   *Psalm 119*   Staying at 645 [his uncle's house in Glen Ellyn, Illinois] these days. En route to New York area for meetings with Bill. Startled at the Lord's instruction coinciding with my need these days. Fearing the power of television last night, Psalms 119:37, "Turn away mine eyes from beholding vanity, quicken me in thy ways" came as counsel this morning. Lost victory in not obeying it tonight at Bob and Margaret's. Sense the powerful *decentralizing* effect it has on my mind and affections. It "quickens" me in ways not God's and defeats the purpose of the prayer to be quickened in ways divine. Lord, grant me a disciplined spirit and an obedient body henceforth.

SEPTEMBER   20–22   Arrived in Moorestown, New Jersey. Came to settled rest about Betty. I love her. The problem from now on is not "whom should I marry?" but "should I marry?" Nearer to her now than ever, yet more confident still that God is leading me away from her, to Ecuador with Pete, and she to the South Seas. [Pete Fleming, an old friend of Jim's, had just received his master's degree and traveled with Jim for a series of speaking engagements.] This is a strange pattern. Fields behind Birdsong [the Howard home] Saturday. Discovered later that this contact was terribly upsetting to her. She wept Sunday and came to peace on Monday.

Preached with Bill at Front Street Missionary meeting in

Plainfield. Felt utterly graceless, ministering from Romans 15:14–22. "Fulfilled the gospel" (v. 19). "Not where Christ was named" (v. 20).

Preached this morning on the resurrection, 1 Corinthians 15, arguments and defense; Acts 17:31; Romans 10:9 at Gospel Hall in Maplewood, New Jersey. Tonight there on Psalms 110:1 as used in the New Testament.

SEPTEMBER 26   Preached last night in Jersey City on pattern principles—"Paulicy"; how that it *exists* (traditions of 1 Cor. 11:2; 2 Thess. 2:15; 3:6; 1 Tim. 1:16), how that we are obliged to follow it (1 Cor. 3; Phil. 4:9), and how that it is universally applicable. Believers seemed warmed and interested in Ecuador.

Kiss me, Heavenly Lover, in the morning.
Be Thou the first to sweeten
This whole day's speech with that warm, honeyed touch
Of Thy caress.
And tenderly, while yet each eye lies unawaked,
Come lightly and impart to them
For day's long hour a heavenly set
To see all things as through a lover's eyes,
By soft caresses from the lips of Him
Who lives in Paradise.
Kiss me, Christ of Beauty, here alone
The two of us, while dawn
Steals down the slopes and
Wakens day's bright eye to smile on me.
Let not its luring draw me from the sense
That I belong to One
Whose first embrace full ravishes,
Who has kissed the son.

SEPTEMBER 27   Preaching every night. Monday at Madison Church House. Bill and I both gave details of the Lord's guidance. Tuesday, Jersey City. Ministered of Pauline traditions. Wednesday, Pete, Bill, and I for the first time together shared our exercise at Kenilworth. Thursday, Tenafly—strange meeting, little liberty.

Cannot seem to get much joy from describing details of our leading. Testimonial speaking is not compelling to my soul. I long to cut loose in some passage and open it up. Still, they must know of our background to pray sensibly for us. This visit to New York has certainly been a blessing from God to show me the *family* relationships and joys. Haven't been here a week yet but feel as though I had met a host, and known him for years. Surely God is good to His *Israel!* How delightful a teacher, but gentle a provider, how bountiful a giver is my Father! Praise, praise to Thee, O manifested Most High.

Called Bett today. She wants me to come down to stay with her tomorrow night after Tidmarsh's farewell in Plainfield. I hesitate as it will complicate things and provide some embarrassment since Pete is already expecting me. Guide me, Lord, let me miss no path I must walk to deal justly.

Later. Went to Moorestown. Sat close, very close as we neared there. She had told her parents the news of our desire and intention, under God, of marriage. They were much more affable and hearty. Mom and Dad came down to Moorestown and took us to the station [the Elliot's had driven Jim east from Portland]. South Seas out! [My own inquiries into South Seas missionary work had proved unfruitful.]

SEPTEMBER 30   Flushing. Spoke from Matthew 28, the Great Commander, the Great Command, and the things commanded, on Saturday night. Sunday in the breaking of bread, the Spirit peculiarly centered our hearts on thoughts of the Father. ". . . how full is Abbah's Name!" Much enjoyed the feast. Ministered from John 17 on the fatherliness of God, Abram and Abraham, and Christ's prayers to the Father. Experienced great liberty on Sunday afternoon in speaking of "Even as the Father hath sent me, so send I you." The preceding display of His wounds indicates that He was sent for suffering and sacrifice—and so were they. The succeeding admonishment, "Receive ye the Holy Spirit," indicates that their power was as His—in dependence upon the Holy Spirit.

OCTOBER 1   Elizabeth, New Jersey. Great joy in a missionary meeting for prayer and testimony. Spoke afterward with Carl Johnson of Congo. He counseled Pete and me thus: (1) never let the sun go down on the slightest miff between us. Walk in the light with no darkness between us; (2) always be willing to abase yourself before a native. "We think and say that we are just being 'firm,' but they know that we are angry"; (3) beware of idols. In going to lead other men away from idols, the Enemy will put them in your own house. His hobby, he said, was hunting; he got to like it better than speaking to souls about Jesus. *Beware, my soul, of idols.*

OCTOBER 6   "Begotten again unto a living hope." Every Jew, because he was born a son of Abraham, was born with great hopes. His were the "adoption" and the glory, and the covenants and the giving of the law, and the service (of God), and the fathers, and so on. His hopes then had high aspects. Alas, however, those hopes were dying. As the nation's history wore on, those hopes seemed more and more distant. Each succeeding generation drifted further from the realization of Jewish hopes. It was a "dying hope," dying as every father in Israel died, dying as the nation's glory faded. But now, says Peter, a "living hope" is ours, because of a begetting with greater implications is ours. Now we come into the inheritance, not of the land promised Abraham, but of that incorruptible, undefiled, and unfading inheritance in the heavens. Because we live through higher means (that is, the begetting of the Spirit), we become inheritors of greater marvels (that is, spiritual possessions). It is ours through greater mercy from God and by the resurrection of Jesus Christ from the dead.

OCTOBER 8   Lake Oswego, Great Bay Harbor, and shore. Keswick Conference picnic supper with just Betts. Happiest birthday ever. Met her pupils [two missionary children whom I tutored for a year]. Philadelphia on Tuesday. Lunch at Wanamaker's.

OCTOBER 16   Music Hall show with her and B. [Bill Cathers].

OCTOBER 17   Beach with Flemings, B., and I, and Betts.

OCTOBER 18   *Psalms 1:1, 2*   The nature of the concerns of the righteous man stand out tonight. It is plainly contrasted with the concerns of the wicked. Note: the nature of the righteous's meditation is *law*, settled, established, absolute. Whereas the other is found bothering with "counsel," a variable of extreme insecurity. Or with "ways," tentative methods of action. Or with the "seat" of the scornful—that is, his position, an unstable, unsettled, and unreliable rest. But the righteous, he delights in *laws*, firm and secure and eternal. Beware, my soul, of regarding lesser controls!

I am discovering Betty all over again these days. She has taken on a new meaning and power—and purity. Last two nights on top of Shelton delightful. Her body, once the thing that disturbed my thoughts of marrying her, seems now to fit the picture well. Thank God for her! Pure and warm and relaxed in my arms—I never guessed it could be. Waiting will be a trial, but loving her purifies me, somehow. "He who loves not lives not," said Raymond Lull. Amen, oh, amen!

OCTOBER 21   Preached at Kenilworth Hall, Kenilworth, New Jersey, on John 8:31: "If you continue . . ." and John 12:34: "Who is this son of man?" Betty and Phil and Marg picked me up afterward, then to New York for Pete and then Franconia, New Hampshire. In the car she pressed my fingers to her lips . . . .

OCTOBER 22   Climbed Bald Mountain. Wind tangling her hair. Kerosine lamp shadows . . . by the fire.

OCTOBER 23   The Flume, the Boiler [the Basin, a natural-rock formation in the Pemigewasset River], Lonesome Lake, the Old Man of the Mountain. Night by the fire. I cried a little at thoughts of leaving her.

OCTOBER 24   Mount Washington. Happy frankness in discussion on the way down. The waterfall that formed two flows, then one, two, and emptied into the pool. Dinner at the hotel in Littleton. Storm at Echo Lake. She wore pearl earrings for me.

OCTOBER 25   She sat at my feet while Pete read some, reclining in black skirt and sweater as Pete read the Ballad of the Northern Lights.

OCTOBER 26   Lake Winnipesaukee, Boston, Providence, the Wagon Wheel, Aunt Bess's for a snack. Night in the living room at Birdsong—talk—oh, such talk! She prayed for my being kept.

OCTOBER 27   She smiled after tears and prayer and told me she loved me. [This was our last time together before Jim sailed for Ecuador in 1952.]

OCTOBER 27, 28   Washington, D.C., with Pfaffs, Maranatha, Bob Smith.

OCTOBER 29   Chicago.

OCTOBER 30   Saint Louis, Maplewood.

OCTOBER 31   Sparta.

NOVEMBER 4   Sense real bitterness at not receiving a letter from her here in Oklahoma City. Pete heard from Olive, and that aggravated me more. Strange, the mixture of suspicion, attributing carelessness to her, and the strong apologies on her behalf that rise at once in my mind. "She had a whole week to write . . . but she may have lost the address" [this is actually

what happened]. "She doesn't care . . . still, she *must*."
Funny, this being-in-love phase again.

Noted "the commandment" of Psalms 133:3 is "life for
evermore." Seems odd that "life" should be a commandment.
It may refer here to perpetual animation, birth, growth, fruit-
fulness, and so on—as is hinted at in the reference to "dew"
upon the grasses of Hermon. There may be a deeper meaning
if this peculiar combination of "commandment" and "life" be
attached to my Savior's words in John 12:50: "And I know that
his commandment is life eternal . . . ." He who allows for the
unity of Psalm 133 provides it on the basis of eternal life. The
word that He spoke (a command from God) was to be the judge
of His hearers, and that word was "eternal life." If they had not
this word realized in experience in the day of judgment, there
would be no escape. Why? Because it was a *command* from God
that they should have received and obeyed.

NOVEMBER 20 *Genesis 6–9*   Home and trying to get back on
a schedule. While reading the flood account this morning, several things suggested themselves. First, the animals must have
had no fear of man until after the flood. They came of themselves to join Noah and his family in the ark. Not until after the
flood subsided did the Lord say, "The fear of you and the
dread of you shall be upon every beast of the earth" (9:2). The
reason seems to be that men became carnivorous, having up to
that time eaten only the food promised Adam (1:29), herb and
seed, which he shared with the animals (1:30). Second, it does
not seem likely that the flood of Noah's day covered the entire
world. God's interest was only the destruction of men. Where
men had not gone, there was no need of the judgment waters.
Land and *earth* are often indistinguishable in Hebrew. There
was no big spread of population until after Babel. Third, it may
be that 9:5 refers further to the beginning of enmity between
man and beast and, also, to war among men. God, promising
never again to destroy by flood, now declares His means of
judgment. "And surely your blood, the blood of your lives,
will I require" (9:5) and this at the hand of beast and man.

Would to God that the nations would understand their present case was nothing else than God's vengeance upon their violence and corruption (6:11)!

I began last night to consider engagement with Betty. Frightens me to think of finally leaping over all the old barriers I've raised against marriage. Is it to be, after all, the conventional life of rugs and appliances and babies? Is Paul's example of single intensity beyond me? Am I at last not one of those who make themselves eunuchs for the Kingdom of heaven's sake? I feel no bitterness, but a sense of regret at losing all the good liberties God has allowed me until now, should I make the promise. No settlement in my mind one way or another, though I feel strongly that for my own stability, for Betty's ease, and for most folks' tongues, I should buy a ring.

Lord, which way? "Thou hast heard the desire of the meek: Thou wilt prepare their heart" (Pss. 10:17). What shall I say to all the liberty I've been given to preach adherence to Pauline method—even to single men working on the field and illustrating it from Pete's intention and my own? Rather, what will men think who have heard me say, "I go single, in the will of God" when, if I were really engaged, my plans would be otherwise? Well, it is in God's hands. He gave direction to speak that way. And after all, an engaged man *is* still single, but purposing to be married. And Paul would have me free from care . . . did he ever love a woman?

NOVEMBER 21   I want her more today than any day since leaving her. I need her to purify my desires, to lift me above lust. I need her counsel, her attitude, her strength, her fingers, her forehead, and her breasts. My God in heaven, how am I made! Oh, that I had never tasted woman at all, that thirst for her should not be so intense now, remembering. It is not good that man should be alone—not this man, anyhow. Frightfully depressed this whole day, a sense of inner wrong from defeated thinking from lust which warred against my soul. A day when things did not go well—all things seemed to betray me, and nothing satisfied—a day in the presence of demons, crafty, cruel demons who fight under camouflage. God deliver! Oh, make me to take Thy ways of escape. Withal—a sense that I should not ake public betrothal.

NOVEMBER 23   Just read again the story of Abraham. Convenient food just now, with this pressing sense of sex need, the want of warmth and woman—tenderness—relief, and children. God "prepared laughter" for Sarah in her old age, whose promises make Abraham himself fall to the ground and laugh because they seemed so goodly and so impossible. This is fitting for my present attitude because I feel now as though it may mean five years of single life yet—these next five resilient years, years when I will most want her, most need her, and better be able to satisfy her—these years I see in the plan now, must be spent alone. Then, maybe after I'm thirty, getting paunchy, wrinkling, and balding even, then the marriage bed! (Mother said the other day, "Who wants to raise a family after they are thirty, especially a woman?" I had no answer. Certainly not me. All I knew to say was, "You raise a family when God wants you to.")

And I believe, I feel sure, that God is doing the *best* for us, and that in the face of what *seems* most unlikely. Perhaps I'm wrong in planning in terms of years, but a man can't feel the "lustihood of his young powers" swell and surge inside him and not be affected by restraining them. It may be that He hasn't planned to make us wait five years, but it certainly looks from here that it can't be any less. Of course, I hope I'm wrong, but if I'm not, then El Shaddai, the God who saw and heard Hagar, considered Sarai's laugh, and disregarded Abraham's one hundredth year—this God is the One I believe to be guiding and governing me in these affairs. And in this, in prospect, I, with Abraham, can laugh.

NOVEMBER 29   On waking, I enjoyed Psalm 16 this morning as it confirms so many things in my experience recently. And knowing that the psalm was experienced by the Messiah makes it doubly happy. My fears about not being able to raise a family if I *wait* to take Betty, since I may have to wait years, this, added to the possibility of tropical sterility and the generally debilitating effects of jungle living, makes real the opening cry of the psalm, "*Preserve me,* O God." The dozens of little arguments that flood me when I think of waiting—the effect of small remarks dropped by Mother occasionally ("Who wants to raise a family after they're thirty," and so on)—amount to considerable force if I let them work on me. But my refuge is not in answering them one by one and arguing them down; my refuge is in Jehovah whom I have asked to preserve me. For now, and always, "He is the portion of my *inheritance* and of my cup; Thou *maintainest* my lot" (comforting in the extreme, that word *maintain*—stronger than the prayer word *preserve*). Relegating all problems directly to the Lord, trusting implicitly in His guidance, for past and future experience produces the remark, "I will bless Jehovah, who hath given me *counsel.*"

My going to Ecuador is *God's counsel,* as is my leaving Betty, my refusal to be counseled by all who insist I should stay and stir up the believers in the U.S. And how do I know it is His counsel? "Yea, my *heart instructeth* me in the night seasons." Oh, how good, for I have known that—my heart speaking to me for God! "My *heart said for* thee, 'Seek ye my face' " (Pss. 27:8 DARBY). No visions or voices, but the counsel of a heart which desires God. And so I sense that I may share the Christ's words, "I have set Jehovah always before me; He is at my right hand, I shall not be moved" (Acts 2:25). Not moved? With all the awful pressure of inward desire to move me to lust? Not moved. With all demonic hatred to move me to fear and doubt? Not moved. Wherefore? He is before me and on my right hand. "*Therefore my heart is glad!*"

I am reading *The Return of the Native.* Poor Hardy! If only he could have once seen the hand of God. The tragic lines of Egden Heath form patterns which resist any idea of the working of the will. If he could once have experienced a well-timed incident that wrought the greatest possible good, perhaps he would not have written as he did. Each event is so meshed with the unreasoning ill, and the reader gets to expect the blackest. Really he does in the negative what poor novelists do in the positive—accentuates improbabilities—only he does it to his heroes' ill; they to the betterment of theirs. Neither are true to life. Granted, fate and tragedy, aimlessness and just missing by a hair are part of human experience, but they are not all, and I'm not sure that they are even a major part, even in the lives of men who know no Designer or design. For me, I have seen a keener force yet—the force of ultimate good working through seeming (and sensed!) ill. Not that there is rosiness ever; there is genuine ill, struggle, dark-handed, unreasoning fate, mistakes, "if onlys," and all the Hardyisms you can muster. But in them I am beginning to discover a plan greater than any could imagine. Witness three years of relations with Betty!

DECEMBER 1   In reading the Scriptures I find a great moral power. Therein am I made aware of two great forces for good in human experience: the *fear* of God and the *grace* of God. Without the fear of God I should not stop at doing evil; the fear of God restrains from evil. Without the grace of God I should have no desire to approach positive goodness. The one is a deterrent from evil; the other an encouragement to good. "Wherewithal shall a young man cleanse his way?" Not so much make up for what is past, but perfect what is future, "by taking heed thereto [from now on] according to thy word" (Pss. 119:9). "These things I am *writing* to you that you may not sin" (1 John 2:1). The Scriptures were written to this very intent: to be for me a means of grace in struggling against sin. Would that Christians read their Scriptures, we should have a holier band for it.

DECEMBER 2   *Psalm 102: the Gethsemane Psalm*   The cry of the psalmist is that he may not be cut off in the midst of his days (v. 24). A man in the prime of life has strong desire to live.

V. 3: My days consume away like smoke.
V. 11: My days are like a shadow that declineth.
V. 23: He shortened my days.

So Christ, in manhood, cried that His days be not cut short. God, hearing, sent an angel to strengthen Him in the words of verses 24–28: "Thou art the same . . . ." Moses' cry in Psalm 90 displays men as their days are consumed under the wrath of God (Pss. 90:9), but Messiah has His cut off in the wisdom of God. For God, considering from heaven, knew that only thus could the prisoners' sighing cease, the condemned know release, the Name of God be praised (vv. 19–22). Christ in the Garden so cried and was considered.

As a pelican, He went where others could not, a seabird in the wilderness.
As an owl, He went at night, and as a sparrow, He went alone (vv. 6, 7).

DECEMBER 5   Terribly depressed after preaching tonight. Felt as though I had no preparation, no liberty, no power. Once I felt compelled to stop during the sermon and tell the people I didn't have a message from God, but then thought better of it, or rather, thrust it from thought altogether. I never want to preach that way again. Lord God Almighty, let me speak "Thy word as going forth out of Thy mouth." How sadly and how slowly I am learning that loud preaching and long preaching are not substitutes for inspired preaching. Oh, it's awful! To see a room full of people, waiting to hear a word from God, and to have no words—and then to try and make up for it by jumbling unripe, untested ideas with old, dry words and know that your heart isn't in it. El Shaddai! Deliver! Worst of all, the people can't seem to tell the difference when I feel the Spirit and when I don't. Either I am a frightful bluff, or the people are utterly undiscerning—maybe all of both.

DECEMBER 6   Sick, almost crazy, with desire for her tonight. My God, what does a man do? Almost I could desire never to have known embrace, or not to have known it so sweetly, than to know and be denied by distance. If all the comforts of family here and the press of meetings engage, what will it be like in Ecuador? God, make me to forget! I remember too keenly to endure much retrospect. Passion, bordering on frenzy, grips me at times—not always, thank heaven, but often enough to make my denial of her for the work's sake a very real, poignant thing.

In this just now I feel more than anywhere the Lord Jesus' requirement, "Except a man forsake . . . ." Well, thank God for the privilege of giving aught up for His sake. But I know from this present sense of need that I cannot do so forever. Or, perhaps, if He requires that, He will teach me disciplines of desire, something I am not now acquainted with. This makes nine days without a letter. Funny that would not have bothered me in the least last Spring. God help me. Help me to keep desiring *her* of all women. It's sure that way. I want my need to be always of *her*, not merely of *woman*—that would lead to awful temptation.

DECEMBER 9   Finished two weeks' meetings at 87th [87th Street Plymouth Brethren Assembly]. General interest, excellent. No certain decisions, but several very good contacts which God will ultimately make His own. Busy weekend. IVCF retreat yesterday morning. Young People at Hinson Baptist tonight and then the Gospel meeting at 87th. Lord, "the work of our hands, establish thou it" (Pss. 90:17).

DECEMBER 10–12   Seattle shopping with Pedro. [Shopping for equipment for Ecuador with Pete Fleming.]

DECEMBER 13–19   Mount Pleasant, Vancouver, Thursday—on "Being Sent" in John: Sent as little saviors (3:17–19) to speak His Word (3:34). Sunday, 24th and Main in the morning: "The Given Glory of John 17:22":

Grace and truth (of His fullness we received [1:14–18]).
Suffering (chap. 12).
Oneness with God (17:22).

Granville Chapel in the evening on John 12:44–50, the last
public announcement of Jesus in the Gospel. "He cried out."

DECEMBER 22   Christ is termed faithful in two instances in
the New Testament. In Hebrews 2:17, a faithful high priest. In
Revelation 1:5, the faithful witness. As a priest, He must know
the power of sin first, that He might be *merciful.* Then, too, He
must know the persistence of sin, that He might fail us in no
event—He must be *faithful.* Finally, He must know the pain of
sin, that He might succor. Had He not in all things been made
like unto His brethren, He could never have known what
mercy was required, or what faithfulness, or what succor.

But this faithfulness is not alone for the people's sake. "He
was faithful *to Him* that appointed Him" (Heb. 3:2). There was
a sense in which the incarnation provided something in God
Himself. Not that God was unmerciful prior to it, nor unfaith-
ful, nor unsuccoring, but that His mercy is now executed
through experience of trial; His faithfulness the more certain
and real from His having had it pressed to the utmost. It is
valuable to note that He is a high priest "in things pertaining
to God," that is, He is faithful and merciful in respect to matters of deity—not merely "before God" or "in the things of
God for us," but merciful in things that relate directly to God.
God's faithfulness is the greater for having been proved; His
mercy more tender from actually having suffered in a body.

Noted tonight Psalms 116:12: "What shall I render to
Jehovah for all his benefits toward me?" The answers are unusual:

1. I will take (what kind of rendering is this?) the cup of
   salvation.
2. I will pay my vows openly.
3. I will offer the sacrifice of thanksgiving.

This represents:

1. A reception of God's offers, my will acting on His provision.
2. A remembrance of His requirements, my body fulfilling its purpose.
3. A recounting of His goodness, my tongue acclaiming His praise.

DECEMBER 24   Just finished *For Whom the Bell Tolls.* A most intriguing work and one raising some problems for a Christian. Realistic, psychological, compactly detailed, it presents a literary landmark for me for its style alone. Would that I could get as aroused about experiencing God in life as these modern writers are aroused at just experiencing life. They make no comment, draw no conclusions, point no moral, simply state things as they are in simple words in up-to-date settings. Perhaps it is for this very lucidity that they hold such grip on one. Must we always comment on life? Can it not simply be lived in the reality of Christ's terms of contact with the Father, with joy and peace, fear and love full to the fingertips in their turn, without incessant drawing of lessons and making of rules? I do not know.

Only I know that my own life is full. It is time to die, for I have had all a young man can have—at least, all *this* young man can have. If there were no further issue from my training, it would be well—the training has been good and to the glory of God. I am ready to meet Jesus. Failure means nothing now, only that it taught me life. Success is meaningless, only that it gave me further experience for using the great gift of God—*Life.* And, Life, I love thee, not because thou art long, or because thou hast done great things for me, but simply because I have thee from God. This writing is part of thee, and I am glad to write; not that there is any purpose in it for others—it is simply part of Life, and Life I have come to love.

7

Ecuador, 1952–1955

The Plymouth Brethren are not a denomination, strictly speaking, and have no mission board or formal organization, their reason being that they do not find such institutions described in the Bible. They attempt to follow as literally as possible the pattern of the New Testament church. Jim was, as they say, "in fellowship" with these Brethren, and went to Ecuador "commended," that is recognized and vouched for by them. No formal authority was exercised over him and his colleagues, Pete Fleming, Bill Cathers, and Ed McCully, neither was there any promise of financial support from the Brethren. Jim went to Ecuador fully trusting that God would direct his activities and supply his needs. He felt at the same time a serious responsibility to report to the Brethren who were his "overseers" in the Lord.

JANUARY 1   This has been a good day, full of visiting and chatting, resting and remembering. Doctor Charles Taylor and family were with us all last night, leaving at noon this morning. No small sign was given me confirming my going to Ecuador via the *Santa Juana* [a Grace Line freighter]. I have been asking God to seal my leaving, not knowing what to expect. Yesterday several checks came in the mail, and I intended to cash them and send a bank check to Kelley for my passage. But the bank was closed when I finally found a parking place and finished other pressing things yesterday afternoon. Today when I picked up some purchases from Tommy Dryden, he gave me a check for $50. I made no special note of it until I got home and put it with those I got in yesterday's mail. Then I discovered that they totaled $315, my exact fare to Guayaquil! All in twenty-four hours, from five separate sources. This is the first of these miracles I am encouraged to expect. Hallelujah! Praise to the King of heavenly coffers. The checks confirmed my leading to Milwaukee last fall, to Sparta this spring, home this summer, and home now, since all came from individuals whose contacts depended upon my being in those places. Wise Guide, my God. This to encourage me for 1952.

In the last two years I made some of life's biggest decisions. In 1950 it was the understanding that I was to go to Ecuador. In 1951 it was the knowledge of my mate in Betty.

JANUARY 10   Last day in Portland. The past week has been very busy—full of visits and interruptions while packing. But God has been good and exceedingly loving-kind toward me. The saints have given unhesitatingly at every turn and every need has been met—even beyond the need. It is as in the wilderness, "For the stuff they had was sufficient for all the work to make it, *and too much*" (Exod. 36:7). Pete will arrive today, and we will drive to Williams tomorrow, Lord, in Your will. That will be the first step away. It is hard to say goodbye, but, as Pete wrote yesterday, "the hand is on the plow." I have had difficulty keeping spiritual pace these last days. Rushing through prayer and scanning the Word only—this is no way to have confidence in the soul. *Still*, God is gracious.

> We change, He changes not;
> Our Christ can never die.
> His love, not ours, the resting place,
> His truth, not mine, the tie.

FEBRUARY 4   White stars breaking through a high mist. Half moon. The deep burn of phosphorus running in the wake.

Long, easy rolling and the push of steady wind. The *Santa Juana* is underway. We've just come from a walk on the upper deck after a meal served in the officers' dining room. Black cod, mashed potatoes au gratin, fresh vegetable salad, and good black coffee. The stateroom is quiet now as Pete begins a little typing. All the thrill of boyhood dreams came on me just now, outside watching the sky die in the sea on every side. I wanted to sail in grammar school and well remember memorizing the sail names from Merriam-Webster's ponderous dictionary in Library (room 8) back in Vestal [grade school in Portland]. Now I am actually at sea, as a passenger, of course, but at sea nevertheless, and bound for Ecuador. Strange—or is it?—that childish hopes should be answered in the will of God for this *now*.

We left our moorings at the Outer Harbor Dock [San Pedro, California] at 2:06 P.M. today. Mom and Dad stood together watching and feeling that *je ne sais quoi*, right at the pier side. Aunt Mabel, Will, and Margaret Taylor with her two stood behind. Dad called Genesis 22:5: "I and the lad will go yonder and worship and come again unto you." I wonder what he meant. As we slipped away, Psalms 60:12 came to mind, and I called back, "Through our God we shall do valiantly." They wept some.

I do not understand how God has made me. I didn't even feel like weeping, and don't even now. Joy, sheer joy, and thanksgiving fill and encompass me. I can scarcely keep from turning to Pete and saying, "Brother, this is great," or "This is the best ever." God has done and is doing all I ever desired, much more than ever I asked. Praise, praise to the God of heaven and to His Son, Jesus. Because He hath said "I will never leave thee, nor forsake thee," I may boldly say, "I will not fear." His presence is real in so many things He has given us, and I can do nothing but sing out "Hallelujah!"

Ed and Marilou cried when we parted yesterday. Thank God for their love. Send them to us, Director of the harvest, in Your wisdom. Pete and I have a real bond with them now. We've spent some time in conversation over matters of interpretation of the Word and assembly order these last two weeks in L.A., and it has knit us all. Dave and Ruth Hunt came out yesterday afternoon to say goodbye in Tujunga. They seem to have been given a heart to receive the things spoken by us, and will pray, I'm sure. Lord, lead them on to godliness and perfection. You have begun a good work in them.

Our stateroom (number 2) was to have had three in it, but we bless God that He had ordered it so that we are alone. It would be a little awkward with another, and the Father knew. "Your Father knoweth . . . ." Ah, we've proved that lately! When the Chrysler was being repaired, we needed a car for running around L.A., and God gave us Bob and Genevieve's Ford. He knew we needed a place to stay when we came, and Lohof's trailer was given us. He knew we needed a nearby bed last night, and Helen and John Brown offered when the ship failed to leave last night. He knew we needed the extra time for equipping and the *Juana's* delay from January 20 until now gave us that time. We needed, too, the breaking of bread at Glendale yesterday morning—the presence of Jesus the Lord was *real*. Thanks, then, to You, Good Lord. I'm glad that the Lord *knows* the way of the righteous. He knows the way that I take.

Oh, well it is forever,
Oh, well forevermore
My nest built in no forest of all this death-doomed shore.
Then let the vain world vanish
As from the ship the strand,
For Glory, Glory dwelleth in Immanuel's Land.

"Rutherford's Hymn"
ANNIE R. COUSIN

FEBRUARY 5 *Leviticus*   Second day out from San Pedro. 10:23 A.M. Pete is lying down after listening to some linguaphone records in Spanish. Breakfast served from 7:30–8:30 is more informal than dinner we discovered. Last night we went in sport shirts, and the other passengers were dressed up. This morning we complied with shirts and ties, and everyone else was in lounge garb. What'll we do at noon?

Finished reading Leviticus this morning. Am still asking God for a key to the book. I am not at all secure in the typical teachings usually drawn from the book, though I'm sure the understanding of it lies in that direction. Certainly the types are more valid here than in the historical narratives.

Generally, I noted the sense of "overtones" in the reading of the statutes. The incidental law seems to imply thinking modes for the keeper of it. A man who habitually concerns himself with being fair to a sojourner, paying tithes for the priests, and honoring his neighbor's rights becomes in time a kind man, thoughtful of others. The danger was in missing these resultant virtues. The Pharisee kept the tithe law but passed over justice, mercy, and faith—the weightier matters of the Law. These "overtones" are what are to be fulfilled in us (Rom. 8:3) who walk in conformity to the spirit of the thing.

It is possible to have the virtue developed from within, without the slaying of beasts or the attendance at festivals, and it is this which is required of the Christian believer, but we must understand the miraculous spiritual nature of the development. God, through the Spirit, coming into a man gives him power to leap through the "ordinance step" to its purpose immediately. Not that I am unconditioned utterly by directives, but the directive may be stated in its abstract and flow to its incidental. Since Christianity is worldwide and must apply to every society, and each culture group varies so greatly, the agrarian and local nature of Hebrew law cannot possibly apply. So we overstep the ceremonial statute, recognizing its validity for the Hebrew and its purpose (to make him godly) in his own civilization, and using the concept of it where it will apply in other cultures, we then apply its "overtone" to whatever situation we face. We thus establish the law. We know it was given for a good end and that it has accomplished that end in showing men their hopelessness and sin by setting forth the character requirement of the Most High.

Each statute is related to the very person of God. They were to honor elders because He who required it said, "I am Jehovah." This attachment of God's name to the legal code should have given the Hebrew the key to the intent of the Law. They were to act in conformity to the laws of the nature of such a God, and that meant, in detail, such and such a statute. This is the great "overtone." God, His name and nature, now was connected to their conduct. Hence the importance of obedience and the horror of disobedience.

FEBRUARY 6   Clouding slightly but warm wind is constant. Reading much of the day. A most instructive work by John Collier was in Pete's footlocker. As a sketch of historico-cultural American Indian problems called *Indians of the Americas*, it includes a great deal of material which should be instructive to our policy in the forests. This quote, from the close of the sixth chapter "The Spanish Rule and Las Casas" caught me up short last night. It may be significant in light of what Tidmarsh has suggested about a Christian Indian colony.

> Colonizer, missionary, moralist, idealist, crusader for causes, it is to the hurt of all that you love, to the defeat of your own purpose and the ruin of men, if you, plunging toward your aim in terms of individuals, aggregations of individuals, or external material results, ignorantly or impatiently bypass the society.

The insolvent problem of Christian morals versus Quichua culture may force us to a common denominator that will be unsatisfactory to both that culture and most orthodox moralists. But there is a solution, I am sure, in terms of *society*, as well as in terms of the individual, and we must expect from God a workable program. Christianity, disruptive in nature, has nonetheless integrating powers for the individual in the culture, though both he and it may expect revolution.

Another interesting book is [D. M.] Baillie's *God Was in Christ*. Stimulating since it is outside a fundamentalist viewpoint, yet not radical, or liberal and not quite neoorthodox. "Catholic" he calls himself!

FEBRUARY 9   Sixth day out, *Sábado*. On *Miércoles* a crew-member developed appendicitis, and we put in at Manzanillo,

Mexico, to get him taken care of. Loaded 130 tons of glass while there. Pete and I spent half the night talking Spanish with some cabdrivers in the town plaza. José, a smooth and smarty twenty-three-year-old, had been to Tijuana and San Diego and knew some English. Andrés, younger and more simple, was impressed with the difference between evangelists and *católicos*. Alexandro, quiet—very quiet—but warm at the parting handclasp. Enjoyed speaking what little Spanish I knew in relation to the Gospel.

Meeting the crew little by little. Two forward watches both have religious relatives and talk about them rather than face personal issues about the Messiah. Gordan MacMurray, our radio officer, is a Christian Scientist, but a most interesting fellow. Captain Lindholm and Willie, the mate, are both sensualists, I fear, one in respect to women, the other in respect to drink. A watch officer, a Romanist, is moody and distant to us and to all (a drunken engine-room hand described him as "a guy with a mean disposition" yesterday). Bill Wilson, youngish and a little nervous, is in his second year at Kings Point, merchant-marine officers' training school. Of our fellow passengers, the Mullards, Valencia-orange growers on their way to visit the Chilean lakes, are the most refined and interesting. Pete had good opportunity to witness to them on deck last night in answer to a question as to our true motives in going among Indians.

FEBRUARY 10 (Sunday)   *Matthew 8, 9; Psalm 65*   This will make our first full week at sea. It has passed terribly fast. Strange that the other passengers seem to get bored waiting around, and we hardly have enough time to get what we want done. Thank God for *purpose* in life. So many contributive purposes come into existence when one works the will of God that there is no excuse for laziness or wasted time. He is redeeming our lives, as well as our souls.

Three Scriptures have been a help these last few hours. On retiring, Pete and I read a psalm in Spanish together and translate as best we can with the English Bible. Last night it was Psalm 65 and verse 5 in Spanish seemed to give us glad en-

couragement: "Con tremendas cosas, en justicia, nos respon-
derás tu, O Dios de nuestra salud, esperanza de todos los tér-
minos de la tierra, y de los mas remotos confines de la mar."
Then in my reading in Matthew, the Spanish word for *east*
applied to our particular locale in the Oriente [the eastern
jungle] faced me as a promise. ". . . Vendrán muchos del
oriente . . ." (Matt. 8:11).

I noticed for the first time that Jesus' compassion on the
multitudes was not only because they were many. In fact, the
real cause of his concern was because they were scattered and
divided and distressed as sheep not having any shepherd
(Matt. 9:36). So is it among our tribes. They merit His mercy
again because they are *scattered,* not because they are so many.
Thus God confirms my way, with many seals in my surroundings, and these encouragements from His Word.

FEBRUARY 12 *1 Corinthians 2* Overnight on the hook off
San José, Guatemala, a six-hour run from Champerico. Passed
the evening with the stevedores up over the holds, with good
practice in Spanish. Unloaded tins, tallow, cinnamon, silicate
of soda, and muriatic acid. Much more diligent crew of workmen here than at Champerico. Learned something of the country's history, geography, and politics. The quetzal, the national bird, is the symbol of liberty, giving its name to their
coinage, and associated in myth with the death of the great
Indian leader who perished in conflict with the Conquis-
tadors. If I ever travel here, I must make sure to see Antigua,
the third largest city, thrice destroyed by the *volcán* "fire and
water." It is Spanish colonial, and there are Indian relics
about.

Pete and I waded into 2 Corinthians 2:14–17 this morning.
No startling revelation, but I'm more sure of the passage from
having "discovered it myself." Still not sure about the savor of
death and life as to their sequence and exact meaning. Seems
to be a reversal of the relation to apply the "death" savor to the
"perishing," and the "life" savor to the saved, but that is the
more easily explained.

FEBRUARY 14   Rolling slightly in a strong breeze, out of sight of land but off Nicaragua. Tuesday afternoon we anchored off La Libertad, El Salvador, and we went ashore with four other passengers. Decided on a trip to the capital, so we hired a station wagon that would take us all. Got a couple of pictures of ox teams en route; it's about an hour's ride up, over nice blacktop road. We left the others and wandered over the town, its back streets and parks. While eating tortillas at the restaurant up from the Nuevomundo Hotel (a place run by the Borgea brothers, if I recall), we were approached by a very pretty little harlot named Emelia. I will always wish I could have spoken clear Spanish. We tried to make plain our desire only to speak her language, and she was willing for a while to walk and speak with us. She took us to the university post office where we bought some cards and then she became embarrassed somehow—curses on my Spanish—and bade us good-bye.

My whole soul went out to her, so young, so sweet faced, and, yet, so enmeshed in an evil net. How long, Lord, will the earth perpetuate its wrongs? Hurry the promise, Lord, that "the earth shall be filled with the glory of the Lord." She epitomizes for me the wrong of earth and men. I could no more have slept with her than died at will—the whole idea violated all that I know and feel. But, oh, I longed to speak about the Savior of harlots, the friend of genuine sinners. God help me in the language for just such cases as these. I am sure she thought us strange men—such as fit no pattern she had seen—but will she ever really know why we refused to have her go find her *"amiga"* for us?

Weighed the hook yesterday in mid-afternoon and rolled on out past the cone-shaped volcanoes into a ravishing sunset. Noted that the sea, like experiencing the will of God, changes its color in distance. Up close it holds its own color, blue green and white. But as it is more distant, it takes on the color of the sky, shining not of itself, but of its cover. Incidents in life, while I am in them, are colored of themselves, their mood is set by the circumstantial context. Only as one moves away from them, can he see another color, the heavenly, shining in them.

The will of God, the hues of heaven, is not always felt as I experience a situation in life, but as it passes from me, I begin to see God over it, and it assumes its beauty from simply being under His sky.

Pete and I talked long last night, mostly about women—Jeanine, Betty and Cammie and Olive. Joy in praying afterward. Pete gave me this from Teasdale ["Let It Be Forgotten"]:

> Let it be forgotten
> As a flower is forgotten,
> A flower, and a fire
> That once was singing gold.
> Let it be forgotten
> Forever and forever,
> Time is a kind friend
> And he will make us old.

FEBRUARY 15 *Numbers 15–21*   Off the Panama coast this morning. Plan to reach Balboa about 9:00 this evening. Days pass quickly with reading, Spanish, and talk. Spent three hours on the flying bridge last night with Bill Wilson, the midshipman, speaking of the things concerning Christ. Lord, open his heart to the Lord Jesus. Give him the honesty to examine the evidence.

Reading Numbers 15–21 today, I noticed the general effect of disobedience and punishment from the slaying of the fearful spies to the capture of Sihon and Og. The more Jehovah punished them, the more hard were their hearts, and the sequence from Korah's rebellion, the succeeding complaint, the plague which killed fourteen thousand, Miriam's death and Meribah, Aaron's death and the fiery serpents, is one of the saddest records in the law. It is interesting that as long as the people were idle, they complained, but when they begin to fight (Arad whipped in 21:3), they begin to sing together. There has been no singing of praise or victory since the Red Sea. Now it begins as the nation becomes warlike, the elders who were disobedient die, and young blood stirs in the ranks.

FEBRUARY 16   Arrived around 10:00 P.M. at the dock at Balboa, Canal Zone, last night. Before we had the *Juana* secured, a redhead in a white shirt was shouting "Fleming and Elliot?" at the purser, Bob Basman, who pointed him up to our deck. He took us home for a cup of Ovaltine, some reading, and prayer. But it took all day today to get acquainted with Sydney Temple [a Plymouth Brethren man who lived in Panama]. He reads the Bible through every year, and started his Old Testament section before 7:00 A.M. Squeezed us some orange juice and took us to the Clubhouse in Diablo for breakfast. His '51 Ford handled admirably at 90 mph once this afternoon, and I got the impression that Syd doesn't ever drive that fast, but excused himself by explaining that there wasn't much straight road on the isthmus—he was only taking advantage of a rare occasion.

First we drove over to Gamboa to visit an aged and ailing sister named Myers. Took a few pictures of Charges Lake and headed for Colón on the Caribbean coast. Met Dr. Gregory in the Bible Society building and ate *chilbena* (?) and papaya salad for lunch at the Clubhouse in Cristóbal. Hunted up Ken Jones at the Colón Hospital and met Jim Young from Louisiana, a believer also interning here with Jones and company. Returned to Panama City and were taken to points of interest down through this end of the Canal Zone.

There is work to be done here, and the brethren at home know nothing of it. Great privileges are given zone workers in Panama and the bilingual situation would be ideal for some. I must do something to dispense with the information now in our possession. It makes me responsible, terribly so! Visited a few other souls and saw the garage they use for a Sunday school at Pueblo Nuevo. Mrs. Du Saire and Mrs. Purcell her daughter (and granddaughter Eunicia) were our hostesses for a brief session of singing and studying tonight. Met a Baptist brother thirty-one years old who is interested, but held back by Sydney's narrow spirit, I fear. Egerton Miller: father of three and brother to Raymond, who is contemplating "seminary" in Costa Rica. Dear, dear children of God, but with no shepherds. Lord, send laborers!

The *Juana* is unloading lumber and flour. Sailing at 6:00 A.M.

FEBRUARY 21   Arrived at Puná, Ecuador, about 9:00 A.M. Ship received at noon. The yacht *Santa Rosita* came alongside sometime after 2:00 and took off our hand baggage, and we came up to Guayaquil on her by 6:00. Our schedule had been wrongly relayed to Quito as Dr. Tidmarsh was not at the dock to greet us. Maximiliano, our self-appointed *cargador* [porter], brought us to the Reed and Reed establishment, which was closed, and then to the apartment of Miss Roble, a C&MA sister working here. She advised the Helbig Hotel, and we came here for a rest, our first night in Ecuador. Disagreeably hot and mosquito infested, the room offered little sleep until early this morning.

FEBRUARY 22 *Deuteronomy 3:24*   "O Lord Jehovah, thou hast begun to show thy servant thy greatness and thy strong hand: for what god is there in heaven and in earth, that can do according to thy works?" Met Dr. Tidmarsh outside the Grace Lines office and with great joy began discussion of the work. Customs this afternoon D.V. Hope to be here over the weekend, then fly to Quito Monday morning before Carnival gets too far along. There are no controls here these last two days prior to Lent and most foreigners pack up and leave— we'll follow suit. Watched them stir cocoa beans with bare feet on the pavements this morning; saw a small boy with a monkey on his head; had my shoes shined by a *lustrador* in the plaza along the river front; argued a man from fifty sucres to twenty-five for a silver bracelet and then refused to buy.

FEBRUARY 24   Left Pension Helbig after discovering that one barge with all the radio and generator equipment did not come up on the night tide. We must be here now until Tuesday morning, so at the kind invitation of the GMU [Gospel Missionary Union] workers, we came to their compound to stay. Met Malcolm Brown and went swimming with him this afternoon. Met Helen Dick, Lloyd and Esther Shrader and Martha Bricker here. Dear Christian folk, and very kind and hospitable. Gave Miss Bricker a back and hip massage tonight—first time I ever rubbed down a woman, and the doing was not near so fearsome as the thinking about it. Hope she feels better! Great council with T. [Tidmarsh] these days. At odd snatches we get in some most interesting conversation. God be praised for an understanding older worker.

FEBRUARY 27 *Ash Wednesday*   Caught the Panagra flight out of Guayaquil yesterday afternoon about 1:30. Clear view of the coastal plain as we came north, but began hitting clouds as we moved toward the mountains. Scudded over the mountains suddenly, catching sight of high ridges not far below. Then, as the clouds cleared again, we saw the great quilt of the plateau, beautiful and quiet with terraced hillsides and occasional buildings. Quito was in sight immediately and our DC-3 bounced down on the runway at about 2:45 P.M. Cathers, Gwen, Rob [Mrs. Tidmarsh and her son], and Dee Short awaited us and brought us home in the Ford pickup from the school at San Miguel. Spent the evening and afternoon chatting about our trip and discussing the work here. Since T. left here, the C&MA have offered Aguano [a small Quichua outpost near Auca territory] (Campo Sauder) for sale to us, and we must have God's direction about going down to look it over. T. feels that the Indians there have had the Gospel and refused it, but owns that it is the springboard for Auca work. Seems to me that Doreen's consistent sense of being sent to the Oriente should be heeded. Especially if [Dorothy] Jones and Betty come down. Barbara and Doreen and Betty and Dorothy have the identical training, the English girls in medicine and the Americans in linguistics. Looks to me as if they ought to split, and since Betty will ultimately be in Oriente work and Doreen feels pressed there, they might be given a chance at Sauder's place. Prayed that God would guide in this situation. [Doreen and Barbara were English missionaries to the Colorado Indians. Dorothy was an American missionary with whom I lived for a few months in both New York and Ecuador.]

Shorts having moved to Santo Domingo, now wonder whether to start a school or simply to open up a pension for school children. This, too, is committed, and we wait on Thee, O Lord, to show unto Thy servants Thy work.

Dee and Marie Short, an American couple, had lived in the jungle near the Colorado Indians, before they moved out to a "white" town. Jim wondered if he and Pete should consider helping the Colorados by starting a school.

MARCH 2　　Lord's Day morning. Great sense of uselessness because of inner failure and sin. Reading in the Law and the psalms, but with no life. My soul refuses comfort and instruction. Revive Thy servant, Lord God; restore his soul. Don't feel that I'm getting anywhere, either in the Word or in Spanish. Failing to reach the people here in a cooped-up home with everybody that we came to reach locked out. Visited last night with Betty Austin and Ross Larsen at the HCJB [missionary radio station] compound. Met Miss Jones and Eleanor Hahn of the British and American Embassy. Doctor Paul Roberts's slides on the work in Ecuador were good—longing, though, for a word from God. All the lesser blessings and comforts fail me. I must have Christ felt in the soul, seen clearly again in my mind. Out of the depths have I called unto Thee, O Lord, hear Thou my cry.

Went to the street with T. yesterday morning; longed to be able to preach, but felt a deadening objectivity in listening—analyzing, watching, wondering, rather than caring, praying, weeping. I need a change of heart, Lord. Began Spanish lessons with Srta. Baleroso on Thursday. Lord, hurry my progress. T. gave me this Friday—Psalms 18:30, "As for God . . . ."

1

> Say not, my soul, "From whence
> Can God relieve my care?"
> Remember that Omnipotence
> Has servants everywhere

2

> God's help is always sure
> His method seldom guessed;

Delay will make our pleasure pure,
Surprise will give it zest.

3

His wisdom is sublime
His heart profoundly kind;
God never is before His time,
And never is behind.

4

Hast thou assumed a load
Which few will share with thee,
And art thou carrying it for God,
And shall He fail to see?

5

Be comforted at heart
Thou art not left alone,
Now thou the Lord's companion art,
Soon thou shalt share His throne.

THOMAS T. LYNCH, 1855

Strange that *words*, even such as these, fail for help.

MARCH 5   Enjoyed reading Deuteronomy 32, 34 and seeing the blessings set on Israel *despite* Jahweh's knowledge of their prompt disobedience. Ah, "the good will of him that dwelt in the bush" (33:16).

MARCH 6   This marks the end of my second week in Ecuador. God has been faithful. Enumerating answered prayer is something I have not often done, but it is fitting tonight. We are here—praise God for that—and all the waiting, asking, and preparing that it involved are over. *He has brought me to this country*, and as I now feel about the Oriente, that it is *lejos* [distant] and problematic from my point of view, I once felt about Ecuador. Take courage, soul, God does nothing by halves. Through customs without opening a *bulto* [piece of baggage] or paying a cent of customs, *direct answers*. And today I asked in faith for three things. First, a Latin young fellow to converse with in Spanish and contact for the Lord. He was in T's study before noon, and I spent an hour and a half with him in the plaza this afternoon. Abdón, he is, from San Miguel. Second, that I could get the recorder to work right. I did—before noon. It was unaffected by all the transportation handling of the barrel. Third, *El Camino Real*, a textbook for Spanish. This has not come yet, but I expect it. For I believe Him who said, "Porque de cierto os digo que cualquiera que dijere a este monte: Quítate, y échate en la mar, y no dudare en su corazón, mas creyere que será hecho lo que dice, lo que dijere le será hecho" (Mark 11:23).

Today T. was going over some of his stored things. He found some old sermon notes and remarked, "I used to preach better sermons than I do now." Can this be confirmation of Dad's fears? I've heard him say, "I think missionaries often fail to go on in the truth to deeper things," implying that the pressure of the work and the constant contact with primitive minds stultifies deep thinking in the Scriptures. God deliver me!

MARCH 8 *Joshua 3*   With T. at the preaching in the market again this morning. Do so long now to be able to assist him in this as his voice gives out and the people seem so intent to hear. Besides, there is this persistent sense of uselessness, the vacancies created by English-context loss seem countless. Spending an hour a day with Abdón, helping him with English. Met and chatted with Misses Hatley and Hernandez, Jehovah's Witnesses who are daily in the plaza. "Lo here" and "lo there . . ." point the heretics, poor earth-centered souls, blind leaders who with those who follow teeter on the brink of "the ditch." There are nine such in Quito now. I don't know how many in Guayaquil, Ambato, and Cuenca. Will the cause of the Christ be forever so weak? Not that we are so few here, we evangelicals, but that we are of such mediocre stock, so distant from the people, so puny in our efforts. Still, He works on with us; oh, that He might work in *power*.

"Lo here . . . lo there" (Matt. 24:23). *Jim classified the Jehovah's Witnesses as false. They were among the heretics who would seek to deceive, identifying one "here" or "there" as Christ. But as blind leaders, they would direct followers into a ditch.*

I am coming to suspicion in the interpretation of the Red Sea, and Jordan crossings which I have learned. They are made to represent two experiences of the believer usually: one, initial deliverance from judgment, and the other, deliverance from unbelieving and wayward flesh. It falls down in two main points. First, two experiences of such deliverance were not God's original intention. Had Israel followed Moses, they would have entered Canaan from the south, with no Jordan to cross; that was the ideal situation, and had Israel followed wholly, no "second" experience would have been necessary. Second, the believers who entered at Jordan were a *separate* group from those who crossed the sea so that the "type" fails in that both experiences did not occur in the life of the same individual in a vast majority of cases.

Now I see in the two crossings the design of God to give authority to *His* chosen leaders. The crossing of the Jordan meant to Joshua what the Red Sea had meant to Moses. "This day (of the crossing) will I begin to magnify thee in the sight of all Israel, that they may know that, as I was with Moses, so shall I be with thee" (v. 3). The people needed confidence in their leader, and this was what Jordan provided. The spiritual lesson that must now be drawn is obvious—not vague at all—as the "second experience" stuff has proved. If a people—any people, an assembly, a mission, or whatever—are to be expected to follow their leader, they must know personal deliverance under that leader's hand. For Joshua to have assaulted Jericho without the confidence, faith, and power that Jordan had provided, there could have been no unity among the people and no courage in the general himself.

Now, in my day, the great trouble in churches is that the people are following teachers who are not their Father's—self- or group-appointed leaders under whose hand they have not been delivered. The confidence and honor that one should be able to place in his leader is gone because we have no leader who brought us through initial obstacles. Let this be a warning not to build on another's foundation, and an encouragement to stick by those who I am personally responsible to because, under God, I am their father in the fight of faith.

MARCH 11	Felt a strange bitterness this evening tending to sullennesss and dissatisfaction with everyone. Coming outside and feeling my barrenness, the beautiful night lured me on a walk. The moon has powers to wash a man inside, and I experienced it tonight—the laving of the spirit by chill air, old mud walls, the smell of eucalyptus, night birds, and moon-burnished clouds. It's a different world over the walls here and up beyond the hill.

MARCH 14	My first night under mosquito netting. Came down from Quito with D. [Dee Short] and company and B. [Barbara] Edwards. Slept here in their rented house in Santo Domingo de los Colorados. Saw my first Colorado in the plaza *esta mañana* [this morning]. Leaving Quito on cobblestone, you climb awhile in view of all three peaks of Pichincha—swallowed in cloud yesterday at least the top third. Suddenly, you see the valleys dropping away below, sunk in mist. Watching, you can see the mist part and the utter green denseness break clear, shot here and there with whites—a dead tree, a flash of waterfall, or a show of smoke. Down, down, down, twisting into canyon heads, past the cascades and smoking *carboneras* [coal bins], squeezing past upcoming trucks, down through the chill mist until it is not chill but steamy. Above, the shouldering mountains swim into cloud now, and you still go down. The drop in total is something around seven thousand feet. It took us six hours in the Juan Yates *camioneta* [pickup truck]. Here in Santo Domingo there is no other missionary for a radius of one hundred kilometers, a fast-growing agricultural center with black, Indian, and *chola* [mixed] population. Short has a great opportunity here; we'll see how he does.

MARCH 17   Living with Short these days and trying to be of some help around as well as sizing up the work and keeping Spanish before me. Most of the time it amounts to plenty of little things—washing dishes, helping with the kids, playing the harmonica in the open air, helping drive the truck. Yesterday we had a good meeting in the *sala* [meeting room] in the plaza—lots of interested men. Then an afternoon trip toward Quinendé in the *camioneta* to visit Scott and Brown, Americans who want Short to ship machinery from Quito for them and are forwarding money for the new truck. D. goes to Quito today to settle for it, and is taking about thirty quintals of corn and cargo to pay for the trip. He insists his trucking takes no time, but it took this whole morning and will kill his afternoon. I am suspicious of this business, but he hopes to make the mission self-supporting. Seems like a hard thing to do with the work so new and the outreach so vast. He's the only evangelical for one hundred kilometers any direction.

MARCH 18–22   Spent these days in San Miguel with Barbara Edwards and Doreen Clifford. First real time in the forests and first contacts with the Indians [the Colorados]. Rode Short's "Recuerdo" [horse's name] down with Norbie while Marie and Stevie and "Chito" followed on the mule. The road is impassable by any sort of vehicle now, with all manner of mud holes. Took almost four hours to go down. Marie returned with the young ones Wednesday and in the afternoon the girls with Marta and Don Gustavo took me to the house of the two albino Colorados—"Alemán." Found the mouth harp of good use in making friends, accompanying Doreen on her autoharp. Discussed location of a school with the Indians. Some interest in a school, and the girls seem determined in faith to start one. They feel that they cannot spend time with the whites in school, wanting only to carry on Sunday meetings and women's work. Thursday I went with Barbara to the home of Patali, supposedly a hundred years old and well versed in all tribal lore. His wife had a tooth that was to have been pulled, but she didn't want to lose it that day as it wasn't bothering. He should be an excellent source of language material, if anyone ever bothers. Friday afternoon we visited Ramón, the big man south of San Miguel. The nuns have been staying with him, and he told us frankly that they did not want to learn. The R.C.s intend to start a school in that area. God hurry Your Word to those folk!

Saturday a dozen men came to the clearing at San Miguel to cut off the brush in preparation for the *Pascua* [Easter]. We fed them soup, *sancocho* [a broth with corn and manioc], and *bala* [a cylinder made of boiled mashed green plantain] to be exact, and made good contact through the instruments and radio. But I am persuaded that only a man will be able to really reach the Colorado. One of them told Marie once, "Well, what can you do about it? You're only a woman." Obviously Short is not the man, as he himself recognizes. The girls are doing a good work medically. I watched them work on a bad skin case of Jose Marillo's, the little yellow-haired boy. And Betty with Dorothy may be able to do something with the language. God, give us men! Returned in the afternoon in less than three hours, the road being somewhat better than when I went in. Met again with the bank employees who are studying English, an alert crowd whom I hope Dee will be given as the nucleus of the work here. His trucker can't get a license so he got nowhere in Quito last week, and he is now selling his old truck piece by piece. Lord, govern in that business. It seems crucial to the work here.

Am able to be of some help in Spanish now, but yearn for fluency. Abdón is down this weekend and had the preaching this morning.

MARCH 27   Returned to Quito in a fruit *camion* [truck] with Abdón on Monday with mixed feelings. Doreen came to Santo Domingo Sunday evening and Abdón was at Short's—the matter between them is unfortunate and they both have my sympathy. It is plain that they still care somewhat for each other and their being in proximity is not an easy thing. Praying, too, these days for Dee as I fear his trucking business is not necessary—even detrimental—to the work down in S.D. Lord, show him *Your* work of individually ministering to some of those *jovenes* [young men] down there—simple-minded Jorge, thoughtful, hot-blooded Olmedo, Nilo, the unpredictable, and all those fellows in the bank yet unsaved.

Enjoying Christ and counsel with the Father these days, though since I have taken to pure Spanish reading of the Scriptures, I feel I have forfeited some of the freshness I once enjoyed from the Word. But it must be, and I have the hope that soon I shall be getting things from the Spirit in still another language.

Began medical course with T. today [a short course in homeopathy].

APRIL 6   The Lord's Day. More inner joy today than for several days. Been reading snatches from several helpful books lately and find they contribute to my soul's good. [John] Owen's *The Glory of Christ;* [John] Gill's *Body of Divinity;* Bernard's *Progress of Christian Doctrine; God Was in Christ.* Enjoyed breaking of bread today, simply remembering Him. One sees clearly the necessity for it here—not to speak of its honor to God, but for one's own soul—to keep one pressing after Christ, pursuing fresh realities, and purifying old ones. Preached this morning in English fellowship on Deuteronomy 18:15: The Prophet. Raised up of God, as a prophet, from among Jews, like Moses. Came fresh and felt liberty. Some commented on being helped, and so I trust the Father honored the Word about His Son. Faithful, He is, faithful and kind.

Betty should be in Ecuador a week from tonight, God willing. Strange that we are led so close together so soon—wonderfully strange! There will be talk, especially at home, but I tend not to care a bit for it here. Let them talk, and God shall lead us on! Faith makes life so even, gives one such confidence in such movements, that the words of men are as wind. Enjoyed Cayambi [one of the snowcaps near Quito] by moonlight across the valley of Guápulo tonight.

APRIL 7   Ascended second knoll above HCJB on Pichincha today with Bill, Pete, Abdón, and Victor, his cousin. Approximately 3,700 feet done in four hours. Beautiful climb with clouds on us at the height of ascent (13,000) cutting off view of Wawa. Spatters of rain descending from which we found shelter under trees which are only occasional. Followed the ridge straight up, except for taking the switchback trail for the last few hundred feet.

Read the story of Dave's death in recent *Brown Gold*. Four arrows in his body, both arms cut off and one foot. Near Bolivian border in Brazil. Only obvious mistake: *He stayed alone in new contact territory.*

APRIL 17   Spent Easter with Short in Santo Domingo. Went down last Thursday and then walked to San Miguel in three and a quarter hours Friday. Watched the Colorado *Sábado de Gloria* ["Saturday of Glory"—fiesta] with interest, although there is very little to watch. Bill and Pete stayed over the Lord's Day, but I came back to S.D. for breaking of bread here. Monday we rode to Quinendé, about eighty kilometers. From there the Quinendé and Blanco rivers form the Esmeraldas and flow to the sea. Banana rafts take off from there for transport to the States and Europe. Wide open for the Gospel and Short has been going down once a week lately. Someone will have to go and live there.

There are times when the testimony of God, by divine purpose, goes on independently of human cooperation. So was it in the days when Israel was not fit for victory over the Philistines in the last days of Eli. God refused to let Israel triumph with the ark, but when it was captured, began to smite Philistia with the power of the ark itself. Let it not be with me that God should have to refuse my privilege in winning with Him in the testimony of the Name, and override all human assistance by carrying on the work without His workers. It has been of great grace that I share in His work; let it not be revoked for my underestimating it. Again, Lord, deliver me from evil. It was moral failure in those who served the testimony at Shiloh that lost the ark and brought the declaration of Ichabod.

Betty is in Ecuador. Difficult to believe, but heartening to have this seal that God is for *us* two.

He who dedicates his services to a revolution ploughs the sea.

SIMON BOLIVAR

APRIL 24

> She came today;
> Stepped off an airplane
> And watched her feet walk down the steps;
> Looked up at friends
> And frowned a little.
> The sun was brighter than the plane,
> That made her frown;
> That, and the not seeing me
> Among the friends.
>
> She hesitated
> Wondering which side the fence
> To walk up toward the building
> Where I was waiting,
> Watching her. And then
> She saw me;
> Came straight on,
> Stepped up and stood
> Before me, wondering
> What I would do.
> I took her hand, smiled
> And said,
> "Sure good to see you."
> So it was, and so it is
> Now that she has come.

APRIL 28   She came to 129 Andalucia at 8:05 for the med course at 9:00—med course: heart disease. Then, 11:00–12:30 behind the American school. "Good of the Lord to stop the rain." "I wouldn't mind sitting down." "How *many* years." "I don't think you know what being alone means."

Having prayed last week that the Lord would arrange a time for us to be alone together, this seemed ideal, and I took the great privilege to embrace. Moved for her. I could not find another woman like her who would wait without commitment indefinitely. God, give her courage.

"Are you happy?"

"I don't know . . . ."

"Is there anything I can do to make you sure?"

"I don't know . . . it's just that it gets worse all the time."

Tears, quiet sobbing.

APRIL 29   Overlooking the Valle de Gúapulo: she seemed small before me, felt almost frail. "Are you comfortable?" "Yes, and happy." Broad daylight!

APRIL 30   Srta. Balereso sick since Tuesday, no classes. Abdón fails to come, so I take these time gaps as providential for time with Betty. Downtown together to get her snaps from photographer. Looked at them on the fountain in the Plaza de Independencia. Gene and Ruth Jordans' [missionaries with radio station HCJB] for supper. Our first real debut into a social evening at a home together—Chavades. She does very well, if a little self-vindictive at times. Seems sure of herself . . . so much more natural than in Portland in '49. Afterward we walked to her house and stopped by a mud wall. Pichincha—smouldering in fog, moon on its back not quite half full.

Spoke of engagement. She thinks I'm inconsistent, Lord, seeming to be self-contradictory so often in speaking plainly of marriage and then seeming to be so unsure about it all. I guess You understand, Lord. So long as I can do a work in reaching a primitive people *better* as a single man, I will stay single. And that brings me to the other thing we've been digging around—the Aucas. I see no reason now to stay single if I'm only sent to Yumbos—Tidmarsh didn't, Cathers hasn't. But Aucas! My God, who is sufficient for them?

MAY 1   Watched our first *corrida de toros* today. This is Ecuadorean "Labor Day" and they had a six-bull fight. Betty and I went with Cathers, Springers, Poole, Jordans, Pete, Bob, Doreen, and Esther Rymer. It was wonderful! The picador action is especially thrilling, while the ballet grace of the cape wielders is really beautiful. I don't know why I love bulls. Nothing has quite the fitness to act *bravo*, it seems to me, as a well-built bull. They do nicely with their front feet striking straight, stiff from the shoulders. The head feint just before the lunge is a clever technique, and although they hardly have a chance to vindicate themselves, they do well for all the confusion they are put to. One feels it a little unjust that the matador has done it so many times before, while the bull is at it for the first time. It is not as spectacular as a good western rodeo, and, of course, somewhat bloodier, but the whole thing seems so fit to the Latin mind—gold braid and blood, exultation at death, paper ribbons and "picks," gracefulness and brutishness, a bull and a pair of ballet shoes. These people are extremists.

MAY 2   Oh, for a heart like David's! For all his obvious powers of leadership, he never goes out to lead the people in battle without consultation with Jehovah. "Shall I go up?" This lack of self-confidence marks him as God's man for guiding others. He would not trust himself; he is rewarded by being entrusted with others. I never noted before this present reading of the books of Samuel in Spanish his zeal for God's anointed, Saul. Refusing himself to lift a finger, he slays those men who take any action against Saul or his house—a complete lack of self-aggrandizement or vindictiveness. He allowed God to press his cause, and the kingdom was established in his hand. Good lessons for the basing of our thoughts about moving to the Aucas—"Shall I go up?"

MAY 4   Dorothy Jones arrived Friday, and it looks like my "larks" of last week are over. [Jim and I were to have few opportunities to see each other alone, as Dorothy lived with me.] Went to street meeting with T. today and Pete, returned to English Fellowship. Ross Larsen and Betty Austin at T's for dinner. D.J. and Betty came over for b.b. [breaking of bread]—refreshing, and, I trust, pleasing to God. Worship is excellent exercise for the soul. Makes a man big inside, makes him feel like he has at last found what he was built for, though he is conscious that he is inept.

Couldn't keep my eyes off Betty. She is attractive in so many ways. I had to catch myself from breaking into a laugh of joy as we all were at Frank Cook's for supper. She knows *so well* how to handle herself in public—artistic in conversation, a ready and refined laugh, and always a soft look for me. Sang with HCJB Coro. [chorus] over the air again, and she has a beautiful voice, too. Well, do I thank God for her; she is on all counts unusual! She brought me three letters from Thomas to read. There is something strong between them, something so like about them that they are closer than any of the other members of the family. They exchange Latin phrases, or hymn quotes, or tidbits from some author I've never read. Felt a strange envy creep over me as I realized what a place he has in her—but it didn't last long. I had to face *it* again—I can never be all she ought to have in a husband. Too dull witted, too slow a reader, too poor a memory. Her ability to hold tiny details in mind over years (she told me what coat I wore at Saint Michael's Cemetery in '48 just yesterday!). Lord, let me make up to her in other ways what I lack in supplying that sort of thing for her. I just wasn't raised a scholiast. She will ultimately have to be satisfied with my body in exchange for what I lack in mind, and I, with her mind in exchange for what used to appear to me a lack in her body. Strange how I am quite satisfied with it now, for once having such boyish fears. Well, *Dios sabe,* and I am persuaded that we will fit when His time comes to join us. Would that it were tonight!

Puzzling all day again Exodus 17:9: "A hand on the throne of Jahweh." Septuagint reads, "With a secret hand the Lord wars against Amalek . . . ." Spanish revision, "Inasmuch as the hand of Amalek is lifted against the throne . . . ." Instruct, Lord.

MAY 5   *2 Samuel 11*   Tingo [a hot-springs resort near Quito] with C. W. Jones and we six. Med course this afternoon. Dinner with Esther Riemer, Evelyn Richner, Ida Weismann (C&MA schoolteacher at Missy. School for Children), Astrid Pearson, Miss Nelson, Vi, Catherine, and we six [all missionaries]. Concerned today with a careless tongue, vain conversation. Betty and I walked home with P. and D., and I was silent, not feeling liberty to touch her. Came home with silence eating inside me and went up on the *azotea* [roof] to think things through with God. Clear, cool night with a little more than half a moon, broken sky, and occasional stars. Gave myself for Auca work more definitely than ever, asking for spiritual valor, good Spanish, plain and miraculous guidance, among other things.

Consolidated my thinking about Betty. Reading of David's sin against Uriah the Hittite I got to thinking over Uriah's attitude. David, obviously thinking he could make Uriah think himself the father of his own impregnation of Bath-sheba, brought him home from war, made him drunk, and all but forced him to his wife's bed. But Uriah stayed with the king's servants and his reason for so doing is, "The ark, and Israel, and Judah abide in booths; and my lord Joab, and the servants of my lord are encamped in the open field; shall I then go into my house, to eat and to drink, and to lie with my wife? As thou livest, and as thy soul liveth, I will not do this thing" (2 Sam. 11:1). It was no *time* to return to his house, though he had the right to do so and the encouragement. It was the *time* for battle, and Uriah was a warrior; there could be no mixing of home goodness and the business of his life. So it came to me. Marriage is not for me now; it simply is not the *time* (I do not say, and never did say, "It is not the *thing* for me"). With tribes unreached which I now believe reachable only by unattached men, "I will not do this thing."

MAY 6 *2 Samuel 12, 13*   Noted in reading 2 Samuel 12 and 13 the comfort, first of Bathsheba by David (12:24), and then of David himself over Amnon's death (13:39). It reminded me of Isaac in Genesis 24:67 who was comforted after the death of Sarah by his espousal with Rebekah. All of these cases are comforts of an earthly sort, giving a peace that the world may give in any case to any man. A mother's death may be assuaged by a wife's love (Isaac). A son's death may be forgotten by a husband's ardent attention (Bath-sheba). Or an heir's death may be eased simply by the fatalistic acceptance of death—David was comforted "seeing he was dead." But the comfort is postgrief and consists in simple replacement of attention. But Paul in 2 Corinthians 1:4 is "comforted by God" *in* his affliction. The Christian believer enjoying Holy Spirit's benefits knows the peace bestowed *not as the world giveth*, not by forgetting or doing, but by accepting conflicts as from God and finding peace *in* war.

MAY 7   Near full moon found us above Arias's [an Ecuadorian family with whom I lodged], under a sparse stand of eucalyptus, after heavy rain. Sky was broken with clouds, and flashed stars, but the horizon was sufficiently clear to see Cayambe, Antisana, and Cotopaxi by moonlight. No night like it so far here in Ecuador. Someone tried to scare us off with gunfire, not knowing what we were doing there—finally came out in a troop with rifles, led by a señora who queried angrily, *"Que pasa?"* [What's happening]. Explaining that we were *"amadores, no mas,"* [only lovers] we obtained our *"desculpe"* [pardon]. Laughable, really.

It was one of those "asked for" times with her, depending on weather conditions which God openly controlled for us. He seems so much "for us" (two) these days. I have not lost one nameable thing by putting her and our whole affair in the simplest way possible into His hands. There has been no careful analyzing, no planning, no worrying over details in the matter. I have simply recognized love in me, declared it to her and to Him and as frankly as I could, told Him I wanted His way in it. There has been no leading thus far to engagement, but the symptoms of a beautiful courtship prevail—not perhaps a routine, or "normal" one, but a good one nonetheless, and withal, a deep sense that it is God directed.

MAY 8   Unasked-for time together today. Unthought. With us it has been "exceedingly abundant above asking or thinking." After getting the girls' papers through, Dorothy volunteered to go home, a most unusual instance. Since we were up at the other end of town, I suggested a brief walk up the

Panecillo, and we were alone again—through the narrow, cluttered streets and up the side hill on a steep track. Rugged, brilliant cloud patterns—everything from heavy thunderheads to fractured, fibrous spinnings in the high blue. Clear view of Quito and environs through the scattered eucalyptus. Discussed girls school in the Oriente, "knit together . . . ."

I can't get her to believe that I am really satisfied with her body. She still has me holding my first impressions stated in our former days together: "banana nose . . . sand paper . . . skinny." I don't know how to explain or clarify the change in this which has come since I really knew that I loved her last September 20. All I know is that it doesn't matter if her breasts are small, or her shoulders are slight, or her nose not finely shaped, or her front teeth set apart. I wouldn't like her any more if they were all "ideal," partly, I think, because she would not be what she is psychologically if she were anything but what she is physically. Conscious of these things, she has become realistic in her outlook on life generally, and has developed a humility through them she might not have had she been built otherwise. This much I know, we were made for each other—if I for "comfort," then she for "speed"—though I have not found her *incómodo* [uncomfortable] in the least! My arms are for her "homing," a place to rest, shelter, shield, and strength. What having her there means to me cannot be said. God has brought her there and prepared her before He brought her. I am *wholly* satisfied with His doing.

MAY 9   Tried to explain to her something of what I wrote about Uriah on May 5 while we were walking downtown today. I don't know why, but it seemed unreasonable to her, and she laughed at me. Flaring back at first, I soon lapsed into silence, and by the time we reached her bus stop downtown, I was seeing only sidewalk and biting my lip. And then I cried, and we walked. I couldn't understand why I was unable to explain sensibly just *why* it was not time for engagement.

I suppose I couldn't say it, because I don't *know* it in words. The knowledge is inward, and it may be that there are no reasons to be given. She says it is enough to know that I know, that I don't have to summon reasons (thanks, Lord, for a girl who not only will *wait* there, but be *happy* to wait there). But somehow it doesn't seem right to have to force her there—though I have done nothing else but that from the beginning. My reasons didn't hold up today, not even to me, and I am now aware that my reasons for not getting engaged are hidden in the counsels of God's Spirit. The same for my reasons for loving her; I can't enumerate them, or at least when I do, they seem puny. There is a bigger reason—it is love itself; it simply *is* so, and the thing itself is given of God. So, for not being engaged, I simply know it is not for now—that knowledge is inward, God given, and to be obeyed at whatever cost; it is so.

There are no explanations except that God leads, and He does not always let a man know why He leads. Faith binds a man to what he knows inside, like coming to Ecuador. The world couldn't shake the persuasion. "The just shall live by faith"—*faith*, not alone in facts and a rational apologetic, but in the reality of the inward work of the anointing which he possesses through the gift of the Holy Ghost. I must maintain a surer belief in the Spirit of God. It is no mere tenet of the faith, that He indwells the believer. He does indwell, and there He does His work of informing the spirit of man.

Then, too, I learned something about Betty today. She makes me feel "on the defensive" in arguments (in the kindest sense of the word). She often sees clearer than I, and faster, to the end of things, and moves ruthlessly and rapidly to state what she sees. From her point of view we ought to be engaged—though she is not trying to force me to it. (This I know, first, because she says so, and I trust her; she fears breaching the will of God for the work; I think she knows how impossible it would be to make me do such a thing with arguments.) When I couldn't explain well why we shouldn't be and I choked up, she immediately changed her attitude and went on the defensive herself, saying she understood, that she was sorry she had said anything, that she hoped I didn't think I would have to produce "reasons" for staying apart. I was sorry I couldn't control myself, because I fear to make her less expressive than she is in these matters. I *want* her answers, suggestions, outlook—no honest man could fear them—and today I may have been too sensitive to them so that she thinks it hurts me to hear her "debate." But I swear it was not against her that I cried, rather against myself—that I could not say what I know, or even against the Lord, that He had left me verbally defenseless. Most surely it was not against her. I kept saying to myself of her, "You're right; you're so damned right . . . but there is nothing for it, nothing to say, nothing to admit . . . I agree with you, but somehow I can't ever make you see what I know . . . ."

MAY 10   Austin-Larsen wedding [Betty Austin and Ross Larsen, missionaries]. *Paseo* [an outing or walk] in the afternoon to discover the route up Pichincha. Found that she is a wonderful mountaineer! Looks nice at weddings, too. She gave me this from George MacDonald [*Unspoken Sermons*] today:

> Where a man does not love, the not-loving must seem rational. For no one loves because he sees why, but because he loves. No human reason can be given for the highest necessity of divinely created existence. For reasons are always from above downward.
> In the main we love because we cannot help it. There is no merit in it: how should there be in any love? But neither is it selfish. There are many who confound righteousness with merit and think there is nothing righteous where there is nothing meritorious. "If it makes you happy to love," they say, "where is your merit? It is only selfishness." There is no merit, I reply, yet the love that is born in us is our very salvation from selfishness. It is the very essence of righteousness . . . That *certain* joys should be joys, is the very denial of selfishness. The man would be a demoniacally selfish man whom Love itself did not make joyful.

MAY 11   Lord's Day. Took S.S. [Sunday school] for Ross Larsen on his honeymoon. Breaking of bread full of joy. HCJB at night. Then with her in the open field. "Hello . . . ."

MAY 13, 14   Decided to climb Pichincha. Left at 2:15 A.M. from here, Wednesday. Betty, Abdón, Pete, Bill, and Rob formed the party. Above the mist over Quito in an hour's walk. Antisana, Cayambe, Cotopaxi all visible by moonlight. Up Pambachupa (valley's tail) during dawn hours. Nearly wept with the beauty of it. Breakfast at 7:30 and 13,300 feet above valley's head in the long grass. Missed true summit, but climbed nearest one this side by 11:00 A.M. Altitude 15,500 feet. Peak awash with mist, chill with wind, stonily ragged, wonderful with Betts. En route home we split from the others, feigned sleep in her arms, and unless I am mistaken, she pressed a kiss on my cheek as I lay there, desperately trying to keep my breathing slow! At least she went through all the motions. "We'll go no more aroving . . . ." "I'm glad you're the kind of man that likes this sort of stuff"—mountain climbing, that is.

MAY 18   Thinking today of the beauty of God's world— although bearing a curse!

MAY 19, 20   Afternoons with Abdón and then Betty over at the *bodega* [storeroom]. Feels like the hungry time of the month for me, and I can't keep my hands off her. The tranquillity of being with her is indescribable, and I find it has a mellowing effect on me, makes me easier in social converse. Also, I find it "sensitizes" me, makes me more alert to feel situations. Praying that God will make me wise enough to treat her right, love her well, and control our playing. And He deigns to do so insofar as I can now measure it. The joy of just loving, giving and taking, waiting and holding is at peak now. True, as she notes constantly, there is a pain in it, being unable to consummate now as we are, but then there is no real love without suffering of some sort. I pity her as I see she worries over the future—loving and losing. God, let me be faithful to her. And lèt me live to love if it please. Yesterday, "Don't you like schoolboys?" "Only one." Today, "Do all men love like this?" How should I know?

Inter-Mission Fellowship Conference began tonight. Abe V. D. Puy on "Make full proof of thy ministry." Personally moving. Thank God for so many knit evangelicals. Lord, preserve our unity!

Street meetings discontinued for a couple of weeks until after elections.

MAY 22   IMF conference last night. I was stimulated by Dr. Turner's word on the parables as given to teach us an appreciation for the person of Christ. Suggested that a larger view—an "I AM" view—of the Lord Jesus would be corrective of many of our problems, in prayer and testimony.

This afternoon I was helped by Ray Rosales (World Mission Prayer League) leading a discussion on methods of approach to jungle Indians:

1. Village approach: usually a linguistic situation governs. Missionary worker right in tribal community having no building except what hut he lives in concentrates on one phase of the work.
2. Itineration approach:
   a. Evangelism and church planting. Missionary may have three "shack stops" where he can live as he moves back and forth through the country.
   b. Evangelism with nationally run schools.
3. Station approach: missionary works in developed centers—building with his own funds.
   a. Chapel method. Indians come to frontier town where missionary lives.
   b. Farm method. Indians come to work on an hacienda run and owned by missionary.
   c. Colony method. Christian socialist town. Missionary is pastor and mayor and owner of all property.

The itineration approach appealed immediately to Pete and me as possible with a base in Shandia. It has more flexibility for true indigenous development.

After evening session (where I smiled to hear Crisman, who has fifty years here, tell of early days and interpret the Church in Proverbs 31), Bill and Pete and D. J. and Betty and I walked home. Bett seemed unusually quiet and hung back. She said later, "I couldn't bear walking home with all five of them!" She was silent much of the way. Blundering into conversation near her place I said, "Well, I'm afraid it's going to be a long, hard road for you." "What?" "Waiting for me." "I'm not waiting for you." That started it. Her wise unwillingness to be syrupy now, struggling with her desire to really be nice, often results in a negative tone that nettles me. Somehow tears explain things that words never can, so when she cried and explained in the fields above Arias's place, it came plainly to me how she really felt. Her restraint from speaking of her love—to me or to anyone—is a hard thing for her, and I must learn to be satisfied with answer responses for now. She cannot be aggressive until engagement, she feels, and I am glad there is that restraint for I feel none. How I thanked God for her! I find He is answering my prayers for wisdom to treat her properly—not through my understanding of how far to go or just how to love her—but through her attitudes, restraints, and liberties. She is a marvel for having the right "feeling" for things, and after I try to figure out her feelings, I find that they are often the best *reasons* for doing or refraining from any given thing.

Engagement for us, as I understand it now, would mean: (1) we would kiss (how I've refrained from this so long I'll never know); (2) she would give me further liberty with her body; (3) she would be free to be aggressive in embrace; (4) I would give her this to read, and she would let me see her diary; (5) she could say what she really feels for me, rather than just having to whisper, "Jim . . . !" and remarking, "If you only knew"; (6) we would throw off our public distance; (7) for my part a more responsible care for her, a sense of divine obligation, first, to protect her from any social inconvenience; second, to preserve my own health and body for *her* (as contrasted with my present attitude of expendibility of my powers); more time spent with her to align attitudes; (8) a definite idea of "when" for marriage; (9) fairly clear guidance about the nature of our future work, as, for instance, I now have with Pete.

MAY 26   Dinner with Ray and Carol Rosales. Stimulating discussion of missionary method as relates to their work in Cuenca among mountain Quichua and ours among the forest folk. Lord, keep me praying for them. Lead them on to full working out of Your will. He is a ready man—instruct him.

Rain and the goat shed with her. Discussion of women in New Testament missionary work—translation as relative to the building of churches and the training of leaders. We finally agreed—silhouette against the goat-shed door. "That's what I like about it. One of the things I didn't expect about being in love was how much *fun* you can have . . . ." Talk about how loving both brings out the boy and matures the man. Came home elated, *very* much in love, and extremely thankful for God's giving me the woman. A happy, full, profitable day. Praise for it. Never noticed how bright her eyes could be before tonight.

MAY 27   Moved to Dr. Hugo Cevallas's home today. A pure Spanish context at last. Thank God! Taking midday meal with Sr. Arias and morning and evening here. Great provision from God to have this place. I want to make the best of it, Lord.

MAY 29   Finished med course at T's. Full Spanish schedule now.

MAY 30   Satan well knows the power of a single gathering center. Jeroboam's idea of other "convenient" places to sacrifice rather than Jerusalem effectively divided the nation of Israel more than any other thing. Right down to the time of Christ where the issue was, simply put, "You say Jerusalem, but our fathers say this mountain." And how other gathering centers have affected Christ's Church since! Any place, or anybody, will do for the worship of Jehovah. The prescribed place and order ordained at Jerusalem under Solomon were thrown aside, with the satanically wise counsel, "Si este pueblo subiere a ofrecer sus sacrificios en la casa de Jehováh in Jerusalem, el corazón de este pueblo se volverá a su señor Roboam rey de Judah . . ." (1 Kings 12:27). A mind faithful to God's mandates will soon make subject a heart to its proper king. Lord, let me walk in Your ways. Jeroboam's divisive powers outlived himself by centuries. Let me gather and scatter.

Walked with Bett above the district of Las Casas. Under the row of eucalyptus in the grass I knew again that I loved her and knew that it was right so to love. Instruction from God has not ceased since Decoration Day four years ago at the lagoon in Wheaton. And, by grace, the next four years will be yet more so. "She will do thee good all the days of thy life."

MAY 31 *1 Kings 13*   The prophet who took someone else's word as divine mandate when he had already gotten his orders, stands as a serious warning. A man, be he never so powerful in his word for God, who dares himself transgress that word, from whatever so piously plausible reasoning, writes his own death warrant. When God leads one way, the voice of an ancient prophet should not move to another. God, O God, preserve me from retracing ground I've covered in obedience.

JUNE 4   Moonlight over Guápulo. "I hope we never lose the wonder." "There's nothing wrong with either of us that one another wouldn't cure."

JUNE 6   *Autocarril* [automotive railroad car] with the girls, Pete and Arias to Otavalo. Refreshing trip winding in and out of the valleys over the railway. Thanks, Lord, for this "extra." Seems as though I feel liberty to allow myself luxuries now in getting acquainted with the country that I must necessarily curtail later. Learning a language means meeting a people in all their circumstances and trips—as long as you are *with* nationals, it will always contribute to the end.

JUNE 7   Up early to see the Otavalo Indian market. Day overcast although hot and dusty. Hired a *colectivo* [large station wagon] and visited Lake San Pablo, shining back great Mount Imbaburra and touched with great white "garcías" [a species of bird, probably a heron]. Side trip to Lake Cuicocha and then to Ibarra for lunch. Enjoyed it much with the group but longed to do it alone with her. Ken and Frances Jones, interning in Panama, went with us. Raining hard when we arrived in Quito.

JUNE 8   Heard brother Crisman (fifty years in Ecuador) at the Second Church in the morning. Lord, let me learn to speak Spanish in fifty years—seems as if no one really gets past the beginner's stage in pronunciation of all the gringos I've met. And none hit the national's genius of language. Giver of the gift of tongues! Let me speak to them as they ought to be spoken to, so they do not have to hide their real reaction with polite praise. Glad to be in a national home—at least to hear it spoken as a living-thought medium—not merely as English translation.

Mist and rain under the slim, sharp silhouetted eucalyptus with her, then the mud-arch doorway out of the wet. Talked of her relation with Dorothy and some of the problems. Lord, I'm asking for the very best for them; let them learn friendship in the full sense. Betty doesn't seem to really want intimacy with D. J.—something my personality will never understand. Let me deal wisely here, Lord, if I should counsel or suggest. Feel very much outside the situation as far as really being able to analyze it, yet somehow so close to it with my feelings for Betty—wanting the very happiest for her, and sensing a certain responsibility to achieve it for her. She admits a problem and confesses that she doesn't know the way through it, but I fear she doesn't really want it solved badly enough. Her natural reserve is strong; she only gets intimate with those who "happen to fit"—or, as she says, "with those friendships that are outright gifts from God." Although she recognizes that some friendships must be made, I think she is not willing to expend the effort to make one with D. J.—mainly because she doesn't really believe that they are a pair, she doesn't think D.

will really be capable of being "made" a comrade.

I agree. D. doesn't look like the right kind of stuff. But, oh, how I want to see Bett happy these waiting years without each other, and an intimate with whom she could share things would be such a boon. Still, she says as I said when D. was en route to New York, they have nothing in common. Outwardly, no. Betty is poetic, fond of nature, penetrating. Dorothy seems superficial, childish, ingenuous beside her. But, Father, they have Christ in common, and I want You to teach them *how to share Him.* I can't expect D. to be for Betty what Pete has been for me, but at least she can be some sort of outlet to confer with, some sort of balance to stabilize all Betty's inwardness. Sure seems like a good problem, Lord. I am waiting to see You work it out.

The discipline of distance has passed into the discipline of proximity for me these days. Living right across the street, eating a meal a day together, on the bus, walking puts me on an entirely different basis than I have ever known with her before. Not only is the problem "how far should I go?" (she usually has that set, thank God), but "how often?" Fighting between two opinions. Should I take all of her I can get now and live on the memory, feeding love full every opportunity that comes? Or should I go cautious, keep it the rare occasion so as not to overdo it—and possibly tire too soon? (So far I've been surprised that I do not tire of holding her; it doesn't get old, but more real, like getting used to a strange place. The shyness goes, and a little of the surprise, but none of the niceness, none of the real joy of being there.) So far the Lord has given a good balance, it seems to me. I don't feel like I've really abandoned my Spanish for her or any of the other big purposes of being in Quito. I've had to keep myself from staying out too late and from going out too often. And love never gets "full" to the point of satiation, although at times I have the sense of having had "just enough for now."

JUNE 11   Moonrise in the scattered brush north of Las Casas. First session with Bett in Quito that kept us out until midnight. She was full of play, and we seemed like children together, laughing and chatting. Once, when I grew quiet, she said, "Talk to me." So we talked—I don't know what of. Standing behind her with her head between my hands and pressed against my legs struck me as a ballet pose—terribly symmetrical for us—until she clasped both legs and tripped me backwards. More genuine *fun* than I've had doing anything for a good long time. How can I show my gratitude to the Lord who provided her for me? Pure grace from Him gave her, and I need more of it to maintain our present happy sense of wanting and having. Never let it get stale, Lord, I want this woman to be the woman of all women for me as long as I want woman.

JUNE 13   Left here at 6:00 A.M. with Abdón, Rob, and Pete for a hike up "Wawa." Climbed until 3:00 P.M. to the ridge running between Rucu and Wawa, made camp, retired early. Up at dawn, wandered over the crater rim until we made the peak around noon. Returned to cache of our equipment, ate lunch, and came home, circuitously by 9:00 P.M. Saturday. Again thankful to God for strength and zest to do such things. I'm sure He made mountains for city-bred boys to climb. Tidmarsh is not too happy about our taking long trips—thinks we ought to be aware that we were not sent here to always be excursioning. But I had liberty to do it: first, because we had an Ecuadorian along for language study; second because we are not tied to any definite work yet; third, because of the freshening effect of the trip.

JUNE 15   *2 Kings 3–6*   Betty and I went to Cooks' for coffee after "Pláticas Dominicales" [a radio program on which we sang sometimes]. Seemed so right and good for us to be visiting together, thought of as a unit, nearly—one invited and the other expected. She suits me fine in public, and in private . . . ! Stars afterward above the house here in the soft, wet grass; the sound of her breathing, the weight of her body, the billow of her hair under her head—seems like she gets nicer every time. Still, we haven't kissed. I can't believe it sometimes, but it's so. Who ever heard of people in love like we are in love sporting as fondly as we do, and as often, who have never met at the lips? Can it really be there will be *more* thrill than now?

Reading 2 Kings these days in Spanish. Noted the reputation of Elisha before he was recognized as the prophet of Israel. He was known as "the one who poured water over the hands of Elijah" (3:11). Lowly beginnings for such an office, but it teaches a thing or two. Even in these days, God's men were trained right alongside others of God's men—in the most intimate and unofficial modes. Pauline method of training workers was a prophetic method. God always has trained through His men directly influencing the instructed by personal, close-up contact. Lord, give me my man to train. And give me the power of life necessary to labor. Gehazi, in training, could not do, even with Elisha's staff, what Elisha did by the power of personal faith in contact with the expired son of the Shunammite. The form brings neither voice nor hearing under the hand of Gehazi. And let me remember the power of God's majority. "Porque mas son los que están con nosotros que los que están con ellos" ["For they that are with us are more than they that are with them"] (6:16). Not only do angelic hosts outnumber human ones, but also, in another realm, divine forces overpower demonic ones. "*Greater* is he that is in you than he that is in the world" (1 John 4:4).

JUNE 20   Read and prayed with Bett in the *quebrada* [ravine] above—first time since Portland, if I remember correctly. Jordan's for lunch (lead Gene forward, Lord. He is full of faith, but needs guidance and method principles from the Word). Much talk with Abdón in the *bodega*. I appreciate him much as he seems to understand many things that one would hardly suspect he had thought of. Mentioned that *pruebas* [trials] came for two reasons: (1) to chastize for sin, (2) to quicken and draw closer in times of spiritual anemia. I found a third, curious cause reading this evening: "For *Thy sake* we are dead men every day . . ." (Rom. 8:36). This refers to "anguish," "hunger," "danger," and so on (Rom. 8:35). Is it then that converse circumstances may be turned satanically against us on these levels—simply because we are His?

JUNE 21   I think I just hurt her. Can't be sure, but the instance makes me feel sorry. We were just looking at the Arias's puppies now. She had told me earlier that she was going to see this Gladys around 2:30 this afternoon—I assumed for study. I was walking away from the backyard, and she came to follow me to the gate when it happened. I said, "What's the idea, making plans for Saturday afternoon with this gal?" Harmless enough, and natural, since we usually are together for *paseo* Saturday afternoon, and I was thinking they were going to study together. Then she explained that she had told Gladys we usually got together for Saturday-afternoon walks and had intended only to include her. Pete joined us. At the gate after a few minutes, Pete walked far enough away for her to say, "So I don't have a right to make my own plans any more?" I said, "A perfect right . . . ." I didn't feel like walking with a group, and Pete was dubious (he's had diarrhea lately and feels low). After saying that I would leave it up to Pete whether he wanted to go and including that it looked like rain and waiting, I said, "Frankly, I don't feel much like going." She turned and walked down the driveway. "See you," Pete said. "I guess so." I knew *then*, at last, that it had hurt her. We were still standing by the gate when she came out, chatting with Dorothy who had come up. She didn't say good-bye with her eyes as she usually does.

Strange that so small a thing makes such an ache. I came home and dropped on my knees. Asked the Lord to take the bitterness out of it for her and to let her know somehow that I love her. Funny, I can't think why I didn't want to go; rain and Pete have never stopped us from afternoon *paseos* so far, and Gladys would have been no problem. Just to be with her has been happiness, and it would be now, if I had been man enough to follow her straight, quick walk to the bus twenty minutes ago.

JUNE 23 Bob Schneider, Wycliffe Bible Translators, made public the news of their recently signed contract with the government to enter tribes in Ecuador and reduce their language to writing. This will bring changes in our plans for the Oriente. Especially does it seem to affect Betty. Where will You send her now, Lord?

JUNE 24 Street meeting in the morning. Confusion of appointments with Betty and Abdón. Found her crying up the road to Pambachupa. Feel like I gave her poor comfort for my blundering having caused her ache. Lord, teach me to understand and care for her.

JUNE 28 Quick trip to Shell Mera with Schneider and Doc Fuller [Dr. Everett Fuller, missionary with HCJB]. Raining and clouded in the whole way down but caught something of the spirit of the Pastaza and the Llanganati range.

JUNE 29 Lord's Day. Street meeting and tract distribution in Puyo. Grateful for interest and receptiveness from the people. Investigated Shell installations that remain—a base for Wycliffe and a hospital for HCJB. First visit to the Pastaza [river] curling and crashing as it breaks out of the mountains. Big, husky country that gives the sense of newness and virginity. Thank God for being sent to such an inheritance; I'm so glad I've been sent to the Oriente, not to the *Sahara!*

JUNE 30 Visited Baños with Al Ryde while the weather held in any survey flying. Getting to know, respect and love Bob and Keitha Wittig.

JULY 1 Flew over Arajuno to the Curaray [river] looking for Auca houses. Down the Nushino to a *guarnición* [Army post] and circled back a little to the south. Nothing. Late trip to Macuma and visit to the Jívaro [the "head shrinker" tribe of Indians] house after dark. Catheter drained three and a half quarts of urine. Hadn't relieved himself for six days. Washed him up and did the dirty work for Schneider who wanted to keep sterile to insert the tube. Marie and Frank Drown most hospitable at Macuma.

JULY 2   Buzzed Shell's deserted field at Ayuy; landed at Villano for lunch in the *guarnición*. Made inquiries about Quichua population in the Canelos region. Estimates uncertain. Would guess one thousand to fifteen hundred. Saw the necessity for our being single to reach these people—too scattered to reach with the mission-station method.

JULY 3   Quito in a clear day—all the mountains visible. Beautiful, my God, beautiful.

JULY 4   No class. Señorita Balereso went to the American Embassy picnic. Met Bett on the way home from visiting Gladys, and we looked at newly arrived Kodaslides. Then to a little field of eucalyptus off to the north above the house. Happy chatting mostly about our families—Ginny, Bert, Jane. Then she chose and executed a position that I never dreamed of—head to head, one lying on the back, the other on the face. Wonderful! Just faces and hands touching. She said, "How can you say you don't know how to be tender?"

JULY 9   Reading 1 Chronicles 16, the praise of David. Verse 11: "Buscad de continuo su presencia" ["Seek his presence continually"]. I have been wondering why the presence of God is not always real. This is one reason: it has not been sought. It is scriptural counsel to see the presence of God, strive for its realization. It does not come "naturally," even to the believer, to sense the presence of God; he must exert seeking faith for it. Verses 13, 19: ". . . Jacob, sus escogidos . . . muy pocos, y estranjeros" ["Jacob, his chosen ones . . . few in number . . . and sojourners"]. It did not seem to puzzle Jacob that he was elected out of many. Seldom does he ever seem to really mention the "to us" obvious problem of divine justice. Rather, his sense of being chosen from among many nations only gave rise to praise. "I have not loved you because you were great . . . but because I loved you" (Deut. 7:7, 8). And often the mention of God's choosing occurs, as here, as motive for praise. Verse 33: "Entonces cantarán los árboles de los bosques delante de Jehová; porque viene a juzgar la tierra" ["Then shall the trees of the wood sing for joy before the Lord, for he comes to judge the earth"]. The wrongs of men against the earth, whether through ignorance or deliberate ravage, will, as suggested here, be judged of God. Careless misuse of God-entrusted land is worthy of judgment, and even the trees of the forest will vindicate God in the day that He judges the earth for the wrongs done in and to it.

JULY 10   3:00 A.M. to 8:00 P.M. with Betty alone. Circled Rucu in hopes of getting to Guagua but were slowed by a valley we didn't know of before. Beautiful day. Saw mountains on the Colombian border as well as Sarahuren for the first time. Returned by the *chorera* [waterfall] route. Slept in each other's arms for a few minutes in the big valley floor behind Rucu. Love is developing to a solid thing with me. A touch is more than sexually arousing. It is conveyer of meaning now.

JULY 11   I wonder sometimes if it is right to be so happy. Day follows day in an easy succession of wonders and joys—simple, good things like food well prepared or play with the children or conversation with Pete, or supply of money for rent and board within hours of its time to be paid. Grace upon grace in the outside sphere of living. But, simply because I am not really studying the English Bible, fresh truth for inner soul refreshment is rare. I am supposed to speak at English fellowship again on Lord's day and find that I must go back to old truth, learned in the work-free days of '49 in Portland, to get solid material for preaching. I was reading my diary notes and noting the contrasting soul soreness of those days with the freedom and joy of these. Those were certainly more productive from a point of view of getting things from the Word;

these are more casual and less fruitful, but for reasons, Spanish must be gotten. I want badly for God to speak as He did then, but I want Him to begin speaking in Spanish, and I am not yet used to that—perhaps not ready for it. So I go on in these days, glad hearted and simple in my thanks, lacking the profundity of material for depth of worship. But I have not left off seeking His depths, and I believe He will take me back to those days of struggling and discovering in the Word. How well I see now that He is wanting to do something in me! So many missionaries, intent on doing something, do forget that His main work is making something of them, not just doing a work by their stiff and misunderstanding fingers. Teach me, Lord Jesus, to live simply and love purely, like a child, and to know that You are unchanged in your attitudes and actions toward me. Give me not to be hungering for the "strange, rare, and peculiar" when the common, ordinary, and regular, rightly taken, will suffice to feed and satisfy the soul. Bring the struggle when I need it; take away the ease at Your pleasure.

JULY 21   Felt condemned yesterday by the Word as I sat down to meditate at the Lord's Supper. "I will not offer any of that which cost me nothing to the Lord," said David (2 Sam. 24:24). I realized that I had paid out nothing last week to really get something to offer the Lord. So as I confessed my sin, the Lord forgave and began to feed my meditation from the Gospels with thoughts of the patience of the Lamb. Prayed with much liberty and worshiped God with joy for this attribute of the Father so wonderfully characterized in the Son. Thought, too, about:

> Limitless Bread from the kitchen of God
> How hast Thou fed His world . . . !
> and   Wine of the Cellars of heaven!
> Grape of the Lord's own vine.

Much refreshed in worship, and thankful for the uplifting character of the feast.

Went to Jan Terry and Kay Evan's for Sunday evening snack—waffles and banana splits. Nobody here suffering much lack! After the program "Pláticas Dominicales," Bett and I went above the *barrio* here for our usual Sunday evening walk. She was sweet last night, chatty and affable with laughter. Talked of all sort of things, from the "Howard belch" to Jane Feely. She was really dressed nicely yesterday; how easily my wonderings about her figure have been dissipated with just looking at it. Well-formed legs, slender waist (and without strappings!), and mild breasts. Not one bit distasteful or even "skinny," as Mom would say. Thanks for all that made yesterday, Lord.

JULY 26   Marveled at my inner weakness yesterday. Felt miserably unworthy to be here as an "administrator of the mysteries of God." Strange that I should—evidently for life—be put to such close contact with Pete and Betty whom I feel are far my intellectual superiors. Spanish studies, for instance. When Betty first arrived and saw Pete and I were studying at the same level, she said, "How did you get so far behind?"—that Pete should be up with me. And now she is competing with us both, right along in the same material! They are both able to correct my grammar and pronunciation, and seem to be able to apply tense rules so much easier than I. Felt weepy and useless yesterday at noon, swept with waves of envy and defeated wonderings about such things.

Ross and Betty Larsens' for supper with Bett, Pete, and Miss Arboleda [an Ecuadorian who taught us Spanish].

Oh, for a faith that sings! Thought of Jehoshaphat in 2 Chronicles 20. Threatened with defeat by a multitude that far outreached his powers of war, he "puso su rostro a buscar a Jehová" ["set his face to seek Jehovah" (v. 3)]. He called a fast for the people and then publicly reminded God of His covenant with Abraham and Solomon. Stating the problem thus put God in a position of responsibility: "Dios nuestro, No los juzgarás tu? Pues nosotros *no tenemos* y *no sabemos quehacer:* mas nuestros ojos están puestos en ti" ["O our God, wilt thou not execute judgment upon them? For we are powerless against this great multitude. We do not know what to do, but our eyes are upon thee" (v. 12)]. Then, after an answer from a prophet, Jehoshaphat, himself humbled and believing, charges his people: "*Creed* en Jehová vuestro Dios, y seréis sequros; *creed* a sus profetas, y seréis prosperados" ["Believe in Jehovah your God, so shall ye be established; believe his prophets, so shall ye prosper"]. And then they broke out singing! Singing in the face of such a problem! Lord God, give me a faith that will take sufficient quiver out of me so that I may sing! Over the Aucas, Father, I want to sing.

JULY 30   I have only now come in from a short hour's trip with her to the post office. She noticed today, as she did not seem to on the twenty-fifth, the spirit of heaviness that comes over me. I told her that I felt weepy, sighful, and that I couldn't tell her why now, but that I would later, when she could do something about it. Also, that it concerned things about her that I didn't want changed; and that I would get over it. Not very clear. It isn't to me either. I don't understand what there is about loving her that makes me such a damned woman. I can hardly begin to describe it; I only know that I feel it strong and that I can't talk of it without twists coming to my mouth. Lips get dry and tears seem to brim at my eyes, and there is a crushing sense in my chest. At the bottom of it is a tremendous weight of sheer unworthiness. I don't feel fit to be in her company; I can't think of things to say if she doesn't readily come back in conversation.

I sense that I am not her better in anything. She is fine in her feelings, but I am gross. She is settled in her thinking about things (she knows that it is inherently wrong to possess a book of nude photographs; I have to puzzle it slowly through making blunders and contradictions). I haven't thought about them seriously. She knows the Spanish word for *tawdry;* I never heard it. She can do a Spanish lesson faster and better, frame and state a clearer sentence in class, give a more sensible reason for an English usage, or ask a more sensible question about a Spanish one. In short, I see that she is my superior, and it frightens me.

Can I bear competition with that sort of woman all my life? And to her, I daresay, it never occurs that her efficiency makes me feel like I'm being beaten, and can't help it, just *can't help it.* I have seen husbands who are excelled by their wives and what piteous things they are, how out of place! Is that what her self-security, calmness, ability, and purity are going to make me when we marry? Great God in heaven, don't allow it! If only she didn't make me feel so small, if only she had had some great defeat in ignorance as I had in Wilma, something that would make one feel at least morally her equal, yet I could not love her if she had, I fear. How is it that she speaks a perfect Spanish *r* and is commended for it by Angelita, and I can't even roll one without twisting my jaw to the side, or do a sensible "flap r." Pilar laughed the other day at my "buenas tarrh des."

I know it would help to talk to her, but can't bear to think of speaking of this thing in daylight when she could see me cry. She wouldn't believe me, anyhow. I don't give the impression of feeling underdog, and I don't usually display any humility that would suggest I felt myself her lesser. But I do. I know she would assure me that she didn't feel that way at all and that she didn't sense any superiority. Superiors usually don't, if they are really superior. But there it is—and I'm none the happier for having written it.

Oh, if only she felt that she could tell me she loved me and why, perhaps that would bolster me somehow. But this constant sense of having to apologize—for my table manners, my grossness, almost for my sex. Oh, it's hard for me; it makes me want to cry. If only she could come to *me* instead of my having always to go to her, letting her control, having to follow so many times when I feel that I should be leading. But what is to be done? She *can't,* simply *can't* do otherwise until engagement—says it just has to be that way now. My God, what a vise I'm in.

JULY 31   Spent some time in 1 Corinthians 7 this morning; it came up in my presleep reading last night. Puzzled over verse 1: "It is good for a man not to touch a woman." Does this have

anything to do with my play with Betty? First the word *good* is
καλόν—"noble," "excellent," "well." Williams says, "It may
be a good thing that a man not marry." The *proper course* for
believing men is not to touch. Second, *a man* is ἄνθρωπος—not
a husband but man: (1) in general, or (2) an unmarried man. It
cannot be a husband because in verses 3 and 4 he encourages
the function of the body in marriage. If there is to be any
restraint in marriage of the physical union, it is to be by consent and only for a set period.

He may be speaking of an unmarried man sharing another's
wife because: (1) of the word ἄνθρωπος (2) of the word γυνή
(cf. v. 34 where a contested reading makes a difference between a wife [γυνή] and a virgin), (3) of the following ideas: (a)
"fornication" (where at least one person is unmarried), (b)
ἑαυτοῦ and ἰδίον—"his own" and "her own special" mate, as
though they may have suggested a plurality of wives or husbands, so as to keep marriage a matter among Christians only,
and the limited number of one sex would force them to
polygamy. If this is his meaning, he should go on to explain
who should ἅπτειν whom, and that is precisely what he does.
He may be saying, "It is only right that an unmarried man
should not handle a woman who is a wife." Also, *touch* ἅπτω
means "handle." The lesser word θίγγειν means "to run the
hand over" (1 John 1:1; Luke 24:39) and the still less potent
(Heb. 12:18; Acts 17:27) means "to grope after" [Jim is in error
here; ψηλαφάω is used in all four references]. The Old Testament LXX usages (Gen. 20:6; Prov. 6:29) may imply adultery or
simply handling, but they are both in the evil sense. This
"touching" is illicit. "It is good for a man not to fondle
another's wife." I conclude in favor of the interpretation that
the Corinthians had asked about wife sharing and that Paul is
answering that such was not good—"let each man have his
own."

It does not apply to my play with Betty. Rather, I am persuaded our case is discussed in verses 35–38 where the subject
is neither "a virgin daughter" (KJV) nor "virginity" (DARBY)
but a "betrothed virgin." And the conclusion is that when I
feel I am not treating her (1) fairly (in withholding marriage),

or (2) uprightly (in going too far outside of marriage), and she is getting older and I want to marry, I do not sin if I follow the dictates of my own desire.

AUGUST 6, 7 She had word the sixth that Ginny was engaged to Bud De Vries on Sunday. Broken up through the whole day. Crying when I came over to ask her for a walk in the evening. We ambled off toward the brush field, keeping silence the whole way, as I listened to her sobbing. Hardly any spirit to enjoy a beautiful moon. "Betty, I know I am asking you to do something that few women in the world are asked to do. And I want to be a help—all I can. Can you tell me what started it?"

"It's not important what started it. The thing that climaxed it . . . I had a letter today . . . ."

"Is Ginny engaged?"

"Yes . . . and two letters from Dave about his new baby . . . (long pauses) . . . it's just that I can't see why they should have it so, and we have it this way."

I cried too. Cried to see her hurt and wondering, cried to share her ache, cried because I honest-to-God didn't know why they should have it that way, and we have it thus. But my tears are no answer to the problem. It was more tears than talk tonight.

Thursday was not much better for her. But we went downtown together, took a taxi up the Panecillo and walked down. She was much freer to chat—her very touch filling me with tenderness. We played in the grass down below the house, and she taught me to "two step" in the street afterward—after midnight! Sense great moving of heart wanting to be fair to her, wanting to marry her, wanting, wanting. But now I feel no guiding from God, not even for engagement. The "years" weigh on me often, awake and going off to sleep, thinking of the length of a year, worrying over the real view I should take of engagement, feeling my previous arguments fall, one by one. Knowing that I will be there one day and glad of it, but knowing that it is not for now. We talk of it freely together, she and I, and my reasoning must be making it worse for her, but I know—reason or not—that now is not the time.

AUGUST 12   Awoke with a hunger for the Word and a breathed prayer of "Feed me, Lord, feed me." Morning reading in Job where I noted the authority Satan may have over robber bands, to control them and restrain them (one servant was left from each loss to tell Job), or over natural forces, a whirlwind that directed itself against the house of Job's eldest son, or over life itself, to kill (he was given power over all that Job had, and he used it to slay). Cleverly, he did not take Job's wife; he needed her for the final thrusts, to jibe at Job to curse God and die. I *must* come to be aware of Satan. He is out to win arguments over me with God. He may never get me into hell, but he may cause God shame in defeating me. Preserve me from the lion, Lord. Let him not swallow me up.

Enjoyed reading an article in *The Witness* about the call of Moses. Oh, for the sense of His presence! Betty weighs on me these days. She is not happy often, not full of that good fruit, joy, and it saddens me to see her living in this defeat— especially when I know that I am the cause. Liberate her, Lord, and me through her. Frequent tears and long silences are heavy things to me who has lived so lightheartedly until now. This worry robs me of the Presence, as I find I want always to be near her, even though I am little help when there, to comfort and chat as I'm able. Not that being near her is robbing of the Presence, but *wanting* to be there when I must study or write alone leaves me with a dissatisfaction. Oh, for a heartiness in the will of God—"doing it from the heart," as Paul says.

I must confess that, though I am sure now that engagement is not for us this summer, the acceptance of that as the will of the Father is no gladdening thing—not that my wants (for her—for the work of God, perhaps among Aucas) conflict. They are not contradictory, but they do not seem to mesh. They have come at the same time, so that instead of fitting into one another, as cogs would, they grind against one another, sometimes with awful concentration.

To have her I am led to hope would mean to have a family. And having a family while attempting to reach Aucas are, to my present knowledge, incompatible. I am beginning to feel that engagement, not involving a family, and being a great help to her, would not be incompatible. But there are one or two things that I hold against it for tonight. I don't like long engagements anyway, and if I can shorten engagement to fewer months by holding off, perhaps until Ed comes, it will be a little easier.

Second, I have enough adjustments to make right now, in going to the forest, to have to increase the emotional strain by leaving a fiancée in Quito. Nor am I sure that I want the public pressure of being thought of as hazarding my *promised* life. It is too soon for me, not having seen the Oriente, to believe that God may not want me there entirely unattached. These reasons seem fearfully inadequate, so I must list the deepest one (and the most inadequate to other folks). I do not *feel* that it is time for engagement. But all the while, I'm mad for her, wanting to be with her night and day, the haunting hunger of body, the loneliness of mind making book study a farce at times and making life itself seem useless without her.

AUGUST 14   My last day in Quito broke clear and cold. I am writing amid suitcases, pack sacks, and rubber bags, while Pete changes his clothes in lieu of a visit to Señorita Balereso. Betty was fevered last night and I visited her in her room. Read *The Big Sky* awhile, then, following her example of bad bedside practice, when I was sick a week ago, I sat on the bed. Pete says he's ready.

AUGUST 15   Left by bus with eighteen boys at 6:00 A.M. from Quito. Sensed again that weak "leaving" sensation as we pulled out into dawn and a clearing day toward the south. Periods of semidesertion as I traveled, sleepiness and silence. But withal a sense of being sent by God and a joy in going as we made the next-to-last run for Shandia—goal of months of plan and desire. Camp began with getting to know the boys' names, dividing them into groups, and getting them to cooperate in behaving. Slept restlessly, with recurrences of last night as she knelt over me in the field. I told her that I had gotten liberty to hope for engagement in less than a year. She said "That's good to know." Feel more and more that my reasons against engagement do not carry the weight of those in favor of it. It will mean years of "promised" life, likely, and that involves some problems, but they do not compare with what I am assigning Betty to in this uncommitted period with her great reserves and pressures. For us both I believe engagement would be a release for easier thinking, both present and for the future. Thinking now of asking Ed to bring a ring.

AUGUST 17　　Sunday.　　Resisting the urge to write as I study for this morning study session with the boys—so much I want to share with her. Hungry for the power of God again and wondering how to have time alone with these little ones pressing around constantly.

AUGUST 20　　Prayed last night that God would give me six sons—boys like these I'm working with to raise for Him. This morning God gave me a break, and four, Napoleon, Danillo, Ruben, and Oswaldo, came crying after the Bible study, and we had a long pray and chat. Believe God gave me four sons.

AUGUST 22　　It is quiet in the bunkhouse. The boys left at 6:20 A.M., and Pete (now dozing in his room) and I are awaiting the arrival of the older fellows this afternoon. Stan has gone down to visit his wife; the Georges (Poole, Sanchez) went back to bed. The week has been a happy one, and I think, under God, a useful one. But it was too short to train sons— one must live with them. Wanting sons these days, wanting to feed them, lift them, have them hound me, beg me in the name of a father. And for me, it looks like no sons are in sight, at least, not my own.

Still, as I was reading Job again (12:10), "en cuya mano está el alma de todo ser viviente" ["in whose hand is the soul of every living being"], I recognized that all I am and have is the Almighty's. He could, in one instant, change the whole course of my life, with accident, tragedy, or any event unforeseen. Job is a lesson in acceptance—not of blind resignation, but of believing acceptance—that what God does is well done. So, Father, with happy committal I give You my life again this morning—not for anything special, simply to let You know that I regard it as Yours. Do with it as it pleases You. Only give me great grace to do for the glory of Christ Jesus whatever comes to me . . ." in sickness and in health!"

AUGUST 23   This waiting for letters again. Waiting, waiting without hope for anything but more waiting, it seems, for God to give me her. It has been more than a week now since I have followed a thought of hers, and, oh, the Lord knows how I miss it. A letter—just to share a single feeling of hers—would be a help, but one wonders just how the mail service down here ever succeeds, and, in weariness, thinks that it doesn't make any difference anyway. If I had just that much of her— one thought to follow—I know that it would satisfy only as long as I followed it, and leave a greater gap of wanting. ". . . when you can't live without her, marry."

AUGUST 26   The first letter came Sunday, full of fresh love and telling me what I wanted to know. She has been given peace. Thanks, Lord God. Woke at 4:00 A.M. after one of those senseless dreams of her. We got on a boat together, going north from Portland, and ended up climbing on the outside of a train and watching Marilou McCully being greeted by a group of girls at one of the stations that fled by. Among them, Shirley Paine! Women washing clothes and bathing in the river at Puyo was not much help as we swam with the *jóvenes* [boys] this morning.

Henry Adams's *Democracy*, a novel satirizing late nineteenth century U.S., has a line of interest (*Time*, Aug. 25, 1952). The woman of the story decided that her love ambition was nothing more than "a blind longing to escape from the torture of watching other women with full lives and satisfied instincts."

AUGUST 29   Shell Mera. Friday. Woke at 3:30 A.M., unable to sleep knowing that she is here. (Came down yesterday with T's.) Up at 4:30 with the boys. Packed, breakfasted, and said good-bye to them all, touched especially by Herman, Armando, Arturo, Raphael and the Luis from Ibarra, and Miguel—who, unsaved, invited me to his home in Quito. Cleaned up and read a little. First Corinthians 13:7: "Love suffers all, believes all, hopes all, endures all." Then came to Wittigs' and readied the flight for Dr. and Pete, whose weight gave him privilege of going in with more of the baggage. I am to wait for Eladio tomorrow and go in on Monday, God willing. But she was here, and we talked odd bits—about the greetings Monday night, about the unfinished letter I gave her because her coming caught me in the middle of it. Then, as we stood, stalling at the kitchen door with the others outside, suddenly we leaned toward each other and pressed hard, face to face, only for an instant. That's all—but, oh, it was a full instant, full of telling things. She came toward me without being pulled, full of quick passion. And we went out to the car together. There were tears wandering in her eyes . . . and I am alone tonight.

AUGUST 30   Job, utterly distressed and knowing that death was his ultimate end: "A la corrupción digo, 'Mi padre eres!' y al gusano, Mi madre y mi hermana!" ["To corruption I say, 'You are my father,' and to the worm, 'my mother and my sister!'"] (17:14). But Messiah, more distressed than Job, and recognizing His position as sin bearer and death bearer for men, stopped not at saying to the worm, "My sister;" but in Psalm 22 He notes in His great distance from the race in becoming sin for His people, "Yo soy gusano" ["I am a worm"].

SEPTEMBER 1   Woke this morning with thoughts for a message to Institute Chapel [the Bible Institute in Shell Mera run by GMU] on "Possible Errors Concerning the Resurrection."

1. That there is none (1 Cor. 15:12).
2. That it will not be a bodily one (1 Cor. 15:35).

But we know that it will be at least as bodily as Christ's was (1 John 3:2). He breathed, talked Hebrew, ate, could be handled, had wounds, and so forth. It may be something besides body—something extra in body—but we know it will not be less than body in the good sense of body. I can never think of this apart from the recurrence of Jonathan Swift's remark—I hope the thought is only jokingly brought up, not blasphemously—"We are not told what they do do in heaven, only what they do not do—they neither marry nor are given in marriage." Christ come and coming in flesh (1 John 4:2; 2 John 7).

3. That it is already past (2 Tim. 2:18).

Instead, I spoke of "El ministerio de reconciliación que Dios nos puso en nosotros" [the ministry of reconciliation that God laid upon us] (2 Cor. 5:18, 19; 1 Tim. 6:20; 2 Tim. 1:14; 2:1, 2). Guarding the ministry in rejecting *discursos vacíos* [empty thoughts]; in faith and love; in the Holy Spirit and in committing it to others. Not much life in preaching, but some help in Spanish.

This afternoon Wittig brought in a man whose neck was cut all the way across the back in a drunken brawl Saturday night. All the way from Sucua. He is here now, waiting for some way to get to Quito. Nothing to do for him. Wish we had the GMC like last week when the little Indian girl shot herself through the eye.

SEPTEMBER 3　　Shandia. As I write, my praise mingles with the steady rush of Jatun Yacu [the river, "Big Water" in Quichua], running like pure silver into the jungle under a full moon. Left Shell Mera at 3:00 P.M. in a sky of scattered clouds, landed at Pano around 3:30 P.M. and made the walk to beautiful Shandia in just two and a half hours. The moon rose just as I stepped into the clearing with Eladio [an Ecuadorian teacher hired for the boys school] and three carriers—prognostically telling me of the faithfulness of God, and reminding me that the moon is round, as I learned in Huntington two years ago Christmastime. Surely life is full in His will and brings promises of good things yet for us here. In spite of my wait since Friday, first for the teacher and then for Wittig, the thought kept recurring as I came along, "Right on time, right on time—God's time." So with much joy we have arrived at last at the destination decided on in the will when at Wycliffe in 1950—and my joy is full, full, full. Oh, how blind it would have been to reject the leading of those ten days, how it has changed the course of life for me and added such a host of joys.

Sopping with sweat this afternoon, I looked up over the notched horizon of hills that hide her up there in Quito, and, perhaps in love for her, or perhaps in self-pity, said, "I can stick it out if I can only stay here." The wildness and grandeur of the jungle was on me and gave again the sense of rugged solidarity, the sense of living alone and still feeling satisfied within—a satisfaction I did not have this past weekend in Shell Mera, wanting her so badly. The forest is not unlike the west around San Miguel, bigger, of course, and emptier, but not much different. The trees with the concave bark, and the roots ribboning down to the ground, the straight hanging vines, the clear, warm creeks—all beautiful, simply beautiful.

Shandia was a mission station in Quichua Indian country (the eastern jungle, known as the Oriente) first occupied by Dr. and Mrs. Wilfred Tidmarsh. Due to injuries suffered by Mrs. Tidmarsh in a plane crash, they had to leave Shandia. Doctor Tidmarsh had sought replacements and found them in Jim and Pete, who moved into the station to learn Quichua, reopen the boys school, preach the Gospel, and rebuild the dilapidated buildings.

SEPTEMBER 8   Psalm 7 is a psalm of justice. The fears of David of being overcome by his persecutors and torn by the *lion*, are first comforted by his remembrance of his own integrity. "Si yo he hecho esto . . . persiga el enemigo a mi alma . . ." ["If I have done this . . . let the enemy pursue my soul"] (vv. 1, 5). The appeal is then made to Jehovah who has ordained justice, that He judge his enemies, and acknowledgement that He will judge the nations, and the plea that he himself be judged according to his own justice. Verse 11 seems a climax: "Dios es un justo juez" ["God is a righteous judge"]. Then, as David expected judgment in conformity with his deeds, he describes the judgment of the wicked, conforming to *his* deeds. "Mas en el fosa que hizo, el mismo cayó" ["He is fallen into the ditch which he made"] (v. 15). Finally, as ever with David, this must all bring praise. "Yo alabaré a Jehová conforme a su justicia" ["I will give thanks unto Jehovah according to his righteousness"] (v. 17).

SEPTEMBER 14   Lord's Day.   A beautiful afternoon and a wonderfully full day. Began this morning with Psalm 19 in which I noted the Spanish *moderno* rendering of "melody" for "line" in the phrase, "Their *line* is gone out into all the earth." More than fifty Indians came to the singing and Gospel teaching this morning, and that after the priest had made special efforts yesterday to get them to the mass. He blundered on us as we were listening to an Indian play a violin in a house downriver where we had gone to watch Venancio [an Indian, hired as handyman] butcher a hog. He refused Pete's hand as he entered, walked to the center of the house, made the brief announcement that all good Christians should go to mass on Sunday, and stalked out the other door. After meeting this morning, Pete and Luis and I sang some choruses in Spanish and Quichua, and, while the men played soccer, I entertained a dozen girls and women reading a sheet of Quichua and dawdling over the organ. Pete was dressing a baby's burned buttocks when I returned to the house. The sick folks attended to, we had coffee with T. and discussed the Romanists' methods and practice here.

Just before lunch we had a little devotional time together. Felt the need of cleansing after our coffee-table talk and sang "Eternal light, eternal light, How pure the soul must be . . . ." T. read Isaiah 6, and I noticed, for the first time that I can recall, that the Lord fills, first, the temple with His train, and then, the earth with His glory. Considered the glory of God in prayer and sang "Behold the Lamb With Glory Crowned." He *fills* the throne, the throne above. Happy remembrance of Him, but without the bread and wine, as we have neither here. It is a serious lack—makes the communal remembrance seem to have no center.

After lunch we rested, read a little of C. S. Lewis's *Perelandra* and then went to visit a boy with a broken wrist three-quarters of an hour downriver. He was drunk last Thursday and, sporting on the beach, fell on a stone. Doc splinted it and slung it, gave an old woman an antimalarial, passed around the candy balls, and we came home for a bath.

Beginning to hear words of the Indians' speech now. Making a good-sized vocabulary list in notebook form from the doctor, studying in the mornings, or doing some small job with the tools. Feel that we must eventually live nearer to the people than we do now to really catch the genius of this fascinating idiom. This house will do for now, but it keeps the Indians' level of living too far below ours for us to really "get next" to them in the psychological sense. We are making friends among them, learning a name or two and, we trust, leaving good impressions.

Praying definitely against the work of the priest, that God will intervene and halt his railings or prove him, by our testimonies, a liar so that the Indians will not listen to him. He has a peculiar power over them, so that, even though they know him to be false in some respects, and even, perhaps, immoral, they attend the mass with a devotion that is hard to explain. May God send His light and liberty among these dear people, and make them fearless in His fear.

SEPTEMBER 18   Went to Pano today. Left 9:30 A.M., visiting sick folk in Indian homes near Talac and Pano. In the one near Talac, a breech baby was born last night. Pete and the doctor went in case of an emergency, and the mother was still hemorrhaging some this morning. Yesterday afternoon I was there with the doctor to check the sequence of labor pains. A little girl was scraping a sloth's toe into a half-gourd to make a potion for the approaching birth. As the woman has had a history of two breech births before, and as the sloth hangs by its toes upside down, the way a baby ought, I wonder if there may not be some connection, otherwise we were given none.

Plane was to come to Pano with mail and money by noon, but as it had not arrived by 3:45, I had to leave with Luis, the cook boy. It did come later, with Miller instead of Conn, and took T. to Mera. Returned in a lovely afternoon, drying path, in two hours and ten minutes. Luis [Venancio's son] complained of stomach pains tonight, and we gave him Alka-Selzer, as his description of them was vague and general. Not much progress in the language, and, except for getting to know the old route to Talac from Pano, I suppose the journey would be described as a "dry run." I was so hoping for mail from Betty. I wonder if she is in Shell Mera tonight.

SEPTEMBER 21   Pete and I alone in Shandia last night. Eladio *paseod* to Tena, and the doctor is in Tena. Things seem freer, better, simpler when Pete and I are alone. We see things alike and enjoy like things so that there is a general air of agreement. But others complicate it. T. injects a mannerism of his that is foreign, or insists on some fear that seems inconsequential. Eladio, of course, cannot even share ideas or appreciate the Word, being a noncommitted hanger-on. But I do thank God for Pete and long for the days when our language training will free us to work together down these rivers, and through the forests.

We spent the day easily. Meeting which Luis took had attendance of some thirty Indians. Afterward the sick folk. Saw Kali Bick [a homeopathic remedy] clean a "punched in" ulcer on a baby's buttocks in twenty-four hours. Came to a beautiful, loose head and pressed out easily. Wrote home and June and Roy McDaniel in Sparta, asking always for prayer for help in the language. It is extremely difficult to get any consecutive study time in. Interruptions are myriad at nearly any hour of the day—buying, selling, treating, working with the men, paying them. It makes language study difficult, and using Luis as an interpreter makes it too easy, so that I don't feel the strong necessity of knowing the idiom. But I know all the same that I must get it—get it good and get it rapidly.

By Thy grace, good Lord, I'm going to.

Just finished a sing out of *IV Hymnal* and *Believer's* and *Little Flock*. Great joy going over "At Even, Ere the Sun Was Set"; "The Lord's My Shepherd"; "And Is It So, I Shall Be Like Thy Son?"; "Souls of Men, Why Will Ye Scatter"; and "Oh, Lord, We Adore Thee"—remembering the sweet last remembrance feast in Glendale and Uncle Bill wanting the second verse repeated.

Noting in 2 Corinthians 13 the possibility of interpreting verse 5 as meaning that "reprobates" have no knowledge of whether they are Christ's or not. We say, you know as to yourself, if Jesus Christ is in you—but Paul adds, "unless indeed ye be reprobate." The believer knows that he knows; the unbeliever knows that he knows not—but the reprobate, the Judas who acted like a believer but was rejected as reprobate for acting like an unbeliever, knows not if he knows or not.

SEPTEMBER 24   Full, happy, useful days, these last two have been. Rising early to get a few moments morning quiet, I am soon busied. The radio at 6:30, breakfast, getting the men going to work, treating the sick, working on the strip until lunch. Then a brief noon rest—I find I really need it, sleeping hard and suddenly just after lunch—usually until the radio contact at 1:45. Then a trip. Today it was upriver in a dugout to the home of Segundo and his brothers. His wife has had swelling, lumps, and blueness with extreme pain in her left breast, with occasional, scanty suppuration. Her extremities ache and are stiff. We gave Phytolaca [a homeopathic remedy], swabbed the area around the nipple with calendula. Noted that they had plastered on *guineo* [a species of banana] to soften up the balls of hardness. Gave Atabrine to some. Then down to the house where the baby was born two weeks ago. Mother has postbirth soreness in midsection—Arnica. Baby was sleeping hard in the afternoon but crying all night—Pulsatilla. Down the river Talac to the house of Luis Capitan. His wife was with aching joints, pain on movement—Rhustox. Dressed a groin burn on a small boy. Noted that they had applied *anelina*, a green ink with which they paint their faces. Across the river there were several children with fevers—Atabrine. Home, a bath in the chill Napo, supper and letter writing, Roylene Alley and Lloyd Hamilton. To bed with a great sense of unity in attitude with Pete. How I thank God for him and our present relation. We were not vainly sent "two by two."

SEPTEMBER 25   Another full day. Began after 6:30 (revised time) radio contact with breakfast. Got the men started on the strip and worked with them for some time. Pete came out to advise me that a woman upriver had come and told him of her husband, dying with fever. Said she had an injection but no way to put it in, and since I've given one or two injections—Pete hasn't given any—he suggested I go. I did, with Luis. Going up we stopped at the house of Angashillu (bird talon) and found him in a cold stage of fever—Arsenicum—and left Atabrine. The farther house had the father and two boys all with 105-degree fevers, and while I was there, the fever broke over the little girl. They had a powder injection of Atabrine, but no distilled water. They were all in fever, and knowing the quinine is not to be applied injectionally when fever is high, I begged off giving it, saying that I had no water to mix it with. Before I left, I had had my first *chicha* in the Indian homes (of *chonta* [a palm fruit] mashed, not mouth made [mashed by pestle rather than by the usual method of chewing and spitting]), and my first cooked chonta fruit. The latter was rich, though woody; the former flat and watery. Returning, I stopped at a hut where a man with fever was lying under flies *a montones* [a mountain of flies] wrapped in a blanket. Atabrine for fever for him and baby. He had boils on his knee and shin—silica. Home to dinner, dismissing the men, and rest. Study this afternoon after a bath.

Ate my first ant yesterday.

SEPTEMBER 28   Lord's Day. Pete is not feeling well— vomiting and diarrhea with gas and what he calls "poopi- ness." The hot afternoon is refreshed by that blessed river breeze. I have just played the four Quichua records to a little friendly Indian named Shilverio and feel like doing some re- cording.

I was thinking Friday again of the quality of love. Pete and I are reading Lewis's *Perelandra* together and a sentence or two occasioned thought:

> Weston: "But the king would love you more . . . if you were like earth women."
> The Lady: "How can one love anything more? That would be like saying that a thing was bigger than itself."

I think this means what I have thought before in terms of love being not a quantity, but a quality, rather. The command is not really, "Love me more," but "love me as . . . ." Love is absurdly measured by any gradient ("I love you, a bushel and a peck!"), and its greatness can only be described in terms of the quality of the giving love of God. "Greater love hath no man than that he should lay down his life for his friends." "As the Father hath loved me, so ought ye to love one another." ". . . *as* Christ loved the church." ". . . as yourself." Quality of loving may vary. I may not "love" in the absolute sense. Only God does so. But I may, and must, love in that essence of attitude of which I am capable in emulating God not measured in terms of smallness or immensity, but in terms of sincerity ("*unfeigned* love of the brethren") and obedience ("the new *commandment* . . ."). But I feel like I don't know where I am going. I am losing power and simplicity and clarity in English with so much concentration on other languages.

The female breast has been so long and so intensely interesting to me that I cannot now explain my "calloused" thoughts about it, as I could not formerly explain my fascination. Twice this past week I have, in medical work, fingered the breasts of young Indians. I confess, with a great deal of surprise, that it does not now raise the slightest suggestion of lust for me. It is not that I have sort of depreciated the breast for having seen it suckled and noted it in all its shapes (U.S. women are brassiered into disgusting uniformity), or that I will not be aroused by her breast when the time comes for it.

But here it is regarded for what it is, a part of the woman's body necessary to make her a good mother, and it has not become an advertising touchstone. I can think of no other way of overcoming what was to me inwardly a great trouble often in the past, except by this frank realism which only the Indian really knows by intuition. We civilized men have to learn it by heart. It is not that I feel they are not attractive—though I am certainly aware of the illusions most moviegoers suffer in that feature of female form—for many of the young women have quite "well-formed," solid breasts pushing out their short blouses, but my whole outlook is transformed. It is what I always wanted to feel and never could before, and perhaps never would here, outside of marriage.

SEPTEMBER 30   An important day for the work here. Radio contacts solid all morning covering the first flight to Shandia. The doctor returned after Bob left him in Pano to come in solo in case of some slipup. Easily a hundred and fifty Indians gathered for the event, the boys running about, the women hooting, the men crowding into the stopped Piper. Praised God for success and rapidity in getting the strip done. He supplied us with funds in time, kept the men working in a good spirit, sustained us with joy in the doing of it. "This God is our God *forever;* He will be our guide until death." The doctor brought bread, meat and vegetables, stock for sugar and lentils—and best of all, honey, peanut butter, candy, and Ritz crackers—birthday stuff from Betty. Praise for her, too, while I'm praising.

OCTOBER 1   Planned the general layout of Shandia with Pete and the doctor, began work on the generator house over the cliff. Pete not feeling well, vomiting and diarrhea, gas in his stomach. I wonder sometimes if he will stick it out. He goes quiet and pale, and I feel sorry for him, but he usually comes out of it. What would I do if he had to leave the forest?

Had a chat with the Lord out on the *pista* [strip] in the cool of the day. Decided finally what I have been thinking for months. Engagement is the best thing for Betts, for me, for the work. Wrote Ed to buy a ring for me and bring it. I am withdrawing all my feelings about long engagements and getting ready for one. When? When God brings Ed. That leaves that question with the God who is going to guide me to death.

OCTOBER 2   Pete worse. Ate little, spent most of the day in bed. Woman with breast abscess visited by doctor today. Abscess opened and draining. That ruins both the mammary glands for good. What of future children? School which began yesterday morning with five boys was up to nine tonight. Thanks be to Him who is Victor for us in the face of Roman treachery.

OCTOBER 3   Heavy rains swelled the river overnight. Canoes, tied on dry banks yesterday afternoon, were rocking on full currents this morning, and the bleached boulders that run between the island and the other shore, white yesterday, are nothing but a swirl of muddy rapids now.

My prayer life these days, for the pressure of so many people (I am embarrassed to hear someone pull aside the door curtain and know they watch me as I pray) has been cut to basics. Minimal praying I find includes asking for Betty, Ed, Bill, Pete, and the doctor. Mother and Dad and occasionally Jane and Bob and Bert, though not daily. Also cries for reality, the presence of God, and a hearing of His voice. Finally, deliverance from evil and progress in the languages. "In God I will praise His Word" (Pss. 56:4, 10).

Afternoon. Betty enclosed a letter from Jan (nee Cunningham—I can never remember names of married friends in cases like this. It must be Brooks) from which I want to copy a few lines with which I agree: "We were most interested in what you had to say about transporting an American culture pattern to another land. Betty, this is what I've been talking about for the past two years!! It is what every American has been doing here in Australia (with one or two exceptions). With it all goes a most repelling attitude of superiority, which is not only expressed in the desire to superimpose American ways and methods on a people who have an already established pattern of life, but in a *personal patronizing* attitude. It is enough to make one weep! And it has caused difficulty in every sphere where Americans have tried to work with Australians (especially in Christian work). That's why I have pleaded that Americans should stay home until and unless they are prepared to impose themselves on other peoples with a much different attitude of mind and heart, with a love that melts all barriers and prejudices and rests in the sure knowledge of a life really devoted to God and not to any national . . . or party spirit . . . ."

OCTOBER 12   This morning's radio contact brought the word suddenly, almost shockingly, of Betty's decision to go to work with Doreen on the Colorado [Indian language]. I don't know why it should disturb me. I had before even hoped she would do so, but it quieted me to almost bitterness, making me feel as though I were saying good-bye all over again. It will be even harder not to have her in Quito, mail service slower, contact even less frequent, and the possibility of seeing her more remote. The Father was told all about it again—how I wanted her, needed her here—and I must confess, the comforts of faith—at least my *poca fe* [little faith]—are not always completely satisfying. But I *believe*, for all it's being poor believing, and know that I will not lose for having believed. That sickly sense of blunted want, of so good a thing denied and so indefinitely denied, comes seeping through all of me when I sit down to think about it. And the thoughts of it come more and more these days, with slighter and slighter stimulus—a glance at the quiet loveliness of her photo, a taste of the peanut butter she thoughtfully sent down, the sugar spoon with *E* on it. O God, having made me thus and led me thus, enable me to endure Thy making and Thy leading. I do not find it easy tonight—a Lord's day spent listening, resting, visiting—to rest in the course of the will. It is harder now than it was for me before. I wonder if for her, too. God, where will it end?

OCTOBER 15   Heavy rains have kept the men from work on the clinic all this week. Spent a good deal of time in language study today. Fear that I am losing ground in Spanish, but don't quite know what to do for it. Lanced Eladio's underarm swelling which would not come to a head but was soft and seemed ready. Made a small medicine shelf in the afternoon, played ball with the schoolboys—now numbering about fifteen—went for a muddy bath in the very swollen Jatun Yacu. Wrote Ron Harris and showed a movie to the schoolboys. Two boys from the priest's school came to play and sleep tonight as they could not cross the river. Give them to us permanently, Lord.

OCTOBER 26   Lord's Day.   In the reading of the psalms, I have noted some of the differences in Asaph's material from that of David. The distinctions are not settled, from lack of thorough study, but so far I have noted these as perhaps significant. David is conscious of his songs and desires as an individual; Asaph is more prone to engage the group entity as his subject, Israel as a whole, or Zion, or the "flock," what I have been taught to call "corporate feeling"—the sensitiveness to the whole of God's saints. Whereas David's opposition was personalized and his defeats poignantly individual, Asaph is concerned with the nation's setbacks, the city's ruins. His is an empathic singing.

Now both of these are valid bases for spiritual exercise. Some of the mystics have entirely neglected "Asaphic" thought in their purging concentration on inner, private communion. The editor of the *Little Flock Hymnal* recognized the problem, at least, in his preface, and, rightly or not, attempted to do something about it in the altering of the number of the first-person pronoun. As the whole of the psalms are commended to us for worship, I take it that there should not be a selectivity principle in public worship—an *I* may serve even there much better than a *we* in any given hymn. But the point is to be conscious of whichever we use—to "feel in" with all the people of God when singing "we," and to sense the full responsibility of a thing sung in using "I." It may be that the conditions of an age will partially determine the singularity or plurality of a writer's work or the character of the writer himself. I assume that both causes are present in the Asaph-David difference.

In these busy days of study, building, working with the school, and tending the numberless interruptions, I find my thoughts of Betty concentrated. Waking, the moments before dressing are crowded with longing, and I suppose I think mostly on going to sleep of what it will be to be engaged. Perhaps more of what it will be like to "get" engaged! And it comes to me the thing that I want most of her—that she should be free to approach me, to be aggressive in her affection. It has been so rare to have her plan the position or make the move that brings us together, that I rather think it will put me somewhere near delirium to have her do what (she has given me to believe) she wants most to do. And can it be that this is what God wants of me—the forwardness of a lover liberated from any restraint?

NOVEMBER 20   Nearly a month since I last made entry. T. has been gone nearly all that time and will not be back in for another week. Bill was in for a visit and confirms guidance we have felt by wanting to make Shandia a permanent base, and wanting to come in soon. The plane turned over on the airstrip and was here a week waiting for repairs. Two Indians died of what we suppose to be yellow fever—Pedro, a sixteen-year-old who was under the priest's care, and Cesar, a baby not a year old, under ours. Henrique, his father, refused penicillin after an injection abscess developed from a quinine shot. Child died just before we were called; camphor and artificial respiration had no effect in revival. We buried him in a semi-planed box under the schoolhouse.

Betty has gone to San Miguel and is at last in something tough enough to match her wits, trying to analyze Colorado. Thank God for that direction, as it will engage her profitably for some time and make the months pass with her not marking time. Sustain her spirit, Lord, and make the time there useful, to her and assuaging to the disappointment that she must feel as keenly as I, or more so. It is no easy thing You have asked us to do, and we depend on You to work in us the doing of it.

The work here is not ripping. We lost a couple of schoolboys—I fear because Eladio is no teacher. The language suffers for the constant interruptions; correspondence lags and visitation is not effective yet with our smattering of Quichua. Visit from Arajuno Indians yesterday made me long to travel in this area, and a visit last Lord's Day to Iluculin fanned the interest we had of a visit upriver to the gorges. There is talk now of putting a road through by here to Latacunga . . . .

NOVEMBER 23 *John 6* When the Jews asked the Lord Jesus for a sign to establish His identity as the One sent from God (John 6:30), they cited as a cause for their questioning the matter of Moses and manna. "Moses gave manna; what do You give?" The "he" in ἀρτον ἐκ τοῦ οὐρανοῦ ἔδωκεν αὐτᾶς φαγεῖν (6:31) they assumed to be Moses, but had they read Psalm 78 properly, they could have predicted Christ's response. For it was not Moses that gave manna, but Yahweh, and as Moses had no need to give a sign, neither had Messiah—*He was Himself the sign!* His very presence there, as Moses' in the desert, was God's proof and seal that He was chosen and sent by Him.

"Moses did not give you bread from heaven," I have always read with the thought stress on the bread, as not being true bread, taking the idea from what follows. But it came to me today that the sentence is introduced by the foregoing mistake about who gave bread, and I feel that Christ's teaching is foremost from this. "It was not *Moses*, it was the *Father*, and He alone gives the true bread." Then He moves on to the discussion of the bread and presents Himself as the Eternal Provision for the world. Their demanding of Him a sign on the basis of Moses' miracle (already provided in the loaves) was unfounded and unnecessary. They, as often as I, overlooked the already-wrought acts of God and turned to a human source for proof of validity of claims and promises.

Reading this afternoon, I was startled with thoughts of things that Christ is not to do—not exactly things that He cannot do, but things that He does not as the Son of Man, in whatever office, undertake. The present confusion among believers between God and Christ, so clearly marked in such things as table prayers in which the Father is thanked for dying for us, or in everyday thinking in which the man Jesus is constantly confused with God in Bible stories retold, and so on, tends to bring one into a position of poorly defined limits in the Godhead. But the Scriptures teach us otherwise. The disciples erred on this very point, relegating to Messiah the right to choose those who sat on His right and left hand (Mark 10:40). But Jesus teaches, "no es mio darlo"—it is not His to give, but another's who appoints and prepares over and above the reign of Messiah.

Not only the positions, but also the inauguration in that Kingdom is controlled by the One above the King, for Matthew 24:36 is evidence that Messiah Himself did not know of that day or hour, and He later told His disciples (Acts 1) that the Father had kept times and seasons in His own right. But most interesting of all to me, and what started my thinking on these things, was the phrase in 1 Corinthians 15:27, "He is excepted, who subjected all to Him . . . ." God the Ruler, from eternity, is pictured as the One actually and now bringing the Kingdom under Christ's power, while Christ *sits* at His right hand. Psalm 110 should have taught me this, for the prophecy is clear, "Sit thou, until I *make* thine enemies thy footstool." Thus in the Kingdom of God, God Himself appoints Christ as executive (". . . even as my Father appointed me a kingdom" [Luke 22:29]), chooses His officers, sets the bounds of it in time, accomplishes its growth, and finally awaits the ultimate act of humiliation, when Christ shall give it all back to Him, when comes the end.

DECEMBER 6   Yesterday Doc T. arrived here on the first flight since the plane turned over. Good to have him here and especially to have his language help, though his attitudes change little on things we would like to forget sometimes. Finances, for instance. Now we are paying his bus fare for the shopping trips he made in Quito. The money comes so freely we can do nothing but let it go freely, and we don't begrudge him the money. It's just that he doesn't seem to be living in faith on the matter and worries over the slightest outlay. They don't seem to be able to rest in God, he and Gwen, and for all I know of their sincerity in His service, I feel they need the Spirit's counsel on this point. He says now that the plane's turning over here has made Gwen put entirely out of her mind coming in here again. I wonder what God has for them—they do not really seem satisfied in Quito.

He brought with him a moving letter from Bett. So moving I sat down and wrote an answer last night and this morning and then forgot to give it to Bob when he flew out after a cargo flight this morning. Some attentive lover, I am. Well, attentive or not, I do love her and feel now that there is no course for me but marriage. I'm not (what I like to think of as) myself these days, not all in what I do, not fully sold out to the activity in hand, and I know it is just the want of her that seems to carry me out of the here and now to the hoped-for there and later. Daily my prayers—almost exclusively, for my prayers have not been long or fervent these days—are over the matter of engagement and all woven round her. I have reached the point again of standing on the faith of the Spirit's guidance as the deciding point, just the liberty, the noncondemnation in knowing that next time I go to Quito, we will be engaged. It seems as if the decision came from me, as it is completely in accord with my wants and the "natural" thing that should follow our years of friendship. But I believe that it is in conformity with God's wants as well, and I believe this in the face of 1 Corinthians 7 and Matthew 19, and everything I've said about the single apostolate. But I cannot write how I know or wherein lies the basis for my faith, no more than I could satisfactorily write my reasons for not being engaged four months ago. And from this I believe in the inner word of the Spirit to the surrendered will. He molds that will to His own within the framework of the will so that the will of the individual is the directed yet still the director; so that "we have the mind of Christ."

DECEMBER 18   The house is full of workmen. Pete is selling from the *bodega*. The doctor is sharpening a plane. I just stepped here into the bedroom to think a moment—about what we're doing here, about progress, about hopes, and prospects. Oh, God, life is slow, for all the action it holds. The clinic work lags—not half a wall finished this whole morning. The widening of the *pista* mouth moves so slackly with such very few men. The language hardly seems more intelligible today than it did three months ago, at least in the lips of many Indians. And Betty—she seems *so* far away, so *far* in the future before she can be enjoyed. What shall I say, Lord? That I am dissatisfied, not pleased with the way You have led me? Almost I would say it. Why cannot I shout orders to the workmen, urge on the projects, *press* ahead with language, hasten marriage? The pattern of life thus in the will seems so to drag, to wait for the nothing that happens, to push quietly up like trees, and to eat slowly away, and the clouds, like slugs, ooze over the fixed sky. It would not be happier otherwise, I suppose, but it seems discouraging this hot afternoon.

DECEMBER 30   Peter and I just returned this afternoon from our first week of Oriente orientation. Most instructive from every point of view. We left here December 24 (Wednesday) with the Pano Indian "Doctor" [his nickname] about 1:20 P.M., walking through rain and chatting over States' Christmas customs, arriving in Pano around 3:30–3:45. Spent a very pleasant Christmas Eve with Henry [Miller, a C & MA Missionary] and his family, listening to carol music, reading the Nativity story. We spent the twenty-fifth with them, lounging in the hammock, reading the "Disciplines of Life," eating roast chicken and duck, opening packages by an artificial tree with honest-to-goodness colored lights. We attended Auca's [the nickname of a Quichua Indian] wedding in Pano in the late morning. Friday we visited down the Pano River with Doctor as far as Wamundi's house, stopping for some time at Puma Rumi—a most interesting archeological artifact from which I copied the following material. [See illustration, page 429.]

The carvings are obviously done by chipping. We had no way of measuring the stone, but I should say it was twenty feet long and perhaps fifteen feet wide. Doctor said it used to be in the forest. The Indians seriously believe that a puma made the stylized paw marks and that the large lower-right-hand figure is the sun in representation. The wide band may

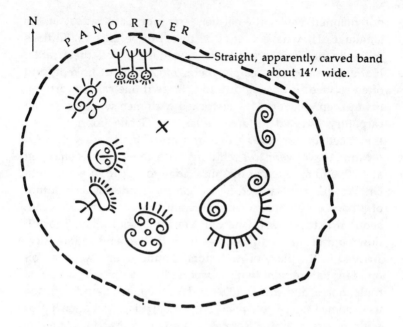

be a natural phenomenon in the rock itself though I could observe no structural change in the rock in the band and beside it. The Indian boy Moises remarked that it was a road or path. I thought the mistake of the overlong body line on the man farthest east (they appear to me to be human stick figures) interesting. It may show that that figure was drawn without first sketching a plan. This may also be supported by the far out of symmetry "sun" figure (I have misdrawn the body line of the other two men figures). There is much more space between the last Ionic figure and the band than I have shown.

Saturday we walked to Tena with the boy Alfonso, stopping at a house at the first river crossing to treat a fever case, and making it in two and one half hours. Spent Lord's Day with Conns, speaking in the morning on John 6: "Labor not for the meat that perishes." I used Spanish; the Indian Pedro, assistant school teacher, translated. Dos Rios [a C & MA Station in Quichua territory] culminated my suspicions that the mission-station approach is ineffective. It is understaffed and not manned well with neither Jerry nor Carol adept at the language. They have a lot of pasture, but because the Indians milk, do not *aprovechar* [take advantage of] all their cattle. Hundreds of fruit trees are there, moss grown, unkept, and often robbed. It does no use to splurge if one cannot carry on his upkeep. Ecuador is overstocked with men who came to do carpentry—Al Ryde, Morrie Fuller, and Gerald Conn. [Jim felt they needed more evangelists and preachers.]

Monday we went to Archidona with the Indian Mona. Left at 8:20, and stopped at the big bridge to talk for a while with Dr. Weyerbauer, lawyer, *hacendado* [hacienda owner], author of a book on ethnology, and aspirant to go to Germany again soon. Side trip over Mishawalli to visit a sick Indian. Took off down a trail through meadows from the hacienda Santa Inez. Arrived in the plaza of Archidona around noon. Met the Colombian hacendado (who purportedly brought in the first mule, horse, and cow in 1902) and Sr. Mejia who kindly treated us to some fine ice-cold *piña* [pineapple] juice. Met and chatted with the Sra. Clotilde Rosales, daughter of Shandia's late *patrono* [white landowner]. Walked a kilometer north in search of *Miel de cana* [cane syrup] for Carol, but the cana is too green for pressing yet. Home to Dos Rios in two hours exactly. Path is sanded and graveled and would be better walked in oxfords and socks than in sockless Keds as we did it. God must show some way of entering this priest-dominated area. There are an estimated three thousand Indians there now, out of an original ten thousand now scattered, according to Mejia. Many more than in the Tena-Napo-Shandia region.

And today we returned home. Two good hours from Dos Rios to Puerto Napo on path like the Archidona one. A beautiful early morning walk. Met the canoe owner there, and a man named Moro who claims he is a believer and wanted us to stay and teach him in the way of the Lord. Less than forty-five minutes of bad, muddy trail brought us to the house of Cesar Paredes, opposite the *embocadura* [mouth] of the Ansuj. Cesar was in Arajuno, and Espinoza treated us to *piña*. We left there at 10:55 and made the house of his sister Rosa by 1:40—two hours and forty-five minutes including a Napo crossing. From there to the mouth of the Talac, it is twenty minutes. We were home at 4:20. One hour forty-five minutes to the Talac mouth. We walked quite fast with Venancio packing a full load. From Dos Rios to Shandia, nine hours, four river crossings, three eat stops, and not many more pauses except at the whites' homes named and visited.

JANUARY 18   Lord's Day evening and I am alone with Eladio in Shandia. The schoolboys have all gone home, and Pete left this afternoon with Dr. Fuller for Pano. We have enjoyed his three days with us—an introduction to clinical diagnosis and minor surgery probably being the outstanding things of interest. I remain unconvinced of orthodox medicine—as of most forms of treatment now. If back adjustment is no cure-all, neither is penicillin, nor are grasshopper eggs [homeopathic pills]. There is so much of value in the three systems that I have contacted that I would do ill to mock any of them or to respect one above another. One must use whichever suits the diagnosis, and when that is decided, it is time to be chiropractor, homeopath, or allopath. And I'm beginning to respect these forest leaves and roots, too. Chewed moss will stop bleeding where tourniquet and compress bandage will not, I have seen.

Being alone gives a moment for reflection. I had thought to be in Quito by now, and in her arms. The last couple of Saturdays I have gone off to sleep saying, "Perhaps in a week, I'll be engaged." But the doctor has come only three times to the radio, and Ed yesterday said that he may be another two weeks yet. Maybe more. Maybe the Lord is having me wait for a full moon to be in Quito—that would be the twenty-ninth. I wonder if that is His design. If He is trying to give me space to consider engagement, I'm afraid He is not having success with me. I've been too pressed for one thing with the work here. But even if I do stop to think if I am being delayed here for guidance, it seems like misspent time. It was all so securely settled, and, seemingly, so long ago, that there *could* be no changing.

It has already happened inside me. I have given myself over

to the love of her, and there is no desire, purpose, or sense in any thought of withdrawal. It only lacks her word, and I could not believe that will not be given with such square-shouldered confidence as I believe I have gotten from God. There is the "It is finished!" tone in my spirit; morally, I am already engaged. There is, or can be, no other woman now for my children and my wife, and there is a quiet glad knowledge in writing it. I have sought slowly the will of God, and the slowness has brought strength into the conviction of it and joy in the realization of it. And how long will it be before Dr. Tidmarsh comes to the radio and says "I'll be down tomorrow"?

JANUARY 26   Yesterday afternoon Ed came to the radio and told us that the doctor would likely be down on Thursday. If Ed comes with him, we will probably go out to Quito a week from today together. It is barely possible that I may be engaged in ten days. Oh, that it were certain, that I held her already after she said yes or whatever she will say. This waiting has built up pressure and released it so many times that I feel it has changed me somehow. I sense an aging and a waning—not of desire but of spirit—as though strength were washed out of me from so many nights standing alone on the cliff and watching so much water pass. It is the oldness of hope deferred, the borderland of hopelessness. A week seems unbearably long this rainy morning; intolerably slow the river runs, though it is in the rush of flood. Pass, water; get on down to the sea. Wash away the Was, the Is, bring down What Is to Be. I'll need special tolerance of things these days, kind Lord, a steeled patience—with rain and poor radio communications and trying schoolboys. Help me this week, and do let it be the last of waiting.

JANUARY 27   I didn't know when I wrote yesterday morning just how full the day was going to be. Even before I wrote, Angel's daughters had come with the news that headed the day's events. Pascualito's (the witch's) daughter's year-old baby had fallen sick the previous night and was lying with fever and difficult breathing. Luis (Angel's son) came at noon and told us to hurry and come. We went together early in the afternoon to find the baby with shallow, rapid, and raspy breathing. We injected penicillin and treated homeopathically with Bryonia. Pete went over to inject Pablo in the next house whom we have been treating for lobar pneumonia for more than two weeks. He is recovering. I stayed and watched the baby, having good language practice with all the family while Pete came home to tend affairs here. About 4:00 P.M. I decided to see the case through the night if it were necessary. A note sent in answer to mine from Peter reminded me that our medical notes said "alleii maseii" flapping was prognostic of bronchial pneumonia. Phos. and Bryonia homeopathically served for nothing. I gave orange juice as the throat seemed dry, steamed with hot rocks and cold water in the area of the child to aid breathing, put melted menthol into the throat, rubbed with Sloan's liniment. The witch was an old woman with herbs and leaves. Around 5:30 I was politely invited out of the house to see a ten-foot snake at Cua's house. It was a *Matolo* [bushmaster], deadly and beautiful. I skinned it, preserved the head, and tried some of the white meat. The Indians refused to eat it but declare that the Archidonas eat it often. It is not tasty, but certainly not disagreeable like some of the meats they do eat.

Back at Pascualito's a bed was made up for me and a "possum" hunt was in process outside as I arrived. Inside I was very nicely and frankly told that they were going to drink *Jayaj wasca* [a hallucinogen] and that I was to stay in my cane bed—much too short, incidentally—without using my lantern until it was over. Had some talk about our country and geography in general before checking the baby for the evening. Symptoms unchanged. We had succeeded in provoking an occasional cough, but could raise no phlegm. There was no temperature to speak of. Listless eyes, restlessness, no crying, raspy, dry breathing.

All lamps were extinguished by 8:30, and the three Indians who were to drink could be heard speaking across the room occasionally. I feigned sleep and drowsed but woke when one of the watchers sleeping on the floor beside me was roused to be alert to listen as the drinking was passed and the swoon speech expected. I heard the quick steady swish beat of what sounded like a bunch of dry leaves being shaken, and from somewhere, I cannot say if it was the same source, as it seemed far away, outside at times, the rather melodious whistle on the three drop-tone pattern so usual among them. This was interspersed with a spitting, retching sound and the curious pop of the smoke blowing on the patient's head, as I had seen done in the afternoon. (I had offered another injection of penicillin but was refused at supper time—the witch insisting that we wait until morning.) The swishing and blowing and whistling were joined by an occasional heavy snore, and I dropped off to sleep.

At eleven I was awakened by Angel's playing the violin. We chatted; I checked the baby at midnight, and was told that the witching had not amounted to much as the drinkers had not taken enough to do much talking. Fever seemed a little higher, breathing and general condition had not changed. I chatted with Angel and Pascualito until 1:00 A.M. and then went off to sleep. The mother and the old woman with herbs were awake and making applications of leaves and tobacco. *Lamparillas* [night lights] and the kerosine lantern made things somewhat less eerie than earlier. I slept until the death wail wakened me at 3:00. No struggle, just quit breathing. Played as per custom until about 5:30. Left a little after six. Made our third small coffin this morning.

JANUARY 31   She said, "I have no reason to hesitate."

FEBRUARY 1   Back Home Hour Chorus sang "I Love You Truly" for us as we entered Studio B for the Sunday evening broadcast. Afterwards—on the *azoteo* [roof].

FEBRUARY 2   Bill and Irene up and living in bodega.

FEBRUARY 3   Lunch with Bill and Irene and McCullys and Emma—house planning.

FEBRUARY 4   Supper with Joe and Betty Springer.

FEBRUARY 6   Hotel Colón—filet mignon with Ed and Marilou.

FEBRUARY 7   Home at Chiavari. Head to head on the carpet.

FEBRUARY 8   Preached on the leaven of Herod at English Fellowship. Walking to Second Church in the evening.

FEBRUARY 9   Dinner with Cevallas. Shopping every morning now.

FEBRUARY 10   Snack dinner before the fireplace at bodega. "Limits and discipline."

FEBRUARY 14   Just came in from Otavalo. Gwen was tired so left us with supper and dishes alone. I am waiting for Rob to come home (he has gone to some school affair) having just kissed Betty good night at the door of her room. She was sleepy tonight—went dozing off while I was reading in this diary and then in my arms and later in my lap. She surprises me sometimes as a lover—a gay ardency, a girlishness I see in her few other times. And oh, how glad I am she knows just how much of herself to give. I could still ask that she be more aggressive with my body, but from what I already know, she will in time do very acceptably. The other night, Tuesday, I believe, we had a lunch together at the bodega and afterward a long discussion about limits to engagement relations—everything from touching her breasts to intercourse. And when I came home so I spoke, "A garden shut up is my sister, my spouse; a spring shut up, a fountain sealed" (Song of Sol. 4:12). She is that until marriage, by her present attitudes. The following night at the bodega she told me that we would not lie down again, choosing a variant restriction I had suggested. We came home, and at the gate she cried—for not having had enough of me that day. We walked up to the fountain and wall above Guápalo and sat on the steps. Thursday we went to Tingo with McCullys and Emma, and in the evening she and I bought wine together. I know I cannot live without her now.

Pondering downtown Romans 1:1: "Set apart unto the gospel of his Son." Paul was separated from a family (wife and "play loving"), a business, the church fellowship in Antioch, and who knows what else, for the progress of the Gospel. How far am I "separated unto the Gospel"?

FEBRUARY 15   Noted the three uses of the word *full* in Isaiah 6:1–5:

1. His train *filled* the temple.
2. The *fullness* of the earth is His glory.
3. The house was *filled* with smoke.

After midnight.   Spent a happy day—at English Fellowship and here at dinner and the breaking of bread with just her and Gwen and me. Ev Fuller came here looking for us yesterday and left a message that we should call him. So we went to the Second Church, and he took us to his place for cake and chocolate. Then he announced what we had feared. Betty's chest X rays showed an active lesion. There are more tests, but the doctors are fairly certain she has T.B. She held a brave face until we got home here, then telling Gwen, her voice broke. In the *sala* [living room] she cried bitterly, hard sobbing and much tears. She fears she can never marry me—says that I can't be nursing a consumptive all my life. Told me that I couldn't kiss her on the lips anymore, but she let me in the hall just now, forgetting, I suppose, that there is a bacteria eating at her lungs and swimming in her sputum.

As for me, things are unchanged. She is the same woman I loved last night before I knew the tubercles were formed in her chest. If I had any plans, they are not changed. I will marry her in God's time, and it will be the very best for us, if it means waiting years. God has not led us this far to frustrate us or turn us back, and He knows all about how to handle T.B. I remember how horrible was the emaciated form of the woman whom I saw autopsied at Sykesville, how utterly unlovable her form. She died of T.B. And I remember the man Ed and I visited in the army hospital near Milwaukee, and what his collapsed lung looked like. And I remember talking with Betty long ago—jokingly—about how she was the T.B. type. And now, if she really has it, it may mean a trip to the States for three or four months, or it may mean a lifetime of being an invalid. I don't know what it means. Only I know that God is in the generation of the righteous and guides their steps aright. Beyond His counsel and will, there is no going. I am there now and want nothing more.

MARCH 2   No, I believe it's the third. Ed left yesterday morning after our first ten happy days in the forest together, and I am alone with Eladio now. Pete went out with malaria on Wednesday last (Feb. 25) and up to Quito with T. on Friday, putting me in close fellowship again with Ed. It is better than ever to be with him, and I almost stand in awe sometimes to think that God has really brought us together. Hurry the rest of our preparation now, Lord, and get us in the language preaching with one another again. With all this planning and building going on, I will certainly enjoy our dreamed-of itineration in the forests.

Monday, a week ago, Betty came to the radio and said, "It was all a mistake . . . ." The T.B. fears are gone. I wonder if God healed her in those ten days or simply proved our faith by a mistake. Whatever, He has done well, and I bless Him for her health, and for my own. Yesterday I picked up a case of conjunctivitis from some Indian and spent a pretty miserable first night in the forest alone—as well as a useless day today. Argyrol and penicillin ointment helped today. Last night boric-acid hot packs. Just now I'm sipping lemonade and wine.

Henry Andi died last Friday afternoon—I cannot tell what from. [The Andi family were squatters in Shandia.] Began vomiting great mouthfuls of bright red blood last Monday. We stopped it with Vitamin K and emetine and gave several shots of gluconate. He was getting along fine until Friday about 3:45 when he vomited again and became exceedingly restless—dangerously so for one so weak. He was gone by 4:30. The first man I ever watched die. And so it will come to me one day, I kept thinking. I wonder if that little phrase I used to use in preaching so much was something of a prophecy: "Are you willing to lie in some native hut to die of a disease American doctors never heard of?" I am still willing, Lord God. Whatever You say shall stand at my end time. But, oh, I want to live to teach Thy Word. Lord, let me live "until I have declared Thy works to this generation."

MARCH 15   Sunday, quiet and relaxing, almost to a point of being useless. Eladio and I have just finished lunch of bean soup, steamed yucca, and boiled corn. An apple and papaya and hot lemonade made fruit, dessert, and a drink.

I've just been reading some love poems and feel as I often have before, how ill-adapted words are to describe love. True, love is a fervor, "humming all night long," a frenzy even, and a sweetness, and I suppose it is well that men try and say it, but I cannot help feeling that all that has ever been said, in poetry or in prose, is nothing more than descriptive; it does not really define or explain love. And I say that, not with any notions of the power of my personal feeling for Betty, but only with a taste in my experience of the reality already exceeding what the poets say. I think it must be that they all miss the point of love's being divine. "Love is of God." Until a man knows that and is enjoying God-given love, he had best not try to write poetry on the subject, for it will surely sound superficial if he begins anywhere else.

I think the poems which come the closest to really explaining love are those whose nature is purposefully simple, and borders on abruptness. As, "Whenas in silks my Julia goes . . . ." There is nothing profound in it, and I am almost sure there was nothing much profound in the love it illustrates. Or Wordsworth's "Lucy." "Oh, the difference to me!" is about as close as a man can get to saying the truth in a love frame of that sort. They approach the reality of their own experience when they are light and abrupt in their writing. Their love is light and very likely abrupt—at both ends. My own experience is that love is such a sweetly sensible thing. Too sweet, really, to write about for other folks to read of (who can make the sucking of her lower lip—a devastating thrill—sound good and right and thrilling, even, on paper?).

So I'll leave off poetry about love, I think, unless I'm struck with inspiration some day. And *sensible*, what shall I say about this? Love is not a slave lord that whips a man out of all other thinking or doing, leaving him only with desire or power to love. Sometimes one is overmastered with desire, and glad of it in the darkness of a lonely night. But it is not always so with me, and he who describes that as love at its peak, I think misses the second point—love is part of man's nature, at least, becomes so when one has lived with it long enough. It is part of my thinking now—this loving of Betty—something I always go back to, not as something old, but as something that I *am* now, and cannot help referring to—a lover. And once a lover, I must recognize all the phases of loving and encourage and develop them.

It is like becoming a man—not only do your sexual organs function, but something else in you functions to control them and decides when it is time to release controls. As one must consciously develop his whole *man*, keeping body fit and mind flexible and heart adoring his Maker, so must one train himself in the new life of a lover. There must be practical exercise of love—those letters must be written. And there must be a certain inner psychological conditioning, a training of the want of her, a warming of the hope for her. And when we see one another again, there will come easily that old joy in her body. I write this observing, not lecturing myself, as all these things are in me at work—quite normal and not having to be forced, paralleling, surprisingly, the experience of becoming a man.

I am still alone these days. Pete will have been gone three weeks if he gets in on Wednesday, and although I miss him, I see really that for this present pattern of life it is not Pete that I need but Betty. Oh, what a delight it would be to do some of these things here with her. What pure joy it would be to come in after a cool river bath and dress in the same room with her!

MARCH 25   Venancio woke us at 12:30 last night to say that an Indian visiting from Tena was in labor and wanted medicine. We gave calaupholum and drowsed through the noise of her crying until just after the baby was born around 2:00. They told us then that she had had it in the woodshed by the school kitchen. Gave ergotrate to the mother. Baby girl doing well this morning.

Storm came up immediately afterward. A solid, heavy rain with thunder and lightning that has lasted until now (mid-morning). The river is rising rapidly, and it looks like our hopes to pour concrete are to be washed out for today. Many of the boys went to sleep down Talac last night and have not come to school this morning yet, so we are holding up devotions. But the most pressing thing on me this morning is an agony of want of Betty. Oh, how I long for her—all of her, her help and counsel and just her presence here, but most of all this morning, for her body. Sleep was fitful with the air mattress at an uncomfortable inflation point, with the birth, the storm, and worries about the cement getting wet out under the shed, but over and through it all the pounding hunger for the feel of her, that left me weak and devastated on rising this morning. I don't know how long I can take this. It leaves me useless to study or pray or read or work. I think sometimes I must have her or simply break in my mind. Every little thing seems to irritate me, and there is nothing that would satisfy me this morning but Betty herself—all of her. Lord God, how long? Little did I know for what I dealt in those days I said I was willing for celibacy—nothing did I know about the power of love for a woman, I believe. So help me, God, I did not know! Had I been aware of what I should feel this morning as the rain falls heavily out of a low sky, I doubt if I would have made any sort of vow of willingness to stay single. Lord, can it be that this must go on for hundreds more rainy mornings and hundreds more fitful nights? How shall I bear it apart from some inwrought miracle of grace? Father, if it is possible that the work here in the Oriente not suffer, and that Your design for the Kingdom plan in the jungle be in no way thwarted or slowed, O merciful God, give me permission to marry her— soon!

Ponme como sello sobre tu corazón!
Como sello sobre tu brazo.
Porque fuerte como la muerte es el amor,
Inexorables como el sepulcro son los celos;
Sus ascuas arden como ascuas de fuego,
Como la misma llema de Jehová!

Muchas aguas no pueden apagar el amor,
Ni los ríos lo pueden anegar:
Si un hombre diere todos los haberes de su casa por el
    amor,
El sería completamente despreciado!

Song of Solomon 8:6, 7

MARCH 29   I haven't gotten over the beauty of this place, Shandia, yet. Even in its moods which are not so pleasant, when the mists hang heavy through the forest, or when the clouds fall in heavy rains—

Relentless as death the marching winds
With hosts of gray-clad rain . . .

Like it came yesterday just as we finished pouring the last concrete pillar—all of it is a loveliness.

But, oh, the wretchedness inside me at times. I wonder if Pete ever really knows the heaviness of desire that I feel. Yesterday walking back fron Angu's house after injecting Augostine (who, praise God, is better after his near death struggle with pneumonia), I was alone in the cool, dark forest, and I knew then how vulnerable I am just now to attacks of fleshly temptations. Even then, I don't know how it would have been had I met an Indian woman alone in the trail. O God, what a ferocious thing is sexual desire, and how often it is on me now. I find that the desire for Betty, sustained and willed, disperses through the whole of me, settles in every thought and diffuses through time into a generalized desire. Just the huge, hot want of woman. It is like food and hunger. When we eat plain food we dream of special food—sundaes and cakes. But when we have no food, we dream of bread and water. So when Bett is within reach, or even within thought reach, when I can imagine or remember well enough, that is solid food, and I think of love fulfilled with her. But when I cannot call up an image close enough or live enough of her, that is not want of food, and the desire generalizes, as I say, and any food at all would suit it seems.

Or I hear of Maldonado boasting in the Plaza of Puerto Napo that he has slept with Sevilla's mother, his wife, all his daughters and now only lacks sleeping with Sevilla himself. I know that it is in me to so do, that I would enjoy different women as I enjoy different views and places, that the mere variety is attractive. And then I remember the constancy, purity, and solidarity of Betty's love, and her saying, "Think how awful it would be to do it with someone else . . ." and then I look down at the narrow trail and am ashamed, deeply ashamed.

APRIL 12   Pete and I spent last week in Dos Rios with Henry Miller and the Conns and Doc T. Spoke in three afternoon adult meetings on eternal life, its source, manifestation, maintenance. Struggling desperately with Quichua, and feel we gained ground in the solid week's listening and studying and trying to speak. There was no real stirring. Lack of united prayer on the part of we ministers of the Word, and a lack of believing faith in what prayer there was accounted for this. I felt too that T's ministry was faulty along the same lines as Stateside evangelicalism. Illustration of the truth is no substitute for a statement of the truth; a story will not do where a sermon fails. Again, it is the exhortation and stern warning to believe without sufficient statement of what is to be believed. But the statement of truth is too deep, "too difficult" in

Quichua, being such a simplified language. Still it is better to make them understand, or try to, that they may know what they are rejecting, than it is to allow them to accept something they do not understand, by pressing more the acceptance than the understanding.

Was touched at the Mishawalli as the believing Indians came to the river's edge to say us good-bye. I was startled to find two of the girls, the cripple Serafina and the *malta* [young woman] Cristina, taking my two hands and leading me, before the rest of the group, to the river and saying, "In every prayer we make we will pray for you . . . ."

APRIL 19   Went to the house of Cuchicara yesterday, once to accompany Venancio in asking for the girl Virginia as a wife for Alejo, and once with Pete and Eladio after dark to ask on our own, the Indians having been refused twice. The old man was not at home last night, so we chatted the thing over with the mother and sisters who, when we left, seemed somewhat favorable. Alejo sold his gin to the rest after the refusals, and Venancio was drunk in Cua's house when we arrived just after dusk. God, deliver that Indian from sin and the power of *Tarago* [Quichua corruption of *trago* (Spanish), "drink"]. [Marriages in the Quichua tribe are always arranged through middlemen.]

Noted yesterday the predominance of judgment in the message of Isaiah. We call him the evangelist of the Old Testament, and rightly so, but our evangelism doesn't learn much from his. The preaching of ultimate justice and the ruin of the wicked is both prior and primary in his prophecy. He who speaks for God, without clarifying the point of His justice and power of His judgment, speaks as no prophet at all.

APRIL 20   I get to feeling a want for something *nice* out here. Everything is so half-done and left-to-be that it makes me feel the need of a really nice piece of work, something fine. Pete's classical records are a help, and I have found the cat with its smooth litheness an outlet. Caught myself stopping to smell and look at a white flower this evening—perhaps for half a minute. To put out of mind warped girders and rough-planed planks, rusted tools and bat-dirtied books, I need something else, and believe that Betty will be a help. The grace of her leg and smoothness of her face; even her wiping off the table or her serving soup in something besides a tin plate; perhaps her ironing a shirt—all these would be a help. To have it done without asking for it and without having to explain how it's done—that would be wonderful!

APRIL 27   Struggling to maintain real faith for the genuine conversion of adult Indians and for confession on the part of schoolboys. Concerned lest my faith not be of the believing sort, as there are fears connected with it, fears as to failure in our work here. Reasoning, what if we don't get converts, what then of New Testament principles of church order? What then of teaching Bible-study method and memorization, translation seminars and Book Study Retreats with young men? And then it fell my turn to teach devotions in school from Mark 11:12–26. I could not teach all the passage with a clear conscience. It says more than I know experimentally about faith. So I settled for an illustration of leafy but fruitless trees. But O Christ, how I want this "speaking to a mountain" faith. This faith that is bold, *publicly* for God. I have prayed in faith for the life of a baby that has hung near death for a week—prayed in front of the schoolboys and thanked God openly for days when it was some better. Now I am going to the house again. It is unconscious, they say. This much I know. A prayer to God asked with whatever reservation in respect of consequences devolving upon the prayer's not being answered cannot be called the prayer of faith.

MAY 2   Pete left yesterday for Quito and dental work. Day broke cool, and I took the opportunity to make a survey of the old trails running from Talac northeast to Pano. Left Luis's house with him, Venancio, Eladio (Pano), Shilvi, and Guiña Malqui, following the ridge northeast that divides the Ichuculin watershed and that of the lower Talac. Rise is gradual enough to make a useful trail until arrival at the headwaters of the Yana Yacu watershed, and there are no streams to cross until then. Looks to me as if it could be made into a useful trail as it runs north northeast continuously, following a ridge that rises to the top of Jatuni Urcu. Wasila Urcu is visible to the northwest in places. Crossing the *cabezeras* [headwaters], it is possible to hit descending ridges—I think we only were on two—that lead on right down to Pano airstrip. But the descent is too rapid and with too many rises in the ridge to make a good trail. It needs more survey from the Achiyacu side, with the hope of finding a good north descent to the valley of the Pano.

MAY 11   Flew out of Shandia at about 10:30 A.M. with Luis Andi. Picked up Gerry Conn in Tena and flew to Shell Mera. Waited for a bus until about 2:00 P.M. and had difficulty getting out of Baños. Made Ambato about 8:00 and Quito after midnight. She had waited up for me at Tidmarshs' until very late, but had gone to bed thinking I stayed in Ambato. Pete let me in, and Doc got up to welcome me. When things were quiet again, I tried to waken her by rattling at the door, leaving the bath water run as a decoy. After some trying I went in and woke her with a kiss. She rose into my arms in one of the warmest embraces I can remember, and it was the beginning of two most intense weeks of embracing.

MAY 12–14   Conference of IMF at HCJB hut. Stimulating words from Rolf of Peru's C&MA. Described the Peruvian Evangelical Church there, and in the evenings spoke on the promises to the overcomers in Revelation 2, 3. Based the messages on "He that hath, shall be given," and interpreted it to mean that the promised rewards were based on present possessions. A man who inherited a place on a throne here knew something of governing or exercising God's authority on earth, and so on. Unusual and helpful.

MAY 15–18   Went to Calderon for a visit with the Reyburns [Dr. William and Marie, anthropologists]. Happy fellowship—Betty worked some on her Colorado with Bill. But the late evenings alone with her by the fireplace were the best. If there was before anything tentative in our loving, it is since then destroyed. Our love is now and always and only the true love I can know, and if I should lose her, there could be nothing again in life like this.

MAY 19–22　　　Shopping in Quito. Dinner with Jordans at the Colón; together at the Sicilian çafe for supper; and there once with Ed and Marilou. Supper and wine at the bodega; *our* rug from the Casa de Akios. Happy days, like none before I've known, and I thank God for the memory of them off here in the forest.

MAY 23–25　　　San Miguel. The peasant blouse, the thin blue dress, and the plaid blouse, and jeans. The shoulder, the leg, and the naked waist.

JUNE 5　　　Finished up the joisting on Ed's house in the morning. Ready now for flooring. That makes three months just getting foundation and undergirding in place. No speed record, but I thank God for even that progress. Went to Pano with the schoolboys in the afternoon for a weekend *paseo*.

JUNE 7　　　Dedicated Millers' baby in the Sunday-morning service—Carl Timothy. May God hear our prayers over him. Preached with liberty and desire on the rich man in hell in Quichua to both schools and attending adults. Came home accompanied to Pawas' house by Carmela and Helena. They asked for baptism, and we had good conversation in the Gospel on the trail. Carmela said they believed today, and I was encouraged of God in hearing it. Make it true faith, and live, Lord, full of love to Christ and desire for service.

JUNE 13　　　I am clean mad for a woman this afternoon. The week's rains looked like they had come to an end as we had the women and boys at work cutting grass this morning, and we started again on the flooring. But we hadn't been out with the tools ten minutes before it started in again, and we had to cover up the lumber and go for cover ourselves. The river is very high and the general outlook is depressing; better said "confining." And, as I said, I want a woman—just one to hold and press against me, to feel and fondle with my lips and fingers. Disgustingly, it could be any woman, as I cannot seem to bring *her* fixedly to mind, and it is just the woman want that plagues me, the craving to feel one close to me. The Indians in the tight skirts and loose blouses bent over with machetes often bring me to this state, and I know of no escape from it except work. If I could just get engaged in hammering or sawing I could get free of it, but under a thatch roof on a rainy Saturday afternoon I know no release. At times this sheer physical *need* is the strongest argument for marriage that I know, stronger than love or social adjustment or anything. When God saw that it was not good for man to be alone, He saw something that is terribly obvious, and He *did not* meet the need by making a second man!

JUNE 14   This may become known as the season of the big flood. It started a week ago nearly and has rained here and in the mountains for five days and nights. Day before yesterday we noticed several large slides on the cliff wall downriver, and in anticipation of a possible sudden rise, we tied the motor-house base and the generator to a rope and knotted it to the orange tree in front of this house—the one T. built—I don't know how long it will be here. This morning at breakfast the Napo was plainly heading for a rampage. We went down to the *cafetal* [coffee grove] below the new house to watch the slides eat away the trail and forest on the east bend. Then we went to the school for services and came out to find the airstrip, too, had begun to peel away. It crested between 10:00 A.M. and noon. The motor platforms and generator are dangling over a sheer wall on the orange-tree rope now. The new house, once thirty yards away from the river wall, is a bare fifteen now. The trail is completely gone, and Protaco's house is quite visible on the clean-cut cliff downstream.

The river was frantic and huge, gnawing off great chunks of earth and stone and forest, burying them in its turbid maw, spewing up stripped bones of trees and growling deep in its guts as it churned up the stones. A fearful thing to see— especially when one is so close to it. I am about fifteen yards from the brink myself now as I write, and although the crest has passed for now, the island is still far from the far shore, flotsam lies crashed against the trees down low, and tons more are rolling by, on the mud-gone-greenish water. The problem is, shall we go on building the new house with all the expensive furnitures, aluminum, and all with the sudden chance of a repetition of today's show? The Indians intimate it hasn't been like this for perhaps thirty years. But who knows when it will come again? Only the God whose voice is upon many waters. And He will show us His will and power. I am going out for a survey of new house sites.

JULY 5   Came in yesterday evening from Pano with four Dos Rios schoolboys loaded with aluminum, after leaving Dos Rios around ten in the morning. Betty came in a week ago to Dos Rios without stopping here, so I was mad to see her by the time we heard from Pano that an invitation was out and a canoe was going downriver with the Bohles from Latacunga. So I went over Wednesday morning, arriving after a lovely two-hour canoe trip from Pano. The Indians were all ahowl that I should have brass sufficient to visit my wife-to-be, and speak of doing so in public, but I felt no restraint in acting as we would normally in Quito or at home. They may as well learn how we feel about one another and how we express it.

They were our three most intimate days ever. House planning and Quichua study—with those silly, spasmodic embraces interspersed and making it all so worthwhile and fun. The evening was spent on the clinic porch. Forget not in age what tenderness you knew there, my soul. Friday it was beach and blond hair and blue sky and bathing suits.

JULY 21   O God, how long must I wait for her? It is day and night now, and momently that the hunger comes over me, a restlessness, an unhappiness, a drive, and a dissatisfaction. They are right who say, "Once you decide it is the thing to do, there is nothing except to do it." I have in my mind, and to Mom and Dad stated that it will be a wedding by Easter of '54. But I am afraid I cannot wait until then—the burning is too strong for her.

I never knew that love would be so intense for me, that it could be constant and strong enough to leave one with this emptiness day and night, in whatever activity. Pete gives me patter about controlling with the will the undisciplined emotions, but it is nonsense. I used to think that, too, that it was all a matter of willing not to be overcome of love that would keep one balanced and protected from "getting silly" over a woman. But what happens when the will itself is affected? The will is stronger even than the emotion in wanting. But I can see no way for marriage during this year. God is giving us what we asked for, single lives, and freedom to move in the Oriente. But here we are building houses. The summer is just getting under way, of course. We couldn't have traveled up until now. But with Ed held up indefinitely in Quito with Marilou having jaundice, and no word from T. about a visit—who knows if we can get away, even by September? August—the constructional part of the house not yet done. Everything says wait—rain, materials lacking, language study calling—but love for her inside me says wait for nothing.

JULY 30   Spent the weekend in Dos Rios—speaking mostly of when we should be married: September, November, January, or March. I have rest about marriage and feel now that January will probably be best, after talking with Pete. He is completely at rest in the whole matter, saying that the will of God for us goes right on, married or unmarried, and that he does not at all feel as though I were leaving him out "in the cold," as some shall if I marry first. On the contrary, he feels that we should be married at different times, as it would complicate housing, and so on here and would tie us up at the same time with details easier handled at separate times. His spirit and attitude are excellent, and although he feels as I do, that we should try out traveling before marriage, he would not at all oppose a wedding in September. He, like me, would hesitate in it. So I will write Betty tonight. It is raining hard and the river is very high again, so there will be no work outside. I feel happy at settling on January for a wedding.

Lord God, and Father, I call upon Thee to enter all the avenues of my life today and to share every detail of it with me. Even as Thou hast called me to share with Thee Thy life, and all the wonders of it. As I am entering Thy treasures, Thou must now come in to possess all mine. As I am to share the destiny, glory, and future affairs of Thy Son, so would I now have Him share this small destiny of earth which is mine, the joys of it, and all its small matters—that we should *be* One, Thou and I, even as we *are* in Christ.

AUGUST 15   Saturday night, unshaven, unbathed (for sheer weariness to walk to the river), and alone. A year ago today I left Quito for Shell Mera. A year ago today it occurred to me that I should have Ed bring a ring. This morning at ten minutes to three I felt we should be married in October and wrote her so right after breakfast. Two weeks have passed since I last wrote and those two weeks have made me older. The day I wrote that prayer on the other page, the Napo wiped out Shandia. The weekend was a weary one, brightened only by Betty's coming here on Sunday. Then it was collecting all the stuff from all the buildings that were and the buildings which were yet to be, sorting it, drying it, storing it somewhere. Ed came on Tuesday. Then it was wondering together over the will, talking, planning, and discarding plans. More sorting, saving, and throwing out. It rained that weekend and took more of the cliff, leaving the moved foundation useless, altering plans again. Doc arrived Monday the twentieth, insisting that Shandia be immediately rebuilt—another disturbing factor. But I decided long ago that I'm not here to please him.

Tuesday we took off the girders of the foundation, and in the night I got my first touch of malaria. Ed and Pete left Wednesday morning, and I spent the day in chills and fever, utter weakness, and quite a lot of pain. Managed to get the girders laid for the storage house halfway down the strip. That night I saw the luminous dial on my watch flash as I rolled and read every hour from midnight to five. Dizziness and headache constant with utter loss of appetite for everything except lemonade, which, for the gallons I have drunk to cool and fill and satisfy me these three days, I regard as a rich mercy from God. There is a teapot on the desk about a third full now.

Yesterday Doc hammered away at Nate and the weather to get out of here and was the distraught doctor eating supper here last night. [Nate Saint, a pilot with the Mission Aviation Fellowship, transported missionaries and their supplies throughout the jungle.] I was near crazy with dizziness and weakness and headache and his constant useless comments ("I'll put up the tent flaps now." "Just *too bad* Nate didn't leave for Macuma half an hour earlier." "Shandia will never seem the same." "Jim, can you come a minute to see where Chaucha wants to build his new house?" [No, I couldn't.] "I've had utopian ideas during the night, and some more practical"). I am persuaded that that esteemed brother has one grave fault: he talks—too fast, too precipitously, and too much.

At supper the mental symptoms of malaria reached their pitch. With the cessation of any physical work (all I could do was sit and tell the men what to do), the mind works overtime. My thoughts were awful. I did not know I loved Betty. I could not sustain two sentences of prayer. I talked impatiently to the men.

It was awful. Slept from 8:00 to midnight. Such a twisting serpentine mass of wretched and uncontrolled ideas I never thought the mind capable of, especially as I knelt in prayer. God forgive me. (Pardoned—just took it in faith.) By 1:30 A.M. I was wide awake and rose to make some lemonade. Then something happened. I was healed (I had prayed to be twice, but not then). My thoughts came clear. I thought we should use Chaucha's house for a school—we had never thought of it. He is abandoning it, but it would serve, I think, for another year, with remodeling. I knew I should marry Betty in October. The Shandia, Puyo, Bella Vista line, one at the road supplying one by air and one by canoe, seemed to me most useful, even God's mind, for our station set up—Puyo manned at first by Marilou while Ed (temporarily) and Pete built Bella Vista.

A second itineration after the present one to Bella Vista projected seemed useless. Why go to hell-and-gone for an idea of putting a station at Cuyabeno where supply lines are mighty wispy when we could, with a little effort, put in three near, but not overlapping, points which would be mutually supporting. Betty and I would rebuild Shandia asking Dad down the end of November for a couple of months to build, with Mother perhaps joining at Christmas. We would live in the tent. I even projected it so far as getting the T's ultimately running Puyo—the rest of us scattering to other parts if new workers came, and if they didn't, having tent itinerant stations air supplied at Arajuna and Villano regions. I ponder if I really was healed.

Now it is cool and growing later than my recent early bedtimes. I may sleep tonight if I stay up a little longer. The walls, studs, door, windows, and roof slats with part of the aluminum are on the storage house. By the great kindness of God I am feeling stronger and enjoying good food. Tonight it was raw carrots, tomatoes, lettuce, and cauliflower (a salad plate! With a little homemade vinegar), vegetable soup, and a snatch of chocolate cake from Shell Mera! God be praised, this is a good night in what used to be Shandia.

Psalms 71:15:

> My mouth shall tell of Thy right doings,
> Of Thy deliverances all the day;
> The number of them
> These "doings" and these "deliverances"
> I know not.

The experience and the translation are my own.

AUGUST 16   A much better day, today. Had meeting of some thirty Indians in the morning air. Thirty couldn't get into anything we've got now. Luis and Lucas preached. The latter has improved immensely this last year, or since I last heard him. First time I ever heard an Indian preach the Resurrection the way it should be preached. Sickly and weak. Treated some folk and folded washing in the kitchen as the tent was too hot to rest in this afternoon. Bathed leisurely alone in the Talac. First time I've felt I could walk that far in a while.

This came to me as I was sitting on the brink after a light supper (yuca [Spanish: manioc], raw carrots, and tea):

> Rivers are strong,
> Tearing down continents,
> Hurtling along:
> And the rivers roll down to the sea.
>
> Mountains are high,
> Shoving up continents,
> Challenging sky:
> And mountains shoulder the sea.
>
> Numberless sands,
> Strapping-in continents,
> Duning in bands:
> And sands all end in the sea.

God, like sea cast,
Shaper of continents,
All that Thou hast
Shall come unto Thee.

PRAYER

Because O God, from Thee comes all, because from Thine own mouth has entered us the power to breathe, from Thee the sea of air in which we swim and the unknown nothingness that stays it over us with unseen bonds; because Thou gavest us from heart of love so tender, mind so wise and hand so strong, Salvation; because Thou art Beginning, God, I worship Thee.

Because Thou art the end of every way, the goal of man; because to Thee shall come of every people respect and praise; their emissaries find Thy throne their destiny; because Ethiopia shall stretch out her hands to Thee, babes sing Thy praise; because Thine altar gives to sparrows shelter, sinners peace, and devils fury; because "to Thee shall all flesh come"; because Thou art Omega. Praise.

Because Thou sure art set to justify that Son of Thine and wilt in time make known just who He is and soon will send Him back to show Himself; because the Name of Jesus has been laughingly nailed upon a cross and is just now on earth held very lightly and Thou wilt bring that Name to light; because, O God of righteousness, Thou wilt do right by my Lord, Jesus Christ, I worship Thee.

SEPTEMBER 23   Shandia again. Fly season coming on and beautiful weather. After finishing the shack late in August, Betty came in from Dos Rios and was with me over the weekend of the twenty-second. Left in good weather about 9:30 the twenty-fourth with Venancio, Shilvi and Maldenado Andi, Shilvi Grifa, Alejo Tapui, and Lucas Cerda. We were stalled at the *chimbadero* [crossing] because Laran had gone off somewhere and left the canoe on the opposite side. He returned drunk after we had gotten the canoe across with the help of two schoolboys. Only made the Ansuj crossing at Ila when heavy storms forced us indoors at the *tambillo* [a small shelter]. Spoke to a Záparo [an Indian of that tribe] who wanted to know if old folks go to heaven when they die when he heard Lucas and we discussing the possibilities of infant redemption.

Pushed on to Boa Yacu for the next night. (From tambillo to Cusha Yacu is one hour's walk.) Met a man named Latico who has a house near Cusha. Nearing Llandia Yacu, the Pituja Yacu enters Ansuj from west. Small streams on trail side called Ichilla Llandiawa or Sangu Llandea by Shilvi G. Indian house at Llandia Pungu was passed at 10:00 A.M. (left at 6:40). Should be one day from Shandia to Llandia. Trail is good to there, then gets muddy and steep. Sapatto Yacu is one hour farther. Basilio's wife's family lives here. Crossed Chambira Yacu on south of priests' cleared land at 11:30. Stopped at the house of Julio Cesar Sanchez, a white sympathetic to the Gospel. Bought a chicken, and he gave us eggs. He wants us to take two children from Tunguratura into school, Orlando Ramiro and Vicente Marcial Frere. Must send him a Bible and New Testament. His daughter Mercedes Vasconez, requested one as well. Reached Boa Yacu in time for bath and had a good rest at the tambillo there.

Left at 6:35 and passed the pastures of Hacienda Cavilan at 7:30. A man named Salvador is owner. Passed Anga Yacu at 7:45 and paused at Yana Yacu at 9:30. Both good-sized streams. Arrived at Puyo Road (kilo 10) at noon, and made Shell at 3:00. Survey flight to Sara Yacu and sought Auca house on Callana River beyond Villano. Rested Thursday, August 27, packing and arranging with Saphiro Vargas for canoes. Walked from Puyo to La Union bridge in one hour twenty minutes where we dickered for two canoes. Used one from Isaac Vargas's house and his son Jorge helped as *boga* [boatman]. Indians live on west side of river and whites have claimed much land on east.

Met a man who claimed to be a "brother" named

Paredes from the white settlement of Vera Cruz. Saphiro Vargas has a wife named Andiria, and she called her daughter Pucho. The daughter called him Doceviro. In Isaac Vargas's house there were two women, Jorge, and small children. Below bridge on west bank there are two houses on a cliff south of the river junction. Victor Vargas and wife Maria Inez Muya are owners of one. Farther west there is a communal house whose head is Atanasio Vargas in a place called Puyupungu. Pascual Santez and Pascualito Yumbo live there as well, and the Jívaro guide Pasmino Shuquillo seemed to be there living near. On east, Eliseo (Elison) Vargas has a house and Ramon Dawa, a Napo, is married into his family (met previously on Puyo Road).

Passed Ulupungu Cucha and Para Chicta just below it. Tsingushimi enters from west and Gonzalvo Vargas lives at this point (Victor's brother). Leandro Vargas (Victor's mother) lives across from a white named Sanchez at Rosario Pungu (from east). I believe trail leaves river here and goes overland to Isaac Vargas's house, following river from here to Indillama. Below this there are three Indian houses on west bank. Walking from here, it is one hour to Livinos and another to Chorera Yacu and one more to Indillama. Two hours below bridge we brought Ana from *Livino* (east bank). Bascuto Santi lives just below him on west bank.

At Chorera Pungu there is an hacienda shack on east and Segundo Yasacama has his house on west. Below the rapids just above Indillama, there is a division called Puma Chicta. Julio Rodriguez and Flores live at Indillama. Met a family just below Indillama at a rapids. Has a house of sorts on east bank, lives in Puyu Chicta south of this rapids called Churu Singana. At another heavy rapids called Guiña Sas, we met Atanasio Vargas en route to Puyu. He returned with us to Bella Vista. There is a house at the mouth of Putuimi (river that comes from Shell) just above Puyupungu that belongs to Pascual Santez.

We stayed in the convent overnight. Found Atanasio and family most eager for a school which would, with boys and girls, probably not number more than twenty. To get the Gos-

pel down the Puyu, even for a year, would be a victory for the
Master and an outreach for the Kingdom, I believe. Pushed on
next morning up the Indian trail to Canelos. Trail takes off the
east side of Puyu river at Changala Yacu. Houses at
Puyupungu:

> Pascualito's two girls
> Arsenio's two girls, two boys
> Guillermo's two boys
> Atenazio's four girls, five boys
> Pascual's one boy

In all, nineteen with a possibility of nine more, from upriver.

Met rain on Saturday the thirtieth. Stayed in leaf lean-to at
Cashape (Tushapi) River. Pushed on to Canelos, arriving at
Dario's house about 4:30 P.M. Stayed the night and Monday at
cuartel under lieutenantship of one Torres. *Captain* Torres is a
landowner who runs a store described by Lt. Torres as *explota-
ción inicua* [an iniquitous exploitation]. Geron, Chief of *bogas*,
secured us three canoes, and we left with the *"comision de
viveres"* [commission of supplies] for the lower Bobonaza
Tuesday morning. Our *boga* was named Luis; his wife,
America. They live on the right bank two or three curves down
river from Canelos.

Caypi River enters on right below Luis's house and Cuya
Sas; below is Cungilla Cocha. At Ishpingo Yacu, Isidro lives.
Passed a *chicta* [a creek which splits from the mainstream and
rejoins it later] which goes to the left and then Mauca Yacu
enters from left. Tiny stream on right, further down is Camatoa
Yacu. Bintami (wife Ataco) Sante has house just above Rayo
Yacu (enters from right). Copala Yacu from left. At Lata Luis
has a *purina wasi* [a house used for short stays]. Capawari Yacu
on right and above Sas by same name. Challua Yacu below on
left. Followed by Charapa Cucha, a wide sharp bend and
Mishquipi Yacu on right. Bimbi has a house on right at Chapiton Cucha. Chapiton Yacu on right and Daniel Wasi below.
Ilipe Wasi on left. Jawlapi Yacu on right is a fair-sized stream.

Bujiu Yacu on left is small. Micacio leaves on left at Waira (Wira) Yacu. Small falls on left called Baranca Yacu. Pucacaspi Yacu on left; Huito Yacu on right and Tsatsapi Yacu on left, a river size. Bolas' house is round and at the mouth of a chicta where we dynamited for fish. Machitona Yacu on right, Umiypi Yacu on left; Guikiwaya Yacu on left and Vintamin has house on right. We stopped for Chicha at Ramon's house on right. Met Venancio Varela below Ramon's. Aya Yacu just above Chambera on right. Chambera Yacu on left. Stayed in Chambera in rather comfortable quarters in the army post. Sergeant Guzman in command.

September 2, Wednesday.   Below Chambera to Sara Yacu. Ishpinga Yacu on left. Domingo Aguindo lives at Nachi Cucha on right. Yara Rumi Yacu and Tiu Yacu come in opposite each other. Ilipe Aguinda lives on right. At Caspi Pitishca just above Pacai Yacu lives a soldier named Tizru. Stopped for milk at Abram Arayou's. Chumbi Yacu enters on right between Aragon and convent Yatapi Yacu, a good-sized river enters on right more than halfway to Sara Yacu from Chambera. Gallo Rumi lies mid-stream—a huge rock just opposite a small stream on right. Baka Yacu enters from left. Below there is a house on left and Chonda Yacu comes in on right.

September 3, Thursday.   Slept in Sara Yacu at cuartel. Sergeant Vermaye in charge. Chicha at Ilipe's house below Sara Yacu. Met old Ignacio on beach at Palanda. Several houses there. Asked for salt. Stayed in a house just above at Pingullu.

September 4, Friday.   Game birds abundant. Slept in house which was abandoned after Jivaro killings here.

September 5, Saturday.   Arrived in Montalvo after two hours' canoeing. Passed the priest's Mashuj Ilacta. Lieutenant Fausto Riquete entertained us. Met W.B.T. [Wycliffe Bible Translators] workers Ralph, Kathy, and Mary who are beginning Záparo. Mighty few of them, it seems to me, but God bless their work. I cannot agree with their policy on covering up their evangelicalism. Stayed over Sunday and visited Indian homes downriver. Quite a concentration of Indians and some desire among them for a school. Priest has peeved them by moving out of Montalvo and carrying his work upriver.

September 7. Left before dawn in rain. Slept in deserted house at Jatun Palisada.

September 8, Tuesday. Flood hit us. Pushed all day through the Yutsu until after dark, made a tarp shelter one hour below Tawai Nambi.

September 9. Waited for Pete's canoe in Tawai. He arrived early afternoon; we waited for water to recede. Watched Adi make pots.

September 10. Made shelter on beach near Yana Alpa, one hour above Munelo.

September 11. Made shelter on island above Jatun Pulaya.

September 12, Saturday. Slept in Sara Yacu Pungu, Atenazio's *purina wasi*.

September 13. Passed Sara Yacu. Met Creeiente. Stayed in empty house one hour up from Sara.

September 14, 15. Slept in Chapiton, Ilipe's house (Auca scare).

September 16. Canelos—Dario's house.

September 17. Chorera Yacu above Indillama.

September 18. Shell.

September 19, Saturday. Shandia.

SEPTEMBER 28   Another characteristic of Ezekiel that was shared with Christ in His ministry—Ezekiel 20:49: "Ah, Senor Jehova! ellos dicen de mi: el no habla sino paraboles." ["Ah, Lord God! They say of me: he speaks not but parables"]. The two who were called "Son of Man" were not understood for their speaking parables.

Jim and I were married October 8, 1953, in a civil ceremony in Quito. We went to Panama and Costa Rica for a honeymoon, and then traveled by dugout canoe to Puyupungu.

DECEMBER 1   It is not raining at the moment but the fresh-cut bamboo slats are chunked with fresh mud, and the other half of the tent, not yet floored, is slippery gum from an all-night rain on Sunday. We had to get this much of the floor in yesterday, and they are supposed to be bringing more bamboo today so perhaps we will be fully foored this week. Betty took matters in her own hands this afternoon while I rested (I am supposed to have had jaundice—almost since the day we arrived, November 11—and am still a part-time bed patient) and put down sticks between the tent and the eight-by-ten mud-floored kitchen, as yet only half walled. She is there cooking now while I sit at the card table, decked with an aster-flowered tea cloth with a centerpiece of white candle and a graceful-leafed little forest flower set off beautifully in a tin can.

Married life is likened to single life as a long stanza of Whitman's is to the first phrase—a continuation, but with the connection only fully appreciated after you've felt the whole piece. It is rich, as I have always known life to be, but richer in its complexities. What intimacy I have known outside marriage is now hardly worthy of the name. The living-together-alone lessons that I have learned with Bill, Pete, and Ed are all of utmost significance in living with Betty, but none of them were such whole-hearted, enthusiastic "cooperators" as she is, indeed, as she has need to be. I never declared my love to them; with her, the affair is public. We have committed ourselves to love each other and are publicly at stake to make good the commitment. I am finding it no effort.

She is just what I always knew her to be, all woman, with her habit of being surprised and shocked at things I do and say (an amusing habit to me, and an incentive to keep saying shocking things), her tendency to use exaggerated words ("horrible," "awful" in tones of utter disgust), and to feel things strongly and with a love for me that I can neither understand nor appreciate, let alone be worthy of. We have had nothing but harmony, from our wedding night in El Panama to the last time we spoke—about the men bringing bamboo to the plaza just now. The "marriage adjustment" is something—if it exists at all—that I am going through effortlessly, unconsciously, even. Such is the love we know.

Have read a few things since being sick: Emily Bronte's *Wuthering Heights;* John P. Marquand's *The Late George Apley;* C. S. Lewis's *Miracles* to the end and reviewing chapters before read. Also a couple of Untermeyer's poetic anthologies. I'm not too excited about Untermeyer and his "helps." He was all right for high school; now he seems a bit pedantic. Bett and I are reading Amy Carmichael's biography together. It stirs me— kept me awake even, in the dark here last night after the candle went out.

JANUARY 20   Puyupungu. Spent a holiday in Shandia from December 19 to January 5 and with much joy. First young men's conference went off with not enough prayer or study; but albeit with the blessing of God. Baptized Georgina Cerda and Carmela Shiwango in Talac on Lord's Day January 3, with great joy and confidence in God. Began work on the airstrip and house site here January 11 but have been discouraged by rain and slowed by personnel problems. Still God helps and progress is visible. Not happy altogether with Lucas as a schoolteacher, but am encouraged with the attention some show to the Word of God. Last night in a little meeting we have Tuesday evenings Atanasio said, "I will die in your words," meaning he would never go back to the priests' side again. I do not know how much he understands, but he does hear some. Praying for a work in the schoolchildren—who now number ten. May start a literacy class for some young fellows when the house is under way and the airstrip finished.

Talking about the Jivaría yesterday, Atanasio said of a great cliff of salt (somewhere in Peru, now) "Ima chari maimanda shamun. Dios saquishca" ["Who knows what it is or where it comes from?" God left it there!]

FEBRUARY 5   Finished the roof of the house and outhouse today. Men wearying some and dropping off work. Only the Lord is constant and sure. It must be by His grace we have accomplished all that we have this past month—both on the airstrip and in the house here.

Sorry for a hasty word, spoken to Lucas a week ago—rather, to his wife on the matter of salt. I guess he didn't understand that we did not bring supplies for them to buy. He says his spirit is changed and that he cannot feel the same again with me in the work. I sat an hour or more with him humbling myself ridiculously before other Indians to try and gain him. God knows if I gained; I strove to be meek. May the Spirit restore us to fellowship again.

Praying for Pablo and Atanasio especially these days. Oh, that God would bring light to their minds and life to their souls! Began literacy class daily with Tito and Benito this week. Tito does well. Perhaps God will give him to me to father in the faith.

Dad's sailing postponed indefinitely now. All awaits Tidmarsh's work with entry permits in Quito. May God clear that part of the way soon.

APRIL 1   Pause late on a rainy afternoon. Gratefully settled in our home in Puyupungu for a week now. Been a long, but not unendurable five months in the tent. God has been faithful, though Satan has fought us to discouragement through long weeks of rain. Men came from Pano, or I would never have gotten the airstrip done by now. Plane landed on three hundred yards of it day before yesterday—the end is still too wet to pass the "stick test." Hope it will drain and harden eventually. Nate seems to think it will. Still employing three men to cut down the approaches. Lots of work remains that will have to be done little by little, ditching and crowning. Pete may come in tomorrow from Shandia for a visit, but Nate won't promise to take him out as the strip is so soft still.

They have begun slandering Lucas about a girl in school— Mamerta. Must face Atanasio and wives with the lies this week. Blessed and given confidence by that word: "Be not overcome of evil, but overcome evil with good." Lucas stands firm, undismayed and hopeful of an outcome for glory.

Stopped literacy work with the schoolchildren for two weeks to give myself to house and airstrip. Must begin again next week. Dad sails this weekend, but am not sure of his arrival.

MAY 30   Lord's day, Puyupungu.   Both Dad and Pete are here with us now, and their presence represents a great deal of answered prayer. Betty and I were able to fly out of Puyupungu strip April 21 in separate flights. We waited a day in Shell for Ed and went on to Quito together the twenty-third. Met Dad with much thanksgiving at Puná on Tuesday 8:00 A.M. April 27. One week took us all through customs and Ed took a truckload of stuff on through to Shell. We spent a week in Quito getting teeth fixed, attending IMF conference, and meeting people, coming down on truck to Shell with GMUers May 14. Betty came here, and I went to Shandia to choose a house site (O God, may it be the right one!). Dad and I were the only ones for it. All the rest wanted us to build on lower ground near the Talac. Came here with Dad and Pete last Wednesday. Things seem to have gone well under Lucas's supervision. I hope he has been faithful in the ministry of the Word. He is off to Puyu now, so I will see what progress has been made tomorrow as we take over the school for a day.

AUGUST 8   Lord's Day.   In Shandia now for several weeks with Ed and Marilou gone out for a rest. Just Dad, Rob, Betty, and me. Working on the house now, pouring cement mostly, and have finished the floor and walls except for surfacing. Preached on "He that does the will of My Father who is in heaven the same is My mother, brother, and sister." How long, Lord, before they understand? Preaching, teaching, and having school all seem vain now as things move so slowly in the Indian soul.

Most of the young men are gone to the coast to work, including our most encouraging believers. God spare them the ravages of civilization and bring them back better men. Questioning now how to open school next year. Cannot feel happy about re-employing Eladio as an unsaved man. Guide me, Lord, as it looks like I will have the responsibility. Lift up my soul, O Lord, for I am cast down. We want to see the Gospel spread, but how can it except it first take root in all the culture—old as well as young, men as well as women? The few baptized girls listen well in meetings and seem to show progress in understanding the ways of God with them. Camilo has gone and Asencio, Luis and Lucas and all the normal and

Institute boys—off for a fast *sucre* [an Ecuadorian monetary unit worth about six cents then]—I hope for nothing worse. But, Lord, is this why we have trained them, that they should leave the forest for white man's culture? Was it not that they should go reaching their own people with the Word? Wherein have we missed in setting before them the wrong ideal that they should regard money as of more worth to seek after than souls? Lead us out of it, Lord, and back to a simple principle of operation. School is a chore; house building, a heaviness now as I see little of what I aimed at accomplished.

JANUARY 16   Cast down on this Lord's Day morning. Just came up from *culto* [meeting] with twenty-five Indians, mostly schoolboys and young women. Felt as though I preached powerlessly, without unction, and the resultant effect was evident. Restlessness, interruptions, playing. Almost no adults come—Vicenti's wife and Cua's and Upuchu's—no adult men. My first thought is that they have tired of the preaching, that they do not enjoy it. I may be preaching too hard. Then I think that I am worried too much during the week with the finishing of the house—right up until Saturday supper. Translated and preached from Titus 1 but felt little life or even continuity in what I said. I have paid dearly for giving up my early quiet time. It is surely obvious in my preaching. Marriage has been a hindrance. Betty doesn't like me to get out of bed amorning without some little loving. Just now she came in "so mad" because somebody stole a *patas muyu* [a type of fruit] from the backyard.

My concerns are other, I fear. House and furnishings *must* take second place now. Getting the Indians out to meetings and individual witness to them has got to be my foremost concern. Elias Cerda wants to be baptized, but he did not come out to meeting today. I must speak personally with Gervacio, Venancio G., and Abelardo as well as to Elias before the young men's conference the fourth of February. I feel resolved now, but don't know how long it will stay strong with me.

Ed's folks should be here Tuesday and Ed with newborn Michael Kirk. Abstinence is not easy in the last months of pregnancy, and I have felt much untamed desire these couple of weeks. God save me through March! [Our daughter Valerie was born February 27, 1955.]

I am sorry to have neglected writing here. Many times fresh thoughts have come, and I have failed to record them so that now they are gone. One concerned the physical and material aspects of Mosaic law. There was no promise of eternal reward. Achan died without mercy, but nothing is said of his soul, in the afterworld. The Law has a spirit of temporality and fixed locality. Promises are mostly concerned with "long life, good days, and dwelling in the land."

Another was a note about the tribal distribution of the judges. Nearly all the tribes participated in that period of leadership: (1) Othniel (Judg. 3:9); Caleb's tribe was Judah (Num. 13:6); (2) Ehud (Judg. 3:15) a Benjaminite; (3) Deborah (4:5, 6)—Ephraim, Naphtali, Zebulun are associated in the victory over Sisera (5:14, 18); (4) Gideon (6:15), Manasseh; (5) Jephthah (Gileadites tribe uncertain (12:4); (6) Ibzan—Bethlehem (12:8), a city of Judah; (7) Elon, Zebulun (12:11); (8) Abdon (12:15), Ephraim; (9) Samson (13:2), Dan.

MAY 16　　This has been a busy morning and one of those that doesn't leave one with a great deal of satisfaction after its doing is all done. Morning reading was in 2 Thessalonians 3: "If any man will not work neither let him eat." Yesterday I had told three girls to come to work; six came to clean two measly *chagras* [cultivated clearings]. Then I went down to put Urpi and son on planting pasture; they achieved a morning's success of perhaps thirty yards, ten feet wide. The men were waiting for tools to be sent for roof leaf. I sent them. More than twenty women brought *plátano* [plantain] and *chicha* [a masticated and fermented drink made of manioc, a staple of the Indian diet] and I outraged them all by buying enough for only two weeks—I had sufficient for one week already—and one *maitu* [leaf-wrapped package] of *chicha* from each one, leaving much unbought, along with a basket of unnecessary sugar cane. Then the change ran out.

Then the workmen on the teacher's house needed *barengas* [two-by-fours] planed. I planed *varengas*, after a session in school on the splendor of Solomon. Then it was sizing and grading over two hundred new *varengas* for the school building. Then the girls arrived who had been cleaning *chagra* and wanted me to buy their *plátano*. Domingo wanted ink powder for *tablas* [boards]. A boy came to buy five-dollars worth of rails for Señora Rosa down river. The workmen had cut a *varenga* too short and needed a hand. Venancio's leg needed massaging, and he wanted to sell me beans (I had to give him some yesterday as he said he had nothing to eat). Had to tell the men to start weaving roof and not to stand about doing nothing. Then they all wanted to work the whole day. Yuyu wanted money for thirty pounds of peanuts, and his mother wanted a sack Ed had not given back to her. Protaco wanted his work money and the gun that Pete sent down from Quito to sell. Pete had been on the radio, and now it is urgent that I write Tidmarsh. Believers' meeting this afternoon. Juan Grifa at Limon Chikta is in bad shape with snakebite. I was there Friday and yesterday and must go again tomorrow—an hour or more both ways. Betty and the baby both have colds. I have just eaten a good lunch.

CASE	SNAKE	COMMENTS	SYMPTOMS
Wangana	Shishin (airstrip)	Little local swelling. Blood loss considerable. Anemia.	Hematoxic (fer-de-lance). Bitten on heel.
Paula	Shishin	Bleeding at gums at capillaries.	Hematoxic. Bitten on foot.
Sabella Andi	Shishin	Bit on finger. Never saw case.	Bitten on hand.
Indi	Pitalala	Dead in forty-eight hours.	Alone in forest.
Carmela's uncle	Shishin(?)	Dead in twenty-four hours.	
Venancio (Cuchicara)	Motolo (Bushmaster)	Tissue destruction— rotting of flesh. Treated with sulfas and penicillin. Hand dried.	Hand. Immobile fingers.
Juan Grifa	Pitalala	Tissue destruction; anemia. Some vomiting of blood.	Ankle.
Orkenia Cerda	Shishin	Cut, sucked. Horse serum injected; retching.	Not much swelling or pain; fear.
Casiano	(unknown)	Dead in twenty-four hours (coast).	Fell flat immediately, had to be carried.

MAY 22   Sunday.   On way to treat Juan Grifa for a *pita lala* [a species of viper] snakebite, Eugenia was bitten by a *shishin* [fer-de-lance]. This leads to a little serpent study tonight:

Gabriel Andi: deformed hand.
Laura Andi: deformed hand.
Maria Cerda: arm amputated by Shell doctors.
White boy in Puyupungu: large watery blister. No ill-effects.
Shilvi Andi: one week in bed. No ill-effects.

JULY 19   Venancio Tapui and I baptized fourteen this morning after the Gospel meeting. No other missionary here, so had the believers in for examining yesterday. It was a four-hour session, and we saw evidence of real discernment on the part of Ascencio, Mariano Andi, Mariano Mamallacta, Horvaco, and Abelardo, as well as Venancio Tapui. I felt lonely in doing it and did it with some fear that I might be mistaken. We decided to ask four young girls to wait, and they were very unhappy this morning. My flesh often lacks the deep feeling that I should experience at such times, and there was a certain dryness to the form this morning, but I cannot stay for feelings. So cold is my heart most of the time that I am most always operating on the basis of pure commandments, forcing myself to do what I do not always feel simply because I am a servant under orders.

And there was enough of the physically distracting this morning to save one from walking on clouds. A part of the cliff gave way, and three girls sat down on the beach amid shrieks and laughter. The schoolboys threw stones in the water. Antonia's son fell headlong off the airstrip onto the beach and set up a great wail just as she was being baptized. Venancio failed to get Carmela Chimbu's face under. A group of mockers from the priest's came by and taunted the baptized ones about bathing with their clothes on. But God is my witness that I have fulfilled His Word as I knew how. These were baptized today:

Bacha Cerda	Basilio Cerda
Alberto Andi	Antonia Andi
Luis Andi	Mariana Grifa
Jimbi Andi	Rosalina Tapui
Juan Andi	Carmela Chimbu
Wakina Andi	Shilverio Andi
Ostanico Andi	Carmelawa Shiwangu

Praise to His Name! He only does wonders.

AUGUST 21   Returned yesterday from Quito after our first run from Puyu to Papallacta. We started in a small truck from Quito on Monday, August 8, with eight boys from Calderon, Benton Rhoades, Alberto Ronquillo, and Ed and me. Arrived and slept on Puyu-Napo road at Kilometer 14. House of one Sr. Molino. [This was an excursion to introduce mountain Indian boys to jungle.]

Tuesday, August 9: Off at 6:00. Mistook trail at end of road, wandered in cleared land until 7:45. Got on trail at 8:00 A.M. Rain and mud. All discouraged. Ate *piñol* and sardines at noon. Arrived at abandoned Indian house 5:00 P.M. Could hear Ansuc but not see it. Trail bad all day.

Wednesday, August 10: Llandia at 8:30. Jimenez friendly, gave us pineapple and limes. Arrived Ila 1:30. Lost several thousand *sucres* when Calderon boys nearly went downriver at the Tambo crossing. Arrived Jatun Yacu 7:00. Shandia 8:30. Tired, some boys with sore feet. All discouraged.

Thursday, August 11: Rested in Shandia. Hectic day. Boys slept in school dorm.

Friday, August 12: Left Shandia at 8:00. Arrived Achi Yacu where Alberto Abuja is making *camino de herradura* [log trail] from Tena to Talac. Boys went on that. Jimbi and I went to see if Jarrín would accompany us to Quito; four went on old trail arriving same time as boys and Ed. Arrived Archidona 4:30. Ate in hotel. Slept in telephone office of Clotilde Rosales. Patron Pancho Mejia helped us secure two mules from Santiago de Nayon.

Saturday, August 13: Waited for mules until 9:30. Met Jarrín who was going back to Pano. Trail good. Country opened along mule trail. Met Indians and whites and priest Morales at *Cotunda*. Must see him again. Maybe a searching soul. Arrived Jundachi 5:00 P.M. Made chicken-and-rice soup. Slept in upstairs. Chilly.

Sunday, August 14: Up the Wacamagas ten kilometers uphill. Reached *Cosanga* 3:30. Slept at house with telephone at Jana Yacu. Met Anna's (from Pano) brother.

Monday, August 15: Baeza eighteen kilometers from Yara Yacu. Passed Sara Yacu and other river without bridge. Follow Cosanga Yacu (headwaters of the Coca) to Baeza. Can see to Sumaco and El Chaco from trail. El Chaco best reached by foot from Borja. About twenty-five kilometers from Baeza. Baeza at noon. Cuyuha at 5:00. Slept in schoolhouse. Cold and windy up whole valley from Baeza. Land not good for much but grazing—sheep and cattle. Awfully swampy. Highland Indians met today. They live above Baeza.

Tuesday, August 16: Left Cuyuha at 7:00. Arrived Papallacta 12:00. Waited on truck until 5:00. Arrived after one flat tire on the *Páramo* [high-grass country of the Andes] in Quito at 10:00. Dick Larson took us to Calderón.

Wednesday, August 17: *Paseo* to markets. Schoolboys bought shoes. Campfire with weiners, buns, punch, potatoes, and ice cream at Flories in Calderón.

Thursday, August 18: Benton drove us past *hacienda* La Concepcion above Lloa by 8:00. We were at crater rim by 11:30. Cloudy and cold. Walked back to near Quito by 4:45 P.M. Venancio Grifa, Cesar, Abelardo, Pedro Tasiwano, and I were only ones to make rim. It's the best way to climb Pichincha.

Friday, August 19: Hector took boys to several ministries and monuments. I shopped.

Saturday, August 20: Left Quito at 7:00. Ambato 11:10. Shell 4:35. Shandia 5:10 P.M. Praise. It's a long run.

OCTOBER 29　First time I ever saw an Auca—fifteen hundred feet is a long ways if you're looking out of an airplane. Nate and Ed have found two sites and have been visiting one and dropping gifts weekly for about a month.

Ed and I flew to Villano with Johnny [Keenan, a MAF pilot] on Thursday and arrived at the Huito Plaza around 4:30 P.M. or later. Met old Carlos Jay—sixty-one, single-toothed, lion-headed, and talkative. Not secure in his patronship. Treated us well. While raised a Lutheran, he is a Catholic Mass attender for convenience rather than conviction and is in league with the Dominicans from Puyo for the house in Huito. He takes care of it. They built it. Indians were drunk and friendly when we arrived. Had a meeting—perhaps forty persons Friday morning on the church benches in the plaza. As we were visiting in the afternoon, a small boy—perhaps ten years old—named Adam, was pulled under, evidently by a boa, and drowned while swimming. The search for recovery of and wake-making over his body spoiled the afternoon meeting we planned. Indians claim a *supai* [demon (Quichua)] got him. Returned with the success of a fair relation established with Jay. The Indians there are certainly not dying to hear the Gospel. Returned to Villano by canoe 6:30–8:15 A.M. Saturday. Nate was waiting for us.

We flew together back to Arajuno, had a little talk about tactics and flew then with the battery loudspeaker and the Auca phrases I got from Dayuma last week in Ila. I repeated the phrases at the first circling of the house at about two thousand feet:

Llaimi punumai—"you will be given a machete."
Wa'ati punum yamwi—"to exchange" (for a lance?).

We saw perhaps eight Indians scurrying about the house. One crossed the river with something on his head and seemed to flash a new machete. I did not see him return even though it looked as though he only went to the *chagra* [plantation]. One rushed into the house and returned with a lance. I took this as evidence that one had gone to get food in exchange and another to get a lance. But when we dropped the machete on the string they tore off both machete and the small basket we had tied on to receive some exchange. One went about the house flailing the piece of canvas the machete was wrapped in.

We hauled in the line (heavy work!) then dropped it again after several tries thinking they may tie something on. It dropped in the water, and they cut off a section of it instead—old green line of the other drops. We pulled it all the way in and set up the loud speaker again, this time using the phrases:

Punimupa—"I like" (you).
Bitimiti punimupa—"I like" (you).
Kyanya punumai—"You will be given a pot."

At this a group raced back into the trees behind the house and one lone man walked to the beach. He cupped his hand. We dropped a small aluminum pot free with ribbons. It contained a yellow shirt and beads. The man on the beach pointed to the place of the fall. Those behind the house got it, and one was soon flailing the yellow shirt. As we approached the drop house, two canoes some distance below it going downstream turned and went upstream hurriedly. I noticed three people come running up through the water onto the beach at one time and a single one with a white cloth another time. Returned via the Curaray looking for possible landing beaches. Hopes not good. Decided to send for a Whittaker landing gear and plan a trip to make an airstrip when it arrives. Guide us, Lord God.

NOVEMBER 8   No special day, this, but reading a bit of poetry always rouses in me the old urge to "record." This afternoon I felt strangely tired and slept an hour or more, I guess. Maybe it was the smell of cement dust in tropic noontime. Abelardo and Mariano and Ascencio poured seven of the pillars for the school building this morning, and my hair is stiff, picking up cement in it, just from standing about telling them how.

Have been thinking about the reasons for some of the attitudes and actions of the Indians these days. I've often been puzzled by the fact that they do not grow food they could and do enjoy. They can't grow a citrus tree, because they won't take time to weed it and trim it. They won't grow rice, because it takes too much effort to scare the birds off at harvest time.

They won't grow pineapple.in quantity, because it's too hard to keep it from going to weeds. They are not "food growers" in the classic primitive sense. They are not long-ranged enough in their views. They cut down trees to get one season's crop of fruit. They kill a vanilla vine to get a single pod. They cut a cinnamon tree to strip the whole bark. They have no concept of conservation. In this they are in the classic sense "food gatherers." But even in this they are not good. Few of them are really good at blow-gun dart shooting. They waste all kinds of ammunition because they are simply not good shots. They are too lazy to walk two days to good hunting grounds. It seems to me that they are in a transition between food gathering (which they do poorly—hunting and fishing are not their real "meat." They would sooner *buy* food) and food growing which they only manage to do. They do not do it well.

In my view of "progress," there seems nothing to do but lead them into the food-growing stage. White intrusion and example points the tribe in that direction. Population growth and settlement will eventually eliminate hunting, fishing, and gathering as a means of living. Conclusion—begin:

1. Teaching conservation and agriculture in the school
   a. Palm-planting projects
      (1) Each grade-a grove of edible palm?
      (2) What about palm oils? For sale.
   b. Sugar-cane culture and refinement.
      (1) How do we make *raspadura* [crude brown sugar]?
      (2) Could the school sell *raspadura?*
   c. School pigs and chickens. How will we get hens?
2. Encourage hunting and fishing
   a. Fish hooks (not dynamite and barbasco [poison used to stun fish]); fly fishing?
   b. Blow-gun target contests.

As a result of this transition, there are some economic factors resulting. The main one is this continuous traveling out to the coast. We lost Jimbi from school today. He took off with

Dionisio Rayo. It is not because he wants money. I offered him S/250 [250 sucres—about $16] a hectare for sowing *potrero* [pasture]. I told Dionisio that Sevilla is paying S/300 a hectare for *potrero*. Jimbi said it was easier to do a hectare on the coast (though they get only S/140), and Dionisio said that it meant he would have to send his wife between here and Ila for food, if he goes to the coast only he is *turmindarishka* [in difficulty, tormented (Quichua)]. But I am inclined to think the truth of the thing lies nearer a statement Kuwa when he left last week. "We go just to *pasear*." In the transition has come the effect of the outside world. How it lives and earns and ruins. They don't come back with a whole lot of money, just a lot of shining stuff. But they feel that they have seen the world. The school-boys agreed not to go to the coast last summer if we went to Quito together. They didn't want to work; they wanted "to see the world" in the limited, possible sense. Conclusion:

1. Take them on long *paseos* so they can see the world with a controlling Christian element. Guayaquil? Colombia? Otavalo? Arajuno? Puyupungu?
2. Teach them how to save money. All important. They are stupid in this. Get a program going for next summer so they can save now.

Valerie is cutting two more teeth today and has been fussy. She pulls herself to a standing position in her crib and playpen by herself. She is a heart wringer for cuteness and makes me want more children.

NOVEMBER 20   Let Hervaco and Venancio have the whole service this morning. Would to God that they could handle everything by themselves.

Finished *Exploration Faucett* today. Another record of back-jungle talk for the most part, but the man saw some things and reported them true. His disappearance fascinates me. Why didn't he give the exact locale of Z, and why didn't he make some way for others to follow him? This latter seems to me his great mistake and the big lesson of the book for me. In dealing with unknown Indians, never burn your bridges and always plan for follow-up contact. He may not have had the money to do this, though I cannot imagine the newspaper would not have granted it in terms of a contract should he fail to return.

Also read parts of *Behind the Ranges* and am resolute to do something about it in my private devotional and prayer life. In studying Spanish I left off English Bible reading, and my devotional reading pattern was broken. I have never restored it. Translation and preparation for daily Bible lessons is not sufficient to empower my soul. Prayer as a single man was difficult, I remember, because my mind always reverted to Betty. Now it's too hard to get out of bed in the morning. I have made resolutions on this score before now but not followed them up. Tomorrow it's to be—dressed by 6:00 A.M. and study in the Epistles before breakfast. So help me, God.

NOVEMBER 26   Spent Friday and Saturday morning (for a day-late Thanksgiving) with Conns and Fullers in Pano. In the afternoon (Ed was in Quito), Nate and I made my second Auca flight.

Flew down the river to the grass shack where there are fenced *chagras* but no people. Noted an increased amount of cutting down the forest and land clearing since my last visit. They seem to know what to do with machetes and axes. On the way up we dropped a pair of pants at the first house because a woman there had on a gray slip—or so it seemed from the air. The second house has a model airplane carved on the house ridge and there we dropped a machete, a pair of short pants, and I saw a thing that thrilled me. It seemed an old man stood beside the house and waved with both his arms as if to signal us to come down. Aucas waving at me to come! At the next house they have made a large clearing and built a bamboo platform on which one—a white-shirted one—stood and waved. Nate dropped a roll of T.P. and several streamered combs into the trees at the edge of the clearing to try and give them the idea that we want those cut down, too. Dropped a machete there, too, with streamers which they got. Dropped a pot and an axe head on the string and they tied something with a red ribbon on, but we lost it trailing it on the way home. Nate was in a hurry as it was late afternoon, and he stepped it up so we lost it. God send me soon to the Aucas.

DECEMBER 31   A month of temptation. Satan and the flesh have been on me hard. How God holds my soul in His life and permits one with such wretchedness to continue in His service I cannot tell. Oh, it has been hard . . . . I have been very low inside me struggling and casting myself hourly on Christ for help. Marriage is divorce from the privacy a man loves, but there is some privacy nothing can share. It is the knowledge of a sinful heart.

These are the days of the New Year's believers' conference on the Sermon on the Mount. Yesterday I preached and was helped on "whoever looks on a woman . . ."!

"Let spirit conquer though the flesh conspire."

Epilogue

The diary ends on December 31, 1955. Two days later Jim and four other men, Pete Fleming, Ed McCully, Nate Saint, and Roger Youderian, went to a little sand spit on the Curaray River which they named "Palm Beach." They set up a camp in hopes of establishing contact with the Auca Indians. On January 6, 1956, their hopes were realized when two women and a man appeared out of the jungle and spent several hours with the missionaries. Verbal communication was not possible, but there was every indication that the Indians were friendly and trusted the missionaries. The Auca man demonstrated complete confidence by accepting a ride in Nate Saint's airplane. Two days later the five men were speared to death.

The story is told in detail in *Through Gates of Splendor*. Jim's biography, *Shadow of the Almighty*, traces the preparation of his own soul for this assignment, and *The Savage My Kinsman* is the story of how Nate Saint's sister Rachel, my daughter Valerie, and I went to live with the Auca Indians in 1958.

The names of the five missionaries—Ed, Pete, Nate, Roger, and Jim—may legitimately be added, it seems to me, to that list in Hebrews 11 of those who responded to God in faith without seeing their reward, for they are among those who "won a glowing testimony to their faith, but they did not then and there receive the fulfilment of the promise. God had something better planned for our day, and it was not his plan that they should reach perfection without us."

This leaves us with an awesome responsibility, surrounded as we are by "these serried ranks of witnesses."

So "let us run the race that we have to run with patience, our eyes fixed on Jesus, the source and the goal of our faith" (Heb. 12:1, 2 PHILLIPS).

477